America in Modern Times

SINCE 1941

America in Modern Times

SINCE 1941

≈

ALAN BRINKLEY

Columbia University

ELLEN FITZPATRICK

Harvard University

OVERTURE
BOOKS

THE MCGRAW-HILL COMPANIES, INC.

New York   St. Louis   San Francisco   Auckland   Bogotá
Caracas   Lisbon   London   Madrid   Mexico City   Milan   Montreal
New Delhi   San Juan   Singapore   Sydney   Tokyo   Toronto

McGraw-Hill

A Division of The **McGraw·Hill** Companies

America in Modern Times: Since 1941

This book is printed on acid-free paper.

1 2 3 4 5 6 7 8 9 0 FGR FGR 9 0 9 8 7 6

ISBN 0-07-007962-5

This book was set in Janson Text by Graphic World.
The editor was Lyn Uhl;
the production supervisor was Leroy A. Young.
The cover was designed by Karen K. Quigley.
Cover art: Bill Jacklin, *Sheep Meadow I*, 1990.
The photo editor was Kathy Bendo.
Project supervision was done by Graphic World Publishing Services.
Quebecor Printing/Fairfield was printer and binder.

Library of Congress Cataloging-in-Publication Data
Brinkley, Alan.
    America in modern times : since 1941 / Alan Brinkley, Ellen Fitzpatrick.
      p. cm.
    Includes bibliographical references and index.
    ISBN 0-07-007962-5
    1. United States—History—1945–   2. United States—
History—1933–1945   I. Fitzpatrick, Ellen F. (Ellen Frances)
II. Title.
E839.B68   1997
973.9—dc20   96-34841

http://www.mhcollege.com

About the Authors

Alan Brinkley is Professor of American history at Columbia University. He is the author of *Voices of Protest: Huey Long, Father Coughlin, and the Great Depression*, which received the American Book Award for History in 1983; *The End of Reform: New Deal Liberalism in Recession and War*; *The Unfinished Nation: A Concise History of the American People*; and *American History: A Survey*, a widely-used college textbook now in its ninth edition. He has received fellowships from the John Simon Guggenheim Foundation, the Woodrow Wilson Center for International Scholars, the National Humanities Center, the American Council of Learned Societies, and the Russell Sage Foundation. His many articles, essays, and reviews have appeared in both scholarly and nonscholarly publications.

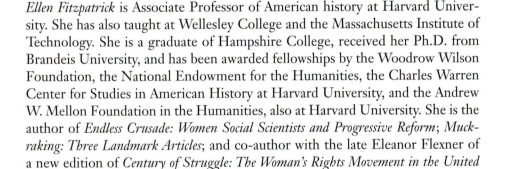

Ellen Fitzpatrick is Associate Professor of American history at Harvard University. She has also taught at Wellesley College and the Massachusetts Institute of Technology. She is a graduate of Hampshire College, received her Ph.D. from Brandeis University, and has been awarded fellowships by the Woodrow Wilson Foundation, the National Endowment for the Humanities, the Charles Warren Center for Studies in American History at Harvard University, and the Andrew W. Mellon Foundation in the Humanities, also at Harvard University. She is the author of *Endless Crusade: Women Social Scientists and Progressive Reform*; *Muckraking: Three Landmark Articles*; and co-author with the late Eleanor Flexner of a new edition of *Century of Struggle: The Woman's Rights Movement in the United States*. She has also written many reviews and articles.

Contents in Brief

Contents

CHAPTER TWENTY-FOUR

From Flexible Response to Vietnam

CHAPTER TWENTY-FIVE

Cultural Revolutions

Preface

In 1941, the United States entered the greatest war in the history of mankind and, in the process, accepted its role as the leading international power in the world. For more than fifty years, America has struggled with the conflicting demands of meeting its responsiblities as a global power—first in a time of armed conflict, then in a long period of "cold war"—and the demands of meeting its social responsibilities at home. Now—as we approach the end of the twentieth century, the Cold War over, our society and economy poised uncertainly at the beginning of a new and still undefined era—it seems appropriate to look back on the last half-century and more of American life and try to see it whole. That, at least, is the purpose of this book: to describe this dramatic period in the history of our nation, to explore the many changes and conflicts that have characterized these years, and to explain as well the continuities that justify considering it a distinct era.

In recounting the history of America in the second half of the twentieth century, we have sought to balance the many stories of frustration, injustice, conflict, and failure of those years with the equally important stories of generosity, progress, and success. We have tried to explain the many forces that have divided Americans, but we have tried as well to describe the equally powerful forces that have united them and made them part of a nation. We have tried to combine the "traditional" story of our nation's history—the story of politics, government, diplomacy, and war—with the "newer" stories of society and culture that explore the experiences of ordinary men and women and the broad demographic and economic changes that have shaped our world. The result, we hope, is an account of enough different approaches to and areas of American history in the last half century to make readers aware of its remarkable diversity. There is much drama in the history of American society over the last one hundred years, much pain, loss, triumph, and above all, determination. The record is there for all Americans to ponder and to learn from as we approach the next century.

Many people have contributed to the making of this book. We wish to thank the scholars and friends who read and commented on various versions of this manuscript, among them Theda Skocpol, Richard White, George Sanchez,

Sonya Michel, William Gienapp, Dennis Skiotis, Charles Poser, Morton Keller, Jacqueline Jones, Martin Nolan, and the members of the women's writing group of which Ellen Fitzpatrick is a part. We wish to thank Thaddeus Russell, Yanek Mieczkowski, and Charles Forcey for their expert assistance with research. We acknowledge the helpful comments of the following reviewers: Ruth Alexander, Colorado State University; Robert Sellen, Georgia State University; Victor Triay, Middlesex Community Technical College; Bruce Schulman, Boston University; Paula Fass, University of California, Berkeley; Ross Evans Poulson, Augustana College; Kevin Byrne, Gustavus Adolphus College; Ira Leonard, Southern Connecticut State University; Francis Kraljic, CUNY-Kingsborough Community College; David Bernstein, California State University, Long Beach; Ronald Tobey, University of California, Riverside. And we are grateful to Peter Labella, Lyn Uhl, Monica Freedman, and Marcia Craig for supporting this project and shepherding it through the editing and publication process at McGraw-Hill.

We hope that readers of this book will feel free to write to us with comments, suggestions, and corrections (either by sending them directly to us or in care of the College Division, McGraw-Hill, 1221 Avenue of the Americas, New York, NY 10020).

Alan Brinkley
Ellen Fitzpatrick

America in Modern Times

SINCE 1941

CHAPTER SIXTEEN

Fighting a Global War

~

The attack on Pearl Harbor thrust the United States into the largest and most terrible war the world has ever known. World War I had cost many lives and had destroyed centuries-old European social and political institutions. But World War II created carnage and horror without precedent in human history. The war raged around the world, drawing in almost every nation in one way or another. It was fought at sea, in the air, and on land. It ended with the deployment of the atomic bomb and the unleashing of other weapons of war of unprecedented destructiveness. It has been estimated that some 60 million people died in the war—most of them civilians. Towns and cities, roads and factories, ancient cathedrals and modern buildings stood in ruins in its aftermath. By its end, World War II had changed the world as profoundly as any event of the twentieth century, perhaps of any century.

Those who served in the American armed forces during World War II endured experiences that no one else can fully measure: discomfort, loneliness, fear, horror, and at times glory. They did so willingly. And they received the gratitude of their nations. These are the men, President Bill Clinton told Americans on the fiftieth anniversary of D-Day, "who saved the world."

The war changed forever the lives of the soldiers who fought it. But it changed American society as well. Unlike the combatants, those Americans who remained at home did not experience the terrible destruction and devastation unleashed in other parts of the globe. Their cities were not bombed, their shores were not invaded, they experienced no massive dislocation. Their economy, unlike almost all others in the world, actually flourished as a result of the war. Veterans who returned home in 1945 and 1946 found their country—at least on the surface—very much like the place they had left four years before. The same could not be said of those returning to Britain, France, Germany, Italy, the Soviet Union, China, Japan, and many other nations.

Nonetheless, for America the war marked an important divide in its history. As the poet Archibald MacLeish noted in 1943: "The great majority of the American people understand very well that this war is not a war only, but an end and a beginning—an end to things known and a beginning of things unknown. We have smelled the wind in the streets that changes weather. We know that whatever the world will be when the war ends, the world will be different." The story of American involvement in the war, therefore, is the story of how the military forces and the industrial might of the United States helped defeat Germany, Italy, and Japan. But it is also the story of the creation of a new world, both abroad and at home.

WAR ON TWO FRONTS

Whatever political disagreements preceded American involvement in World War II, there was a striking unity of opinion once the nation had entered the war—"a unity," as one member of Congress proclaimed shortly after Pearl Harbor, "never before witnessed in this country." Even so, President Roosevelt set out to ensure that American commitment to the war effort would not waver despite the costs. "We are now in this war. We are all in it—all the way," Roosevelt instructed the nation just two days after Pearl Harbor. "Every single man, woman, and child is a partner in the most tremendous undertaking of our American history."

The "United Nations"

The partnership Americans relied upon most during the war was the one formed with its Allies. It has been said that the war was fought with British intelligence, American power, and Soviet blood. Although that sentiment grossly simplifies the complexities of the war effort, each of the Allies did, in fact, make a distinctive contribution to the war effort.

The attempt to coordinate British and American strength had begun even before Pearl Harbor when Roosevelt and Churchill had met to draft the Atlantic Charter. Shortly after the American declaration of war, the two leaders met again, in Washington, to plan Allied strategy for the war. (The Soviet Union, then engaged in fierce fighting on the eastern front in Europe but determinedly neutral in the Pacific war, did not participate in this early conference.) Through late December and then into January, British and American officials worked in what became known as the Arcadia Conference to hammer out military goals. Concerned lest the United States focus its attention primarily on defeating Japan, a tactical decision that Churchill believed might well doom the western Allies, the prime minister pressed Roosevelt to make the defeat of Germany America's first priority. Roosevelt readily agreed, despite the popular pressure in America to move quickly to avenge Pearl Harbor.

The Arcadia Conference was also notable for Allied agreements to make planning of the war a joint enterprise under the authority of a Combined Chiefs of Staff, incorporating British and American military leaders. The Allies agreed to pool their munitions and their shipping resources; administrative control over them was assigned to another joint authority. Some American military leaders chafed at the stress on sharing responsibility for strategic planning with the British. General Joseph Stilwell complained of Roosevelt, "The Limeys have his ear, while we have the hind tit." But Roosevelt partly allayed such concerns by ensuring that the Combined Chiefs of Staff had their headquarters in Washington.

Perhaps most importantly, on January 1, 1942 the United States, Britain, the Soviet Union, and 23 other nations issued a "Declaration by the United Nations." In it, the Allies affirmed commitments that Britain and America had articulated in the Atlantic Charter, most pointedly their joint mission to defeat the Axis powers. Equally critical, they promised not to make a separate peace. Together, the Allies declared, they were "now engaged in a common struggle against savage and brutal forces seeking to subjugate the world."

The first, troubled months of 1942 severely tested their unity and confidence. Despite soaring rhetoric, impressive displays of patriotism, and a dramatic flurry of activity, the Allies reeled in the face of the Axis assault. Defeat seemed a real possibility as Britain struggled to regain its footing after a near collapse in 1940, and as the Soviet Union shouldered the enormous weight of battling the Nazis on the eastern front. Also ominous, Allied strongholds in the Pacific were falling one after the other to the forces of Japan. The first task facing the United States, therefore, was less to achieve victory than to stave off defeat.

Containing the Japanese

Ten hours after the strike at Pearl Harbor, Japanese airplanes attacked the American airfields at Manila in the Philippines, destroying much of America's remaining air power in the Pacific. Three days later Guam, an American possession, fell to Japan; then Wake Island and Hong Kong. The great British fortress of Singapore in Malaya surrendered in February 1942, the Dutch East Indies in March, Burma in April. In the Philippines, American and Filipino soldiers fought desperately to hold the Bataan Peninsula in the winter of 1942 despite a lack of food and supplies.

On April 9, wasted by hunger and disease, the soldiers on Bataan surrendered to the Japanese. What followed for thousands of captured American and Filipino soldiers was a terrible "death march" toward prisoner of war camps. Along the way, nearly 10,000 died from starvation and murder. "You found all kinda bodies along the road," one American GI remembered. "Some of 'em bloated, some had just been killed. If you fell out to the side, you were either shot by the guards or you were bayoneted and left there." Incarceration in

BATAAN DEATH MARCH.   American soldiers carry the bodies of their compatriots
in slings as they march toward Bilibad Prison during the 1942
Bataan Death March in the Philippines.

terrifying prison camps followed for those who survived the march. By May 6
the island of Corregidor, once the command post of General Douglas
MacArthur himself, had surrendered as well. The soldiers on the remaining islands followed suit by June 9. This was the first wholesale surrender of American field forces in a foreign war in American history.

Faced with such defeats, American strategists planned two broad offensives to turn the tide against the Japanese. One, under the command of General
Douglas MacArthur, would move north from Australia, through New Guinea,
and eventually back to the Philippines. The other, under Admiral Chester
Nimitz, would move west from Hawaii toward major Japanese island outposts in
the central Pacific. Eventually military plans called for the two offensives to
come together in an invasion of Japan.

The Allies scored an important victory, for morale at least, in April 1942
when U.S. B25 bombers flew from the naval carrier *Hornet* on missions that
struck the heart of the enemy's homeland—Tokyo. Although the raids inflicted
minimal damage, their psychological impact on Japanese leaders was important.
They suggested a kind of vulnerability in the interior of Japan many enemy
strategists had not anticipated. A month later, the Allies achieved their first important Pacific war victory in the Battle of the Coral Sea, just northwest of

Australia. On May 7–8, 1942, American forces launched a series of air strikes against Japanese carriers that struck one light carrier, inflicted serious damage on a heavy carrier, and destroyed planes aboard another. Although the Americans lost a large carrier, the *Lexington*, they succeeded in turning back the enemy as the Japanese withdrew from a planned landing at Port Moresby, New Guinea. What was to all appearances a tactical draw was in fact a strategic victory for the United States as the Japanese retreated. The events in the Coral Sea were also notable for the unusual character of the hostilities. The two fleets never saw each other in battle; the entire action was fought by planes launched at sea from the decks of the carriers—a practice that became central to modern naval warfare.

A month later, there was a far more important turning point in the Pacific war. Determined to extend their perimeter, draw the American navy into battle, and perhaps eventually seize the Hawaiian Islands, the Japanese prepared to invade Midway Island, an American outpost about a thousand miles northwest of Hawaii. Their strategic plans were notable for their complexity and even eccentricity. While Admiral Isoroku Yamamoto himself led the Japanese combined fleet toward Midway Island, the Japanese simultaneously undertook a diversionary operation in the distant Aleutian Islands, off Alaska, and occupied two uninhabited islands.

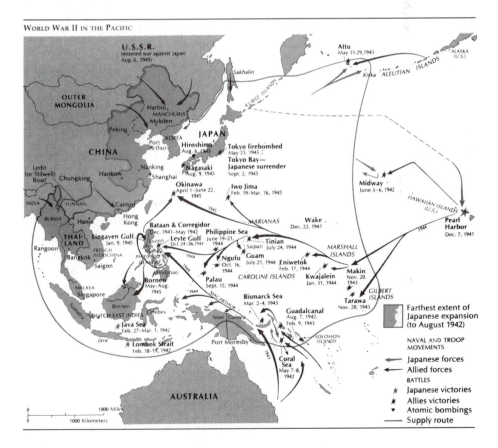

WORLD WAR II IN THE PACIFIC

The battle for Midway was another story. For four days from June 3 to June 6, 1942, the Americans and Japanese fought bitterly for the tiny spit of land. The Japanese amassed an armada that included several battleships, aircraft carriers, over 200 airplanes, and assorted additional submarines, minesweepers, and transport craft. The American forces were much smaller in number, but two miscalculations made the Japanese vulnerable to them. First, the Japanese dispersed their fleet into several separate formations that weakened their capacity to support the main invasion group poised to strike Midway. Second, unknown to the Japanese, Admiral Nimitz had advance knowledge of the enemy strategy because the United States had cracked the Japanese naval code and used the intercepted information to plan their encounter with the enemy at Midway. Three American carriers were thus able to surprise the Japanese, by launching strikes at enemy carriers when aircraft were gathered on the decks ready for launching. A series of initial American aircraft raids failed to inflict much injury, but a second wave of dive bombers inflicted devastating damage on the enemy. When the smoke cleared, three out of four Japanese carriers were in flames. American planes sank a fourth Japanese carrier later in the battle, although not before enemy planes severely damaged the USS Yorktown. Despite great losses, the United States could declare a clear victory.

The Battle of Midway was of great significance to the Allied cause. By sinking four Japanese carriers, the United States managed to wrest the initiative in the Pacific war from the Japanese. They crippled planned Japanese offensive operations in the South Pacific and Indian Ocean. And although the Japanese made minor changes in their codes, they failed to prevent further intelligence interceptions that would greatly assist the Allies. The battle's most important consequence, however, was to vindicate the "Europe first" strategy. Had the Americans been defeated by the Japanese at Midway, the nation would have been forced to reconsider its commitment to focus its primary attention on the defeat of Germany. As it was, the "miracle at Midway" became a reminder of American victory for the duration of the war.

The Americans took the offensive for the first time months later in the southern Solomon Islands, to the east of New Guinea. In August 1942, American forces assaulted Guadalcanal in an effort to dislodge the Japanese who were beginning to build an airfield there. A ferocious struggle, which included terrible savagery on both sides, followed. For six months, the battle raged as U.S. Marines fought the enemy on land. In the meantime, both sides fought relentlessly for control of the seas to replenish troops and supplies that dwindled daily. Slowly, however, the tide turned in favor of the Americans. In late December, the Japanese began to abandon the island, and in early February the fight for Guadalcanal finally shuddered to a close. The young American soldiers who had fought so doggedly felt, some claimed, like old men after the savage action they had seen.

In successfully defending the Solomon Islands, American forces had denied the Japanese control over areas of the Pacific that were crucial to the Axis hopes for victory. By mid-1943, in both the southern and central Pacific, the initiative had shifted to the United States, and the Japanese advance had come to a stop. The Americans, with aid from Australians and New Zealanders, now began the slow, arduous process of moving toward the Philippines and Japan itself.

Holding Off the Germans

In the European war, the United States had less control over its military operations. It was fighting in cooperation with Britain in the West; and it was trying to conciliate its new ally, the Soviet Union, as well. Differences emerged early among the Allies about the best strategy for the defeat of Germany. Britain and the United States both envisaged a landing in western Europe, but the proposed timing failed to satisfy the Russians. The Soviet Union was shouldering (as it would throughout the war) the greatest burden in the struggle against Germany, fighting alone to drive back the Nazis in the East and suffering enormous military and civilian casualties. They wanted the Allied invasion to proceed at the earliest possible moment. They saw the establishment of a second European front as a way to ease the tremendous German pressure on them.

American strategists at first proposed starting immediately to amass a large invading force in England that would cross the Channel and confront the Germans in decisive battle in Europe. But Churchill argued that the Allies were not ready for the invasion, that they needed more time to assemble the munitions— and perhaps most critically the landing craft—they would need. A premature invasion, he warned, might fail and doom the Allied war effort. Finally, in the summer of 1942, British views prevailed. Roosevelt agreed to postpone the invasion of northwestern Europe. But the Allies were still determined to take some immediate action, and they decided to launch an offensive on the periphery of the Nazi empire in hopes that it might weaken the Germans before the great invasion of Europe.

In the fall of 1942, the British and Americans opened an offensive in North Africa against Nazi forces under the command of Field Marshall Erwin Rommel, the legendary "Desert Fox." The British Eighth Army confronted Rommel's forces at El Alamein and forced the Germans to retreat from Egypt. On November 8, Anglo-American forces landed at Oran and Algiers in Algeria and at Casablanca in Morocco—areas under the Nazi-controlled French government at Vichy—and began moving east toward Rommel. The Germans threw the full weight of their forces in Africa against the inexperienced Americans and inflicted a serious defeat on them at the Kasserine Pass in Tunisia. But under the stern command of General George S. Patton, American troops regrouped and began an effective counteroffensive. With the help of Allied air and naval power and the aid of British forces attacking from the east under Field Marshall Bernard Montgomery (the hero of El Alamein), the Allied offensive finally drove the last Germans from Africa in May 1943.

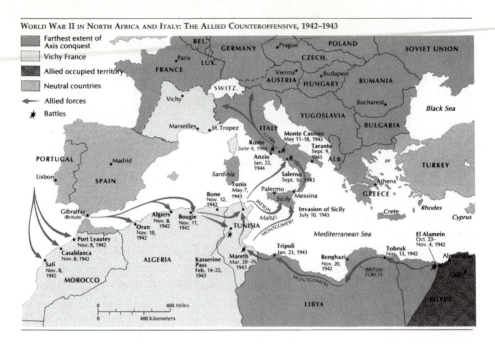

WORLD WAR II IN NORTH AFRICA AND ITALY: THE ALLIED COUNTEROFFENSIVE, 1942–1943

By then the Allies had decided to delay the planned cross-channel invasion until 1944, despite continued protests from the Soviet Union. The threat of a Soviet collapse had now diminished, for during the winter of 1942–1943, the Red Army had successfully held off the Nazis during a major German assault at Stalingrad in southern Russia. Hitler had committed enormous forces to the battle and had suffered appalling losses. Stalingrad constituted a crushing and humiliating blow to the Nazis in a winter of defeat that ultimately paralyzed the Germans' eastern offensive.

The Soviet victory had come at a terrible cost. The German siege of Stalingrad had decimated the civilian population of the city and devastated the surrounding countryside. Indeed, throughout the war, the Soviet Union absorbed losses far greater than any other warring nation—a fact that generations later continued to haunt the Russian memory and affect Soviet policy. As one Russian soldier who survived the winter offensive recalled: "Of my generation, out of a hundred who went to fight, three came back. Three percent. . . . I look at my children and grandchildren and I think: only centimeters decided whether they should be on this earth or not." His narrow escape made the soldier "recollect the phrase: 'The bullet that killed us today goes into the death of centuries and generations, killing life which didn't come to exist yet.'"

The Soviet success in beating back the German offensive provided a backdrop for discussions between Britain and America about Allied strategy. In a January 1943 meeting with Churchill in Casablanca, Roosevelt agreed to a British plan for an Allied invasion of Sicily. For many years after, there would be much debate about the wisdom of British enthusiasm for focusing attention on the Mediterranean. General Marshall opposed the invasion of Sicily, arguing that it would further delay the vital invasion of France. But the British argued that it would be far more difficult for the Germans to reinforce their armies in Italy than in France—an assumption that the long, tortured Allied campaign in Italy would subsequently challenge. On July 10, 1943, American and British soldiers landed in southeast Sicily; thirty-eight days later, they had conquered the island and were moving onto the Italian mainland. In the face of these set-backs, Mussolini's government in Rome collapsed; the dictator himself fled to northern Italy.

Mussolini's successor, Pietro Badoglio, eventually committed Italy to the Allies; but as he delayed, the Germans wrested critical positions in northern and central Italy from Italian troops. The Nazis then moved eight divisions into the country and established a powerful defensive line south of Rome. The Allied offensive on the Italian peninsula, which began on September 3, 1943, soon bogged down, especially after a serious setback at Monte Cassino that winter. In the months that followed, the fighting in Italy remained extremely harsh and exhausting as the Allies tried in vain to break the German line. For the soldiers in the Italian theater, the fighting began to resemble the terrible stalemate that had emerged during World War I. Meanwhile in Anzio, north of the German line, where the Allies had landed in January 1944, the Nazis pinned the landing forces to the beachhead and tried to push them back into the sea. The Allies resisted strenuously. Not until May 1944, however, did they succeed in resuming their northward advance in Italy. On June 4, 1944, two days before the Allied landing in Normandy, American troops liberated Rome; Allied forces moved onward in the ensuing months in an effort to drive the Germans out of central Italy.

The invasion of Italy aided the Allied war effort in several important ways. As Churchill had hoped, it cemented Allied control of the Mediterranean, tied up German forces, and permitted the Allies to establish air bases from which to launch further assaults on central Europe. But it proved extremely costly in men and resources, and it contributed to the postponement of the invasion of France by as much as a year, deeply embittering the Soviet Union. Some Russian leaders believed that the United States and Britain were deliberating delaying to allow the Russians to absorb the brunt of the fighting.

The postponement also gave the Soviets time to begin moving toward the countries of eastern Europe; and that fueled Allied fears. Roosevelt worried that without the Allied invasion of France, the Soviets might well make a separate peace with Germany. Nor did the president want to see the Soviet army move across Europe, occupying the continent while it secured victory. For these reasons, among others, Roosevelt insisted at Allied meetings in Quebec in August of 1943 that the British accept May 1, 1944 as a target date for the Allied invasion of France, which was given the codename "Operation Overlord."

America and the Holocaust

In the midst of this intensive fighting, the leaders of the American government were confronted with one of history's great horrors: the Nazi campaign to exterminate the Jews of Europe—the Holocaust. As early as 1942, high officials in Washington had incontrovertible evidence that Hitler's forces were rounding up Jews and others (including Poles, gypsies, homosexuals, and communists) from all over Europe, transporting them to concentration camps in eastern Germany and Poland, and systematically murdering them. (The death toll would ultimately reach 6 million Jews and approximately 4 million others.) News of the atrocities was reaching the public as well, and pressure began to build for an Allied effort to end the killing, or at least to rescue some of the surviving Jews.

The American government consistently resisted almost all such entreaties. Although Allied bombers flew missions within a few miles of the most notorious death camp at Auschwitz in Poland, pleas that the planes be directed to destroy the crematoria were rejected as militarily unfeasible or as an unjustifiable diversion of resources needed for more crucial operations. American officials made a similar judgment about the proposal that the Allies try to destroy railroad lines leading to the camps, even though the Air Force was already engaged in heavy bombing of industrial sites in the area.

The United States also resisted pleas that it admit large numbers of the Jewish refugees attempting to escape Europe—a pattern of refusal established well before Pearl Harbor. One ship, the *St. Louis,* had arrived off Miami in 1939 carrying nearly 1,000 escaped German Jews, only to be refused entry and forced to return to Europe. Throughout the war, the State Department did not even use up the number of visas permitted by law; almost ninety percent of the quota remained untouched. One opportunity after another to assist the imperiled Jews was either ignored or rejected. In January of 1944, the Roosevelt administration finally responded to criticism that its passivity constituted a deliberate evasion of responsibility. It created the War Refugee Board and gave it the mission of trying to evacuate Jews from Axis-occupied territories and of intervening to assist refugees. But, the agency lacked the resources and the authority to save more than a few people.

In the end, there is no way to know how many of Hitler's victims might have been saved by more forceful action on the part of the United States and Britain. But at least some lives might well have been spared had the Allies acted sooner and more decisively. The western leaders justified abandoning the Jews to their fate by concentrating their attention solely on the larger goal of winning the war. Any diversion of energy and attention to other purposes, they apparently believed, would distract them from the overriding goal of victory. They believed that even though some, at least, were fully aware of the moral gravity of the Holocaust. Churchill himself said in 1944 that "there is no doubt that this is probably the greatest and most horrible single crime ever committed in the whole history of the world." Allied troops finally reached the concentration camps in the spring of 1945, liberated those who survived and made it impossible at last for the world to ignore the magnitude of the horror. But the memory of the Holocaust—an unspeakable crime against humanity and, many believe, against God—survives still as a terrible reminder of the human capacity for evil.

THE DEFEAT OF THE AXIS

By the middle of 1943, America and its allies had succeeded in stopping the Axis advance both in Europe and in the Pacific. In the next two years, the Allies themselves seized the offensive and launched a series of powerful drives. The costs were high and the fighting fierce, but Allied operations now led inexorably toward victory.

Bombing Campaigns

By early 1944, American and British bombers were attacking German industrial installations and other targets almost around the clock, drastically cutting production and impeding transportation. Targeting problems were formidable despite the popular myth that Allied pilots could "put a bomb in a pickle barrel." American pilots conducted daylight "precision bombing" raids that managed to inflict devastating damage on some German fuel supply depots and industrial plants, but these raids ultimately proved less important for the specific targets they hit than for the psychological impact of the extraordinary damage they imposed. British fliers also began night-time saturation bombing raids that resulted in tremendous damage to major cities and the deaths of large numbers of civilians.

Especially devastating was the massive bombing of such German cities as Hamburg, Dresden, and Berlin. In July and August 1943, over 700 Allied planes dropped incendiary bombs mixed with high explosives on Hamburg, the second largest industrial city in Germany. They produced an enormous conflagration that consumed 6,000 acres of land, half the city, and killed nearly 100,000 people as buildings collapsed and fire raged out of control. Nearly a million people were left homeless. A February 1945 incendiary raid on Dresden unleashed a firestorm that destroyed three-fourths of the previously undamaged city and killed approximately 135,000 people, almost all civilians. Kurt Vonnegut, then an American prisoner of war in Dresden, described the scene the day after the bombing in his novel *Slaughter house five:* "The sky was black with smoke. The sun was an angry little pinhead. Dresden was like the moon now, nothing but minerals. The stones were hot. Everybody else in the neighborhood was dead."

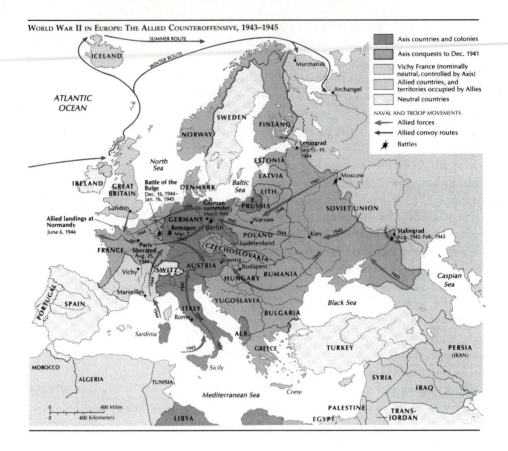

WORLD WAR II IN EUROPE: THE ALLIED COUNTEROFFENSIVE, 1943–1945

Military leaders claimed that the bombing raids destroyed industrial facilities, demoralized the population, and cleared the way for the great Allied invasion of France in the late spring. In truth, the effectiveness of much of the bombing campaign was due less to its precision than to the unrelenting pounding it inflicted on the enemy. The bombing forced the German air force (the *Luftwaffe*) to relocate much of its strength in Germany itself and to engage Allied forces in the air. The air battles over Germany considerably weakened the *Luftwaffe* and made it a much less formidable obstacle to the Allied invasion than it might once have been. But the saturation and incendiary bombings also eroded the distinction, once important to strategists, between military and civilian targets in warfare.

Operation "Overlord": The Liberation of France

By the spring of 1944, an enormous invasion force had been gathering in England for two years: almost 3 million Allied troops, including British, Canadian, and American forces, and the greatest array of naval vessels and armaments ever assembled in one place. The fear and tension were palpable among the troops in the staging areas on the morning of June 6, 1944, and among their leaders. The day before, Dwight D. Eisenhower, who served as commander, had scribbled a note to be read in the event of failure: "Our landings in the Cherbourg-Havre area have failed to gain a satisfactory foothold and I have withdrawn the troops. My decision to attack at this time and place was based on the best information available. If any blame or fault attaches to this attempt, it is mine alone." Instead, as the vast armada moved into action on the morning of June 6, one of the great triumphs of the entire Allied campaign was about to unfold.

The landing came not at the narrowest part of the English Channel, where the Germans had expected and prepared for it, but along sixty miles of the Cotentin Peninsula on the coast of Normandy. Over 1 million Allied soldiers had been committed to the operation, and the enormous scale of the invasion soon became apparent. While airplanes and battleships offshore bombarded the Nazi defenses, 4,000 vessels landed troops and supplies on the beaches. (Three divisions of paratroopers had been dropped, chaotically but not ineffectively, behind the German lines the night before.) Fighting was intense along the beach, but the Allies' superior air and sea power, as well as the determined assault of their landing forces, gradually prevailed. By June 18, American troops had reached the port city of Cherbourg, where intense battle, accompanied by the pounding of enemy shore batteries by the 14-inch guns of Allied battleships, forced a German surrender there near the end of June. The German forces had then been dislodged from virtually the entire Normandy coast.

D-DAY.   American troops disembark from a Coast Guard landing barge during the invasion of Normandy. Up ahead on Omaha Beach, the men who preceded them lie flat against the sand as German machine guns try to stop the Allied advance.

For the next month, further progress remained slow. But in late July in the battle of Saint-Lô, General Omar Bradley's First Army smashed through the German lines. George S. Patton's Third Army, spearheaded by heavy tank attacks, then moved through the gap Bradley's troops had created and began a drive into the heart of France. On August 25, Free French forces arrived in Paris and liberated the city from four years of German occupation. Eisenhower ordered two divisions of American troops to follow the French in marching into Paris, in a demonstration that German occupation of the city was truly at an end. Meanwhile, Allied forces succeeded in invading southern France. As the Nazis retreated, some key French collaborators followed them, watching the Allied occupation of France with fear and dismay. By mid-September the Allied armies had driven the Germans almost entirely out of France and had seized the city of Antwerp in Belgium.

The Battle of the Bulge

The great Allied drive came to a halt, however, at the Rhine River in the face of a refortified line of German defenses, the coldest winter ever recorded in Western Europe, and formidable Allied problems with moving supplies. In mid-December 1944, German forces struck in desperation along fifty miles of front in the Ardennes Forest. In the Battle of the Bulge (named for a large bulge that appeared in the American lines as the Germans pressed forward), German tanks drove fifty-five miles toward Antwerp before they were finally stopped at Bastogne. In the snow when the siege lifted, one soldier recalled, "dead bodies, German prisoners and burning tanks" were scattered in the forest. At the battle's end some 70,000 Americans and 80,000 Germans were dead, wounded, or unaccounted for. Nearly 8,000 Americans had been seized as prisoners of war. Still, the German gamble in deploying some of their last reserves to this arena failed. The Allies could replace the men they had lost; the Germans could not. Their offensive only hastened the Nazi defeat. Even so, the fierce fighting proved a chastening experience for the Americans. "I now live among trees," one veteran of the Battle of the Bulge reported fifty years later, "and every winter on days when the boughs are covered with snow, I think of the Ardennes."

The Battle of the Bulge ended serious German resistance in the West. Now attention shifted to the eastern front. While the Anglo-American forces had been fighting their way through France, Soviet forces had swept westward into Central Europe and the Balkans. In late January 1945, the Red Army began another great winter offensive toward the Oder River inside Germany. In early spring, they were ready to launch a final assault against Berlin. By then, American forces were pushing toward the Rhine from the west. Early in March, the First Army captured the city of Cologne, on the river's west bank. The next day, in a remarkable stroke of good fortune, the Allies discovered and seized an undamaged bridge over the river at Remagen; American troops now swarmed across the Rhine. Before long, Patton's army too had breached the river barrier. Now the Allies were within striking distance of the heart of Germany. In the following weeks the British commander, Field Marshall Montgomery, also pushed into Germany with a million troops. The Ninth Army to the north joined with the First Army to the south to complete the encirclement of German soldiers in the Ruhr by mid-April. Now surrounded, 300,000 German soldiers abandoned the fight in the largest surrender of the war. Their commander committed suicide.

The Death of Roosevelt

Amid all this fighting, a single death far from the front shocked the American people and momentarily renewed Hitler's hopes for victory. Through the war years, Roosevelt's health appeared to those who knew him well to be declining. The burden of his responsibilities showed as the president's face reflected new lines of worry and fatigue. In 1944, physicians discovered that Roosevelt was suffering from a serious heart disease; his high blood pressure revealed rapidly worsening arteriosclerosis. Publicly, the White House managed to sustain the facade that the president was healthy. To admit otherwise might have jeopardized his re-election that year to an unprecedented fourth term. Nonetheless, rumors persisted that the 62-year-old president was seriously ill.

In February 1945 at the Yalta Conference, British observers expressed shock at the deterioration in Roosevelt's appearance. "The President appears a very sick man," Churchill's personal physician reported. "I give him only a few months to live." Upon his return to Washington, Roosevelt himself sought to quiet persistent talk about his wellbeing with a quip about the far more taxing political perils he faced. "I was not ill for a second, until I arrived back in Washington, and there I heard all of the rumors which had occurred in my absence." But on April 12, 1945, at his retreat in Warm Springs, Georgia, Roosevelt died of a massive cerebral hemorrhage. For many Americans, Roosevelt had become virtually synonymous with the presidency. After dying in the midst of the war, the president was eulogized as a soldier who had fallen in battle like those he led so valiantly. His successor, Vice President Harry Truman, now assumed the burden of seeing the war to a close.

Victory in Europe

Any hopes the Germans harbored that the death of Roosevelt would somehow stall the Allies were soon thoroughly crushed. As April 1945 wound down, the German resistance collapsed on both the eastern and western fronts. By month's end the Nazis were also beating a hasty retreat in Italy, as Allied troops swarmed north toward the Alps. Italian partisans captured Mussolini and his mistress near Lake Como in northern Italy and—despite clear instructions to the contrary from Allied commanders—shot him in the back on April 28. His body was then transported to Milan and hung in a public square face downwards. The German forces who remained in Italy surrendered.

In Germany, American forces moved eastward faster than they had anticipated and could have beaten the Russians to Berlin and Prague. By then, however, the Allied conference at Yalta had reached agreement on the postwar division of Germany into several zones of occupation, each assigned to one of the Allied forces. To cross the Elbe and drive toward Berlin would have resulted in many additional casualties for the British and Americans. Eisenhower concluded there would be little advantage in doing so since the territory captured would fall within the already-designated Soviet occupation zone. The Allied high command decided instead, with some British reluctance, to halt the advance along the Elbe River in central Germany to await the Russians. That decision enabled the Soviet Union to occupy eastern Germany and Czechoslovakia and paved the way for many Cold War tensions in later years.

On April 30, as Soviet forces approached his headquarters, Adolf Hitler committed suicide in his bunker, along with his long-time mistress Eva Braun, whom he had married the day before their deaths. Hours before his death, Hitler continued to defend the achievements of his Third Reich. Powerless now to avert a Nazi defeat, he lashed out at his generals and the German people, blaming them for his own failure. In the meantime, the battle for Berlin, by one estimate, resulted in nearly a half million casualties. On May 8, 1945, the remaining German forces surrendered unconditionally. VE (Victory in Europe) Day prompted great celebrations in Western Europe and in the United States, tempered by the knowledge of the continuing war against Japan.

The Pacific Offensive

Allied strategy for the defeat of Japan had taken shape in 1944 after critical victories in the Pacific inspired hope that a successful attack on Japan might soon be possible. In February 1944, American naval forces under Admiral Nimitz won a series of victories in the Marshall Islands and cracked the outer perimeter of the Japanese Empire. Within a month, the navy had destroyed other vital Japanese bastions. American submarines, in the meantime, were decimating Japanese shipping and crippling the nation's domestic economy. By the summer of 1944, the already skimpy food rations for the Japanese people had been reduced by nearly a quarter; there was also a critical gasoline shortage.

A frustrating struggle was in progress in the meantime on the Asian mainland. The Americans, in particular, wanted to keep China in the war for both political and strategic reasons. Toward that end, Burma became a theater of war in part to ensure open supply routes to China. In 1942, the Japanese had forced U.S.

VICTORY IN EUROPE.   Rumors of Germany's unconditional surrender led crowds to throng in New York's Times Square on May 7, the day before the official surrender. Despite lack of White House confirmation, those gathered celebrated the impending end of war in Europe.

General Joseph W. Stilwell out of Burma and had moved their own troops as far west as the mountains bordering on India. For a time, Stilwell supplied the isolated Chinese forces continuing to resist Japan with an aerial ferry over the Himalayas. In 1943, finally, he led Chinese and a few American troops back through northern Burma and reopened the Burma Road. By then, however, the Japanese had launched a major counteroffensive and had driven so deep into the Chinese interior that they threatened the terminus of the Burma Road and the center of Chinese government at Chungking. These difficulties turned the Allies away from their proposed plans to stage their assault on Japan from air bases in China.

Instead, Allied attention in the Pacific came to focus on a series of islands. In mid-June 1944, an enormous American armada struck the heavily fortified Mariana Islands and, after some of the bloodiest operations of the war, captured Tinian, Guam, and Saipan, 1,350 miles from Tokyo. This led to the fall of General Tojo, the leader of Japan's wartime government. But the Americans paid dearly for their victory. At Peleliu over 7,000 American soldiers were killed or wounded in the costliest amphibious assault in American history (measured in casualties). One Marine later recalled his reactions as he watched his fellows being slaughtered by machine gun fire on the beach: "We were expendable. It was difficult to accept. We come from a nation and a culture that values life and the individual. To find oneself in a situation where your life seems of little value is the ultimate in loneliness. It is a humbling experience."

On October 20, General MacArthur's troops landed on Leyte Island in the Philippines. The Japanese now used virtually their entire fleet against the Allied invaders in three major encounters—which together constituted the decisive battle of Leyte Gulf, the largest naval engagement in history. American forces held off the Japanese onslaught and sank three Japanese battleships and four carriers, as well as an array of other vessels, all but destroying Japan's capacity to continue a serious naval war.

Still, as American forces advanced closer to the Japanese mainland early in 1945, imperial forces seemed to redouble their resistance. The depth of their determination became tragically apparent in the battle of Iwo Jima. The United States viewed the tiny volcanic island, only 750 miles from Tokyo, as an ideal place to establish fighter bases for use during future assaults on the Japanese. To defend the island, the Japanese had established elaborate fortifications, many of which were underground caves. On February 16, 1945, American battleships began to bombard the shore, smoking out some Japanese gun emplacements. The U.S. Marines landed on Iwo Jima February 19 and began nearly a month of extraordinarily harsh fighting. The volcanic ash that covered the surface of the island slowed their advance. By February 24, however, a small band of resolute Marines planted an American flag atop Mt. Suribachi, a scene that gave hope to other soldiers who glimpsed the stars and stripes waving high above the battleground. The event became the source of one of the most famous photographs of World War II and was later memorialized in a monument constructed in Arlington, Virginia. By the end of March, Iwo Jima had been secured, but only after the costliest single battle in the history of the Marine Corps. The Marines suffered over 20,000 casualties. Of the 20,000 Japanese troops defending the island, only 200 were alive when the battle ended. This ferocious fighting gave support to American strategists' fears that a very high price would be extracted in the assault on Japan.

With the new B29 heavy bomber at its disposal, the Air Force began in March to launch a series of nighttime bombing raids—"a rain of death"—on the cities of Japan. Among the most devastating was the firebombing of Tokyo on the night of March 9 and in the early morning hours of the 10th. Over 100,000 people died in the firestorm; the firebombing of Tokyo was probably the single costliest event in human lives during World War II. Indeed, the U.S. Strategic Bombing Survey ventured that "probably more persons lost their lives by fire at Tokyo in a 6-hour period than at any time in the history of man." Swept by high wind, the fire destroyed everything in its path. Those watching the planes above Tokyo described scenes of eerie tranquility: B29s with their "long, glinting wings" standing out like "black silhouettes gliding through the fiery sky to

IWO JIMA. Marines from the 5th Division's 28th Regiment
plant the Stars and Stripes on Mount Suribachi after the
battle of Iwo Jima. This photograph, a reenactment
of a prior event, became one of the most famous images
of the war and the inspiration for the monument
that stands in Arlington, Virginia.

reappear farther on, shining golden against the dark roof of heaven or glittering
blue, like meteors, in the searchlight beams spraying the vault from horizon to
horizon."

Less than one month later, the Allies invaded Okinawa, the last island they
planned to take before their assault on Japan. Yet here too, on this island only
370 miles south of Japan, there was evidence of the strength of the Japanese resistance in these last desperate days. The invasion began on April 1, 1945. For
weeks, Marine and Army troops struggled to subdue the enemy. Week after
week, the Japanese sent *kamikaze* (suicide) planes against American and British
ships, sacrificing thousands of planes and pilots while inflicting substantial damage. One naval officer described the stunning sight as a *kamikaze* flew toward his
target, an American battleship off the coast of Okinawa: "Set afire and burning
fiercely he seemed to be almost on top of us and still headed for the bridge when

we got the door closed and backed into the pilot house. . . . When the scream of the plane became almost as loud as the chatter and rap of the guns, I assumed it was time to gather round and hold a little prayer meeting." When the plane hit the deck, eleven sailors died along with the pilot. The U.S. Navy sustained its highest causalities of the entire war in Okinawa.

On shore, the fighting led to widespread death and destruction. Japanese troops launched desperate nighttime attacks on the American lines. United States soldiers used flamethrowers to burn the enemy out of their caves and garrisons. The United States and its allies suffered approximately 75,000 casualties, including General Simon Buckner, who commanded the operation, before finally capturing Okinawa in late June 1945. Over 100,000 Japanese, among them tens of thousands of civilians, died in the siege.

Many Allied military planners were now convinced that the same kind of bitter fighting would await Americans in Japan itself. But others were beginning to hope that such an invasion might not be necessary. Relentless Allied attacks had badly damaged, although not entirely destroyed, the Japanese capacity to wage war. In July 1945, for example, American warships stood off the shore of Japan and shelled industrial targets (many already in ruins from aerial bombings) with impunity. The brutal firebombing of Tokyo and other Japanese cities had also damaged industrial sites and inflicted—at the very least—a major psychological blow on the Japanese homefront.

In addition, moderate Japanese leaders, who had long since decided that the war was lost, were increasing their power within the government and looking for ways to bring the war to an end. After the invasion of Okinawa, Emperor Hirohito of Japan appointed a new premier and gave him instructions to work for peace. Although the new leader could not persuade military leaders to give up the fight, he did try, along with the Emperor himself, to obtain mediation through the Soviet Union. The Russians showed little interest in playing this role, but other developments made their participation superfluous in any case.

Whether the moderates could ultimately have prevailed is a question about which historians and others continue to disagree. In any case, their efforts were ultimately irrelevant. For in mid-July, American scientists demonstrated to their government a new weapon of awesome power. On July 16, near Alamagordo, New Mexico, they conducted a successful test of an atomic bomb.

The Manhattan Project

The Manhattan Project, as the scientific endeavor to build an atomic bomb was known, grew out of concerns that the Germans were developing new weapons of extraordinary power for their war against the Allies. In 1939, scientists including the Italian physicist Enrico Fermi and the German mathematician Albert Einstein (then living in exile in America) passed word to the U.S. government that Nazi scientists had learned how to produce atomic fission in uranium. Acquiring that knowledge, they warned, was the first step toward the creation of an atomic bomb, a weapon more powerful than any ever previously devised. The United States and Britain immediately began a race to develop the weapon before the Germans did.

Over the next three years, the U.S. government secretly poured nearly $2 billion into the Manhattan Project—a massive scientific effort conducted at hidden laboratories in Oak Ridge, Tennessee; Los Alamos, New Mexico; Hanford, Washington; and other sites. (Its name had emerged earlier, when many of the atomic physicists had been working at Columbia University in New York.) Hundreds of scientists, many of them not fully aware of what they were working on, labored feverishly to complete two complementary projects. One (at Oak Ridge and Hanford) was the production of fissionable plutonium, the fuel for an atomic explosion; the other (at Los Alamos, under the supervision of J. Robert Oppenheimer) was the construction of a bomb that could use the fuel.

The scientists pushed ahead much faster than anyone had predicted. By 1944, the United States government knew that the Germans were not progressing with their own atomic bomb project. The war in Europe, in fact, ended before scientists at Los Alamos were ready to test the first bomb. But the Japanese war continued, and the scientists worked on. Just before dawn on July 16, 1945, at a place they named "Trinity," scientists gathered to witness the first atomic explosion in history. Those who saw the blast described a blinding flash of light brighter than any ever seen on earth. Physicist I. I. Rabi explained: "It blasted; it pounced; it bored its way right through you. It was a vision which was seen with more than the eye. It seemed to last forever. You would wish it would stop; altogether it lasted about two seconds . . . and we looked toward the place where the bomb had been; there was an enormous ball of fire which grew and grew and it rolled as it grew." Over the cold morning desert, now boiling from the heat of the flash, a huge billowing mushroom cloud shot up. Brilliant red, white, purple, and green colors appeared in the atmosphere. The eighteen-kiloton blast had left a crater 1200 feet in diameter. The steel tower from which the bomb had been suspended was vaporized. The blast shattered a window 125 miles away from the bomb site. As the ball of fire dispersed in the atmosphere and "washed out with the wind" the scientists made their way back to their base camp. "A few people laughed, a few people cried," J. Robert Oppenheimer recalled. "Most people were silent. I remembered the line from the Hindu scripture, the *Bhagavad-Gita:* . . . 'Now I am become Death, the destroyer of worlds.'"

The implications of the atomic bomb were momentous for human history and, as Oppenheimer's comment suggests, many of the scientists who worked on the bomb project were fully conscious of that fact. They were mindful of the war that had inspired the bomb project; their years of work had paid off. Some expressed exhilaration that "the gadget" had worked. "The war is over," a brigadier general greeted General Leslie Groves, director of the bomb project, after the blast. "Yes, after we drop two bombs on Japan," Groves responded. But some scientists, among them J. Robert Oppenheimer, were already troubled by the implications of what they had done. In the end, it would be left to others to decide when and where to deploy the terrible weapon the Manhattan Project had developed—or whether to deploy it at all.

Hiroshima and Nagasaki

News of the explosion reached American leaders at a critical juncture in the Allied war effort. Okinawa had been secured at enormous cost, long-formulated plans for an invasion of Japan were on the verge of unfolding, and word of internal dissension in Tokyo over surrender had reached the American government through decoded radio messages. President Harry S. Truman was in Potsdam, Germany, attending a conference of Allied leaders, when he received word that the atomic bomb test had succeeded. On July 26 as two unassembled bombs —code named Fat Man and Little Boy—were en route to the Pacific, Truman issued the Potsdam Declaration signed jointly by the British and Nationalist China. The document demanded the unconditional surrender of Japan, warning soberly that "the alternative for Japan is prompt and utter destruction."

Some within the Japanese government favored acceptance of the Allied ultimatum, but others resisted stubbornly. By the time the deadline Truman imposed arrived, the peace forces in Japan had not yet been able to persuade key military leaders to give up. Some Japanese still believed they could inflict such severe casualties on Allied forces when they attempted to land in Japan that the Americans would agree to a negotiated settlement on terms more favorable to the Japanese than a surrender. Others stressed the possibility that the Soviets would come through as intermediaries and produce a settlement agreeable to Japan. In the most wildly optimistic of scenarios, some hoped that the Soviet Union might actually join forces with the Japanese against the United States. The disagreement and delay contributed to tragedy. When the Japanese failed to meet the deadline, Truman ordered the military to deploy the new atomic weapons against them.

Controversy has raged for decades over Truman's decision to deploy the bomb. Critics have questioned the president's motives, his good faith, and his honesty in explaining his actions. Many have argued that the atomic attack was unnecessary, that Japan would have surrendered had the United States agreed to a settlement that would have allowed it to retain its Emperor (something which the United States ultimately permitted in any case). Others insist the Japanese would have given up anyway if the United States had waited only a few more weeks. Still others consider the American deployment of the bomb as an unacceptably immoral act. Whatever Japanese intentions, they assert, the United States should not have used a weapon with such devastating consequences for human history. For the most part, these arguments emerged in hindsight. But some made the case before the bomb was used, including one physicist who wrote to Truman shortly before the attack: "This thing must not be permitted to exist on this earth. We must not be the most hated and feared people in the world."

HIROSHIMA.   Where once a lively city stood, nothing but rubble remains. At the center of Hiroshima, depicted here, the devastation of the atomic bomb appears total.

For American and British leaders, however, there were few moral qualms about deploying the bomb. From the very beginning of the bomb project, the Allies had considered it not an abstract scientific effort, but an attempt to create a practical weapon of war. Once the bomb was successfully tested, few in authority doubted that it should now be used. Truman believed he faced a clear-cut military decision. A weapon was available that would end the war quickly; he could see no reason not to use it.

Some critics of Truman's decision have argued that motives beyond defeating Japan were at work. With the Soviet Union poised to enter the war in the Pacific, did the United States want to end the conflict quickly to forestall an expanded communist presence in Asia? Did Truman use the bomb as a weapon to intimidate Stalin, with whom he was engaged in difficult negotiations? No conclusive evidence is available to support (or definitively refute) either of these accusations.

There is, however, no question that in August 1945 the goal of an immediate end to the war figured centrally in Allied thinking. Both the British and the Soviets supported the American decision to drop the bomb on Japan. On August 6, 1945, after a few days of weather delays, an American B29, the *Enola Gay*, took off for Japan with "Little Boy" in its bomb bay. The plane dropped the atomic bomb, as planned, over the Japanese city of Hiroshima. In an instant, it completely incinerated a four-square-mile area at the center of the previously undamaged city. "Where we had seen a clear city two minutes before," one crew member aboard the *Enola Gay* recounted, "we could now no longer see the city. We could see smoke and fires creeping up the sides of the mountains." The whole "turbulent mass," another reported, "looked like lava or molasses covering the whole city, and it seemed to flow outward up into the foothills where the little valleys would come into the plain, with fires starting up all over."

On the ground, thousands died in an instant from the heat. At the center of the blast, buildings imploded, animals disappeared, every vestige of life vanished in a matter of seconds. More than 80,000 civilians died almost at once, according to later American estimates. For those who survived, a terrible quiet and a fearful darkness seemed to settle on the city. Left to the living was the herculean task of coming to terms with the physical, emotional, and material toll the atomic bomb inflicted. Some survived to find themselves maimed, burned, and blinded. Others would suffer from the crippling effects of radioactive fallout. For many who experienced it, the enormity of the event seemed to defy understanding. "I thought it might have been something which had nothing to do with the war," one survivor explained. It seemed like "the collapse of the earth which it was said would take place at the end of the world."

For many American soldiers, the bomb seemed to represent just the opposite. Aware of the enormous death toll exacted in the grueling Pacific island battles, they awaited the expected invasion of Japan acutely aware that further horror lay ahead. As writer Paul Fussell, an Army infantryman during the Second World War, explained, where one stood during the war determined much of one's reaction to Hiroshima. "I was a 21-year-old second lieutenant leading a rifle platoon. . . . When the bombs dropped and news began to circulate that . . . we would not be obliged to run up the beaches near Tokyo assault-firing while being mortared and shelled, for all the fake manliness of our facades we cried with relief and joy. We were going to live. We were going to grow up to adulthood after all."

Hiroshima stunned the government in Tokyo, which could not at first agree on how to respond to the catastrophe. The Japanese foreign minister continued his efforts to pursue negotiations with the Soviet Union, a tack that soon led to bitter disappointment. Instead of brokering a settlement, the Soviets notified the Japanese on August 8 that they, too, would be at war with Japan as of the following day. That night, just after midnight, the Soviet army attacked Manchuria. Meanwhile the United States dropped leaflets and sent radio transmissions warning the Japanese people that another bomb would soon be dropped if their country did not immediately surrender. And on August 9, an American plane deployed a second atomic weapon—this time on the city of Nagasaki—inflicting horrible damage and over 30,000 deaths on another devastated community. Finally, the Emperor intervened to break the stalemate in the cabinet, taking to the radio to ask his people to "endure the unendurable" and give up the struggle. On August 14, the Japanese government announced that it was ready to give up. On September 2, 1945, on board the American battleship *Missouri* anchored in Tokyo Bay, Japanese officials signed the articles of surrender.

The greatest and most terrible war in the history of mankind had finally come to an end. The United States emerged from it not only victorious, but in a position of unprecedented power, influence, and prestige. It was a victory, however, that few could greet with unambiguous joy. Fourteen million combatants had died in the struggle. Many more civilians had perished, from bombings, from disease and starvation, and from genocidal campaigns of extermination. The United States had suffered only light casualties in comparison with many other nations, but the cost had still been high: 322,000 dead, another 800,000 injured. And despite the sacrifices, the world continued to face an uncertain future, menaced by the new threat of nuclear warfare and by an emerging antagonism between the world's two strongest nations—the United States and the Soviet Union—that would darken the peace for many decades to come.

CHAPTER SEVENTEEN

Wartime Society and Culture

∼

"War is no longer simply a battle between armed forces in the field," an American government report of 1939 concluded. "It is a struggle in which each side strives to bring to bear against the enemy the coordinated power of every individual and of every material resource at its command. The conflict extends from the soldier in the front line to the citizen in the remotest hamlet in the rear." These statements describe very well the impact of World War II on American society.

Although the United States had experienced many wars before, not since the Civil War had the nation experienced so consuming a military experience as World War II. American armed forces engaged in combat around the globe for nearly four years. The American economy became integrally bound up with the effort to supply troops, sustain the Allied war effort, and otherwise support the waging of war in remote battlefields. Families coped with the long absence of loved ones, often by rearranging men's and women's traditional roles, at least for the time being. The war also imposed great challenges on the United States' character as a pluralist society. In all of these ways, and many others, the war had a transforming effect on American society.

THE WARTIME ECONOMY

World War II had its most profound impact on American domestic life by ending at last the Great Depression. By the middle of 1941, the economic problems of the 1930s—unemployment, deflation, industrial sluggishness—had virtually vanished in the great wave of wartime industrial expansion.

The Return of Prosperity

The most important agent of the new prosperity was federal spending, which after 1939 was pumping more money into the economy each year than all the New Deal relief agencies combined had done. In 1939, the federal budget had been $9 billion, the highest level it had ever reached in peacetime; by 1945, it had risen to $100 billion. Largely as a result, the gross national product soared: from $91 billion in 1939 to $166 billion in 1945. Personal incomes in some areas grew by as much as 100 percent or more. In the face of a wartime shortage of consumer goods, many wage earners diverted much of their new affluence into savings. That practice would later help keep the economic boom alive in the postwar years.

The impact of government spending was perhaps most dramatic in the West, which had long relied heavily on federal largesse. The West Coast, naturally, became the launching point for most of the naval war against Japan; and the government created large manufacturing facilities in California and elsewhere to serve the needs of the military. Altogether, the government made almost $40 billion worth of capital investments (factories, military and transportation facilities, highways, power plants) in the West during the war, more than in any other region. Ten percent of all the money the federal government spent between 1940 and 1945 went to California alone. Other western states also shared disproportionately in war contracts and government-funded capital investments. By the war's end, forty-five percent of California's personal income was derived from the federal government.

The activities of one important entrepreneur, Henry J. Kaiser, illustrate the extent and character of the western economic boom. During the 1930s, Kaiser's construction companies had built some of the great western dams. In the process, he became a great favorite of many members of the Roosevelt administration. During the war, Kaiser singlehandedly steered billions of federal dollars and funds into vast capital projects in the West. He helped build the infrastructure to support major centers for shipbuilding, steel, magnesium, and aluminum production.

Kaiser also pioneered in providing health care plans for the over 125,000 war workers he employed in California. Even before the war, he had begun to provide medical assistance to his employees. But the war sharpened his determination and led Kaiser to mount an aggressive public relations campaign in favor of prepaid health insurance programs. At Kaiser's shipbuilding plants, medical clinics were established to provide extensive services ranging from preventive care to free house calls to emergency and specialist services—benefits Kaiser believed added to his workers' productivity and to the success of his business. During the war, Kaiser ran the largest prepaid health program in the nation, an achievement that earned him the enmity of the American Medical Association, who doggedly opposed what they derided as "contract medicine." The Association threatened to expel doctors who worked for the Kaiser plan and in the end fought Kaiser in the courts, where they received a stunning rebuke from the judicial system. The innovative health care program inaugurated during the war by Kaiser provided at least some workers with a valued fringe benefit for their service in the wartime economy, a benefit that became part of many union contracts in the postwar years.

By the end of the war, the economy of the Pacific Coast and, to a lesser extent, other areas of the West had been transformed. The Coast had become the center of the growing American aircraft industry. New yards in southern California, Washington State, and elsewhere made the West a center of the shipbuilding industry. Los Angeles, formerly a medium-sized city notable chiefly for its film industry, now became a major industrial center as well. Once a lightly industrialized region, parts of the West were now among the most important manufacturing areas in the country. A part of the country that had once lacked adequate facilities to support substantial economic growth now stood poised to become the fastest growing region in the nation after the war.

Labor During the War

The war had an ambiguous impact on American workers. The economic growth it created lifted millions of workers out of unemployment and poverty; but the war also produced conflict between organized labor's desire to advance the status of working men and women, by strikes if necessary, and the nation's demand for a stable labor force devoted first and foremost to the needs of war production. In addition, an astronomical industrial accident rate cost the lives of thousands of workers on the home front who labored on complex machinery many were not experienced in operating. Indeed, by one estimate, casualties among industrial workers in 1942–1943 exceeded that of American soldiers in battles by a ratio of twenty to one.

Among the more stunning developments of the war was the way in which it eliminated almost overnight the terrible rates of unemployment of the 1930s. Instead, the war created a serious labor shortage. The armed forces removed over 15 million men and women from the civilian work force at the same time that the demand for labor was rising rapidly. Nevertheless, the civilian work force increased by almost twenty percent during the war. The 7 million who had previously been unemployed accounted for some of the increase; the employment of many people previously considered inappropriate for the work force—the very young, the elderly, and most importantly, several million women—accounted for the rest.

The war also gave an enormous boost to union membership, which rose from about 10.5 million in 1941 to over 13 million in 1945. But it created important new restrictions on the ability of unions to fight for their members' demands. Not long after the attack on Pearl Harbor in December 1941, Roosevelt established the War Labor Board (WLB) in an effort to enlist the cooperation of labor and industry in ensuring the smooth working of the wartime economy. The government was principally interested in preventing inflation and keeping production moving without disruption. It managed to win important concessions from union leaders on both scores. One was the so-called Little Steel formula, which set a fifteen percent limit on wage increases. Another was the "no-strike" pledge, by which unions agreed not to stop production in wartime. In return, the government provided labor with a "maintenance-of-membership" agreement, which ensured that the thousands of new workers pouring into unionized defense plants would be automatically enrolled in the unions. The agreement ensured the continued health of the union organizations, but in return workers had to give up the right to demand major economic gains during the war.

Organized labor responded to the war with outspoken patriotism. The new head of the CIO, Phillip Murray, exhorted his membership to "heed the call of the Commander in Chief and Work, Work, Work, PRODUCE, PRODUCE,

WORKING FOR VICTORY.   A welder works on a ship nearing completion during World War II. Aside him a propaganda poster celebrates the virtues of free labor in American society. Organized labor exhorted their members to devote themselves to war production, but some wildcat strikes broke out during the war among the rank and file who chafed at rising corporate profits and price increases.

PRODUCE." Still many rank-and-file union members, and some local union leaders, resented the restrictions imposed on them by the government and the labor movement hierarchy. They observed with dismay the rise in profits accrued by many corporations and wartime price increases even as their wages lagged behind, chained to the "Little Steel formula." Despite the no-strike pledge, there were nearly 15,000 work stoppages during the war, mostly wildcat strikes unauthorized by the union leadership.

Labor militancy was especially evident among coal miners. In 1942, eighty coal towns in Pennsylvania struggled in the face of rising food costs (one estimate pegged the increase at 125 percent) and grueling and dangerous working conditions. For their pains, mine workers earned only an average of forty dollars per week, considerably less than workers in other industries that posed fewer dangers and provided better working conditions. On January 1, 1943 anthracite mine workers in Pennsylvania walked out, defying their union's leaders and a back to work order by the War Labor Board. John L. Lewis, the United Mine Workers' president, then changed course and supported his membership. Lewis harshly attacked the "miserably stupid Little Steel formula for chaining labor to the wheels of industry without compensation for increased costs, while other agencies of government reward and fatten industry by charging increased costs to the public purse."

What followed was a series of strikes, including four national labor actions, that provoked the wrath of industry and government. The War Labor Board charged that Lewis gave "aid and comfort to our enemies"—a none too subtle suggestion of treason—while the military newspaper, the *Stars and Stripes*, denounced Lewis for his presumed selfishness: "Speaking for the American soldier—John L. Lewis, damn your coal-black soul." Even liberal journals such as the *Nation* attacked Lewis and his striking workers, arguing that their walkout "was irresponsible and unpatriotic and unjustified, no matter what the miners' grievances." Nonetheless the miners stood firm. When industry and government threatened to send in troops to break the strike or even draft striking workers into the Army, the miners brazenly faced the threat down. "What will they do" they responded to the threat to bring soldiers into the mines, "dig coal with their bayonets?"

In May 1943 Congress reacted to the unrest by passing, over Roosevelt's veto, the Smith-Connally Act (or War Labor Disputes Act). The legislation required unions to wait thirty days between calling a strike and actually beginning it (a so-called cooling-off period). It empowered the president to seize a struck war plant. And, it made it a crime for union officials to advocate strikes in defense plants. Even so, coal miners continued to challenge the "Little Steel formula." In November 1943, they finally won a wage increase in an important concession from the federal government.

But the costs of success were high. By the winter of 1943 a civilian coal shortage, to which the miners' strike had only partially contributed, left many Americans on the East Coast without adequate heating supplies for the winter.

When they turned to fuel coordinator Harold Ickes for assistance, he blamed the shortage on the unusual demands of the war. "We can fuel all of the people some of the time," he said, "and fuel some of the people all the time. But in war we can't fuel all of the people all of the time." Many others, however, blamed organized labor. A railroad strike that winter forced Roosevelt to seize some of the nation's rail lines. In the end, the railway workers, too, won important wage concessions. But, public animosity toward labor rose rapidly during the rest of the war, and many states passed laws to limit union power.

Stabilizing the Boom and Financing the War

The fear of deflation, the central concern of the 1930s, gave way during the war to concerns about inflation, particularly after prices rose twenty-five percent in the two years before Pearl Harbor. In October 1942, Congress grudgingly responded to the president's request and passed the Anti-Inflation Act, which gave the administration authority to control prices, wages, salaries, and rents throughout the country. Enforcement of these provisions was the task of the Office of Price Administration (OPA), led first by Leon Henderson and then by Chester Bowles. In part because of the office's success, inflation was a much less serious problem during World War II than it had been during World War I.

Even so, the OPA was never popular. There was widespread resentment of its controls over wages and prices. And there was only grudging acquiescence in its complicated system of rationing scarce consumer goods: coffee, sugar, meat, butter, canned goods, shoes, tires, gasoline, and fuel oil. Black-marketing and overcharging grew to proportions far beyond OPA policing capacity. One OPA study concluded in 1944 that some fifty-seven percent of American businesses failed to observe price controls.

From 1941 to 1945, the federal government spent a total of $321 billion—twice as much as it had spent in the entire 150 years of its existence to that point, and ten times as much as the cost of World War I. The national debt rose from $49 billion in 1941 to $259 billion in 1945. The government borrowed about half the revenues it needed by selling $100 billion worth of bonds. It raised much of the rest by radically increasing income taxes through the Revenue Act of 1942, which established a ninety-four percent rate for the highest brackets and, for the first time, imposed taxes on the lowest income families as well. To simplify collection, Congress enacted a withholding system of payroll deductions in 1943.

Wartime Production

The search for an effective mechanism to mobilize the economy for war began as early as 1939 and continued for nearly four years. One failed agency after another attempted to bring order to the mobilization effort. Finally, in January 1942, the president responded to widespread criticism by creating the War

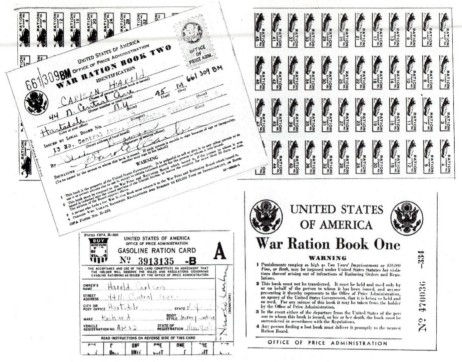

RATIONING. A sample of rations books from World War II prepared by the Office of Price Administration (OPA). Ration Book One warns of the stiff penalties that could be imposed for violating ration regulations—10 years in jail, a $10,000 fine or both.

Production Board (WPB), under the direction of former Sears Roebuck executive Donald Nelson. In theory, the WPB was to be a "superagency," with broad powers over the economy. In fact, it never had as much authority as its World War I equivalent, the War Industries Board. And the genial Donald Nelson never displayed the administrative or political strength of his 1918 counterpart, Bernard Baruch.

Throughout its troubled history, therefore, the WPB found itself constantly outmaneuvered and frustrated. It was never able to win control over military purchases; the Army and Navy often circumvented the board entirely in negotiating contracts with producers. It was never able to satisfy the complaints of small business, which charged (correctly) that most contracts were going to large corporations. Gradually, the president transferred some of the WPB's authority to a new office located within the White House: the Office of War Mobilization, directed by former Supreme Court Justice and South Carolina Senator James F. Byrnes. But the OWM was only slightly more successful than the WPB.

Despite the administrative problems, the war economy managed to meet almost all the nation's critical war needs. Enormous new factory complexes sprang up in the space of a few months, many of them funded by the federal government's Defense Plants Corporation. An entire new industry producing synthetic rubber emerged to make up for the loss of access to natural rubber in the Pacific. By the beginning of 1944, American factories were, in fact, producing more than the government needed. Their output was twice that of all the Axis countries combined. There were even complaints late in the war that military production was becoming excessive, that a limited resumption of civilian production should begin before the fighting ended. The military staunchly and successfully opposed almost all such demands.

WAR AND DIVERSITY

In addition to the imposing military and economic challenges it raised, the war placed new strains on the nation's social fabric, calling into question many traditions of racial, ethnic, and gender identity. For some groups straining against longstanding social and cultural restrictions, the war created opportunities to press their case for equality and opportunity. For others, most notably Japanese Americans, the war produced new levels of oppression. The war itself created few lasting solutions to the problems of racial and ethnic prejudice and sexual inequality, but it helped ensure that America would not be able to ignore those problems much longer.

African Americans and the War

During World War I, many African Americans had eagerly seized the chance to serve in the armed forces, believing that their patriotic efforts would win them an enhanced position in postwar society. They had been cruelly disappointed. As World War II approached, blacks were again determined to use the conflict to improve their position in society. This time, however, they actively pressed demands for economic justice and political equality from the start.

One of the most important initiatives occurred in the summer of 1941 when A. Philip Randolph, president of the Brotherhood of Sleeping Car Porters (a union with a predominantly black membership), began to insist that the government require companies receiving defense contracts to integrate their work forces. The demand stemmed from evidence of widespread racial discrimination in defense industries. Aircraft factories routinely excluded African Americans, or segregated black and white workers. In the construction industry, thousands of African-American craftsmen were denied work despite a vocal attempt by many companies to recruit skilled workers. Randolph, along with Walter White of the NAACP and T. Arnold Hill of the National Urban League, pressed the issue on President Roosevelt at a meeting in 1940. Despite his evident sympathy, Roosevelt offered only vague assurances that he would explore their grievances.

When five months had lapsed with no sign of action from the president, Randolph formed the idea of organizing a massive march on Washington by

African Americans to dramatize their call for jobs in defense factories and for integration of the armed forces. Randolph's promise to bring 100,000 black demonstrators to Washington produced great anxiety in the Roosevelt administration. Roosevelt was afraid both of the possibility of violence and of the certainty of political embarrassment. Many intermediaries, including First Lady Eleanor Roosevelt, attempted to persuade Randolph to cancel the march in exchange for modest concessions. But Randolph rejected these appeals. Instead, he seized on the idea of an executive order banning discrimination, which had surfaced in one high level New Deal conference. With that goal in mind, Randolph met Roosevelt face to face in late June 1941.

The meeting had important consequences. Roosevelt rejected the idea of integrating the armed forces, stressing the problems such an order would create given the likelihood of impending war. Instead he urged Randolph to accept his personal assurance that the chief executive would work hard to persuade industry to integrate their labor force voluntarily. Randolph did not flinch. Instead, he calmly told Roosevelt that he had come "to ask you to say to white workers and to management that we are American citizens and should be treated as equals. We ask no special privileges; all we ask is that we be given equal opportunities with all other Americans for employment on those industries that are doing work for the government." This could be accomplished, Randolph stressed, if

A. PHILIP RANDOLPH.   A. Philip Randolph is pictured with Eleanor Roosevelt and New York Mayor Fiorello LaGuardia a year after the war's end. During the war, Randolph had pressured Roosevelt into addressing discrimination against African Americans with some limited, though highly symbolic, success.

the president made it "a requirement of any holder of a government contract that he hire his workers without regard to race, creed, or color." Moved both by the moral weight of Randolph's plea and by his fear of the consequences of ignoring it, Roosevelt instructed three assistants to draft an Executive Order which, after some delay, he then signed. Randolph responded by cancelling the March on Washington.

Executive Order 8802 turned out to be largely a symbolic victory. It did ban discrimination by management and labor in industries that held defense contracts. And, it mandated the establishment of a Fair Employment Practices Committee to investigate discrimination against blacks in war industries. However, the FEPC's enforcement powers, and thus its effectiveness, were severely limited. As complaints began to come in, the committee found itself hamstrung in its efforts to mediate disputes between workers and the industries that employed them. In its entire history, the FEPC never recommended cancellation of a defense contract for racial discrimination. Its own chairman asserted at one public hearing in Alabama that "there is no power in the world—not even in all the mechanized armies of the earth, Allied and Axis—which could now force the southern white people to the abandonment of the principle of social segregation." Still, despite its disappointing performance, the creation of the FEPC created an important precedent. For the first time in many years, the federal government had intervened publicly and institutionally on behalf of equality for African Americans and had issued an unequivocal statement condemning racial discrimination.

The demand for labor in war plants greatly increased the migration of blacks from the rural areas of the South into industrial cities—a migration that continued for more than a decade after the war and brought many more African Americans into northern cities than the first Great Migration of 1914–1919 had done. Of the more than six million African Americans who left the South for the North between 1910 and 1970, five million came after 1940.

The migration had profound consequences for African Americans. It permitted many of them to improve their economic conditions. It also helped create an infrastructure of community organizations and church groups that would provide a foundation for the burgeoning postwar civil rights movement. Finally, it drew attention to extensive de facto segregation outside the South, as racial discrimination soon confronted many of the new migrants who searched for employment and housing opportunities in northern cities. At times that hostility resulted in violence, as a major race riot in 1943 demonstrated. On a hot June day in Detroit, a series of altercations between blacks and whites at a city park escalated into a full-scale riot. Two days of violence left thirty-four people dead, twenty-five of them blacks, and over 500 wounded. Both the mayor and the governor blamed the city's African-American community for the riot.

Despite such signs of conflict and tension, the leading black organizations redoubled their efforts during the war to challenge segregation. The Congress of Racial Equality (CORE), organized in 1942, mobilized mass popular resistance to discrimination in a way that the older, more conservative organizations had never done. Randolph, Bayard Rustin, James Farmer, and other, younger black leaders helped organize sit-ins and demonstrations in segregated theaters and restaurants. In 1944, they won a much-publicized victory by forcing a Washington, D.C. restaurant to agree to serve blacks.

Pressure for change was also growing within the military. At first, the armed forces maintained their traditional practice of limiting blacks to the most menial assignments, keeping them in segregated training camps and units, and barring them entirely from the Marine Corps and the Army Air Corps. Gradually, however, military leaders were forced to make adjustments—in part because of public and political pressures, but also because they recognized that these forms of segregation were wasting manpower. By the end of the war, the number of black servicemen had increased sevenfold, to 700,000; some training camps were at least partially integrated; blacks were serving on ships with white sailors; and more African-American units were being sent into combat. These changes created tensions of their own. In some of the partially integrated army bases—Fort Dix, New Jersey, for example—riots occasionally broke out when African Americans protested having to serve in segregated divisions. Substantial discrimination survived in all the services until well after the war. But within the military, as within the society at large, the traditional pattern of race relations was slowly eroding.

Native Americans and the War

For Native Americans, the war also gave evidence of new opportunities and of the persistence of racial tensions. Approximately 25,000 Native Americans performed military service during World War II. Many of them served in combat (among them Ira Hayes, one of the men who raised the American flag at Iwo Jima and became part of the legendary photograph and, later, war memorial). Others worked as "code-talkers," working in military communications and speaking their own languages (which enemy forces would be unlikely to understand) over the radio and the telephones.

The war also made its presence felt in the lives of those Native Americans who remained civilians. Little war work reached the tribes, and government subsidies dwindled. These developments increased the pressures for assimilation. As many talented young people left the reservations—some to serve in the military, even more (over 70,000) to work in war plants—contact with white society increased in ways that also spurred assimilation. For some, such exposure awakened a taste for the material benefits of life outside the reservations. It has been estimated that the average income of Indian households tripled during World War II. These improved economic conditions encouraged some Indians to remain in western cities when the war was over. Others found that employment opportunities that had been available to them during the fighting became unavailable once the war was won; many returned to the reservations.

The wartime emphasis on national unity undermined support for the revitalization of tribal autonomy that the Indian Reorganization Act of 1934 had launched. New pressures emerged to eliminate the reservation system and require the tribes to assimilate into white society—pressures so severe that John Collier, the energetic director of the Bureau of Indian Affairs who had done much to promote the reinvigoration of the reservations, resigned in 1945.

Mexican-American War Workers

World War II played an important role in enlarging the Mexican-American population. Large numbers of Mexican workers entered the United States during the war in response to labor shortages on the Pacific Coast, in the Southwest, and eventually in almost all areas of the nation. Indeed, Mexicans formed the second largest group of migrants to American cities (after blacks) in the 1940s. In Los Angeles, the population of Mexicans grew to nearly 400,000 during the war. Some migration was shaped by an agreement between the American and Mexican government in 1942 by which *braceros* (contract laborers) would be admitted to the United States for a limited time to work at specific jobs. American employers in some parts of the Southwest began actively recruiting Hispanic workers.

The war also influenced the kinds of work Mexican immigrants did. During the Depression, many Mexican farm workers had been deported to make room for desperate white workers. The wartime labor shortage caused farm owners to begin hiring them again. More important, however, Mexicans were able for the first time to find significant numbers of factory jobs. And over 300,000 Mexican Americans served in the United States military.

The sudden expansion of Mexican-American neighborhoods created tensions and occasionally conflict in some American cities. White residents of Los Angeles became alarmed at the activities of Mexican-American teenagers, many of whom were joining street gangs (*pachucos*). The gang members were particularly distinctive because of their style of dress, which featured long, loose jackets with padded shoulders, baggy pants tied at the ankles, long watch chains, broad-brimmed hats, and greased, ducktail hairstyles. (It was a style borrowed in part from fashions in Harlem.) The outfit was known as a "zoot suit." For those who wore them, as for many adolescents, their style of dress became a symbol of rebellion against and defiance toward conventional, white, middle-class society.

Eventually, the rebellion of these young Mexican Americans led to confrontation. As Los Angeles newspapers decried a non-existent crime wave supposedly created by Mexicans, an ordinance cleared the City Council that banned the wearing of zoot suits. The law permitted law enforcement officials to sweep through the barrios of Los Angeles and arrest, search, or detain Mexicans virtually at will. The Los Angeles county sheriff insisted that Mexicans had "a biological pre-disposition to criminal tendencies." In 1942, the apparently accidental death of a young man named Jose Diaz led to the arrest of twenty-two young Mexicans who were accused of murdering him. Over half of them were convicted and sentenced to life imprisonment on flimsy evidence before their convictions were overturned two years later.

In June 1943, animosity toward the "zoot suiters" produced a four-day riot in Los Angeles, after a rumor circulated that a group of Mexicans had beaten a white American serviceman. Several white soldiers stationed in the city joined with other white Angelenos and retaliated by indiscriminately beating young Mexicans wearing zoot suits. In subsequent days other riots followed in nearby southern Californian communities. The city police did little to restrain the white rioters in Los Angeles, who grabbed Hispanic teenagers, tore off and burned their clothes, cut off their ducktails, and beat them. But when Hispanics tried to fight back, the police moved in and arrested them. One soldier who observed the scene was horrified by the bloodshed, beatings, and rioting. "This is a form of class war," he concluded.

Chinese Americans and the War

For Chinese Americans, World War II produced a reversal, to some extent, of the blatant rejection many faced in American society earlier in the twentieth century. In fact, the American military alliance with China during World War II significantly enhanced both the legal and social status of Chinese Americans. In 1943, partly to improve relations with the government of China, Congress finally repealed the Chinese Exclusion Acts, which had barred almost all Chinese immigration since 1892. President Roosevelt, in supporting the reform, invoked the demands of the war as he urged the Congress to end exclusion. "By the repeal of the Chinese exclusion laws, we can correct a historic mistake and silence the distorted Japanese propaganda." The legislation that passed, however, did not entirely eliminate restrictions of Chinese immigration. The new quota for Chinese immigrants was minuscule (105 a year). Still, a substantial number of Chinese women—over 4,000 in a three-year period—managed to gain entry into the country through other provisions covering war brides and fiancées. And, perhaps most significantly, permanent residents of the United States of Chinese descent were finally permitted to become citizens.

Racial animosity toward the Chinese by no means disappeared during the war, but it did decline—in part because government propaganda and popular culture both began presenting positive images of the Chinese (partly to contrast them with the Japanese). As Chinese Americans (like African Americans and other previously marginal groups) began taking jobs in war plants and other booming areas suffering from labor shortages, they moved out of the relatively isolated world of the Chinatowns. The war offered an important opportunity for economic mobility as many Chinese gained access to higher-wage jobs than the service positions they had so often occupied in the American economy. On the West Coast and in the East, Chinese men and women labored in aircraft factories and shipyards. Indeed, some fifteen percent of shipyard workers in the San Francisco area in 1943 were Chinese.

Chinese Americans displayed a deeply felt patriotism in countless ways during World War II. The day after Pearl Harbor, and the formation of the United States–China alliance, a newspaper in San Francisco's Chinese community published a letter to "Mr. Hitler, Hirohito & Co." that boasted: "Chinatown is proud to be a part of Freedom's legion in freeing all the decent people of the world." The entire Chinese community in most cities worked hard and conspicuously for the war effort. A higher proportion of Chinese Americans (twenty-two percent of all adult males) were drafted than of any other national group. To men of our generation," one Chinese American explained, "World War II was the most important historic event of our times. For the first time we felt we could make it in American society."

The Internment of Japanese Americans

World War I had produced in America a virtual orgy of hatred, vindictiveness, and hysteria, as well as widespread and flagrant violations of civil liberties. World War II did not. The government barred from the mails a few papers it considered seditious, among them Father Coughlin's anti-Semitic and profascist *Social Justice*; but there was no general censorship of dissident publications. A few Nazi agents and American fascists were jailed; but there was no major assault on people suspected of sympathizing with the Axis. The most ambitious effort to punish domestic fascists, a sedition trial of twenty-eight people, ended in a mistrial, and the defendants went free. Unlike during World War I, the government generally left socialists and communists (most of whom strongly supported the war effort) alone.

Nor was there much of the ethnic or cultural animosity that had shaped the social climate of the United States during World War I. Americans continued to eat sauerkraut without calling it "liberty cabbage." They displayed little hostility toward German and Italian Americans. Instead, they seemed to share the view of their government's propaganda: that the enemy was less the German and Italian people than the vicious political systems to which they had been subjected.

But there was a glaring exception to the general rule of relative ethnic tolerance: the treatment of the small, politically powerless group of Japanese Americans. From the beginning, Americans adopted a different attitude toward their Asian enemy than they did toward their European foes. They attributed to the Japanese people certain racial and cultural characteristics that made it easier to hold them in contempt. The Japanese, both government and private propaganda encouraged Americans to believe, were a devious, malign, and cruel people. The infamous attack on Pearl Harbor seemed to many to confirm that assessment.

This racial animosity soon extended to Americans of Japanese descent. There were not many Japanese Americans in the United States—only about

127,000, most of them concentrated in a few areas in California. About a third of them were unnaturalized, first-generation immigrants (Issei); two thirds were naturalized or native-born citizens of the United States (Nisei). The Japanese in America, like the Chinese, had long been the target of ethnic and racial animosity; and unlike members of European ethnic groups, who had encountered similar resentment, Asians seemed unable to dispel prejudice against them no matter how assimilated they became. Many white Americans continued to consider Asians (even native-born citizens) "foreigners" who could never become "real" Americans. Partly as a result, much of the Japanese-American population in the West continued to live in close-knit, to some degree even insular, communities. Nativists used the existence of such communities as further evidence that the Japanese were, as they should be, outsiders to American life, alien and potentially menacing.

Pearl Harbor inflamed longstanding suspicions and transformed them into active animosity. Wild stories circulated about how the Japanese in Hawaii had helped sabotage Pearl Harbor and how Japanese Americans in California were conspiring to aid an enemy landing on the Pacific Coast. There was no evidence to support any of these charges; but according to Earl Warren, then attorney general of California, the apparent passivity of the Japanese Americans was more evidence of the danger they posed. Because they did nothing to allow officials to gauge their intentions, Warren claimed, it was all the more important to take precautions against conspiracies.

There was some public pressure in California to remove the Japanese "threat," but on the whole, popular sentiment was more tolerant of the Nisei and Issei (and more willing to make distinctions between them and the Japanese in Japan) than was official sentiment. The real impetus for taking action came from the government. Secretary of the Navy Frank Knox, for example, said shortly after Pearl Harbor that "the most effective fifth column work of the entire war was done in Hawaii," a statement that later investigations proved to be entirely false. General John L. DeWitt, the senior military commander on the West Coast, claimed to have "no confidence in [Japanese-American] loyalty whatsoever." When asked about the distinction between unnaturalized Japanese immigrants and American citizens, he said, "A Jap is a Jap. It makes no difference whether he is an American citizen or not."

In February 1942, in response to pressure from military officials like DeWitt and Knox and West Coast political leaders like Warren (and over the objections of the attorney general and J. Edgar Hoover, the director of the FBI), the president authorized the army to "intern" the Japanese Americans. He created the War Relocation Authority (WRA) to oversee the project. More than 100,000 people (Issei and Nisei alike) were rounded up, told to dispose of their property however they could (which often meant simply abandoning it), and taken to what the government euphemistically termed "relocation centers" in the "interior."

In fact, they were facilities little different from prisons, many of them located in the western mountains and the desert. "Suddenly," one evacuee recalled,

EVACUATING JAPANESE AMERICANS.   During World War II, anxiety about the loyalty of Americans of Japanese ancestry resulted in the evacuation and internment of more than 100,000 Japanese residing in the United States. Most were American citizens. The experience of gathering up one's belongings, abandoning home and property, and moving to "relocation" centers was painful and disorienting, as this photograph of an evacuation center in San Francisco in 1942 suggests.

"you realized that human beings were being put behind fences just like on the farm where we had horses and pigs in corrals." Conditions in the internment camps were not brutal, but they were harsh, uncomfortable, and—at first at least—disorienting. As one of those interned later recalled: "We did not know where we were. No houses were in sight, no trees or anything green—only scrubby sagebrush and an occasional low cactus, and mostly dry, baked earth." Government officials, on the other hand, talked of the internment centers as places where the Japanese could be socialized and "Americanized," much as many officials had at times considered Indian reservations places for training Native Americans to become more like whites.

But like Indian reservations, the internment camps were more a target of white economic aspirations than of missionary work. The governor of Utah, where many of the internees were located, wanted the federal government to turn over thousands of Japanese Americans to serve as forced laborers. Washington did not comply, but the WRA did hire out many inmates as agricultural laborers.

The internment never produced significant popular opposition. For the most part, once the Japanese were in the camps, other Americans (including their former neighbors on the West Coast) largely forgot about them—except to make strenuous efforts to acquire the property they had abandoned. Even so, conditions slowly improved beginning in 1943. Some young Japanese Americans left the camps to attend colleges and universities (mostly in the East—the WRA continued to be wary of letting Japanese return to the Pacific Coast). Others were permitted to move to cities to take factory and service jobs (although again, not on the West Coast). Some young men joined and others were drafted into the American military; a Nisei army unit fought with distinction in Europe. In 1944, the Supreme Court ruled in *Korematsu* v. *U.S.* that the relocation was constitutionally permissible. In another case the same year, it barred the internment of "loyal" citizens, but it left the interpretation of loyalty to the discretion of the government.

Nevertheless, by the end of 1944, most of the internees had been released; and early in 1945, they were finally permitted to return to the West Coast— where they faced continuing harassment and persecution, and where many found their property and businesses irretrievably lost. For many years following, survivors of the camps and their descendants attempted to direct national attention to the injustice they had endured and the economic losses they had sustained. A report by the Presidential Commission on the Wartime Relocation and Internment of Civilians issued in 1983 finally agreed. The internment, the report asserted, "was not justified by military necessity" but rather shaped by "race prejudice, war hysteria and a failure of political leadership." The report went on to conclude: "A grave injustice was done to American citizens and resident aliens of Japanese ancestry, who without individual review or any probative evidence against them, were excluded, removed and detained by the United States during World War II." In 1988 Congress voted to award reparations in the form of a single $20,000 cash payment to those internees who were still alive, a number that represented approximately half of those who were relocated and interned during the war years.

WOMEN, WAR, AND THE FAMILY

World War II affected women and the family in ways that few Americans could have anticipated before the war began. The demands of the wartime economy for new workers made it necessary for employers to turn to women, including many who had not worked for wages before. The absence of wage-earning men in many families made it necessary for women to work to support themselves and their children. As in many other areas of American life, gender roles felt the transforming effects of war.

Women and Wage Work

The participation of women in the American labor force had been growing throughout much of the twentieth century. But until World War II, most white women who worked were single and young. (Married African-American women with children had long worked for wages.) World War II altered these patterns in striking ways. Some 6 million new women workers joined the labor force during the war. Of these new workers, sixty percent were thirty-five-years-old or older, and seventy-five percent were married. One third of the new women workers had children under fourteen at home. Overall, the number of women in the work force increased by nearly sixty percent during World War II. Women accounted for a third of paid workers in 1945 (as opposed to a quarter in 1940).

The war did more than simply expand the number of women working for wages, however. It also redefined, at least temporarily, the kinds of work many women did, drawing them into roles from which they had previously been largely barred, either by custom or by law. Most notably, many women obtained high-wage work in industrial jobs that were once the nearly exclusive domain of men. The shortage of available male workers resulted in the hiring of women as ship riveters, keel binders, crane operators, stevedores, and tool and die makers, among other traditionally male jobs. More commonly, women found work in aircraft factories and defense plants, where they worked on assembly lines.

In the end, however, most women workers during the war were employed not in factories but in service-sector jobs. Above all, they worked for the government, whose bureaucratic needs expanded dramatically alongside its military and industrial needs. Washington, in particular, was flooded with young female clerks, secretaries, and typists—known as "government girls"—most of whom lived in cramped quarters in boarding houses, private homes, and government dormitories and worked long hours in the war agencies. Public and private clerical employment for women expanded in other urban areas as well, creating high concentrations of young women in places largely depleted of young men. The result was the development of distinctively female communities, in which women, often separated for the first time from home and family, adjusted to life in the work force through their association with other female workers.

Reconfiguring Gender Roles

Women have played important roles on the home front in all American wars. But World War II was especially important for the ways in which it reshaped traditional gender roles and stereotypes. The War Manpower Commission churned out an enormous amount of propaganda that both challenged and confirmed

WOMEN'S WAR WORK. "Rosie the Riveter," memorialized
in a popular song and a drawing prepared for the *Saturday
Evening Post* by Norman Rockwell, served as a symbol of
women war workers who assumed unorthodox jobs in
industry to take up the slack from absent male workers.
These real-life "Rosies" were welders at a war production
plant in New Britain, Connecticut. The war provided many
women with lucrative jobs in industry that had long been
closed to them. After demobilization, however, many
"Rosies" lost these higher paying jobs and returned to
more traditional women's employment.

many traditional images of women's proper roles. Suddenly a woman's "proper place" was not necessarily in the home—it was in the workplace, laboring for victory. At the same time, however, government films encouraged women to believe that warwork was not dissimilar to housework; both were well within the reach of women's innate competence. "Instead of cutting the lines of a dress, this woman cuts the pattern of aircraft parts," a narrator explained in one such movie, *The Glamour Girls of '43*.

The best-known symbol of women war workers was Rosie the Riveter, sketched by Norman Rockwell for a 1943 cover of the *Saturday Evening Post*. Decked out in overalls, her chest studded with victory pins, protective goggles perched high on a curly head of red hair, Rosie seemed at once the all-American girl and a vigorous, even brawny, specimen of the nation's toughest and most hard-working industrial craftsmen. A popular song told the story of Rosie the Riveter, who "kept a sharp lookout for sabotage, sitting up there on the fuselage. That little frail can do, more than a male can do." Women of independence and courage also appeared in films and even comic strips. The first episode of *Wonder Woman* by Charles Moulton appeared in 1941. "At last, in a world torn by the hatred and wars of men," Moulton wrote, "appears a *woman* to whom the problems and feats of men are mere child's play."

But while economic and military necessity eroded some objections to women's presence in the workplace, many obstacles and prejudices remained. Most factory owners continued to categorize jobs by gender. Female work, like male work, was also categorized by race: black women were usually assigned more menial tasks, and paid at a lower rate, than their white counterparts. Most African-American women, for instance, found it difficult to enter the higher-wage industrial jobs newly open to women during the war, even though twice as many black women were working in industry during the war than had been working there before 1941.

In addition to gender segregation and racial discrimination, the workplace also reflected the persistence of traditional ideas about men's and women's roles. Recruiting materials that described women's factory work as akin to household work reflected stereotypical views of women's capacities. Many employers treated women in the war plants with a combination of solicitude and patronization, which was helpful to them in some respects but was also an obstacle to winning genuine equality within the work force. Important wage differentials among men and women industrial workers still existed despite urging from the National War Labor Board that men and women be paid equally for equal work. Finally, even the most fervent official advocacy of new economic roles for women stressed the temporary nature of the wartime emergency. Most men, at least, assumed that when the war was over, women would return to their domestic sphere.

Still, women did make important inroads in the workplace during the war. They joined unions in substantial numbers, and they helped erode at least some of the prejudice, including the prejudice against mothers working, that had previously kept many of them from paid employment. Women had been working in industry for over a century, but during the war many new women workers gained a measure of confidence in themselves and an appreciation for wage work that they did not leave behind. "They were hammering away that the woman who went to work did it temporarily to help her man," one nurse recalled. "I think a lot of women said, Screw that noise. 'Cause they had a taste of freedom, they had a taste of making their own money, a taste of spending their own money, making their own decisions. I think the beginning of the women's movement had its seeds right there in World War Two." Although many years would pass before the women's movement provided a means for organizing those who shared such sentiments, the war left an important impression on an entire generation of women, as well as the sons and daughters they helped to raise.

War and the American Family

Women's new opportunities for wage work during the war produced new problems and concerns in American society. Many mothers whose husbands were in the military had to combine working with caring for their children. The scarcity of childcare facilities or other community services meant that some women had no choice but to leave young children—often known as "latch-key children" or "eight-hour orphans"—at home by themselves. Although federal funds were provided for some childcare centers under the Lanham Act (1943), very few women defense workers were able to take advantage of the limited assistance provided. The nation appeared to adapt readily to the necessity for women to leave the home and enter the workplace. But far less apparent was any systematic effort to address the need for childcare that the female entry into the workplace made inevitable. Many women were themselves uneasy with the idea of daycare and preferred to rely, when possible, upon their mothers and their extended families to watch over their children. But many women were left to shoulder by themselves the burdens that the combination of motherhood and wage work imposed.

Although little was done to address the need for childcare, much public discussion and debate focused on the American family during the war years. Social critics and public officials expressed anxiety that the family was deteriorating as a result of women's work. FBI Director J. Edgar Hoover warned that the absence of women from the home was fueling a vicious circle of neglect and crime. "There must be no absenteeism among mothers," Hoover insisted. "Her patriotic duty is not on the factory front. It is on the home front." Fear of juvenile delinquency grew especially pronounced as young boys appeared to be engaging in petty crime at a rapidly rising rate. For many children, however, the distinctive experience of the war years was not crime but work. More than a third of all teenagers between the ages of fourteen and eighteen were employed late in the war, causing some reduction in high school enrollments.

The return of prosperity and the coming of the war helped increase the rate and lower the age of marriage. Some couples married quickly before the husbands shipped out; when the men returned, many met newborn sons and daughters for the first time. They thus adjusted to marriage and children simultaneously. Others were eager to marry and begin their families as soon as they were demobilized. The war made life seem tenuous, and the lure of the stability of family proved especially powerful. Some of these young marriages were unable to survive the pressures of wartime separation, and the divorce rate rose rapidly. More notably, the birth rate began to rise precipitously—the first sign of what would become the great postwar "baby boom."

WAR AND THE NEW DEAL

The war's transforming impact on economy and society was no less evident in the arena of politics. When the war began, the New Deal already appeared to be in eclipse. The political casualties sustained by Roosevelt during the court-packing debacle, the recession of 1937, the growing suspicion of organized labor—all these things and many more suggested an underlying shift in the political winds. Still, it was not entirely clear when the war began what would happen to New Deal initiatives and ideas. For many American liberals, the war led to a reassessment of cherished beliefs and ideals. When the war was over, New Deal reform bore little resemblance to the spirited and idealistic movement that took form early in the 1930s.

"Dr. Win-the-War"

Late in 1943, Franklin Roosevelt publicly suggested that "Dr. New Deal," as he called it, had served its purpose and should now give way to "Dr. Win-the-War." The statement reflected the president's own genuine shift in concern: that victory was now more important than reform. But it reflected, too, the political reality that had emerged during the first two years of war. Liberals in government were finding themselves unable to enact new programs. They were even finding it difficult to protect existing ones from conservative assault.

Within the administration itself, many liberals found themselves displaced by the new managers of the wartime agencies, who came overwhelmingly from large corporations and conservative Wall Street law firms. But the greatest threat came from conservatives in Congress, who seized on the war as an excuse to do what many had wanted to do in peacetime: dismantle many of the achievements of the New Deal. They were assisted by the end of mass unemployment, which decreased the need for such relief programs as the Civilian Conservation Corps and the Works Progress Administration (both of which were abolished). They were assisted, too, by their own increasing numbers. In the congressional elections of 1942, Republicans gained forty-seven seats in the House and ten in the Senate. Roosevelt continued to talk bravely at times about his commitment to social progress and liberal reform, in part to bolster the flagging spirits of his traditional supporters. But increasingly, the president quietly accepted the defeat or erosion of New Deal measures in order to win support for his war policies and peace plans. He also accepted the changes because he realized that his chances for reelection in 1944 depended on his ability to identify himself less with domestic issues than with world peace.

The Election of 1944

Republicans approached the 1944 election determined to exploit what they believed was resentment of wartime regimentation and privation and unhappiness with Democratic reform. They nominated as their candidate the young and vigorous governor of New York, Thomas E. Dewey. Roosevelt was unopposed within his party; but Democratic leaders pressured him to abandon Vice President Henry Wallace, an advanced New Dealer and hero of the CIO, and replace him with a more moderate figure. Roosevelt reluctantly acquiesced in the selection of Senator Harry S. Truman of Missouri. Truman was not a prominent figure in the party, but he had won acclaim as chairman of the Senate War Investigating Committee (known as the Truman Committee), which had compiled an impressive record uncovering waste and corruption in wartime production.

The conduct of the war was not an issue in the campaign. Instead, the election revolved around domestic economic issues and, indirectly, the president's health. The president was, in fact, gravely ill. It may not be too much to say that he was dying. But the campaign seemed momentarily to revive him. He made several strenuous public appearances late in October, which dispelled popular doubts about his health and ensured his re-election. That he had succeeded was apparent on election day. "It is going to be a census rather than an election," Harry Hopkins predicted to a British diplomat. When the votes came in, it was not the landslide some New Dealers anticipated. But Roosevelt won handily, capturing 53.5 percent of the popular vote to Dewey's forty-six percent and winning 432 electoral votes to Dewey's ninety-nine. Democrats lost one seat in the Senate, gained twenty in the House, and maintained control of both.

The Eclipse of Reform

Despite the robust support Roosevelt received in the election of 1944, there would be no return to the broad interest in domestic reform and the imaginative array of programs that had characterized his first term. President Roosevelt continued to speak of the importance of federal activism in ensuring the economic well-being of the American people. He spoke in 1944 of "a second Bill of Rights under which a new basis of security and prosperity can be established for all." In fact, the older agenda of liberal reform appeared to inspire little enthusiasm as the war came to a close.

Many liberals who had stood behind the New Deal shifted their attention to new concerns during the war. As the world confronted the bloody consequences of totalitarian regimes, few liberals felt comfortable pressing a vision of a powerful state. The antimonopoly critique of the early New Deal also rang hollow as businessmen and finance capitalists played an important role in mobilizing national resources to sustain the war effort. Instead, those who embraced the goal of liberal reform focused more attention on stabilizing the American economy and helping it grow. Active fiscal policy and other programs designed to produce full employment were important means toward that end.

By 1945, the concerns that had animated reform in the 1930s had not disappeared. But they now reflected the nation's experience with a decade of depression, a period of vibrant reform, and total war. In the postwar years, prosperity and progress would remain central themes in American political life. Those goals would be much influenced by a new sense of the United States' role in the world.

CHAPTER EIGHTEEN

Waging Peace

~

The defeat of the Axis powers, most Americans believed, was a great victory for freedom and the prospects for international stability. Yet even before the end of World War II, tensions between the United States and the Soviet Union, who had been fighting as allies, began to darken the prospects for peace. Once the hostilities were over, those tensions grew quickly. And before long the two nations were locked in what became known as a "Cold War"—a tense and dangerous rivalry that would cast its shadow over international affairs for more than forty years. The Cold War also had profound effects on American domestic life, ultimately producing the most corrosive outbreak of antiradical hysteria of the century. America in the postwar years enjoyed enormous power in the world and great prosperity at home. It also experienced uncertainty and upheaval.

THE COLD WAR

Few issues in twentieth-century American history have aroused more debate than the question of the origins of the Cold War. Some have claimed that Soviet duplicity and expansionism created the international tensions, others that American provocations and imperial ambitions were at least equally to blame. Most historians agree, however, that wherever the preponderance of blame may lie, both the United States and the Soviet Union contributed to the atmosphere of hostility and suspicion that quickly clouded the peace.

Historical Tensions

In retrospect, the enmity between the Soviet Union and the United States after war seems less surprising than their wartime alliance. For throughout the decades before the war, the two nations had viewed each other with deep mutual mistrust and sometimes outright hostility.

The reasons for American hostility toward the Soviet Union were both obvious and many. As early as the 1890s, the two nations clashed over Russian efforts to develop parts of Manchuria, a goal some American diplomats saw as antithetical to the American interest in keeping Asian markets open for competition. Another source of hostility was World War I and the decision of the new Soviet regime in 1917, in one of its first official acts, to negotiate a separate peace with Germany. That left the West to fight the Central Powers alone.

In addition, the ideological underpinnings of the Soviet state ran directly counter to the ideas and values celebrated by American capitalism and democracy. The Soviet Union had called openly and continually for world revolution and the overthrow of capitalist regimes (even if it did little before World War II actively to advance that goal). Finally, there were the realities of the totalitarian state Stalin had overseen. The Stalinist policies and purges of the 1930s and 1940s—among them a brutal campaign of extermination against real and imagined opponents of the regime—had caused the deaths of millions of people. Knowledge of these events caused understandable revulsion in the West. Stalin, like Hitler, was one of the great tyrants of modern history; and in 1939, these two tyrants had agreed to the short-lived Nazi-Soviet Pact, freeing Germany to launch World War II.

Soviet hostility toward the United States had deep roots as well. The United States had opposed the Russian revolution in 1917 and had sent troops into Russia at the end of World War I to work, Soviet leaders believed, to overthrow their new government. Furthermore, the West had excluded the Soviet Union from the international community throughout the two decades following World War I; Russia had not been invited to participate in either the Versailles Conference in 1919 or the Munich Conference in 1938. The United States had refused to recognize the Soviet government until 1933, sixteen years after the revolution. The Soviet Union viewed such attempts to marginalize it, even to deny its integrity as a state, as acts of deep hostility. Finally, just as most Americans viewed communism with foreboding and contempt, so did most Russian communists harbor deep suspicions of and a genuine distaste for industrial capitalism. There was, in short, a powerful legacy of mistrust on both sides.

Postwar Visions

In some respects, the experience of World War II helped to soften that mistrust. Both the United States and the Soviet Union tended to depict each other during the war less as a dangerous potential foe than as a brave and dauntless ally. Americans expressed open admiration for the courage of Soviet forces in withstanding the Nazi onslaught and began to describe Stalin not as the bloody ogre of the purges but as the wise and persevering "Uncle Joe." The Soviet government, similarly, praised both the American fighting forces and the wisdom and courage of Franklin Roosevelt.

In other respects, however, the war deepened the gulf between the two nations. The Soviet invasion of Finland and the Baltic states late in 1939, once the war with Germany had begun in the West, angered many Americans. So did Soviet wartime brutality—not only toward the fascist enemies but toward supposedly friendly forces such as the Polish resistance fighters. Stalin harbored even greater resentments toward the American approach to the war. Despite repeated assurances from Roosevelt that the United States and Britain would soon open a second front on the European continent, thus drawing German strength away from the assault on Russia, the Allied invasion did not finally occur until June 1944, more than two years after Stalin had first demanded it. In the meantime, the Russians had suffered appalling casualties—some estimates put them as high as 20 million. It was a small step for Stalin to believe that the West had deliberately delayed the invasion to force the Soviets to absorb the brunt of fighting the Nazis.

At the heart of the tensions between the Americans and the Soviets in the 1940s, however, was a fundamental difference in the way the great powers envisioned the postwar world. The vision many Americans embraced was one first openly outlined in the Atlantic Charter in 1941, and later popularized through a 1943 book by Wendell Willkie entitled *One World*. It foresaw a world in which nations abandoned their traditional belief in military alliances and spheres of influence and governed their relations with one another through democratic processes. An international organization would serve as the arbiter of disputes and the protector of every nation's right of self-determination. The United States also called for an open economic world, in which it would have free access to international markets—particularly in Europe, which Americans assumed would rebuild along capitalist lines after the war.

Roosevelt publicly embraced much of the "One World" vision, and he devoted considerable energy to making the case to the American people for the participation of the United States in a new postwar international order. In his 1945 State of the Union message, Roosevelt issued a stern warning: "In our disillusionment after the last war, we gave up the hope of achieving a better peace because we had not the courage to fulfill our responsibilities in an admittedly imperfect world. We must not let that happen again, or we shall follow the same tragic road again—the road to a third world war." At the same time, Roosevelt believed that Britain, the Soviet Union, the United States, and perhaps to a lesser extent China ought to play especially important roles in postwar international relations. Whatever his public rhetoric, privately he remained a realist who understood the postwar world would be shaped by the major powers. But he also believed that a new international organization—ultimately embodied in the United Nations—would provide a means of arbitrating differences among the Great Powers peacefully.

The Soviet Union viewed the postwar world very differently. Stalin had signed the Atlantic Charter, but the Soviet Union was determined to create a secure sphere for itself in eastern Europe as protection against possible future aggression from the West. Having twice been invaded by Germany through Poland, the Soviet Union intended to forestall that eventuality from ever occurring again. Controlling Poland and destroying the ability of the Germans to wage war figured prominently on the Soviet postwar agenda. Although the British soon would condemn what they viewed as contemptible expansionism by the Soviet Union, they too were not entirely enamored of Roosevelt's "One World" vision. Britain had always been uneasy about the implications of the self-determination ideal for its own enormous colonial empire. Both Churchill and Stalin tended to envision a postwar structure in which the great powers would control areas of strategic interest to them, and in which something vaguely similar to the traditional European balance of power would re-emerge.

These differences of opinion were particularly important because the "One World" vision Roosevelt promoted had, by the end of the war, become a fervent commitment among many Americans. Thus when Britain and the Soviet Union began to balk at some of the goals the United States was advocating, the debate seemed to become more than a simple difference of opinion. It became an ideological struggle for the future of the world. By the end of the war, Roosevelt was able to win at least the partial consent of Winston Churchill to his principles. But although he believed at times that Stalin would similarly relent, he never managed to steer the Soviets from their determination to control eastern Europe and from their vision of a postwar order in which each of the great powers would dominate its own sphere of influence. Gradually, the differences between these two positions would turn the peacemaking process into a form of warfare, fought not with guns but with threats, bellicose rhetoric, and at times, actively hostile actions hidden behind the thin veneer of diplomacy.

Wartime Diplomacy

Serious strains began to develop in the alliance with the Soviet Union as early as 1942, a result of Stalin's irritation at delays in opening the second front and his resentment of the Anglo-American decision to invade North Africa before Europe. In this deteriorating atmosphere, Roosevelt and Churchill met in Casablanca, Morocco, in January 1943 to discuss Allied strategy. (Stalin had declined Roosevelt's invitation to attend.) The two leaders could not accept Stalin's most important demand—the immediate opening of a second front—but they tried to reassure him by announcing they would accept nothing less than the unconditional surrender of the Axis powers. It was a signal that the Americans and British would not negotiate a separate peace with Hitler and leave the Soviets to fight on alone.

In November 1943, Roosevelt and Churchill traveled to Teheran, Iran, for their first meeting with Stalin. By now, however, Roosevelt's most effective bargaining tool—Stalin's need for American assistance in his struggle against Germany—was almost gone. The German advance against Russia had failed;

Soviet forces were now launching their own westward offensive. Meanwhile, new tensions had emerged in the alliance as a result of the refusal by the British and Americans to allow any Soviet participation in the creation of a new Italian government following the fall of Mussolini. To Stalin, at least, the "One World" doctrine already seemed to be a double standard: America and Britain expected to have a voice in the future of eastern Europe, but the Soviet Union was to have no voice in the future of the West.

Nevertheless, the Teheran Conference seemed in most respects a success. Roosevelt and Stalin established a cordial personal relationship. Stalin agreed to an American request that the Soviet Union enter the war in the Pacific soon after the end of hostilities in Europe. Roosevelt, in turn, promised that an Anglo-American second front would be established within six months. All three leaders agreed in principle to a postwar international organization and to efforts to prevent a resurgence of German expansionism.

On other matters, however, the origins of future disagreements were already visible. Most important was the question of the future of Poland. Roosevelt and Churchill were willing to agree to a movement of the Soviet border westward, allowing Stalin to annex some historically Polish territory. But on the nature of the postwar government in the portion of Poland that would remain independent, there were sharp differences. Roosevelt and Churchill supported the claims of the Polish government-in-exile that had been functioning in London since 1940; Stalin wished to install another, procommunist exiled government that had spent the war in Lublin, in the Soviet Union. The three leaders avoided a bitter conclusion to the Teheran Conference only by leaving the issue unresolved.

The Yalta Conference

For more than a year after Teheran, the Grand Alliance among the United States, Britain, and the Soviet Union alternated between high tension and warm amicability. In the fall of 1944, Churchill flew by himself to Moscow for a meeting with Stalin to resolve issues arising from a civil war in Greece. In return for a Soviet agreement to cease assisting Greek communists, who were challenging the British-supported monarchical government, Churchill consented to a proposal whereby control of some parts of eastern and central Europe would be divided between Britain and the Soviet Union. "This memorable meeting," Churchill wrote to Stalin after its close, "has shown that there are no matters that cannot be adjusted between us when we meet together in frank and intimate discussion." To Roosevelt, however, the Moscow agreement was evidence of how little the Atlantic Charter principles seemed to mean to his two most important allies.

In February 1945, Roosevelt joined Churchill and Stalin for a great peace conference in the Soviet city of Yalta. The meeting began in an atmosphere of some gloom. The American president, his health visibly failing, sensed resistance to his internationalist dreams. The British prime minister, already dismayed by Stalin's willingness to make concessions and compromises, warned even before the conference met that "I think the end of this war may well prove to be more disappointing than was the last." Stalin, whose armies were now only miles from Berlin, was aware of how much the United States still wanted his assistance in the Pacific. He was confident and determined.

On a number of issues, the Big Three reached mutually satisfactory agreements. In return for Stalin's promise to enter the war against Japan, Roosevelt agreed that the Soviet Union should receive the Kurile Islands north of Japan; that it should regain southern Sakhalin Island and Port Arthur, both of which Russia had lost in the 1904 Russo–Japanese War; and that it could exercise

THE BIG THREE AT YALTA.   Churchill, Roosevelt, and Stalin meet in the Soviet Crimea at Yalta to discuss the shape of the postwar order in February 1945. Churchill and Stalin were alarmed by President Roosevelt's gaunt appearance and his apparent weariness during the meeting—evidence of physical deterioration that would lead to the president's death two months later. By the end of the Allied leaders' next meeting— at Potsdam, Germany, in July—only Stalin would remain in power. By then, Truman had succeeded Roosevelt, and Clement Atlee had succeeded Churchill as prime minister of Great Britain after Atlee's Labour party won a postwar election.

some influence (along with the government of China) in Manchuria. The negotiators also agreed to accept a plan for a new international organization, a plan that had been hammered out the previous summer at a conference at Dumbarton Oaks, in Washington, D.C. The new United Nations would contain a General Assembly, in which every member would be represented; a Security Council, with permanent representatives of the five major powers (the United States, Britain, France, the Soviet Union, and China), each of which would have veto power; and temporary delegates from several other nations. These agreements became the basis of the United Nations charter, drafted at a conference of fifty nations that opened in San Francisco on April 25, 1945. The United States Senate eventually ratified the charter in July by a vote of eighty to two (a striking contrast to the slow and painful defeat it had administered to the charter of the League of Nations twenty-five years before).

On other issues, however, the Yalta Conference either left fundamental differences unresolved or papered them over with weak and unstable compromises. Fundamental disagreement remained about the postwar Polish government. Stalin, whose armies now occupied Poland, had already installed a government composed of the procommunist "Lublin" Poles. Roosevelt and Churchill insisted that the pro-western "London" Poles be allowed a place in the Warsaw regime. Roosevelt wanted a government based on free, democratic elections— which both he and Stalin recognized the pro-western forces would win. Stalin agreed to a vague compromise. He promised to offer an unspecified number of places in the government to pro-western Poles, and he consented to hold "free and unfettered elections" in Poland. He made no commitment to a date for them. They did not take place for more than forty years.

Nor was there agreement about the future of Germany. Stalin wanted to impose $20 billion in reparations on the Germans, of which Russia would receive half. Roosevelt and Churchill agreed only to leave final settlement of the issue to a future reparations commission. A more important difference was in the way the leaders envisioned postwar German politics and society. In 1944, Roosevelt and Churchill had met in Quebec and had agreed to a plan, crafted by the American secretary of the treasury, Henry Morgenthau, for the "pastoralization" of Germany—dismantling its industry and turning it into a largely agricultural society. By the time of the Yalta meeting, however, Roosevelt had changed his mind. He seemed now to want a reconstructed and reunited Germany—one that would be permitted to develop a prosperous, modern economy while remaining under the careful supervision of the Allies. Stalin wanted a permanent weakening of Germany.

The final agreement was, like the Polish accord, vague and unstable. The United States, Great Britain, France, and the Soviet Union would each control its own "zone of occupation" in Germany—the zones to be determined by the position of troops at end of the war. Berlin, the German capital, was already well inside the Soviet zone. But because of its symbolic importance, it would itself be divided into four sectors, one for each nation to occupy. At an unspecified date, the nation would be reunited; but there was no agreement on how the reunification would occur. As for the rest of Europe, the conference produced a murky accord on the establishment of interim governments "broadly representative of all democratic elements." They would be replaced ultimately by permanent governments "responsible to the will of the people" and created through free elections. Once again, no specific provisions or timetables accompanied the agreements.

The Yalta accords, in other words, were less a settlement of postwar issues than a set of loose principles that sidestepped the most divisive issues. Roosevelt, Churchill, and Stalin returned home from the conference each apparently convinced that he had signed an important agreement. But the Soviet interpretation of the accords differed so sharply from the Anglo-American interpretation that the illusion endured only briefly. In the weeks following the Yalta Conference, Roosevelt watched with growing alarm as the Soviet Union moved systematically to establish procommunist governments in one eastern European nation after another and as Stalin failed to make the changes in Poland that the president believed he had promised. But Roosevelt did not abandon hope. He continued to believe the differences could be settled to the day he died.

AN EMBATTLED PEACE

Harry S. Truman, who became president upon Roosevelt's death, had almost no familiarity with international issues. Nor did he share Roosevelt's faith in the flexibility of the Soviet Union. Roosevelt had believed that Stalin was, essentially, a reasonable man with whom an ultimate accord could be reached—a belief he was beginning to question at the time of his death, but one he had not yet abandoned. Truman, in contrast, sided with those in the government (and there were many) who considered the Soviet Union fundamentally untrustworthy and viewed Stalin himself with suspicion and loathing.

Potsdam

Truman had been in office only a few days before he decided to "get tough" with the Soviet Union. Stalin had made what the new president considered solemn agreements with the United States at Yalta. The United States would insist that he honor them. Dismissing the advice of Secretary of War Stimson that the Polish question was a lost cause and not worth a world crisis, Truman met on April 23 with Soviet Foreign Minister Molotov and sharply chastised him for violations of the Yalta accords. "I have never been talked to like that in my life," a shocked Molotov reportedly replied. "Carry out your agreements and you won't get talked to like that," said the president.

In fact, Truman had only limited leverage with which to compel the Soviet Union to carry out its agreements. Russian forces already occupied Poland and much of the rest of Eastern Europe. Germany was already divided among the conquering nations. The United States was still engaged in a war in the Pacific and was neither able nor willing to engage in a new conflict in Europe. Truman insisted that the United States should be able to get "85 percent" of what it wanted, but he was ultimately forced to settle for much less.

He conceded first on Poland. When Stalin made a few minor concessions to the pro-western exiles, Truman recognized the Warsaw government, hoping that noncommunist forces might gradually expand their influence there. Until the 1980s, they were not able to do so. Other questions remained, above all the question of Germany. To settle them, Truman went to Potsdam, in Russian-occupied Germany, in mid-July to meet with Churchill (who was replaced as prime minister by Clement Atlee in the midst of the negotiations) and Stalin. Truman reluctantly accepted adjustments of the Polish–German border that Stalin had long demanded; he refused, however, to permit the Russians to claim any reparations from the American, French, and British zones of Germany. The result, in effect, was to confirm that Germany would remain divided, with the western zones eventually united into one nation, closely allied with the United States, and the Russian zone surviving as another nation, with a pro-Soviet, communist government. Soon, the Soviet Union was siphoning between $1.5 and $3 billion a year out of its zone of occupation.

The China Problem

Central to American hopes for an open, peaceful world policed by the great powers was a strong, independent China. But even before the war ended, the American government knew that those hopes faced a major, perhaps insurmountable obstacle: the Chinese government of Chiang Kai-shek. Chiang was generally friendly to the United States, but he had few other virtues. His government was corrupt and incompetent. His popular legitimacy was feeble. And Chiang himself lived in a world of almost surreal isolation, unable or unwilling to face the problems that were threatening to engulf him. Ever since 1927, the nationalist government he headed had been engaged in a prolonged and bitter struggle with the communist armies of Mao Zedong. So successful had the communist challenge grown that Mao was in control of one fourth of the population by 1945.

At Potsdam, Truman had managed to persuade Stalin to recognize Chiang as the legitimate ruler of China; but Chiang was rapidly losing his grip on his country. Some Americans urged the government to try to find a "third force" to support as an alternative to either Chiang or Mao. A few argued that America should try to reach some accommodation with Mao himself. Truman, however, decided reluctantly that he had no choice but to continue supporting Chiang. That was in part because of the strength in the United States of forces committed to him, including the formidable publisher of *Time* and *Life* magazines, Henry Luce, the son of Chinese missionaries and an inveterate defender of Chiang. The pro-Chiang forces came to be known as the "China Lobby," and for thirty years they helped shape American policy toward Asia.

In the last months of the war, American forces diverted attention from the Japanese long enough to assist Chiang against the communists in Manchuria. For the next several years, as the long struggle between the nationalists and the communists erupted into a full-scale civil war, the United States continued to send money and weapons to Chiang, even as it was becoming clear his cause was lost. But Truman was not prepared to intervene more directly to save the nationalist regime.

Instead, the American government was beginning to consider an alternative to China as the strong, pro-western force in Asia: a revived Japan. Abandoning the restrictive occupation policies of the first years after the war (when General Douglas MacArthur had governed the nation), the United States lifted all limitations on industrial development and encouraged rapid economic growth in Japan. The vision of an open, united Asia had given way, as in Europe, to an acceptance of the necessity of developing a strong, pro-American sphere of influence.

The Containment Doctrine

By the end of 1945, the Grand Alliance of World War II was in shambles, and with it any realistic hope of a postwar world constructed according to the Atlantic Charter ideals Roosevelt and others had supported. Instead, a new American policy was slowly emerging. Rather than attempting to create a unified, "open" world, the West would work to "contain" the threat of further Soviet expansion. The United States would be the leading force in that effort.

The new doctrine emerged in part as a response to events in Europe in 1946. In Turkey, Stalin was trying to win some control over the vital straits to the Mediterranean. In Greece, communist forces were again threatening the pro-Western government; the British had announced they could no longer provide assistance. Faced with these challenges, Truman decided to enunciate a firm new policy. In doing so, he drew from the ideas of the influential American diplomat George F. Kennan, who earlier that year had warned from Moscow, in a famous cable known as the "long telegram," (and later in an article published under the pseudonym "X" in *Foreign Affairs*) of the Soviet threat to American postwar goals. The United States, Kennan argued, faced in the Soviet Union "a political force committed fanatically to the belief that with the U.S. there can be no permanent modus vivendi." The only answer for the United States, then, was "a long-term, patient but firm and vigilant containment of Russian expansive tendencies."

On March 12, 1947, Truman appeared before Congress and used Kennan's warnings as the basis of what became known as the Truman Doctrine. "I believe," he argued, "that it must be the policy of the United States to support free peoples who are resisting attempted subjugation by armed minorities or by outside pressures." In the same speech he requested $400 million—part of it to bolster the armed forces of Greece and Turkey, another part to provide economic assistance to Greece. Congress quickly approved the measure.

The American commitment ultimately helped ease Soviet pressure on Turkey and helped the Greek government defeat the communist insurgents. More important, it established a basis for American foreign policy that would survive for over forty years. On the one hand, the Truman Doctrine was a way of accommodating the status quo: It accepted that there was no immediate likelihood of overturning the communist governments Stalin had established in eastern Europe. On the other hand, the Truman Doctrine was a strategy for the future. Communism was an innately expansionist force, the new theory argued, and it must be contained within its present boundaries. Its expansion anywhere could be a threat to democracy everywhere because, as Secretary of State Dean Acheson argued, the fall of one nation to communism would have a "domino effect" on surrounding nations. It would, therefore, become the policy of the United States to assist pro-western forces in struggles against communism whether that struggle directly involved the Soviet Union or not.

Rebuilding Europe

An integral part of the containment policy was a proposal to aid in the economic reconstruction of western Europe. There were many motives: humanitarian concern for the European people; a fear that Europe would remain an economic drain on the United States if it could not quickly rebuild and begin to feed itself; a desire for a strong European market for American goods. But above all, American policymakers believed that unless something could be done to strengthen the shaky pro-American governments in the nations of western Europe, they might fall under the control of their rapidly growing domestic communist parties.

Important initial steps toward supporting economic reconstruction took place at the Bretton Woods Conference in 1944, when the United State established the International Monetary Fund (IMF) and the World Bank. The organizations were capitalized at over $7 billion each and were authorized to make loans to promote international recovery, investment, trade, and a stable world currency. Although the organizations emerged out of Anglo-American plans, the United States provided the lion's share of the funds and therefore expected to have a deciding role in what was done with them. The Soviets attended the Bretton Woods Conference, but they chose not to participate in either fund. Some elected officials grumbled, but Congress approved the plan in July 1945 by a large margin.

After the war, these initial moves to address European economic recovery were joined by a far more ambitious plan. In a June 1947 speech at Harvard University, Secretary of State George C. Marshall announced a program to provide economic assistance to all European nations (including the Soviet Union) that would join in drafting a program for recovery. Although Russia and its eastern satellites quickly and predictably rejected the plan, sixteen western European nations eagerly participated. Whatever domestic opposition there was largely vanished after a sudden coup in Czechoslovakia in February 1948 established a Soviet-dominated communist government there. By now public opinion polls in the United States revealed a widespread popular belief that the Soviet Union appeared to be seeking world domination. Partly as a result, a conservative Congress approved in April 1948 the creation of the Economic Cooperation Administration, the agency that would administer the Marshall Plan, as it became known. Over the next three years, the Marshall Plan channeled over $12 billion of American aid into Europe, helping to spark a substantial economic revival. By the end of 1950, European industrial production had risen sixty-four percent, communist strength in the member nations had declined, and opportunities for American trade had revived.

GEORGE C. MARSHALL AT HARVARD, 1947. Secretary of State George C. Marshall is escorted through Harvard Yard en route to the commencement ceremony, where he received an honorary degree. Later that day, in a speech to Harvard alumni, he presented the Truman administration's proposal to aid in the postwar reconstruction of Europe. Its official name was the European Recovery Program, but it was better known as the Marshall Plan.

Protecting National Security

That the United States had fully accepted a continuing commitment to the containment policy became clear in 1947 and 1948 when Congress enacted a series of measures to maintain American military power at near wartime levels. In 1948, at the president's request, Congress approved a new military draft and revived the Selective Service System. In the meantime, the United States, having failed to reach agreement with the Soviet Union on international control of nuclear weapons, redoubled its own efforts in atomic research, elevating nuclear weaponry to a central place in its military arsenal. The Atomic Energy Commission, established in 1946, became the supervisory body charged with overseeing all nuclear research, civilian and military alike.

Particularly important was the National Security Act of 1947, which created several new instruments of foreign policy. A new Department of Defense would oversee all branches of the armed services, combining functions previously performed by the war and navy departments. A National Security Council (NSC), operating out of the White House, would advise the president on foreign and military policy. A Central Intelligence Agency (CIA) would be responsible for collecting information through both open and covert methods and, as the Cold War continued, for engaging secretly in political and military operations overseas on behalf of American goals. The National Security Act, in other words, gave the government (and particularly the president) expanded powers with which to pursue the nation's international aims. It centralized in the White House control that had once been widely dispersed; it enabled the president to take warlike actions without an open declaration of war; it created vehicles by which the government could at times act politically and militarily overseas behind a veil of secrecy; and it created the framework for the subsequent growth of the national security state.

The Road to NATO

At about the same time, the United States was also moving to strengthen the military capabilities of western Europe. Convinced that a reconstructed Germany was essential to the hopes of the West, Truman reached an agreement with England and France to merge the three western zones of occupation into a new West German republic (which would include the American, British, and French sectors of Berlin, even though that city lay well within the Soviet zone.) Stalin interpreted the move as a direct challenge to his hopes for a subdued Germany and a docile Europe. He was especially alarmed because, at almost the same moment, he was facing a challenge from inside what he considered his own sphere. The government of Yugoslavia, under the leadership of Marshall Josip Broz Tito, broke openly with the Soviet Union and declared the nation an unaligned communist state. The United States offered Tito assistance.

Stalin responded quickly to the American plans for Germany. On June 24, 1948, he imposed a tight blockade around the western sectors of Berlin. If

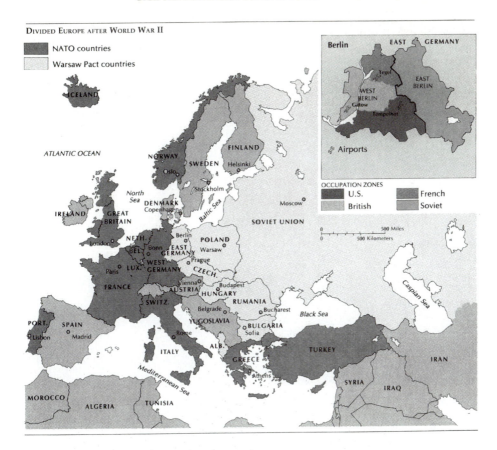

DIVIDED EUROPE AFTER WORLD WAR II

NATO countries
Warsaw Pact countries

ATLANTIC OCEAN

ICELAND

NORWAY   SWEDEN   Helsinki   FINLAND
Oslo

North
Sea   Stockholm

IRELAND   GREAT   DENMARK
BRITAIN   Copenhagen

London   NETH.   Berlin
BEL.   Bonn   EAST   POLAND   Moscow
GERMANY   Warsaw
Paris   LUX.   WEST   Prague
GERMANY   CZECH.

FRANCE   Vienna   Budapest
AUSTRIA   HUNGARY

SWITZ.   Belgrade   RUMANIA
YUGOSLAVIA   Bucharest

PORT.   SPAIN   Rome   BULGARIA   Black Sea
Lisbon   Madrid   Sofia

ITALY   ALB.
GREECE   TURKEY   IRAN
Athens

MOROCCO   SYRIA   IRAQ
ALGERIA   TUNISIA

SOVIET UNION

Baltic Sea

Caspian Sea

Mediterranean Sea

Berlin   EAST   GERMANY
Tegel
EAST
BERLIN
WEST
BERLIN
Gatow
Tempelhof

Airports

OCCUPATION ZONES
U.S.   French
British   Soviet

500 Miles
500 Kilometers

Germany was to be officially divided, he was implying, then the country's western government would have to abandon its outpost in the heart of the Soviet-controlled eastern zone. Truman refused to do so. "We are in Berlin by the terms of the agreement," Truman asserted, "and the Russians have no right to get us out by either direct or indirect pressure." Unwilling to risk war through a military response to the blockade, the president instead ordered a massive airlift to supply the city with food, fuel, and other necessities. The airlift continued for more than ten months, transporting nearly 2.5 million tons of material, keeping a city of 2 million people alive, and transforming West Berlin into a symbol of the West's resolve to resist communist expansion. In the spring of 1949, Stalin lifted the now ineffective blockade. And in October, the division of Germany into two nations—the Federal Republic in the West and the Democratic Republic in the East—became official.

The crisis in Berlin accelerated the consolidation of what was already in effect an alliance among the United States and the countries of Western Europe. On April 4, 1949, twelve nations signed an agreement establishing the North Atlantic Treaty Organization (NATO) and declaring that an armed attack against one member would be considered an attack against all. The NATO countries

THE BERLIN AIRLIFT.   Children standing amid the rubble of postwar Berlin gather to
watch American planes bringing food and supplies to their beleaguered city in 1948.
The Soviet blockade of West Berlin was intended to force the western
allies to abandon the city, but it only increased their resolve, and
that of the Berliners themselves.

would, moreover, maintain a standing military force in Europe to defend against
what many believed was the threat of a Soviet invasion. The American Senate
quickly ratified the treaty, which fused European nations that had been fighting
one another for centuries into a strong and enduring alliance. It also spurred the
Soviet Union to create an alliance of its own with the communist governments
in eastern Europe—an alliance formalized in 1955 by the Warsaw Pact.

The Hardening of Tensions

For a time, Americans believed that their initial achievements had turned the tide
of the battle against communism. But a series of events in 1949 eroded that confidence and launched the Cold War in new directions. Deeply alarming was the
collapse of Chiang Kai-shek's nationalist government in China, which occurred
with startling speed in the last months of 1949. Chiang fled with his political allies and the remnants of his army to the offshore island of Formosa (Taiwan), and
the entire Chinese mainland came under the control of a communist government

that many Americans believed to be an extension of the Soviet Union. Few poli-cymakers shared the belief of many members of the China Lobby that the United States should now commit itself to the rearming of Chiang Kai-shek. But neither would the United States recognize the new communist regime, which created the People's Republic of China on October 1, 1949. The Chinese mainland would remain almost entirely closed to the West for a generation. The United States, in the meantime, would devote increased attention to the revitalization of Japan as a buffer against Asian communism, ending the American occupation in 1952.

The year 1949 also brought an end to the American atomic monopoly. An announcement in September that the Soviet Union had successfully exploded its first atomic weapon, years earlier than predicted, shocked and frightened many Americans. Meanwhile in the highest levels of the United States government a debate was already underway about whether to pursue production of a hydrogen

THE CHINESE REVOLUTION.   Chinese troops march through
the city of Beijing in 1949, carrying banners and accompanied
by a propaganda truck carrying a portrait of Mao Zedong.
The triumph of communist forces in China alarmed many
Americans; the United States did not recognize the People's
Republic of China and Mao's regime until the 1970s.

bomb, a thermonuclear weapon that would be at least ten times as destructive as the bombs dropped on Hiroshima and Nagasaki. Although an advisory committee of the Atomic Energy Commission recommended in January 1950 against the new bomb, Truman decided to approve development of it. "It is part of my responsibility as Commander in Chief of the Armed Forces," the President announced, "to see to it that our country is able to defend itself against any possible aggressor."

Forced to make a series of momentous decisions amid rapidly changing world and domestic events, Truman called for a thorough review of American foreign policy. The result was a National Security Council report, commonly known as NSC-68, which recommended an important shift in the American position. The April 1950 document argued that the United States could no longer rely on other nations to take the initiative in resisting communism. It must itself establish firm and active leadership of the noncommunist world. And it must move to stop communist expansion anywhere it occurred, regardless of the intrinsic strategic or economic value of the lands in question.

Perhaps most significantly, the report called for a major expansion of American military power, with a defense budget almost four times the previously projected figure. The United States and its allies needed to amass military strength "to a point at which the combined strength will be superior . . . , both initially and throughout a war, to the forces that can be brought to bear by the Soviet Union and its satellites." In 1949 Truman had proposed a reduction in military spending for 1950 and 1951. Now he was faced with a stark choice: increase military preparedness and defense spending or, NSC-68 warned, face the potential "destruction not only of this Republic but of civilization itself."

As Truman pondered the report in the summer of 1950, North Korea invaded South Korea. That event erased whatever remaining doubts the president may have had about the wisdom of the new approach to foreign policy. NSC-68, he directed, should be considered "a statement of policy to be followed over the next four or five years." Programs designed to realize its objectives should "be put into effect as rapidly as feasible." In the aftermath of Truman's decision, and amid U.S. intervention in Korea, American military spending increased threefold. The trend proved a lasting one, as defense expenditures remained high for the next 40 years. But the more important result of NSC-68, and the shift in policy it helped create, was to establish the United States clearly and decisively—in its own mind at least—as the policeman of the world.

CHAPTER NINETEEN

Cold War America

~

International crises were not the only frustrations Americans encountered in the aftermath of World War II. The United States in the late 1940s faced the formidable challenge of adapting its wartime economy to the new demands of peace. It also experienced a series of wrenching crises in trying to adapt its domestic political life to the escalating demands of the Cold War.

THE FAIR DEAL

Despite all the weighty diplomatic decisions President Truman faced in the middle to late 1940s, he decided as well to address the unfinished business of the New Deal—to launch a program of reform that would, he believed, complete the structure Roosevelt had begun. Within days of the Japanese surrender, Truman proposed a broad "twenty-one point" reform agenda in a message to Congress. It called for federal housing assistance, a rise in the minimum wage, tax reform, farm aid, broader unemployment insurance, and an invigorated Fair Employment Practices Committee. "We want to see the time come when we can do the things in peace that we have been able to do in war," he had said in July 1945. "If we can put this tremendous machine of ours . . . to work for peace, we can look forward to the greatest age in the history of mankind."

Truman soon faced formidable problems in advancing his goals for American society. Gone were the Depression conditions that had made the New Deal so popular. Instead, there were new obstacles and challenges that undermined Truman's reform initiatives.

A Peacetime Economy

One immediate problem was economic reconversion—shifting the nation's economy from war production to peacetime activity. The bombs that destroyed Hiroshima and Nagasaki ended the war months earlier than almost anyone had predicted. As a result, the nation was propelled suddenly into a process of adapting to peace. The lack of planning was soon compounded by a growing popular impatience for a return to "normal" economic conditions—which meant an end to such wartime restrictions as rationing and price controls. Under intense public pressure, the Truman administration attempted to hasten economic reconversion, despite dire warnings by many planners and economists. The result was a period of great economic instability.

But the problems of the postwar economy were not the ones most Americans had feared. There had been many predictions that peace would bring a return of Depression unemployment, as war production ceased and returning soldiers flooded the labor market. But no general economic collapse occurred in 1946—for several reasons. Government spending dropped sharply and abruptly, to be sure; $35 billion of war contracts were canceled at a stroke within weeks of the Japanese surrender. But increased consumer demand soon compensated. Consumer goods had been generally unavailable during the war, so many workers had saved a substantial portion of their wages and were now ready to spend. A $6 billion tax cut pumped additional money into general circulation. The Servicemen's Readjustment Act of 1944, better known as the GI Bill of Rights, provided economic and educational assistance to veterans, increasing spending even further.

This flood of consumer demand ensured that there would be no new depression, but it did contribute to more than two years of serious inflation. During that period prices rose at rates of up to fifteen percent annually. In the summer of 1946, the president vetoed an extension of the wartime Office of Price Administration's authority, thus eliminating price controls. (He was opposed not to the controls, but to congressional amendments that had weakened the OPA.) Inflation soared to twenty-five percent before he relented a month later and signed a bill little different from the one he had rejected.

Compounding the economic difficulties was a sharp rise in labor unrest, driven in part by the impact of inflation. By the end of 1945, there had already been major strikes in the automobile, electrical, and steel industries. In April 1946, John L. Lewis again led the United Mine Workers out on strike, shutting down the coal fields for forty days. Fears grew rapidly that without vital coal supplies, the entire nation might virtually grind to a halt. Truman finally forced the miners to return to work by ordering government seizure of the mines. But in the process, he pressured mine owners to grant the union most of its demands, which he had earlier denounced as inflationary. Almost simultaneously, the nation's railroads suffered a total shutdown—the first in the nation's history—as two major unions walked out on strike. Truman lashed out bitterly at the unions. Although he was "a friend of labor," Truman said, he could not tolerate a situation in which labor leaders could "completely stifle our economy and ultimately destroy our country." In the end, Truman faced down the striking workers. By threatening to use the army to run the trains, Truman pressured them back to work after only a few days.

The problems of reconversion fell particularly hard on the millions of women and minorities who had entered the work force during the war. With veterans returning home and looking for jobs in the industrial economy, employers viewed many women, African Americans, Hispanics, Chinese, and other war workers as temporary employees who ought to give up their jobs to make room for returning soldiers. Some war workers left the work force voluntarily, including women who wanted to return to their homes to care for their returning husbands and for their children. But as many as eighty percent of women workers wanted to continue working. Many lost the jobs they had gained during the war but managed to remain in the work force. Postwar inflation, the pressure to meet the rising expectations of a high-consumption society, and the rising divorce rate (which left many women responsible for their own economic well-being) all combined to create a high demand for paid employment among women. As they found themselves excluded from industrial jobs, women workers instead moved into other areas of the economy (above all, the service sector). Virtually all black, Hispanic, and Asian males needed to remain in the work force as well. Most did so, but often in less skilled and less lucrative jobs than those they had occupied during the war.

Repudiating the Fair Deal

Despite problems with economic reconversion, Truman remained committed to enacting domestic reform measures. Indeed within weeks of announcing his "twenty-one point plan" he added several other ambitious proposals: federal aid to funding for the St. Lawrence Seaway (which was to link the Great Lakes to the Atlantic Ocean), nationalization of atomic energy, and perhaps most significantly, national health insurance. The latter had been a dream of welfare-state liberals for decades, but one deferred in 1935 when the Social Security Act was written. In unveiling such sweeping plans, the president was declaring an end to the wartime moratorium on liberal reform. He was also symbolizing, as he later wrote, "my assumption of the office of President in my own right."

But most of Truman's domestic programs (which he later labeled the "Fair Deal") fell victim to the same public and congressional conservatism that had crippled the last years of the New Deal. Indeed, that conservatism seemed to be intensifying. At the same time, the president was losing the confidence of much of the public—and even of many liberals. Truman was subject to daily criticism in the press; he fared little better among elected officials in Washington. Increasingly his critics portrayed Truman as bumbling and ill fitted for the momentous responsibility of the American presidency. Invidious comparisons between Truman and Franklin Roosevelt worsened the president's plight. One joke, which began with the question of what Roosevelt would do if he were still alive, ended with the punch line: "I wonder what Truman would do if he were alive."

By October 1946 public opinion polls indicated that only forty percent of Americans approved of the president's performance. Before long even that dismal approval rating had sunk to only thirty-two percent. The president himself privately expressed frustration with the pressures of office—"I would rather be *anything* than president," he told his press secretary in 1946. To his mother he confessed, "When I make a mistake it's a good one." As the November 1946 congressional elections approached, the Republicans made use of a simple but devastating slogan "Had Enough?" When the votes were counted, the Republican party had won control of both houses of Congress.

The new Republican Congress quickly moved to reduce government spending and chip away at New Deal reforms. The president bowed to what he claimed was the popular mandate to lift most remaining wage and price controls, and Congress moved further to deregulate the economy. Inflation rapidly increased. When a public outcry arose over the soaring prices for meat, Senator Robert Taft of Ohio, perhaps the most influential Republican conservative in Congress, advised consumers to "Eat less," and added, "We have got to break with the corrupting idea that we can legislate prosperity, legislate equality, legislate opportunity." True to the spirit of Taft's words, the Republican Congress quickly applied what one congressman described as a "meat-axe to government frills." It refused to appropriate funds to aid education, increase Social Security, or support reclamation and power projects in the West. It defeated a proposal to raise the minimum wage. It passed tax measures that cut rates dramatically for high-income families and only slightly for those with lower incomes. Only vetoes by the president finally forced a more progressive bill.

The most notable action of the new Congress was its assault on the Wagner Act of 1935. Conservatives had always resented the new powers the legislation had granted unions; and the labor difficulties during and after the war had sharply intensified such resentments. The result was the Labor-Management Relations Act of 1947, better known as the Taft-Hartley Act. It made illegal the so-called closed shop (a workplace in which no one can be hired without first being a member of a union). And although it continued to permit the creation of so-called union shops (in which workers must join a union after being hired), it permitted states to pass "right-to-work" laws prohibiting even that. Repealing this provision, the controversial Section 14(b), remained a goal of the labor movement for decades. The Taft-Hartley Act, like the wartime Smith-Connally Act, also empowered the president to call for a "cooling-off" period before a strike by issuing an injunction against any work stoppage that endangered national safety or health. Outraged workers and union leaders denounced the measure as a "slave labor bill." Truman vetoed it. But both houses easily overruled him the same day.

The Taft-Hartley Act did not destroy the labor movement, as many union leaders had predicted. But it did damage weaker unions in relatively lightly organized industries such as chemicals and textiles; and it made much more difficult the organizing of workers who had never been union members at all, especially women, minorities, and most workers in the South.

The Election of 1948

Despite the 1946 election results, Truman and his advisers still believed the American public was not ready to abandon the achievements of the New Deal. As they planned strategy for the 1948 campaign, therefore, they placed their hopes on an appeal to enduring Democratic loyalties. Throughout 1948, Truman proposed one reform measure after another. He again endorsed housing programs, a rise in the minimum wage from forty to seventy-five cents, farm support, aid to education, and national health insurance.

Most remarkably, on February 2 he sent the first major civil-rights program of the century to the Congress. Noting that "not all groups enjoy the full privileges of citizenship," Truman asserted that "the federal government has a clear duty to see that all the Constitutional guarantees of individual liberties and equal protection under the law are not denied or abridged anywhere in the Union." Truman asked for passage of a federal law against lynching, a ban on the poll tax, protection of voting rights, a ban on discrimination in interstate travel, a new Fair Employment Practices Commission, the end of racial discrimination in the military, and redress of the wrongs inflicted on Japanese Americans who had been interned during the war "solely because of their racial origin." Many of these proposals had come from the report of a presidential Civil Rights Commission that had made a deep impression on Truman. When southern Democratic congressmen heaped criticism on Truman for his civil-rights program, the president reminded one that he himself had Confederate ancestors and was thoroughly familiar with "Jim Crowism." But, Truman continued, "my very stomach turned over when I learned that Negro soldiers, just back from overseas, were being dumped out of army trucks in Mississippi and beaten. Whatever my inclinations as a native of Missouri might have been, as president I know this is bad. I shall fight to end evils like this."

While Congress ignored or defeated all of Truman's reform proposals, the president built campaign issues for the fall. There remained, however, the problem of the public's perceptions of Truman himself—the assumption among much of the electorate that he lacked stature, that his administration was weak and inept. Also troubling were deep divisions within the Democratic party. At the Democratic Convention that summer, two factions abandoned the party altogether. Southern conservatives reacted angrily to Truman's proposed civil-rights bill and to the approval at the convention of a civil-rights plank in the platform (engineered by Hubert Humphrey, the mayor of Minneapolis). They walked out and formed the States' Rights (or "Dixiecrat") party, with Governor Strom Thurmond of South Carolina as its presidential nominee. At the same time, the party's left wing formed a new Progressive party, with Henry A. Wallace as its candidate.

Wallace supporters objected to what they considered the slow and ineffective domestic policies of the Truman administration, but they resented even more the president's confrontational stance toward the Soviet Union. It attracted the support of, among others, those on the left sympathetic to communism.

In addition, many Democratic liberals unwilling to leave the party attempted to dump the president in 1948. The Americans for Democratic Action (ADA), a coalition of liberals, tried to entice Dwight D. Eisenhower, the popular war hero, to contest the nomination. Only after Eisenhower had refused did liberals bow to the inevitable and accept the nomination of Truman. The Republicans, in the meantime, had once again nominated Governor Thomas E. Dewey of New York, whose substantial re-election victory in 1946 had made him one of the nation's leading political figures. Austere, dignified, and presumably competent, he seemed to offer an unbeatable alternative to the president. Polls showed Dewey with an apparently insurmountable lead in September, so much so that some opinion analysts stopped taking surveys. Dewey conducted a subdued, statesmanlike campaign and tried to avoid antagonizing anyone.

Only Truman, it seemed, believed he could win. As the campaign gathered momentum, he became ever more aggressive, turning the fire away from himself and toward Dewey and the "do-nothing, good-for-nothing" Republican Congress, which was, he told the voters, responsible for fueling inflation and abandoning workers and common people. To dramatize his point, he used his acceptance speech at the Democratic convention to call Congress into special session in July and give it a chance, he said, to enact the liberal measures the Republicans had recently written into their platform. Congress met for two weeks and, predictably, did almost nothing.

The president traveled nearly 32,000 miles and made 356 speeches, delivering blunt, extemporaneous attacks on his opponents. He had told Alben Barkley, his running mate, "I'm going to fight hard. I'm going to give them hell." And he was true to his word. He called for repeal of the Taft-Hartley Act, increased price supports for farmers, and strong civil-rights protection for blacks. (He was the first president ever to campaign in Harlem.) He sought, in short, to recreate much

ELECTION OF 1948	(53% of electorate voting)		ELECTORAL VOTE	POPULAR VOTE (%)
		Harry S. Truman (Democratic)	303	24,105,695 (49.5)
		Thomas E. Dewey (Republican)	189	21,969,170 (45.1)
		Strom Thurmond (States' Rights)	39	1,169,021 (2.4)
		Henry A. Wallace (Progressive)	—	1,156,103 (2.4)
		Other candidates (Socialist, Prohibition, Socialist Labor, Socialist Workers)	—	272,713

ELECTION OF TRUMAN.   Few pundits believed Truman would beat Dewey in the election of 1948. Public opinion polls showed Truman lagging far behind his opponent. In this famous photograph, Truman exuberantly displays the Chicago Tribune's erroneous headline reporting the results of the election. In fact, Truman had defeated Dewey in a narrow victory.

of Franklin Roosevelt's New Deal coalition. To the surprise of virtually everyone, including nearly all the polls, media pundits, and political experts, he succeeded. On election night, he won a narrow but decisive victory: 49.5 percent of the popular vote to Dewey's 45.1 percent (with the two splinter parties dividing the small remainder between them), and an electoral margin of 303 to 189. Democrats, in the meantime, regained both houses of Congress by substantial margins. It was the most dramatic upset in the history of presidential elections.

The Fair Deal Revived

Despite the Democratic victories, the Eighty-first Congress was little more hospitable to Truman's Fair Deal reform than its Republican predecessor had been. But Truman did win some important victories, to be sure. Congress raised the legal minimum wage from forty cents to seventy-five cents an hour. It approved an important expansion of the Social Security system, increasing benefits by seventy-five percent and extending them to 10 million additional people. And it passed the National Housing Act of 1949, which provided for the construction of 810,000 units of low-income housing accompanied by long-term rent subsidies. (Inadequate funding plagued the program for years, and it reached its initial goal only in 1972.)

But on other issues—national health insurance and aid to education among them—Truman made no progress. Nor was he able to persuade Congress to accept the civil-rights legislation he proposed in 1949. Southern Democrats filibustered to kill the bill. Truman did proceed on his own to battle several forms of racial discrimination. He ordered an end to discrimination in the hiring of government employees. He began to dismantle segregation within the armed forces. And he allowed the Justice Department to become actively involved in court battles against discriminatory statutes. The Supreme Court, in the meantime, signaled its own growing awareness of the issue by ruling, in *Shelley* v. *Kraemer* (1948), that the courts could not be used to enforce private "covenants" meant to bar blacks from residential neighborhoods. The achievements of the Truman years made only minor dents in the structure of segregation, but they were the tentative beginnings of a federal commitment to confront the problem of racism.

There was less to celebrate in Truman's attempt to advance national health insurance. Through much of his presidency Truman had endorsed the importance of ensuring that all Americans had access to decent medical care and security from the ravages of catastrophic illness. His program to redress existing shortcomings called for the creation of more hospitals, greater support for public health, maternal and child health programs, federal aid for medical research and education, and most sweepingly, prepaid health insurance for all Americans. The program would be funded, Truman proposed, by a four percent increase in the Social Security tax raised through payroll deductions. Those not covered by Social Security would be covered by general federal funds.

Although Congress failed to act on the legislation when Truman first proposed it, the president renewed his call for action during the 1948 campaign and in his first State of the Union address after his re-election. What followed was a bitter debate in which the American Medical Association fiercely resisted the President's reform program. The AMA denounced national health insurance as "socialized medicine," characterized it as an attack on the free enterprise system, and charged that the government was attempting to control the medical profession. The organization devoted over $3 million to lobbying against national health insurance. Part of their campaign included public relations messages designed to "educate" the public about dangers they claimed a mandated federal program would pose. Whether because of such lobbying or for other reasons, the public in fact displayed little enthusiasm for Truman's program. In 1949, polls indicated that only thirty-six percent of Americans favored the legislation.

Health insurance slowly made headway, nonetheless, but as private rather than public programs. Voluntary programs increased, and many unions succeeded in winning coverage as a fringe benefit. By 1950, some fifty-one percent of Americans had coverage for hospital charges, although fewer than fifteen percent had insurance that covered in-hospital physician fees. Fewer than 3 million American workers were covered by negotiated health insurance plans in 1948; by 1954 that figure had risen to some 12 million. As more large employers provided some form of health coverage to their employees, commercial insurance companies also became much more involved in providing health-related plans. But the voluntary programs and commercial insurance plans left many Americans without coverage; and the cost of insurance for those within the covered pool steadily grew.

Despite the failure of national health insurance, there was significant progress in spurring hospital construction. The Hill-Burton Act passed by Congress in 1946 provided the states with federal money to build both public and private hospitals. Between 1947 and 1971, Hill-Burton would result in almost 30 billion dollars devoted to hospital construction, and a significant expansion of the number of hospital beds in the United States.

These measures fell far short, however, of what Truman had envisioned. Not until 1965 did the federal government provide national health insurance—and then only for the aged. The roots of that later success were evident to President Lyndon Johnson, who traveled to Independence, Missouri to sign the bill in Truman's presence. "You have made me a very, very happy man," the eighty-one-year-old former president would tell Lyndon Johnson.

THE KOREAN WAR

Truman's domestic policies had a difficult time from the beginning in competing against the growing national obsession with the Soviet threat in Europe. In 1950, a new and more dangerous element of the Cold War emerged and all but killed hopes for further Fair Deal reform. On June 24, 1950, the armies of communist North Korea swept across their southern border in an invasion of the pro-western half of the Korean peninsula to the south. Within days, they had occupied much of South Korea, including Seoul, its capital. Many Americans believed that the Soviet Union had engineered the North Korean invasion. Almost immediately, the United States committed itself to the conflict: the first military engagement of the cold war.

A Divided Country

The Korean War reflected a kind of political instability that was far from uncommon in the post–World War II period. Both the United States and the Soviet Union had sent troops into Korea by the end of 1945, and neither was willing to leave. Instead, they divided the nation, supposedly temporarily, along the thirty-eighth parallel. The Russians finally departed in 1949, leaving behind a communist government in the North with a strong, Soviet-equipped army. The Americans left a few months later, handing control to the pro-western government of

Syngman Rhee, anticommunist but only nominally democratic. He had a relatively small military, which he used primarily to suppress internal opposition.

The relative weakness of the South offered a strong temptation to nationalists in the North Korean government who wanted to reunite the country. The temptation grew stronger early in 1950 when the American government implied that it did not consider South Korea within its own "defense perimeter." The role of the Soviet Union in initiating the invasion remains unclear, but the Soviets supported the offensive once it began.

The Truman administration responded quickly. On June 27, 1950, the president ordered limited American military assistance to South Korea; and on the same day he appealed to the United Nations to intervene. The Soviet Union was boycotting the Security Council at the time (to protest the council's refusal to recognize the new communist government of China) and was thus unable to exercise its veto power. As a result, American delegates were able to win United Nations agreement to a resolution calling for international assistance to Syngman Rhee's government in South Korea. On June 30, the United States ordered its own ground forces into Korea, and Truman appointed General Douglas MacArthur to command the UN operations there. (Several other nations provided assistance and troops, but the "UN" armies were, in fact, overwhelmingly American.)

The intervention in Korea was the first expression of the newly expansive American foreign policy outlined in NSC-68. But the administration soon went beyond NSC-68 and decided that the war would be an effort not simply at containment but also at "liberation." After a surprise American invasion at Inchon in September had dislodged the North Korean forces from the South and sent them fleeing back across the thirty-eighth parallel, Truman gave MacArthur permission to pursue the communists into their own territory. His aim, as an American-sponsored UN resolution proclaimed in October, was to create "a unified, independent and democratic Korea."

The Costs of Invasion

For several weeks, MacArthur's invasion of North Korea proceeded smoothly. On October 19, the capital, Pyongyang, fell to the UN forces. Victory seemed near, until the new communist government of China—alarmed by the movement of American forces toward its border—intervened, as it had been threatening to do. By November 4, eight divisions of the Chinese army had entered the war. The UN offensive stalled and then collapsed. Through December 1950, outnumbered American forces fought a bitter, losing battle against the Chinese divisions, retreating at almost every juncture. Within weeks, communist forces had pushed the Americans back below the thirty-eighth parallel once again and had captured the South Korean capital of Seoul a second time. By mid-January 1951, the UN armies had stalled the North Korean advance; and by March, the UN armies had managed to regain much of the territory they had recently lost, taking back Seoul and pushing the communists north of the

THE KOREAN WAR, 1950–1953

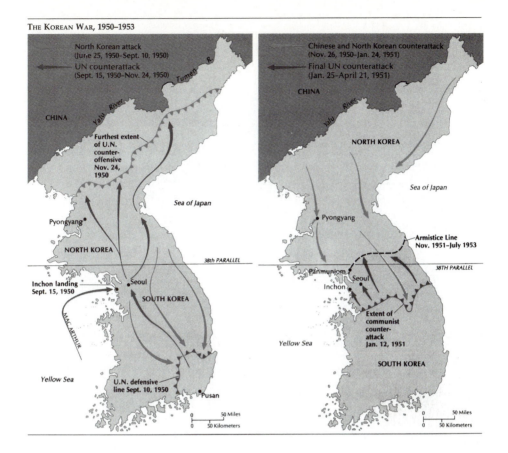

thirty-eighth parallel once more. But with that, the war degenerated into a protracted stalemate.

From the start, Truman had been determined to avoid a direct conflict with China, which he feared might lead to a new world war. Once China entered the war, he began seeking a negotiated solution to the struggle; and for the next two years, he insisted that there be no wider war. But he faced a formidable opponent in General MacArthur, who resisted any limits on his military discretion. The United States was fighting the Chinese, he argued. It should, therefore, attack China itself, if not through an actual invasion, then at least by bombing communist forces massing north of the Chinese border. In March 1951, he indicated his unhappiness in a public letter to House Republican leader Joseph W. Martin that concluded: "There is no substitute for victory." His position had wide popular support.

The Martin letter came after nine months during which MacArthur had resisted Truman's decisions and balked at the president's orders not to make his objections public. The release of the Martin letter, therefore, struck the president as intolerable insubordination. On April 11, 1951, he relieved MacArthur of his command.

KOREAN WAR.   As American soldiers march toward engagement with
the enemy, South Korean women and children flee in the opposite
direction. The Korean War, precipitated by a North Korean invasion of
South Korea, reflected the contradictory pressures of the Cold War as
the United States struggled both to stop communist aggression and, at
the same time, to limit the scale of military intervention.

There was a storm of public outrage. Sixty-nine percent of the American
people supported MacArthur, a Gallup poll reported. When the general returned
to the United States later in 1951, he was greeted with wild enthusiasm. His televised farewell appearance before a joint session of Congress—which he concluded by saying "Old soldiers never die, they just fade away"—attracted an audience of millions. Public criticism of Truman finally abated somewhat when a
number of prominent military figures, including General Omar Bradley, publicly
supported the president's decision. But substantial hostility toward Truman remained.

In the meantime, the Korean stalemate continued. Negotiations between
the opposing forces began at Panmunjom in July 1951, but the talks—and the
war—dragged on until 1953.

Limited Mobilization

Just as the war in Korea produced only a limited American military commitment abroad, so it created only a limited economic mobilization at home. Still, the government did try to control the wartime economy in several important ways.

First, Truman set up the Office of Defense Mobilization to fight inflation by holding down prices and discouraging high union wage demands. When these cautious regulatory efforts failed, the president took more drastic action. Railroad workers walked off the job in 1951, and Truman ordered the government to seize control of the railroads. That helped keep the trains running, but it had no effect on union demands. Workers ultimately got most of what they had demanded. In 1952, during a nationwide steel strike, Truman seized the steel mills, citing his powers as commander in chief. But in a six to three decision, the Supreme Court ruled that the president had exceeded his authority, and Truman was forced to relent. A long and costly strike followed, and the president's drastic actions appeared to many to have been both rash and ineffective.

The Korean War gave a significant boost to economic growth by pumping new government funds into the economy at a point when many believed a recession was about to begin. But the war had other, less welcome effects. It came at a time of rising insecurity about America's position in the world and intensified anxiety about communism. As the long stalemate continued, producing 140,000 American dead and wounded, frustration turned to anger. The United States, which had recently won the greatest war in history, seemed unable to conclude what many Americans considered a minor border skirmish in a small country. Some began to believe that something must be deeply wrong—not only in Korea but within the United States as well. Such fears contributed to the rise of the second major campaign of the century against domestic communism.

THE CRUSADE AGAINST COMMUNISM

The question of why so many Americans came to believe that their government, and their nation, were riddled with communist subversives remains a subject of much controversy among historians. No single factor explains why these concerns by the early 1950s had reached the point of near hysteria. There are, nonetheless, several factors that clearly played a part in fueling the campaign against domestic enemies.

Communism itself was obviously one factor in fueling the fears of Americans. Stalin's atrocities, the expansionism of the Soviet Union in the postwar period, and perhaps most notably, American setbacks in the battle against communism (the Korean stalemate, the "loss" of China, the Soviet development of an atomic bomb) certainly made fertile ground for those who would plant suspicions about domestic communism. The idea of a communist conspiracy within

American borders, aided and abetted by traitors and spies, offered a convenient explanation of why the United States had not always prevailed in the Cold War abroad. But other important factors, rooted in events in American domestic politics, contributed to the rise of the anticommunist fervor as well.

Early Investigations

At least initially, a good deal of the anticommunist furor emerged out of infighting among the Democratic and Republican parties and their battles for political control in the late 1940s. Beginning in 1947 (with Republicans temporarily in control of Congress), the House Committee on Un-American Activities (HUAC) held widely publicized investigations to prove that, under Democratic rule, the government had tolerated (if not actually encouraged) communist subversion. The committee turned first to the movie industry, arguing that communists had infiltrated Hollywood and tainted American films with propaganda. Writers and producers, some of them former communists, were called to testify. Several who became known as "friendly witnesses" agreed to cooperate with the committee and in their testimony named associates and colleagues who, they claimed, had been involved in left-wing politics. Others refused to cooperate with what they viewed as an inquisition. Among them were several leading directors and screenwriters known as the "Hollywood Ten." When these men declined to answer questions about their own political beliefs and those of their colleagues, they were jailed for contempt. As the investigations continued, others were barred from employment in Hollywood when the film industry, attempting to protect its imperiled public image, adopted a blacklist of those of "suspicious loyalty."

More alarming to the public was HUAC's investigation into charges of disloyalty leveled against a former high-ranking member of the State Department, Alger Hiss. In 1948, Whittaker Chambers, who admitted he had once been a communist agent and was now a conservative editor at *Time* magazine, told the committee that Hiss had passed classified State Department documents through him to the Soviet Union in 1937 and 1938. When Hiss sued him for slander, Chambers produced microfilms of the documents (called the "pumpkin papers," because Chambers had kept them hidden in a pumpkin in his garden) that he claimed Hiss had given to the Soviets. Hiss could not be tried for espionage because of the statute of limitations (a law that protects individuals from prosecution for most crimes after seven years have passed). But largely because of the relentless efforts of Richard M. Nixon, a freshman Republican congressman from California and a member of HUAC, Hiss was convicted of perjury and served several years in prison. The Hiss case not only discredited a prominent young diplomat; it cast suspicion on a generation of liberal Democrats and made it possible for many Americans to believe that communists had actually infiltrated the government.

The Federal Loyalty Program

Partly to protect itself against Republican attacks and partly to encourage support for the president's foreign policy initiatives, the Truman administration in 1947 initiated a widely publicized program to review the loyalty of federal employees. Truman himself had some doubts about the program. He believed that America was "perfectly safe so far as communism is concerned—we have far too many sane people." But he yielded to political pressures when he issued Executive Order 9835 establishing the Federal Employees Loyalty and Security Program. Although precedents for such screenings existed during war, no such program had ever been enacted in peacetime.

The program had two important elements. First, it gave the attorney general authority to draw up a list of subversive organizations. Membership in or even support for listed groups could then be used to determine the "loyalty" of federal employees. Second, the program provided the means for the federal government to investigate its own employees for suspicion of political subversion.

THE PUMPKIN PAPERS.   According to Whittaker Chambers, these hollowed out pumpkins held microfilms of classified State Department papers passed to him by Alger Hiss. Chambers claimed Hiss had passed the "pumpkin papers," as they were called, through him to the Soviet Union.

In August 1950, the president went further and authorized sensitive agencies to fire people deemed no more than "bad security risks." By 1951, more than 2,000 government employees had resigned under pressure, and 212 had been dismissed.

Whatever Truman's political intentions, the employee loyalty program seemed to add legitimacy to those leveling accusations of subversion against the government. The anticommunist frenzy quickly grew so intense that even a Democratic Congress felt obliged to bow to it. In 1950, Congress passed the McCarran Internal Security Act, which required all communist organizations to register with the government and publish their records while creating additional restrictions on "subversive" activity. Truman vetoed the bill. Congress easily overrode his veto.

The Rosenberg Case

The anticommunist crusade reached new levels of intensity with revelations of an alleged conspiracy within the United States to pass atomic secrets to the Soviet Union. Many believed the plot accounted for the Soviet success in creating an atomic weapon in 1949, earlier than most Americans had expected. In 1950, Klaus Fuchs, a young British scientist, seemed to confirm those fears when he testified that he had delivered to the Russians details of the manufacture of the American bomb. The case ultimately settled on an obscure New York couple, Julius and Ethel Rosenberg, members of the Communist party, whom the government claimed had been the masterminds of the conspiracy. The case against them rested in large part on testimony by Ethel's brother, David Greenglass, a machinist who had worked on the Manhattan Project. Greenglass admitted to channeling secret information to the Soviet Union through other agents (including Fuchs). His sister and brother-in-law had, he claimed, planned and orchestrated the espionage. The Rosenbergs denied any part in the conspiracy, but they were convicted and, on April 5, 1951, sentenced to death. A worldwide movement in support of the Rosenbergs took form in the next two years; many legal appeals were also filed on their behalf to no avail. They died in the electric chair on June 19, 1953, proclaiming their innocence to the end.

All these factors—the HUAC investigations, the Hiss trial, the loyalty investigations, the McCarran Act, the Rosenberg case—combined with concern about international events to create a fear of communist subversion that by the early 1950s seemed to have gripped virtually the entire country. State and local governments, the judiciary, schools and universities, and labor unions all sought to purge themselves of real or imagined subversives. A pervasive fear settled on the country—not only the fear of communist infiltration but the fear of being suspected of communism. It was a climate that made possible the rise of an extraordinary public figure, whose behavior at any other time might have been dismissed as preposterous.

McCarthyism

Joseph McCarthy was an undistinguished, first-term, Republican senator from Wisconsin when, in February 1950, he suddenly burst into national prominence. In the midst of a speech in Wheeling, West Virginia, he raised a sheet of paper and claimed to "hold in my hand" a list of 205 known communists currently working in the American State Department. No person of comparable stature had ever made so bold a charge against the federal government; and in the weeks to come, as McCarthy repeated and expanded on his accusations (and altered his numbers accordingly), he emerged as the nation's most prominent leader of the crusade against domestic subversion.

Within weeks of his charges against the State Department, McCarthy was leveling accusations at other agencies. After 1952, with the Republicans in control of the Senate and McCarthy the chairman of a special subcommittee, he conducted highly publicized investigations of subversion in many areas of the government. His unprincipled assistants, Roy Cohn and David Schine, sauntered arrogantly through federal offices and American embassies overseas looking for evidence of communist influence. One hapless government official after another appeared before McCarthy's subcommittee, where the senator belligerently and often cruelly badgered witnesses and destroyed public careers. McCarthy never produced solid evidence that any federal employee was a communist. But a growing constituency adored him nevertheless for his coarse, "fearless" assaults on a government establishment that many considered arrogant, effete, even traitorous. Republicans, in particular, rallied to his claims that the Democrats had been responsible for "twenty years of treason," that only a change of parties could rid the country of subversion. McCarthy, in short, provided his followers with an issue into which they could channel a wide range of resentments: fear of communism, animosity toward the country's "Eastern establishment," and frustrated partisan ambitions.

For a time, McCarthy intimidated all but a few people from opposing him. Even the highly popular Dwight D. Eisenhower, running for president in 1952, did not dare speak out against him, although he disliked McCarthy's tactics and was outraged at, among other things, McCarthy's attacks on General George Marshall. Instead, as Eisenhower campaigned with McCarthy in Wisconsin he joined the attack on communist subversion in government, stressing the damage that had been done by Democratic administrations who "had poisoned two decades of our national life" by tolerating communism. A disgusted Harry Truman expressed dismay that Eisenhower did not publicly defend General Marshall. "I thought he might make a good president," Truman said of Eisenhower after his Wisconsin speech, "but that was a mistake. In this campaign he has betrayed almost everything I thought he stood for." Eisenhower, Truman insisted, "knows or he ought to know, how completely dishonest Joe McCarthy is. He ought to despise McCarthy; just as I expected him to—and just as I do."

The Republican Revival

Instead, public frustration over the stalemate in Korea and popular fears of internal subversion combined to make 1952 a bad year for the Democratic party. Truman, whose own popularity had diminished almost to the vanishing point, wisely withdrew from the presidential contest. The party united instead behind Governor Adlai E. Stevenson of Illinois. Stevenson's dignity, wit, and eloquence made him a beloved figure to many liberals and intellectuals. But those same qualities seemed only to fuel Republican charges that Stevenson lacked the strength or the will to combat communism sufficiently. McCarthy described him as "soft" and took delight in deliberately confusing him with Alger Hiss.

NIXON AND EISENHOWER. General Eisenhower greets his running mate Richard Nixon, shortly after Nixon's "Checkers" speech explaining alleged financial improprieties. Though privately critical of Nixon, Eisenhower stood by him. The two men went on to crush the Democratic ticket of Stevenson and Kefauver in the election of 1952.

Stevenson's greatest problem, however, was the Republican candidate opposing him. Rejecting the efforts of conservatives to nominate Robert Taft or Douglas MacArthur, the Republicans turned to a man who had no previous identification with the party: General Dwight D. Eisenhower, military hero, commander of NATO, president of Columbia University in New York. He chose as his running mate the young California senator who had gained national prominence through his crusade against Alger Hiss: Richard M. Nixon.

Eisenhower and Nixon were a powerful combination in the autumn campaign. While Eisenhower attracted support through his geniality and his statesmanlike pledges to settle the Korean conflict (at one point dramatically promising to "go to Korea" himself), Nixon effectively exploited the issue of domestic subversion. After surviving early accusations of financial improprieties (which he effectively neutralized in a famous television address, the "Checkers speech"), Nixon went on to launch harsh attacks on Democratic "cowardice," "appeasement," and "treason." He spoke derisively of "Adlai the appeaser" and ridiculed Secretary of State Dean Acheson for running a "cowardly college of communist containment." And he missed no opportunity to publicize Stevenson's early support for Alger Hiss as opposed to Nixon's own role in exposing Hiss. Eisenhower and Nixon both made effective use of allegations of corruption in the Truman administration and pledged repeatedly to "clean up the mess in Washington."

The response at the polls was overwhelming. Eisenhower won both a popular and electoral landslide: fifty-five percent of the popular vote to Stevenson's forty-four percent, 442 electoral votes to Stevenson's eighty-nine. Republicans gained control of both houses of Congress for the first time in two decades. The election of 1952 ended twenty years of Democratic government. And, while it might not have seemed so at the time, it also signaled the end of some of the worst political turbulence of postwar era.

CHAPTER TWENTY

The Culture of Postwar Prosperity

≈

D uring the 1950s the United States enjoyed a period of exceptional abundance that shaped the nation's social, economic, and even physical landscape in profound ways. Postwar prosperity helped produce a widespread sense of national purpose and self-satisfaction. And it permitted many Americans to live in much greater comfort and with a much stronger sense of personal security than they ever had before.

As throughout American history, not everyone shared equally, or even at all, in the postwar prosperity. Many people lagged far behind the vaunted middle-class standard of living that some Americans now considered virtually a birthright and trumpeted as the "American Dream." In fact more than 30 million Americans lived in poverty in the early 1950s. Significant minorities—most prominently the ten percent of the American people who were African American, but also Hispanics, Asians, and others—continued to suffer social, political, and economic discrimination. American women, too, faced significant obstacles to personal and professional fulfillment.

Indeed, the very things that made America so successful in the 1950s also contributed over time to a restlessness with the nation's enduring social problems. Gunnar Myrdal, a Swedish sociologist who spent several years studying American social problems, wrote in 1944: "American affluence is heavily mortgaged. America carries a tremendous burden of debt to its poor people." Ultimately, the paradox of poverty and inequality among plenty helped move the nation into more turbulent times in the 1960s. Even in the culture of prosperity, signs of problems to come were already visible.

THE ROOTS OF PROSPERITY

Perhaps the most striking feature of American society in the 1950s and early 1960s was the booming, almost miraculous, economic growth that made even the heady 1920s seem pale by comparison. It was a better balanced and more widely distributed prosperity than that of thirty years earlier. It was not, however, as universal as some Americans liked to believe.

Economic Growth

By 1949, despite the continuing problems of postwar reconversion, an economic expansion had begun that would continue with only brief interruptions for almost twenty years. Between 1945 and 1960, the gross national product grew by 250 percent, from $200 billion to over $500 billion—a striking rebuke to the widespread predictions in 1945 that the GNP would decline once the demands of war production ended. Unemployment, which during the Depression had averaged between fifteen and twenty-five percent, remained at about five percent or lower throughout the 1950s and early 1960s. Inflation, in the meantime, hovered around three percent a year or less.

The causes of this growth were varied. Government spending, which had ended the Depression in the 1940s, continued to stimulate growth through public funding of schools, housing, veterans' benefits, welfare, and the $100 billion interstate highway program, which began in 1956. Above all, there was military spending. Economic growth peaked (averaging 4.7 percent a year) during the first half of the 1950s, when military spending was highest because of the Korean War. In the late 1950s, with spending on armaments in decline, the annual rate of growth declined by more than half, to 2.25 percent.

Technological progress also contributed to the boom. Advances in production techniques and mechanical efficiency helped boost worker productivity more than thirty-five percent in the first decade after the war, a rate far higher than that of any previous era. The development of electronic computers, which first became commercially available in the mid-1950s, began to improve the performance of some American corporations. And technological research and development itself became an increasingly important sector of the economy, expanding the demand for scientists, engineers, and other highly trained experts.

The fruits of this scientific and technological research were especially evident in the developing computer industry. The first computers were created by scientists and engineers working for the military during World War II, primarily to help decipher enemy codes. After the war, the International Business Machines Corporation (IBM) and scientists at Harvard developed a more advanced computer, the Mark I, which also served military needs. By 1954, however, IBM and other companies were developing computers for non-military use by government agencies and, more important, private business. Although most Americans did not come into direct and regular contact with computers until the 1980s, the new machines were having a substantial effect on the economy long before then.

The postwar "baby boom" also contributed to economic growth. During World War II, the national birth rate began to reverse a long pattern of decline

EARLY IBM COMPUTER.   One of the early computers built by International Business Machines (IBM), this Naval Ordinance Research Calculator (NORC) was composed of vacuum tubes, resistors, condensers and crystal rectifiers arranged in circuits. Created for the navy, the machine was heralded for its "tremendous speed"—plodding, though it was, by the standards of later computers.

as more young Americans started families. The baby boom peaked in 1957. The nation's population rose almost twenty percent in the decade, from 150 million in 1950 to 179 million in 1960. Americans with large, young families proved to be avid consumers in the postwar economy.

In addition, the rapid expansion of suburbs—whose population grew forty-seven percent in the 1950s, more than twice as fast as the population as a whole—helped stimulate growth in several important sectors of the economy. The number of privately owned cars (more essential for suburban than for urban living) more than doubled in a decade, sparking a great boom in the automobile industry. Demand for new homes helped sustain a vigorous housing industry. The construction of roads, which was both a cause and a result of the growth of suburbs, stimulated the economy as well.

Because of this unprecedented growth, the economy grew nearly ten times as fast as the population in the thirty years after the war. And while that growth was far from equally distributed, it affected most of society. The average American had over twenty percent more purchasing power in 1960 than in 1945, and more than twice as much as during the prosperous 1920s. By 1960, per capita in-

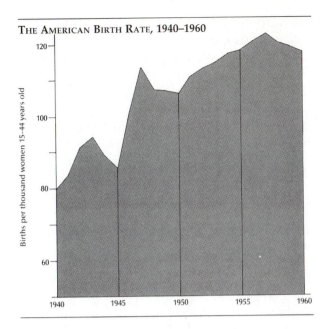

The American Birth Rate, 1940–1960

come (the average income for every individual man, woman, and child) was over 1,800 dollars—500 dollars more than it had been fifteen years before. Family incomes had risen even more. The American people had achieved the highest standard of living of any society in the history of the world.

The Growth of the American West

No region of the country experienced more dramatic changes as a result of the new economic growth than the American West. Its population expanded dramatically; its cities boomed; its industrial economy flourished. Before World War II, most of the West had been, economically at least, an appendage of the great industrial economy of the East—providing it with raw materials and agricultural goods. By the 1960s, some parts of the West had emerged as among the most important (and populous) industrial and cultural centers of the nation.

As during World War II, much of the growth of the West was a result of federal spending and investment—spending on the dams, power stations, highways, and other infrastructure developments that made economic development possible; and the military spending that continued to flow disproportionately to factories in California and Texas, many of them built with government funds during the war. But other factors played a role as well. The enormous increase in automobile use after World War II (a result, among other things, of suburbanization and improved highway systems) gave a large stimulus to the petroleum industry and contributed to the rapid growth of oil fields in Texas and Colorado, and the metropolitan centers serving them: Houston, Dallas, and Denver.

State governments in the West invested heavily in their universities. The University of Texas and University of California systems, in particular, became among the nation's largest and best; as centers of research, they helped attract technology-intensive industries to the region. Climate contributed as well. Once they had the infrastructure (and, most important, the water supplies) to sustain large populations, and once air-conditioning became widely available, southern California, Nevada, and Arizona, in particular, attracted many migrants from the East because of their warm, dry, and sunny climates. The growth of Los Angeles after World War II was an especially remarkable phenomenon. More than ten percent of all new businesses in the United States between 1945 and 1950 began in Los Angeles. The population of the city exploded to make the city one of the largest in the country by 1960.

New Economic Theories

The exciting (and to some surprising) discovery of the power of the American economy contributed to the confident, at times complacent tone of much American political life in the 1950s. During the Depression, politicians, intellectuals, and others had often questioned the viability of capitalism. In the 1950s, those doubts seemed to disappear. The postwar economy became a source of national confidence in several ways.

One was the belief that Keynesian economics made it possible for government to regulate and stabilize the economy without intruding directly into the private sector. The British economist John Maynard Keynes had argued as early as the 1920s that by varying the flow of government spending and managing the supply of currency, the state could stimulate the economy to cure recession and dampen growth to prevent inflation. The experience of the last years of the Depression and the first years of the war had seemed to confirm this argument. And by the mid-1950s, Keynesian theory was rapidly becoming a fundamental article of faith—not only among professional economists but among much of the public. The most popular economics textbook of the 1950s and 1960s, Paul Samuelson's *Economics*, imbued generations of college students with Keynesian ideas. Armed with these fiscal and monetary tools, economists now believed, it was possible for the government to maintain a virtually permanent prosperity. The dispiriting boom and bust cycle that many had long believed to be a permanent feature of industrial capitalism could now be banished for-ever. Never again would it be necessary for the nation to experience another Depression.

If any doubters remained, they found ample evidence to dispel their misgivings during the brief recessions the economy experienced during the era. When the economy slackened in late 1953, Secretary of the Treasury George M. Humphrey and the Federal Reserve Board worked to ease credit and make money more readily available. The economy quickly recovered, seeming to confirm the value of Keynesian tactics (even though Humphrey and the Board did not explicitly endorse them). A far more serious recession began late in 1957 and continued for more than a year. This time, the Eisenhower administration ignored the Keynesians and adopted such deflationary tactics as cutting the budget. The slow, halting nature of the recovery, in contrast with the rapid revival in 1954, seemed further to support the Keynesian philosophy.

In addition to the belief in the possibility of permanent economic stability was the equally exhilarating belief in permanent economic growth. As the economy continued to expand far beyond what any observer had predicted was possible only a few years before, more and more Americans assumed that such growth knew no bounds. A comforting thought in itself, this assumption also made possible a new outlook on social and economic problems. In the 1930s, many Americans had argued that the elimination of poverty and injustice would require a redistribution of wealth—a limitation on the fortunes of the rich and a program to distribute income and wealth more fairly. By the mid-1950s, most reformers abandoned the scarcity model that focused on equitably distributing a limited supply of wealth, resources, and income. Instead they came to believe that the solution to economic deprivation lay in increased production. The affluent would not have to sacrifice in order to eliminate poverty. The nation would simply have to generate more abundance, thus raising the quality of life of even the poorest citizens to a level of comfort and decency.

The Keynesians never managed to remake federal economic policy entirely to their liking. Political obstacles consistently limited the ability of even the most committed Keynesians to use fiscal and monetary policies as they wished; and the increasingly complex modern economy did not always respond as quickly to Keynesian policies as the theory behind them suggested it should. Still, the new economics gave many Americans a confidence in their ability to solve economic problems that previous generations had never developed.

Capital and Labor

Centralization, which had been a conspicuous feature of industrial capitalism since the late nineteenth century, continued and even accelerated after World War II. There were more than 4,000 corporate mergers in the 1950s. A relatively small number of large-scale organizations continued to control an enormous proportion of the nation's economic activity. This was particularly true in industries benefiting from government defense spending. As during World War II, the federal government tended to award military contracts to large corporations. In 1959, for example, half of all defense contracts went to only twenty firms. But the same pattern repeated itself in many other areas of the economy, as corporations moved from being single-industry firms to becoming diversified conglomerates. By the end of the decade, half the net corporate income in the nation was going to only slightly more than 500 firms, or one-tenth of one percent of the total number of corporations.

A similar consolidation occurred in the agricultural economy. Increasing mechanization reduced the need for farm labor, and the agricultural work force declined by more than half in the two decades after the war. Mechanization also endangered one of the most cherished American institutions: the family farm. By the 1960s, relatively few individuals could any longer afford to buy and equip a modern farm; and much of the nation's most productive land had been purchased by financial institutions and corporations.

Corporations enjoying booming growth attempted to stave off strikes that interfered with their operations. Since the most important labor unions were now so large and entrenched that they could not easily be suppressed or intimidated, business leaders made important concessions to them. As early as 1948, Walter Reuther, president of the United Automobile Workers, obtained a contract from General Motors that included a built-in "escalator clause"—an automatic cost-of-living increase pegged to the consumer price index. In 1955, Reuther persuaded the Ford Motor Company to provide a guaranteed annual income to auto workers. A few months later, steelworkers in several corporations won a guaranteed annual salary as well. By the mid-1950s, factory wages in all industries had risen substantially, to an average of eighty dollars per week. Some workers also now received substantial additional benefits, among them health insurance and paid vacations.

By the early 1950s, in other words, large labor unions had developed a new kind of relationship with employers, a relationship sometimes known as the "postwar contract." Workers in steel, automobiles, and other large unionized industries received generous increases in wages and benefits; in return, the unions tacitly agreed to refrain from raising other issues—issues involving control of the workplace and a voice for workers in the planning of production. The postwar "contract" had the support of the National Labor Relations Board, whose mediators (many drawing from their experience in World War II) believed the purpose of labor relations was to maintain industrial peace and promote the general health of the economy, not to defend or expand the "rights" of workers. The contract served the corporations and the union leadership well; many rank-and-file workers, however, resented the abandonment of efforts to give them more control over the conditions of their labor.

Also troubling were the number of industrial jobs in some major industries that disappeared as a result of the new technologies that automated production. Even as the labor movement enjoyed impressive successes in winning better wages for its members, its share of the labor force dropped—from an all-time high of thirty-six percent in 1953 to thirty-one percent by the end of the decade. After a crucially important, but fleeting, time of growth, organized labor faced retrenchment.

Still, the economic successes of the 1950s helped pave the way for a reunification of the labor movement. In December 1955, the American Federation of Labor and the Congress of Industrial Organizations ended their twenty-year rivalry and merged to create the AFL-CIO, under the leadership of George Meany. But success also bred stagnation and corruption in some union bureaucracies. In 1957, the powerful Teamsters Union became the subject of a congressional investigation; and its president, David Beck, was charged with the misappropriation of union funds. Beck ultimately stepped down to be replaced by Jimmy Hoffa, whom government investigators pursued for nearly a decade before finally winning a conviction against him (for tax evasion) in 1967. The union that had spearheaded the industrial movement in the 1930s, the United Mine Workers, similarly, became tainted by violence and suspicions of corruption. John L. Lewis's last years as head of the union were plagued by scandals and dissent within the organization. His successor, Tony Boyle, was convicted of complicity in the 1969 murder of Joseph Yablonski, the leader of a dissident faction within the union.

While the labor movement enjoyed significant success in winning better wages and benefits for workers already organized in strong unions, the majority of laborers who were as yet unorganized made fewer advances. Total union membership remained relatively stable, at about 16 million, throughout the 1950s. Lack of growth reflected in part a shift in the work force from blue-collar to white-collar jobs, as well as new obstacles to organization. The Taft-Hartley Act and the state right-to-work laws that it spawned made it more difficult to create new unions, or new units of existing unions, powerful enough to demand recognition from employers.

In the American South, in particular, impediments to unionization remained enormous. The CIO had launched a major organizing drive in the South shortly after World War II, targeting the poorly paid workers in textile mills in particular.

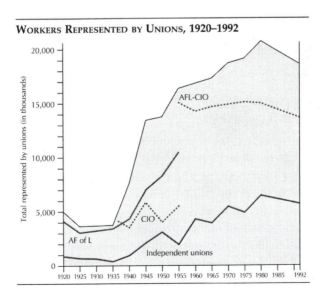

WORKERS REPRESENTED BY UNIONS, 1920–1992

But "Operation Dixie," as it was called, was a failure—as were most other organizing drives there during the postwar period. Antiunion sentiment appeared so powerful in the South—not just among employers, but also among politicians, the press, local police, and many others—that almost all organizing drives encountered crushing and usually fatal resistance.

A PEOPLE OF PLENTY

Among the most striking developments of the postwar era was the rapid extension of a middle-class life style and outlook to large groups of the population previously insulated from it. Several things contributed to the homogenizing of American middle-class culture in the 1950s. The new prosperity of social groups previously living on the margins, the growing availability of and fascination with consumer goods, the rise of television, and perhaps above all, the massive population movement from the cities to the suburbs all played a part in shaping middle-class culture. During the 1950s the American middle class appeared to be a larger, more powerful, more homogeneous, and more dominant force than it had ever been before.

The new prosperity, in fact, inspired some Americans to see abundance, and a set of middle-class values associated with it, as the key to understanding the American past and the American character. Leading intellectuals argued that American history had been characterized by a broad "consensus." "However much at odds on specific issues," the historian Richard Hofstadter wrote in *The American Political Tradition* (1948), Americans have "shared a belief in the rights of property, the philosophy of economic individualism, the value of competition; they have accepted the economic virtues of capitalist culture as necessary qualities of man." David Potter, another leading American historian of the era, published an influential examination of "economic abundance and American character" in 1954. He called it *People of Plenty*. For the American middle class in the 1950s, at least, it seemed an appropriate label.

The Consumer Culture

At the center of middle-class culture in the 1950s, as it had been for many decades before, was consumerism. Increased prosperity, the growing variety and wide availability of new products, and the adeptness of advertisers helped create an insistent demand for products that fueled the consumer culture. The growth of consumer credit, which increased by 800 percent between 1945 and 1957 through the development of credit cards, revolving charge accounts, and easy-payment plans also fed consumption. Prosperity revived the American love affair with the automobile; Detroit responded to the boom with ever-flashier styling and accessories. Consumers also found themselves drawn to new products such as dishwashers, garbage disposals, television, "hi-fis," and (later) stereos. To a

THE SUBURBAN CONSUMER.   This 1953 advertisement for a Whirlpool washing machine shows one of the many consumer appliances that were then moving within reach of the average American consumer. Women were a particularly important target of advertisers, as this picture suggests; and manufacturers tried to associate their products with the comfortable, middle-class suburban lifestyle to which women in the 1950s were encouraged to aspire.

striking degree, the prosperity of the 1950s and 1960s was consumer, as opposed to investment, driven.

National marketing and advertising made possible the rapid spread of great national consumer crazes. For example, children, adolescents, and even some adults became entranced in the late 1950s with the "hula hoop"—a large plastic ring kept spinning around the waist. The popularity of the Walt Disney–produced children's television show, The *Mickey Mouse Club* created a national demand for related products such as Mickey Mouse watches and hats. It also helped produce the stunning success of Disneyland, an amusement park near Los Angeles that recreated many of the characters and events of Disney entertainment programs. The Disney technique of turning an entertainment success into an effective tool for marketing consumer goods was not an isolated event. Other entertainers and producers soon began to do the same.

The Suburban Nation

A third of the nation's population lived in suburbs by 1960. The growth of suburbs resulted not only from increased affluence, but from important innovations in home building, which made single-family houses affordable to millions of new people. The most famous of the suburban developers, William Levitt, came to symbolize the new suburban growth with his use of mass-production techniques to construct a large housing development on Long Island, near New York City. This first "Levittown" (there would later be others in New Jersey and Pennsylvania) consisted of several thousand two-bedroom Cape Cod-style houses, with identical interiors and only slightly varied facades, each perched on its own concrete slab (to eliminate excavation costs), facing curving, treeless streets. Levittown houses sold for under $10,000 and they helped meet the enormous postwar demand for housing, which had been developing during more than a decade of very little construction. Young couples—often newly married war veterans eager to start a family, assisted by low-cost, government-subsidized mortgages provided by the GI Bill and other federal programs—rushed to purchase the inexpensive homes, not only in the Levittowns but in similar developments that soon began appearing throughout the country.

Why did so many Americans want to move to the suburbs? One reason was the enormous importance postwar Americans placed on family life after five years of war in which families had often been separated or otherwise disrupted. Suburbs provided families with larger homes than they could find (or afford) in the cities and thus made it easier to raise larger numbers of children. They allowed privacy. They offered security from the noise and dangers of urban living. They created space for the new consumer goods—the cars, boats, appliances, outdoor furniture, and other products—that advertisers helped persuade many middle-class Americans they needed for fulfillment.

For many Americans, suburban life also helped provide a sense of community that some found it difficult to find in large, crowded, impersonal urban areas. In later years, the suburbs would come under attack for their supposedly stifling conformity, homogeneity, and isolation. But in the 1950s, many people were attracted by the idea of living in a community populated largely by people of similar age and background and found it easier to form friendships and social

LEVITTOWN.   This aerial view of Levittown, a vast postwar suburban development on Long Island, shows its carefully laid out streets with their identically designed houses. Communities such as Levittown had enormous appeal for many young middle-class families after World War II, who needed affordable housing and wanted to raise their children in the comfort of the suburbs.

circles there than in the city. Women in particular often valued the presence of other nonworking mothers living nearby to share the tasks of child raising.

Another factor motivating white Americans to move to the suburbs was race. In an era when the African-American population of most cities was rapidly growing, many white families fled to the suburbs to escape the integration of urban neighborhoods and schools. There were some African-American suburbs. But most black families remained in the cities or the countryside. That was in part because suburban housing was too costly, too distant from employment opportunities, and too far removed from public transportation for people of limited means. Suburbs were often also closed to African Americans (and other minorities, including Jews) through discriminatory selling practices and racial "covenants." Even prosperous black families often could not acquire homes in wealthy suburbs because of formal and informal barriers.

Many suburban neighborhoods appeared to be very homogeneous. But they were far from uniform. A famous study of one Levittown revealed a striking variety of occupations, ethnic backgrounds, and incomes there. Still, the Levittowns and inexpensive developments like them ultimately became the homes of mainly lower-middle-class people one step removed from the inner city. Other, more affluent suburbs became enclaves of wealthy families. Around virtually every city, a clear hierarchy emerged of upper-class suburban neighborhoods and more modest ones, just as such gradations had emerged years earlier among urban neighborhoods.

The Suburban Family

For professional men (who tended to work in the city, at some distance from their homes), suburban life generally meant a rigid division between their working and personal worlds. For many middle-class women, it meant an increased isolation from the workplace. The enormous cultural emphasis on family life in the 1950s strengthened popular prejudices against women entering the professions or occupying any paid job at all. Many middle-class husbands considered it demeaning for their wives to be employed. And many women themselves shied away from the workplace when they could afford not to work for wages, in part because prevailing ideas about motherhood encouraged women to stay at home with their children.

One of the most influential books of the postwar era was a famous guide to child rearing: Dr. Benjamin Spock's *Baby and Child Care*, first published in 1946 and reissued repeatedly for decades thereafter. Dr. Spock took a child-centered approach to raising babies, as opposed to the parent-centered theories of many previous childcare experts. Mothers, he instructed, should devote their energies to helping their children learn and grow and realize their potential. All other considerations, including the mother's own physical and emotional requirements, were subordinate. Dr. Spock at first envisioned only a very modest role for fathers in the process of childrearing, although he changed his views on this (as on many other issues) over time.

Thus, many American women faced heavy pressures—both externally and internally imposed—to remain in the home and concentrate on raising their children. Some women, however, had to balance these pressures against other, contradictory ones. As expectations of material comfort rose, many middle-class families needed a second income to maintain the standard of living they desired. As a result, the number of married women working outside the home actually increased in the postwar years—even as the social pressure for them to stay out of the workplace grew. By 1960, nearly a third of all married women were part of the paid work force. Many women thus balanced competing and, at times, conflicting popular expectations.

The experiences of the 1950s worked in some ways to diminish the power of feminism, which some argue ebbed to its lowest point in nearly a century. But they also produced conditions that would very soon create the most powerful feminist movement in American history. The increasing numbers of women in the workplace did much to spur growing demands for equality—at home, on the job, in politics and society—that would become central to the feminist crusades of the 1960s and 1970s.

The 1950s also saw a surge in women's voluntary activities and associations. Many middle-class women who were homemakers became involved in public life through their work with such organizations as the League of Women Voters, the Red Cross, YWCAs, and PTAs. By the late 1950s and early 1960s, some participated actively in more political movements, including civil-rights crusades and anti-nuclear demonstrations, some of them organized by mothers. In all of these associations, women gained organizational and political skills that would later be useful in supporting feminist causes. The growing frustrations of still other women, both in the home and the workplace, created a heightened demand for female professional opportunities that would do much to spur the women's liberation movement.

The Birth of Television

Television, perhaps the most powerful medium of mass communication in history, was central to the culture of the postwar era. Experiments in broadcasting pictures (along with sound) had begun as early as the 1920s, but commercial television appeared only shortly after World War II. It experienced a phenomenally rapid growth. In 1946, there were only 17,000 television sets in the country; by 1957, there were 40 million—almost as many sets as there were families. More people owned television sets, according to one report, than refrigerators (a statistic strikingly similar to one in the 1920s that revealed more people owning radios than bathtubs).

The television industry emerged directly out of the radio industry. All three of the major networks of the 1950s and 1960s—the National Broadcasting Company, the Columbia Broadcasting System, and the American Broadcasting Company—had begun their lives as radio companies. The television business, like radio, relied upon advertising. The need to attract advertisers determined most programming decisions; and in the early days of television, sponsors often played a direct, powerful, and continuing role in determining the content of the programs they chose to sponsor. Many early television shows came to bear the names of the corporations that paid for them: the *GE Television Theater*, the *Chrysler Playhouse*, the *Camel News Caravan*, and others. Proctor and Gamble and other companies actually produced daytime serials known as "soap operas," because their sponsors were almost always companies making household goods targeted at women.

The impact of television on American life was rapid, pervasive, and profound. By the late 1950s, television news had replaced newspapers, magazines, and radios as the nation's most important vehicle of information. Television

THE BIRTH OF TELEVISION.   Popular culture in America was transformed
during the post-World War II era with the advent of commercial
television. Here two young people watch one of the many popular shows
of the period, *Hopalong Cassidy*, on the family television.

advertising helped create a vast market for new fashions and consumer
goods. Televised athletic events gradually made professional and college sports
one of the important sources of entertainment (and one of the biggest
businesses) in America. Television entertainment programming, almost all of
it controlled by the three national networks (and their corporate sponsors),
replaced movies and radio as the principal source of diversion for American
families.

Much of the programming of the 1950s and early 1960s created a common image of American life—an image that was predominantly white, middle-
class, and suburban. That image was epitomized by such popular situation
comedies as *Ozzie and Harriet* and *Leave It to Beaver*. Programming also reinforced the concept of gender roles that many Americans embraced unthink-
ingly. Situation comedies, in particular, almost always showed families in which,
as the title of one of the most popular put it, *Father Knows Best*, and in which
women were almost always mothers and housewives striving to serve their children and please their husbands. Often however, the programs cleverly transmitted a more subtle message. In programs such as *Donna Reed*, the apparently
deferential mother was actually a woman of great sensitivity and intelligence
who exerted the real power in the suburban family. The wacky situations in
which Lucille Ball found herself in *I Love Lucy* often revolved around her character's desire to escape domesticity, find a decent job, and contribute to the
family income.

Television also conveyed other more complex images: the gritty, urban working-class families in Jackie Gleason's *The Honeymooners;* the childless show-business family of the early *I Love Lucy;* the unmarried professional women in *Our Miss Brooks* and *My Little Margie.* Television did not seek only to create an idealized image of a homogeneous suburban America. It also sought to convey experiences at odds with that image, but to convey them in warm, unthreatening terms—taking social diversity and cultural conflict and domesticating them, turning them into something benign and even comic.

Yet television also, inadvertently, created conditions that could accentuate social conflict. Even those unable to share in the affluence of the era could, through television, acquire a vivid picture of how the rest of their society purportedly lived. Families of limited means or children with an absent parent, whether through death, divorce, or some other misfortune, sometimes measured themselves against the idealized world presented in television families. Real life rarely resembled the world men, women, and children inhabited on television. At the same time that television was reinforcing the homogeneity of the white middle class, it also contributed to a sense of alienation and powerlessness among groups excluded from the world it portrayed.

Science and Space

In 1961, *Time* magazine chose as its "man of the year" not an individual but "the American Scientist." It was an indication of the widespread fascination with which Americans in the age of atomic weapons viewed science and technology. Major medical advances accounted for much of that fascination. Jonas Salk's vaccine to prevent polio, which the federal government provided to the public free beginning in 1955, virtually eliminated polio from American life in a few short years. Other dread diseases such as diphtheria and tuberculosis also all but vanished from society (at least for a time) as new drugs and treatments emerged. Infant mortality declined by nearly fifty percent in the twenty-five years after the war; the death rate among young children fell significantly as well (although both such rates were lower in western Europe). Average life expectancy in those same years rose by five, to seventy-one years.

Other innovations reinforced the American veneration of science and technology: the jet plane, the computer, synthetics, new types of commercially prepared foods, and, especially, developments in aerospace and aviation. Nothing better illustrated the nation's reverence for scientific expertise than the popular enthusiasm for the American space program. The program began in large part because of the Cold War. When the Soviet Union announced in 1957 that it had launched a satellite—Sputnik—which was orbiting the earth in outer space, the American government (and much of the American public) reacted with alarm, as if the Soviet achievement were evidence of massive American failure. Strenuous efforts began to improve scientific education in the schools, to develop more research laboratories, and above all, to speed the development of America's own exploration of outer space.

The centerpiece of that exploration was the manned space program, established in 1958 with the selection of the first American space pilots, or "astronauts," who quickly became the nation's most revered heroes. On May 5, 1961, Alan Shepard became the first American launched into space (several months after a Soviet "cosmonaut," Yuri Gagarin, had made a similar, and longer, flight). John Glenn (later a United States senator) became the first American to orbit the globe on February 2, 1962 (again, only after Gagarin had already done so). For John F. Kennedy, the space program seemed the last great frontier. He committed the nation to landing a man on the moon before the end of the 1960s. Although Kennedy himself did not live to see the fulfillment of his promise, in the summer of 1969 Neil Armstrong and Edwin Aldrin became the first men to walk on the surface of the moon.

For nearly two decades the manned space program was a source of enormous pride and great interest to many Americans. The optimism and faith in the

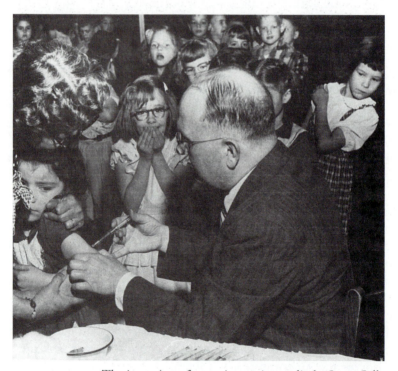

SALK VACCINE.   The invention of a vaccine against polio by Jonas Salk was one of the most exciting medical breakthroughs of the postwar period. In 1955, the federal government sponsored national inoculation of children with the new Salk vaccine. Among the first to receive the shots were these school children in Lancaster, Pennsylvania who apparently viewed the event with mixed emotions.

ALAN SHEPARD.   The first American launched into space,
Alan Shepard was caught by this photographer just
moments before his capsule was sealed. Shepard's brief 302
mile suborbital flight on May 5, 1961 was the first of the
Project Mercury Program.

National Aeronautics and Space Administration (NASA), which ran the program, was badly damaged, however, by the tragic explosion of the *Challenger*
space shuttle on January 28, 1986. The worst disaster in the history of the American manned space program claimed the lives of a crew that included Christa
McAuliffe, a young public school teacher who had been selected for the honor
of being the first ordinary citizen to participate in the space program. Until that
moment, Americans had sometimes questioned the expense of the space program; but few had doubted the evidence it gave of American scientific genius,
technological know-how, and daring.

The Organized Society

The growing emphasis on scientific expertise and rationalization had its institutional counterpart in large-scale organizations and bureaucracies, which greatly

increased their influence over American life in the postwar era. White-collar workers came to outnumber blue-collar laborers for the first time, and an increasing proportion of them worked in corporate settings with rigid hierarchical structures. Industrial workers also confronted large bureaucracies both in the workplace and in their own unions. Consumers discovered the frustrations of bureaucracy in dealing with the large national companies from whom they bought goods and services. More and more Americans were becoming convinced that the key to a successful future lay in acquiring the specialized training and skills necessary for work in large organizations, where every worker performed a particular, well-defined function.

The American educational system responded to the demands of this increasingly organized society by experimenting with changes in curriculum and philosophy. Elementary and secondary schools gave increased attention to the teaching of science, mathematics, and foreign languages—all of which educators considered important for the development of skilled, specialized professionals. The National Defense Education Act of 1958 (passed in response to the Soviet Union's Sputnik success) provided federal funding for development of programs in those areas. Universities in the meantime expanded their curricula to provide more opportunities for students to develop specialized skills. The idea of the "multiversity"—a phrase coined by Clark Kerr, the chancellor of the University of California at Berkeley, to describe his institution's curricular diversity—represented a commitment to making higher education a vehicle for training specialists in a wide variety of fields.

As in earlier eras, Americans reacted to these developments with ambivalence. Harsh criticism of the debilitating impact of bureaucratic life on the individual slowly became one of the central themes in popular and scholarly debate in the postwar period. William H. Whyte, Jr., produced one of the most widely discussed books of the decade: *The Organization Man* (1956), which attempted to describe the special mentality of the worker in a large, bureaucratic setting. Self-reliance, Whyte claimed, was losing place to the ability to "get along" and "work as a team" as the most valuable trait in the modern character. Sociologist David Riesman made similar observations in *The Lonely Crowd* (1950), in which he argued that the traditional "inner-directed" man, who judged himself on the basis of his own values and the esteem of his family, was giving way to a new "other-directed" man, more concerned with winning the approval of the larger organization or community.

A group of young poets, writers, and artists generally known as the "beats" (or, by derisive critics, as "beatniks") became the most caustic critics of bureaucracy, and of middle-class society in general. They produced slashing attacks on what they considered the sterility and conformity of American life, the meaninglessness of American politics, and the banality of popular culture. Allen Ginsberg's dark, bitter poem *Howl* (1955) decried the "Robot apartments! invincible suburbs! skeleton treasuries! blind capitals! demonic industries!" of modern life.

Jack Kerouac produced what may have been the central document of the Beat Generation in his novel *On the Road* (1957), an account of a cross-country automobile trip that depicted the rootless, iconoclastic lifestyle of Kerouac and his friends.

Other, less starkly alienated writers also used their work to express misgivings about the enormity and impersonality of modern society. Saul Bellow produced a series of novels—*The Adventures of Augie March* (1953), *Seize the Day* (1956), *Herzog* (1964), and others—that chronicled the difficulties American Jewish men had in finding fulfillment in the modern urban world. J. D. Salinger wrote in *The Catcher in the Rye* (1951) of a prep-school student, Holden Caulfield, who could not find anything in society—school, family, friends, city— that seemed genuine and worthy of admiration or commitment.

THE "OTHER AMERICA"

It was relatively easy for white, middle-class Americans in the 1950s to believe that the world they knew—a world of economic growth, personal affluence, and cultural homogeneity—was the world virtually all Americans knew; that the values and assumptions they shared were ones that most other Americans shared, too. But such assumptions were false. Even within the middle class, there was considerable restiveness among women, intellectuals, and many others who found the consumer culture somehow unsatisfying, even stultifying. More important, large groups of Americans remained outside the circle of abundance and shared neither the affluence nor, in many cases, the values of the middle class.

Outside the Affluent Society

In 1962, the socialist writer Michael Harrington published an influential book called *The Other America*, in which he chronicled the continuing existence of poverty in America. The conditions he described were not new. Only the attention he brought to them was.

The great economic expansion of the postwar years reduced poverty dramatically. But it did not eliminate it. At any given moment in the first two decades after World War II, more than a fifth of all American families (over 30 million people) continued to live below what the government defined as the poverty line in 1960 (down from a third of all families fifteen years before.) Many millions more lived just above the official poverty line but with incomes that gave them little comfort and no security.

Many of the poor experienced poverty intermittently and temporarily. Eighty percent of those classified as poor at any particular moment were likely to have moved into poverty relatively recently and might move out of it again as soon as they found a job—an indication of how unstable employment could be at the lower levels of the job market. But approximately twenty percent of the poor were people for whom poverty was a prolonged, debilitating experience, from which there was no easy escape. That included approximately half the nation's elderly and a large proportion of African Americans and Hispanics. Native Americans constituted the single poorest group in the country, a result of government policies that had undermined the economies of the reservations and had driven many Indians into cities, where some lived in a poverty worse than that they had left.

This hard-core poverty rebuked the assumptions of those who argued that economic growth would eventually lead everyone into prosperity, that, as many claimed, "a rising tide lifts all boats." It was a poverty that the growing prosperity of the postwar era seemed to affect hardly at all, a poverty, as Harrington observed, that appeared "impervious to hope."

Rural Poverty

Among those on the margins of the affluent society were many rural Americans. In 1948, farmers had received 8.9 percent of the national income; in 1956, they received only 4.1 percent. In part, this decline reflected the steadily shrinking farm population; in 1956 alone, nearly ten percent of the rural population moved into or was absorbed by cities. But it also reflected declining farm prices. Because of enormous surpluses in basic staples, commodity prices fell thirty-three percent in those years, even though national income as a whole rose fifty percent at the same time. Even many farmers who managed to survive economically experienced substantial losses of income at the same time that the prices of many consumer goods rose.

Not all farmers suffered equally as a result of these conditions. On the contrary, some substantial landowners weathered, and even managed to profit from, the changes in American agriculture. Others moved from considerable to only modest affluence. But the agrarian economy did produce substantial numbers of genuinely impoverished people. African-American sharecroppers and tenant farmers were shrinking in number, but those who remained lived at or below subsistence level throughout the rural South—in part because of the mechanization of cotton picking beginning in 1944, in part because of the development of synthetic fibers that reduced demand for cotton generally. (Two-thirds of the cotton acreage of the South went out of production between 1930 and 1960.)

Migrant farmworkers, a group concentrated especially in the West and Southwest and containing many Mexican-American and Asian workers, lived in similarly dire circumstances. In rural areas without much commercial agriculture—such as the Appalachian region in the East, where the decline of the coal economy reduced the one significant source of support for the region—whole communities experienced desperate poverty, increasingly cut off from the market economy. All these groups were vulnerable to malnutrition and even starvation.

The Inner Cities

As white families moved from cities to suburbs in vast numbers, more and more inner-city neighborhoods became vast repositories for the poor, "ghettos" from which there was no easy escape. The growth of these neighborhoods owed much to a vast migration of African Americans out of the countryside (where the cotton economy was in decline) and into industrial cities. More than three million black men and women moved from the South to northern cities between 1940 and 1960, many more than had made the same journey during the Great Migration during and after World War I. Chicago, Detroit, Cleveland, New York, and other eastern and midwestern industrial cities experienced a great expansion of their black populations—both in absolute numbers and, even more, as a percentage of the whole, since so many whites were leaving for the suburbs at the same time.

Similar migrations from Mexico and Puerto Rico expanded poor Hispanic neighborhoods in many American cities at the same time. Nearly a million Puerto Ricans moved into American cities (the largest group to New York) between 1940 and 1960. Mexican workers crossed the border in Texas and California and swelled the already substantial Latino communities of such cities as San Antonio, Houston, San Diego, and Los Angeles (which by 1960 had the largest Mexican-American population of any city in the United States, approximately 500,000 people).

Why these inner-city communities, populated largely by racial and ethnic minorities, remained so poor in the midst of growing affluence has been the subject of considerable, and very heated, debate. Some analysts have stressed the structural impediments to mobility many of the inner-city poor faced. A lack of jobs, training programs, and decent wages, combined with persistent inequality and racial prejudice, fueled persistent poverty. Other critics have insisted that the new migrants were at least in part victims of their own pasts; that the work habits, values, and family structures they brought with them from their rural homes were poorly adapted to the needs of the modern, industrial city. Still others have focused on the inner city itself—its crippling poverty, its lack of strong educational or service institutions, its crime, its violence, its apparent hopelessness. These conditions, they argue, created a "culture of poverty" that is reproduced generation after generation in a relentless cycle that offers no easy escape from those trapped within it.

Whatever the reasons, it is indisputable that inner cities were filling up with poor minority residents at the same time that the unskilled industrial jobs they were seeking were diminishing. Employers relocated factories and mills from old industrial cities to new locations in suburbs, smaller cities, and even abroad—places where labor was cheaper and other costs were lower. Even in the factories that remained, automation reduced the number of unskilled jobs. The economic opportunities that had helped earlier immigrant groups rise up from poverty were unavailable to most of the postwar migrants. At the same time, historic patterns of racial discrimination in hiring and housing doomed many members of these communities to continuing, and in some cases increasing, poverty.

For many years, the principal policy response to the poverty of inner cities was "urban renewal": the effort to tear down buildings in the poorest and most degraded areas. In the twenty years after World War II, urban renewal projects destroyed over 400,000 buildings, among them the homes of nearly 1.5 million people. In some cases, urban renewal provided new public housing for poor city residents—some of it considerably better than the housing they left. More often, however, urban renewal was better at eliminating "blights" than at helping the people who lived in them. In many cases, urban renewal projects replaced "slums" with middle- and upper-income housing (part of an often futile attempt to keep middle-class people from leaving the inner city), office towers, commercial buildings, or—in Los Angeles—a baseball stadium for the Los Angeles Dodgers, recently relocated from Brooklyn, on the site of a Mexican *barrio*.

Inner-city poverty also appeared to contribute greatly to a rising juvenile crime rate. Indeed, "juvenile delinquency" remained one of the few results of poverty that middle-class Americans discussed and worried about with any consistency. A 1955 book, *One Million Delinquents*, called juvenile crime a "national epidemic" and described the existence of a troubling inner-city youth subculture, peopled by embittered, rebellious adolescents with no hope of advancement and no sense of having a stake in the structure of their society.

For much of the 1950s, the persistence of crime, inequality, and poverty struck a discordant note in American society. Many Americans turned a blind eye to such problems and to the manifestations of unrest increasingly apparent in the nation's cities. Before long, however, one of the most powerful social movements in the twentieth century would force the nation to confront the persistence of injustice in contemporary society. However much critics liked to characterize the 1950s as an "age of conformity," those years also gave rise to a powerful civil rights movement that would soon transform American society.

CHAPTER TWENTY-ONE

The Fight for Racial Justice

~

The early postwar period—a period often characterized as one of stability and conformity—gave rise to one of the great social movements in American history. Throughout the twentieth century, African Americans had engaged in a long struggle to gain equal rights in American society. Amid much discouragement, generation after generation sought privileges that most Americans enjoyed simply by virtue of being citizens. But they faced formidable barriers, a result of a long history of economic, political, and social discrimination. Formal, legalized segregation remained entrenched in the American South at midcentury. In the rest of the nation, less visible but often equally pernicious forms of racial prejudice were a part of life for many African Americans.

Throughout American history, black men and women had employed many different strategies, tactics, and ideas to overcome the injustices they faced. But the 1950s became an important watershed in the long drive for racial equality. A civil rights movement of tremendous force, power, and determination began to challenge the very roots of racial oppression in American society. Before the decade was over, the segregation by law that many white Americans had defended or had tolerated for decades was suddenly on the defensive. More subtle forms of racial prejudice, and the persistence of inequality, would also become matters of national debate and, for some, priority.

RACIAL INEQUALITY AT MIDCENTURY

By the mid-twentieth century, African Americans had achieved some important milestones in the long quest for an end to racial discrimination and for equality of opportunity. The agitation of leaders from W. E. B. DuBois in the early twentieth century to A. Philip Randolph in the 1940s, and the long commitment of groups such as the NAACP and, later, the Congress of Racial Equality (founded in 1942) had done much to expose the history, character, and dynamics of inequality. They had also demanded concrete legal and political changes in American society.

There was no question that the life fortunes of many African Americans had improved vastly by midcentury. The booming wartime economy and postwar prosperity had boosted the standard of living for countless black workers and their families. Migration had provided some with a better way of life, a route out of some of the worst conditions imposed by segregation. Rising challenges to racial discrimination were succeeding in leveling some barriers to integration. The integration of the military, important court decisions, Randolph's success in pressuring the federal government, and even such symbolic events as Jackie Robinson's celebrated integration of major league professional baseball in 1947 suggested that sweeping change was in the wind.

At the same time, racial discrimination and oppression were still the norm in American society at midcentury. The remaining barriers to equality were steep. Most obvious was the tradition of legalized segregation in the South—a way of life that stifled opportunities for and inflicted great pain on black Americans, poisoned race relations, and prevented the exercise of basic constitutional rights.

Poverty and Inequality

One of the most important sources of racial oppression in mid-twentieth century America was the persistence of severe economic inequality. During the 1930s, the crop lien system had largely collapsed as a result of the Great Depression and New Deal agricultural policies. The growing availability of new mechanized agricultural technology in the early 1940s—most notably tractors and the mechanical cotton picker—further hastened the demise of sharecropping. But tenant farming was by no means extinct in the United States by 1950. Many white planters, most notably in Mississippi, spurned the mechanical devices and continued to rely on tenant farm labor. Nor had the economic changes in southern agriculture necessarily improved the standard of living for the impoverished white and black farmers who had been caught in the lien system. Some former tenants left the land and found good industrial jobs in southern and northern cities. But many others found only menial jobs in industry, while still others became migrant workers and engaged in an exhausting and endless struggle to piece together a living wage. Black migrants traveled up and down the Mississippi Valley and the East Coast as the season and the needs of the economy dictated, just as migrants had been doing for many years in the West.

Most African Americans who remained in the rural South continued to work for white land owners. In Clarendon County, South Carolina, where one of the first challenges to school segregation would be mounted, seven out of ten residents in 1950 were African Americans. Virtually all lived on farms and made

PICKING COTTON. This photograph of African-American
men picking cotton in Mississippi was taken in 1957.
Such workers were paid around 2 1/2 cents per pound of
cotton picked—or $5 a day.

their livings through agricultural work. Most were tenant farmers. White citizens, the majority absentee landlords, owned nearly eighty-five percent of the farm land in Clarendon County. Two thirds of those who lived in Clarendon County survived on less than 1,000 dollars a year. For most, life was shaped by grinding poverty.

Public education in Clarendon County also reflected gross inequality. Most Africans Americans in the county did not have more than four grades of schooling. Children who did attend were taught in segregated schools that, for black children, were often little more than falling-down shanties. The taxpayers in the county spent approximately 179 dollars for every white child attending a public school in 1949–1950 and 43 dollars for each black pupil. Many defended the system by arguing that whites paid more taxes and therefore deserved better schools. These conditions—although especially terrible in Clarendon County— were far from uncommon in the American South at midcentury. In Mississippi, nearly ninety percent of nonwhite families lived below the poverty level as late as 1960. Only seven percent of African Americans had completed high school. In 1964 the state of Mississippi was spending an average of under 23 dollars per black school pupil and approximately 82 dollars per white schoolchild.

Voting

African Americans might have sought remedies for such injustices in the political system, but here, too, the legacy of Jim Crow laws was strong. The great majority of southern blacks had no access to the ballot. Some legal challenges to restrictive voting laws had succeeded in the early twentieth century, and the Supreme Court had outlawed a system that restricted primary voting to whites only in 1944. But many discriminatory practices survived. The selective use of poll taxes and literacy clauses continued to prevent or discourage the registration of black voters. In 1940, only three percent of eligible black voters in the South were registered. Some officials frankly admitted that they employed any tactic necessary to disqualify black voters, including open defiance of the courts. In Mississippi, one election official explained turning away an African American who had attempted to vote in the primary by saying that "in the southern states it has always been a white primary, and I just couldn't conceive of this darkey going up there to vote."

By the late 1950s, much had changed. But some eighty percent of potential black voters in the South still were not registered. As late as 1962 in five Mississippi counties with black residential majorities, not a single African American was a registered voter. Active efforts to stifle black demands for voting rights actually grew stronger as those demands increased. In parts of the South, whites used considerable violence to uphold prevailing customs.

The Realities of Segregation

Segregation of the races remained the most visible manifestation of inequality at midcentury. Signs reading "white" and "colored" directed the races to separate drinking fountains, restrooms, and sections of movie theaters (for black Americans, usually the balcony). Segregation in transportation, housing, health care, public accommodations, school, and work was the norm throughout the American South. Outside the South, African Americans faced less formal but still corrosive racial discrimination in cities, clubs, labor unions, professions, housing, and countless other areas of life. In 1947, twenty-four hospitals run by the Veterans Administration maintained separate wards for black patients; nineteen such hospitals in the South had no facilities at all for black veterans. In the 1960s civil rights activists were still attempting to force the desegregation of hospitals that denied beds to African Americans and staff appointments to black physicians.

Prevailing attitudes reflected the persistence of racial bigotry. Surveys conducted at midcentury suggested that increasing numbers of white Americans supported desegregation. And by 1956 the vast majority of white Americans surveyed rejected the view that black Americans were intellectually inferior to whites. But that did not always mean support for specific desegregation efforts. When white Americans were asked in a 1958 survey whether they would move if a black person moved next door to them, nearly sixty percent said no. But

SEGREGATION. Signs directing African-American men and women to separate facilities were commonplace in the American South. Here a young African-American man waits in the "colored" section of a bus station. Once aboard the bus, he would have been expected to occupy a seat in a "colored only" section to the rear of the vehicle. One of the crucial challenges to Jim Crow laws mandating segregation would occur in public transportation.

when asked what their response would be if "great numbers" of blacks moved into the neighborhood, over fifty percent replied that they would definitely leave their homes. Such responses reflected continued, if not growing, discomfort as white and black Americans confronted some of the manifest problems in American race relations. And in the South, there was relatively little evidence in polls, or elsewhere, of even this limited commitment to racial equality.

CHALLENGING SEGREGATION IN EDUCATION

The challenge to segregation in the 1950s focused early on the nation's public school system. The Supreme Court's 1896 decision in *Plessy* v. *Ferguson* provided the legal bulwark for segregation for half a century. But the Plessy decision had sanctioned segregation where the races were provided with equal facilities despite separation by race. However, segregated schools, and the funds provided for them, were usually grossly unequal. In the 1930s and 1940s, the NAACP succeeded on a number of occasions in demonstrating to the courts that certain segregated educational facilities were not, in fact, equal. But not until the 1950s would a challenge to the entire concept of "separate but equal" be successfully mounted.

Brown v. Board of Education

The case that succeeded in finally overturning *Plessy* v. *Ferguson* decision was *Brown* v. *Board of Education of Topeka, Kansas*. The Brown decision was the culmination of many decades of effort by black opponents of segregation. Particularly important were a group of talented lawyers, many of them trained at Howard University in Washington by the great legal educator Charles Houston, who worked to fight segregation through the NAACP's Legal Defense Fund. Thurgood Marshall, William Hastie, James Nabrit, and others spent years filing legal challenges to segregation in one state after another, nibbling at the edges of the system, and accumulating precedents to support their assault on the "separate but equal" doctrine itself. In one day in 1950, the Supreme Court sustained three challenges to segregation mounted by Marshall and his associates. In none of these decisions, however, did the Court revisit and strike down the Plessy decision.

The goal then became to secure an unambiguous ruling that would demolish the entire intellectual and legal edifice that upheld the "separate but equal" doctrine. Beginning in late 1949 and 1950, Marshall and his colleagues started to mount several challenges against school boards in various parts of the country including Delaware, South Carolina, Virginia, the District of Columbia, and Kansas. Their complaints argued segregation's inherent inequality. The Kansas suit was filed against the Board of Education of Topeka, Kansas by the NAACP on behalf of Oliver Brown. Brown's eight-year-old daughter Linda had to travel several miles to a segregated public school every day, even though she lived virtually next door to a white elementary school.

When these various challenges to school segregation came before the Supreme Court of the United States, they were all docketed under the name of Oliver Brown—hence giving the case its name. Oral arguments in the cases were heard in late December of 1952. Thurgood Marshall and the other NAACP lawyers presented familiar data to demonstrate inequitable expenditures for black and white public education. But they went further this time. Marshall introduced new studies by social scientists that demonstrated, he argued, that not only were there no differences in the learning potential of black and white schoolchildren (challenging a claim long used to defend school segregation), but that segregation did irreparable harm to black schoolchildren. In an eloquent closing argument James Nabrit, who argued for the plaintiffs in the District of Columbia, summarized the position of the NAACP: "We submit that in this case, in the heart of the nation's capital, in the capital of democracy . . . there is no place for a segregated school system. This country cannot afford it, and the Constitution does not permit it, and the statutes of Congress do not authorize it."

Marshall's opponent, the South Carolina lawyer John W. Davis (who had been the 1924 Democratic nominee for president) argued passionately that the Court had no reason to question the logic of the Plessy decision. He ridiculed the social scientific findings presented by the plaintiffs. And he invoked the importance of states rights, local rule, and custom in his efforts to dissuade the justices from tampering with segregation. "Is it not the height of wisdom," he asked the Court, that education "should be left to those most immediately affected by it, and that the wishes of the parents, both white and colored, should be ascertained before their children are forced into what may be an unwelcome contact?"

The Court was divided on how to decide the case, and most pointedly about whether to overturn the Plessy decision. They thus instructed the parties to return for reargument. But before reargument occurred in December of 1953,

A VICTORY IN BROWN V. BOARD OF EDUCATION. George E. C. Hayes (*left*), Thurgood Marshall (*center*) and James Nabrit, Jr. (*right*) smile with evident pride on the steps of the United States Supreme Court after learning the Court had sustained their challenge to school segregation in *Brown* v. *Board of Education*. The May 17, 1954 landmark decision represented a crucial victory in the long battle to dismantle legalized segregation.

Chief Justice Fred Vinson died and had been replaced by President Eisenhower's nominee, former California governor Earl Warren. Vinson had opposed overturning Plessy, but Warren felt differently. Further, he pressed hard for the Court to hand down a unanimous decision in the case. To do otherwise, he believed, would invite resistance. For months after reargument, the Court failed to make a ruling. But finally, on May 17, 1954, the Court spoke. "We conclude," Chief Justice Warren said as he read the unanimous decision, "that in the field of public education the doctrine of 'separate but equal' has no place. Separate educational facilities are inherently unequal. . . . Any language in *Plessy* v. *Ferguson* contrary to these findings is rejected."

The following year, in May 1955, the Court issued another decision, popularly known as "Brown II," that addressed the question of how to implement desegregation (although the words "desegregation" and "segregation" never appeared in the ruling). This time the Court rejected the NAACP's position, which had insisted upon immediate desegregation. Instead, the decision took a more gradual approach to implementing the 1954 order. The court gave local school boards the responsibility of drawing up desegregation plans, and it ordered federal district courts to supervise compliance. No date was set for achieving desegregation. The court asked only that "the defendants make a prompt and reasonable start at full compliance" and—in a phrase subject to much interpretation—that the schools be desegregated "with all deliberate speed." The justices had said that segregation was wrong; but they left it to communities and lower-level officials and judges to decide how to eliminate it.

Massive Resistance

What followed was a painful struggle in many states and localities to come to terms with school desegregation, a process that still continues. In some communities, for example Washington, D.C., compliance came relatively quickly and quietly. In many of the border states, desegregation had begun in 1954 shortly after the announcement of the first Brown decision. Several hundred school districts in ten states had started peacefully to integrate their school systems. When Brown II was announced, however, momentum slowed perceptibly.

Strong local opposition (what came to be known in the South as "massive resistance") helped produce long delays and bitter conflicts in many communities. Some school districts ignored the ruling altogether. Others attempted to circumvent it with purely token efforts at integration. More than 100 southern members of Congress signed a "Declaration of Constitutional Principles" in 1956 denouncing the Brown decision as an unwarranted—indeed illegal—intervention in local and state affairs by the federal government. They urged their constituents to defy the Brown decision. Southern governors, mayors, local school boards, and nongovernmental pressure groups (including hundreds of White Citizens' Councils) all worked to obstruct desegregation. The "pupil placement laws" that many school districts enacted allowed school officials to place students in schools according to their scholastic abilities and social behavior. Such laws were transparent devices for maintaining segregation; but in 1958, the Supreme Court (in *Shuttlesworth* v. *Birmingham Board of Education*) refused to declare them unconstitutional.

By the fall of 1957, only 684 of 3,000 affected school districts in the South had even begun to desegregate their schools. In those that had complied, white resistance often produced angry mob actions and at times, violence. Many white parents simply withdrew their children from the public schools and enrolled them in all-white "segregation academies"; some state and local governments diverted money from newly integrated public schools and used it to fund the new, all-white institutions. The Brown decision, far from ending segregation, had launched a prolonged battle between federal authority and state and local governments.

The Eisenhower administration was not eager to commit itself to that battle. The president himself had greeted the Brown decision with skepticism and once said it had set back progress on race relations "at least fifteen years." "It's all very well to talk about school integration," Eisenhower added,"—if you remember you may also be talking about social *dis*integration." More pointedly, Eisenhower refused to endorse the Supreme Court decision publicly. But events in the South forced the administration's hand.

Little Rock

In September 1957, Eisenhower faced a case of direct state defiance of federal authority. Federal courts had ordered the desegregation of Central High School in Little Rock, Arkansas, a process that was to begin with the admission of nine African-American students to a school attended by some 2,000 white pupils. Other educational institutions in Arkansas had already begun the process of desegregation peacefully, some even before the Brown decision. In addition, many facilities in Little Rock had been integrated by the mid 1950s, including the city's bus and park system. The head of the NAACP in Little Rock, Daisy Bates, praised the community in 1954 as a "liberal southern city." Some local white-run newspapers wrote sympathetically of desegregation. There was reason to believe, in short, that desegregation plans might go forward in the city without incident.

Instead the desegregation of Central High School soon became a crisis with national implications. As the date for the admission of the black students approached, local white citizen organizations began whipping up popular opposition. The governor of the state, Orval Faubus, was in the midst of a re-election campaign and chose to seize upon the desegregation order to galvanize support among white voters. The night before Central High was due to open in September 1957, Faubus indicated he would defy the desegregation order, citing the need to maintain order and prevent violence. (In fact, no violence had been expected, although it soon followed Faubus's act of defiance.) The governor called in the Arkansas National Guard to "protect" the school. When the nine black pupils arrived on September 4, they were met by the guard who announced that "Governor Faubus has placed this school off limits to Negroes." Elizabeth

LITTLE ROCK–1957. Elizabeth Eckford, one of nine African Americans admitted as part of a plan to desegregate Little Rock's Central High School, met a mob shouting epithets when she arrived at the school on September 4, 1957. To the left, Arkansas National Guardsmen called out by Governor Faubus to "protect" the school, stand by watching.

Eckford, the first African American to try to enter the school, was greeted with shouts and racial slurs—including the chilling cry "Lynch her!"—from an angry white crowd. With bayonets poised, the guardsmen prevented the black students from entering the high school.

The federal district court immediately issued a decree demanding that their desegregation order be enforced unless Faubus could produce some compelling reason to the contrary. Again the students attempted to enter Central High; again they were met at the door by National Guardsmen who barred them from entering. By now the Justice Department and President Eisenhower were forced to confront the situation. The Justice Department filed a petition for an injunction to require desegregation plans to continue and to remove the National Guardsmen. President Eisenhower privately attempted to persuade Faubus to stop his resistance, but to no avail. On September 20, a federal court issued the injunction and ordered the removal of the Guard. Faubus announced that he would comply, but then left the state for a long weekend.

On Monday September 23, the "Little Rock Nine," as the black students became known, entered the school amid a hostile crowd estimated to be near 1,000. "What I felt inside," one of the students later recalled, "was stark raving fear—terrible, wrenching, awful fear. . . . I had known no pain like that because I did not know what I had done wrong. You see, when you are fifteen years old and someone's going to hit you or hurt you, you want to know what you did wrong. Although I knew the differences between black and white, I didn't know the penalties one paid for being black at that time." Although police safely escorted the pupils through the crowd, a melee occurred outside the high school. A mob of angry white protesters, supplemented by segregationists who had traveled to Little Rock from other parts of the South, gathered, taunting the students and shouting racial epithets. When the black pupils actually entered the building, one screamed, "They're in the school! Oh my God, they're in the school!" Some white students began to file out, encouraged by the shouts of protesters who yelled through the windows, "Don't stay in there with them."

The disturbance led city authorities to remove the black students for their own safety. Little Rock's mayor then turned to the Eisenhower administration for assistance. Federal troops, he asserted, were needed to prevent violence and to restore order. Eisenhower had little choice but to deal head on with this defiance of a federal court order. At stake now was not just peace, order, and a desegregation plan; the situation represented a challenge to the authority of the federal government. On September 24, Eisenhower federalized the Arkansas National Guard and sent U.S. army troops from the 101st Airborne Division to Little Rock to restore order. The troops were not there, Eisenhower stressed later that evening to the nation, to "enforce integration, but to prevent opposition by violence to orders of a court." Whatever "personal opinions" some Americans might hold regarding the Brown decision, Eisenhower explained, could not justify mob action. The following day the troops led the first black students into Central High. Tensions remained, and the National Guardsmen stayed in the school for the remainder of the year—this time to protect the black students. But Central High had been desegregated.

"MOVING ON TO VICTORY"

The challenge to school segregation was a critical milestone in the burgeoning civil rights movement. But it was only one of many simultaneous efforts to advance toward racial justice. Throughout the South, African Americans and white sympathizers began to challenge the humiliating practices and traditions that were central to segregation. With considerable courage and growing mass mobilization, those who participated in the civil rights movement sought to dismantle, brick by brick, the solid walls of segregation.

The Montgomery Bus Boycott

On December 1, 1955, Rosa Parks, an African-American seamstress and an active member of the local chapter of the NAACP, was arrested in Montgomery, Alabama, when she refused to give up her seat on a city bus to a white passenger. Although the vast majority of the passengers using the city bus lines in Montgomery were black, they were forced to pay their fare at the front of the bus, then walk to the rear door and enter there. In addition, when the white sections near the front of the bus were filled, black passengers were expected to give up their seats and stand so that white passengers could ride comfortably. These demeaning practices had become a way of life for many black and white passengers. But for many African Americans who complied, they were a daily indignity that was hard to tolerate.

In 1943, Mrs. Parks had refused to enter a segregated bus by the back entrance. Now the very same bus driver who had put her off the bus then for that infraction loomed over her. "If you don't stand up, I'm going to have to call the police and have you arrested," he said. "You may do that," Mrs. Parks replied calmly. Parks was arrested and taken to the city jail. Soon word spread among Montgomery's black community that Mrs. Parks had been detained.

Although on that particular day, Mrs. Parks had decided spontaneously to resist the order to move because she was tired, resistance to segregation in public transportation was not new in 1955, even in Montgomery. In the early 1950s some African Americans in Baton Rouge, Louisiana, had attempted to integrate city bus lines, organizing a short-lived boycott in the process. In Montgomery in 1953, a young English professor at a local black college, Jo Ann Robinson, had also attempted to mobilize fellow members of the Women's Political Council, a group of black professional women, after a humiliating instance in which Robinson had been berated by a white bus driver for sitting in the all-white section. Robinson, civil rights activist E. D. Nixon, and members of the Women's Political Council had then tried to persuade the city commissioners to end segregation on the buses, but to no avail. By 1955, the Council, which Jo Ann Robinson now led, was planning a boycott of the city bus lines. Three times in 1955 other women in Montgomery had been arrested for refusing to leave their seats. But although civil rights activists hoped to use one such incident to challenge the segregation law, none of these cases, for various reasons, seemed entirely suitable to serve as a test case.

When Rosa Parks resisted, however, the moment appeared ripe for broad-scale action. Mrs. Parks was a highly respected, even revered woman in the Montgomery African-American community with much experience in the civil rights movement. (The summer before her act of defiance, she had attended an inter-racial workshop at the Highlander Folk School in Tennessee designed to assist activists in their efforts to change and improve race relations.) E. D. Nixon persuaded Mrs. Parks to permit her arrest to be made into a test case for desegregation. Together, Nixon, Jo Ann Robinson, and the Women's Political Council began to mobilize a mass boycott of the city's bus lines. They printed over 35,000 handbills asking the black citizens of Montgomery not to ride the buses "to work, to town, or anywhere." Crucial to the outcome was the support of black ministers, among them Reverend Martin Luther King, Jr., the young pastor of the Dexter Avenue Church and new to Montgomery. King and his fellow ministers spoke from their pulpits about the bus boycott's significance and the importance of compliance.

When the city bus lines rolled on the first day of the boycott, they were virtually empty of black riders. A sign tacked up at a bus stop captured the spirit of the moment. "PEOPLE DON'T RIDE THE BUSES TODAY. DON'T RIDE IT FOR FREEDOM." Soon a group of ministers and civil rights activists met and formed an organization, the Montgomery Improvement Association, to work toward keeping up the boycott's momentum. At a mass meeting, King—who had agreed (after some initial reluctance) to serve as head of the Montgomery Improvement Association—exhorted Montgomery's black citizens to seize the momentum of the boycott and force an end to segregation. "One of the great glories of democracy is the right to protest for right," he said in one of his first major public speeches. "If you will protest courageously and yet with dignity and Christian love, when the history books are written in future generations the historians will pause and say, 'There lived a great people—a black people—who injected new meaning and dignity into the veins of civilization.' This is our challenge and our responsibility."

The Montgomery bus boycott lasted for 381 days despite considerable hardship to the working people of the African-American community. Black workers who needed to commute to their jobs (the largest group consisted of female domestic servants) formed carpools to ride back and forth to work, or simply walked, at times over long distances. The boycott put economic pressure not only on the bus company (a private concern) but on many Montgomery merchants. The bus boycotters found it difficult to get to downtown stores and tended to shop instead in their own neighborhoods. Merchants complained they were losing millions of dollars as the boycott wore on. Day in and day out, week after week, for over a year, most African Americans in Montgomery did not ride on the city's bus system. In June 1956 a federal district court responded to cases filed by several Montgomery women and ruled against segregation on the bus

MONTGOMERY BUS BOYCOTT. African Americans walk to work through the streets of Montgomery during the bus boycott. The boycott lasted for over a year until the courts ruled that segregation on common carriers was unconstitutional.

lines. Segregation on "common carriers," they held, violated the equal protection clause of the Fourteenth Amendment. In November, the Supreme Court affirmed the court's decision. Segregation on the buses, the justices ruled, was unconstitutional. The boycotters had won.

Among the most important accomplishments of the Montgomery bus boycott was its success in demonstrating the effectiveness of the boycott as a form of protest. Another was its elevation to prominence of Martin Luther King, Jr., who was destined to become one of the great figures in modern American history. The son of a prominent Atlanta minister, King had attended Crozier Theological Seminary and Boston University, where he earned a Ph.D. in theology. Despite his initial reluctance to become a civil rights activist, he soon became consumed by the movement.

King's approach to black protest was based on the doctrine of nonviolent civil disobedience—that is, of passive resistance even in the face of direct attack. He drew from the teachings of Mahatma Gandhi, the Indian nationalist leader; from Henry David Thoreau; and from Christian doctrine. And he embraced an approach to racial struggle that captured the moral high ground for his supporters. He urged African Americans to engage in peaceful demonstrations; to allow themselves to be arrested, even beaten, if necessary; and to respond to hate with love. For the next thirteen years—as leader of the Southern Christian Leadership Conference, an inter-racial group he helped found shortly after the bus boycott—he was highly influential and widely admired, surely the most visible leader in the civil rights movement.

But King's celebrated role—crucial though it was—should not overshadow the extraordinary contributions men and women from all walks of life made to the civil rights movement. Some of the great heroes and heroines were people who never gave speeches, never appeared in headlines, never received any public recognition. The domestic servants who walked instead of rode Montgomery's buses, the young schoolchildren who faced taunts and jeers in the battle for school desegregation, the countless men and women who attended rallies, ran printing presses, marched, and silently demonstrated—all helped make possible the civil rights movement. The movement they joined soon spread throughout the South and throughout the country. Soon after Montgomery, bus boycotts occurred in Tallahassee, Florida, as well as Birmingham and Mobile, Alabama.

Civil Rights Legislation

For the most part, the pressure for change came from African Americans who used the courts and, increasingly, boycotts and other demonstrations to move the public and the institutions of government. But white leaders also began to respond to black demands. Their support was slow to emerge and often grudging when it came. But the national political leadership was gradually moving on the issue of race. President Eisenhower completed the integration of the armed forces, which he had originally opposed. His attorney general pushed the president to support a broad civil rights bill. In 1957, Congress passed the first civil rights legislation since the end of Reconstruction. Majority leader Lyndon Baines Johnson of Texas played an important role in shepherding this compromise bill through the Senate.

Both Eisenhower and Johnson felt particularly strongly about emphasizing voting rights in the legislation, and they helped block more ambitious bills. The law the president signed established a Civil Rights Division within the Justice Department and authorized the attorney general to file injunctions against the infringement of voting rights. The bill also created a Commission on Civil Rights that had powers to investigate and report on civil rights violations. In the end, however, the Civil Rights Act of 1957 was a weak bill, with few mechanisms for enforcement. Two years after it had passed, obstacles to black voter registration still appeared largely intact. The Civil Rights Commission seemed unable to do much to change the discriminatory practices it uncovered.

In 1958, some fifty bombings of black churches, synagogues, and schools occurred in the South. President Eisenhower continued to assure white southerners that he did not support active intervention in desegregation by the federal government, but he also expressed abhorrence of violence and lawlessness by extremists. When a synagogue in Atlanta was bombed in 1958, for example, Eisenhower said in a news conference: "I was raised to respect the word 'Confederate'—very highly, I might add—and for hoodlums such as these to describe themselves as any part or relation to the Confederacy of the mid-nineteenth century is, to my mind, a complete insult to the word." As politicians attempted to balance the concerns of conservative white southern voters with their sense that the civil rights challenge could not be spurned, civil rights activists recognized that much of the momentum for reform would have to come from a mass, grassroots social movement.

Causes of the Civil Rights Movement

Given the many periods of struggle against racial injustice, it is worth asking why such an unprecedentedly powerful movement emerged in the 1950s and early 1960s—and not earlier or later. Several factors helped spur African-American protest in the postwar years. There was, first, the legacy of World War II itself, which had provided considerable momentum to the struggle against inequality. Millions of black men and women had served in the military or worked in war plants during the war. African-American leaders had invoked that record of service to demand change, and the government, however haltingly, had responded. There was, in fact, considerable continuity between the civil rights crusades of the 1940s and those of the 1950s.

The black migration that the war and the collapse of sharecropping helped produce was another important factor in fueling the civil rights movement. When African Americans moved from farms to southern cities, they escaped the isolation of rural life and the close supervision and often harsh control of many white planters. They also created a strong infrastructure of urban churches, community organizations, and social and professional groups. That infrastructure would eventually play a crucial role in the civil rights movement. Migration

BLACK MIGRATION, 1950–1980

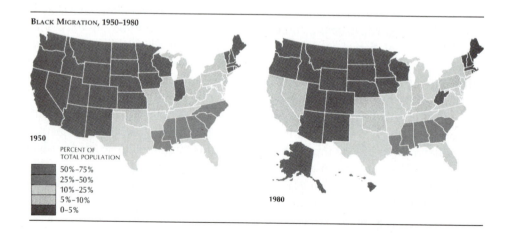

1950

PERCENT OF
TOTAL POPULATION

50%–75%
25%–50%
10%–25%
5%–10%
0–5%

1980

also encouraged some African Americans to challenge the entrenched traditions of segregation. The willingness to pull up stakes, to change one's life, and to take new risks affirmed for many a new sense of freedom and possibility. Finally, northern migration made African Americans a vital factor in post–World War II American politics. The ability of African Americans in northern cities to vote and to create their own political organizations prompted many party leaders to attend more closely to their demands.

The growth of an urban black middle class, which had been developing for decades but which expanded rapidly after the war, also proved important to civil rights activism in the postwar period. A powerful group of leaders, including ministers, educators, professionals, and students at black colleges and universities (which had grown significantly in the previous decades), provided tremendous force to the movement. These men and women with education, a strong stake in society, and often a sense of generational boldness felt increasingly empowered to challenge the racial caste system. Their actions built momentum and provided cohesion as the civil rights movement unfolded. They helped ensure that the message of protest would be heard nationally.

In addition to the forces that were inspiring African Americans to mobilize, there were other forces at work encouraging many white Americans to support the movement once it began. Some whites simply acted on a conviction that the racial injustices in American society were not compatible with democracy. The Cold War made racial injustice particularly embarrassing for those who believed that American society ought to provide a model to the world of democratic institutions. Labor unions with substantial black memberships played an important part in supporting (and funding) the civil rights movement. White ministers and churches also responded to the religious appeal that was so central to the movement. Finally, white business leaders North and South began to see the wisdom of challenging segregation. Efforts to prompt northern businesses to invest in the South and relocate industry there prompted some southern business leaders to support modifications of segregation.

Whatever its causes, the civil rights movement had become by 1960 a force that had already done much to change the contours of American society. It would continue to expand as the United States moved into the turbulent 1960s.

CHAPTER TWENTY-TWO

Eisenhower Republicanism

~

wight D. Eisenhower was the least experienced politician to serve in the White House in the twentieth century. He was also among the most politically successful presidents of the postwar era. At home, he pursued essentially moderate policies, avoiding most new initiatives but accepting the work of earlier reformers. Abroad, he continued and even intensified American commitments to oppose communism but brought to some of those commitments a measure of restraint that his successors did not always match. Eisenhower served in the presidency during a time when the United States was at peace and enjoying economic prosperity. His tenure as president also coincided with rising social and political pressures that he largely avoided but that his successors would have to grapple with for many years to come.

THE HERO AS PRESIDENT

Eisenhower was the first Republican elected to the presidency since 1928. He showed no special interest in the reform agenda that had so absorbed his two immediate predecessors. Nor, as a man who had seen more than his share of bloodletting and the horrible costs of war, was he inclined to pursue an actively interventionist foreign policy. "The trouble with Eisenhower," General Douglas MacArthur complained privately on the eve of the president's election, "is that he doesn't have the guts to make a policy decision. He never did have the guts and he never will." He made this complaint after Eisenhower had responded coolly to MacArthur's suggestion that the president order atomic weapons dropped on North Korea and a full-scale bombing campaign against China to end the Korean War. Some interpreted Eisenhower's caution in both the domestic and international arenas as evidence of timidity and lack

446

of vision. Many others admired Eisenhower's inclination to conciliate conflicting interest groups and to proceed cautiously, although firmly, in the Cold War. But there could be little doubt that Eisenhower enjoyed tremendous popularity. He would be among the few postwar presidents to serve out two full terms.

From the Army to the White House

Eisenhower came to the presidency a celebrated military hero of the Second World War. His parents had been pacifists, and it may have seemed in some measure an act of rebellion when their young son chose to attend West Point for his education. But if so, it was one of a very few rebellious acts in a life committed to working smoothly and effectively within established institutions. Eisenhower did well, but not spectacularly, at the Military Academy; he graduated in 1915, determined to make a successful career in the army.

Although Eisenhower sought overseas combat duty in World War I, he spent most of the war in the United States as a commander of training camps. The war ended a week before he was due to arrive in Europe. A man of considerable personal warmth and shrewd political sense, Eisenhower caught the attention of the right officers early on and rose rapidly through the ranks. By 1933, General Douglas MacArthur had selected Eisenhower as his administrative assistant.

When war broke out in Europe again, Eisenhower quickly earned a series of important commands. In December 1941 he became the chief aide to General George Marshall, Army Chief of Staff. By 1942 his effective work in military planning led to his appointment as commander of Allied forces in North Africa. Not long after that, he became the Supreme Allied Commander in Europe, charged with leading the great invasion of the continent. Before World War II, Eisenhower had never commanded troops in battle. By 1944, he was in command of the greatest invasion force in history.

His fame derived less from brilliant contributions to military strategy—others were far more distinguished than he in that respect—than from his great aptitude for organizing men, resources, and military power and from his tremendous appeal as a public figure. British General Bernard Montgomery's dismissive assessment of Eisenhower's World War II performance—"nice chap, no soldier"—was harsh. But Eisenhower's unassuming personal style and his interest in the men he commanded did as much to inspire the affection of Americans as did his purely military achievements.

After a brief period serving as Army Chief of Staff when the war was over, Eisenhower became the president of Columbia University in 1947. He had virtually no experience in academic life but the job gave him great visibility. In 1951, after he had declined overtures from both political parties to run for president in 1948, the general moved back into the military when Truman appointed him the first Commander of NATO.

When Eisenhower responded to the urging of Republican power brokers and agreed to be drafted as the party's presidential candidate in 1952, he did not even begin to campaign until June. In the fall, he left the dirty work to his running mate, Richard Nixon, and used his smile and his geniality to stand largely above the fray. He ran less as a Republican than as an emblem of American military greatness. He established himself as a firm but not zealous advocate of fiscal conservatism and anticommunism and an apostle of cautious moderate change. Many Americans apparently believed he would preserve the peace and restore tranquility to American society. For the most part, he did not disappoint them.

"What's Good for General Motors . . ."

The first Republican administration in twenty years staffed itself mostly with men drawn from the same quarter as those who had staffed Republican administrations in the 1920s: the business community. But many American businesses had developed a very different social and political outlook by the 1950s from that of their predecessors of earlier decades. Above all, many of them had reconciled themselves to at least the broad outlines of the Keynesian welfare state the New Deal had launched and, indeed, had come to see it as something that actually benefited them—by helping maintain social order, by increasing mass purchasing power, and by stabilizing labor relations.

To his cabinet, Eisenhower appointed wealthy corporate lawyers and business executives, who were unapologetic about their backgrounds—"eight millionaires and a plumber," the liberal *New Republic* magazine caustically remarked. (The plumber was Secretary of Labor Martin Durkin, president of the plumbers' union, who soon resigned.) Charles Wilson, president of General Motors, assured senators considering his nomination to be Secretary of Defense that he foresaw no conflict of interest between his new post and his old because he was certain that "what was good for our country was good for General Motors, and vice versa." But missing from most members of this business-oriented administration was the deep hostility to "government interference" that had so dominated corporate attitudes three decades before.

Eisenhower's leadership style, which stressed delegation of authority to subordinates, helped enhance the power of his cabinet officers and others. Secretary of State John Foster Dulles was widely believed to be running American foreign policy almost single-handedly (although it has since become clear that the president was far more deeply involved in international decisions than was often apparent at the time). Eisenhower's chief of staff, former New Hampshire governor Sherman Adams, exercised broad authority over relations with Congress and strictly controlled access to the president—until he left office in disgrace, near the end of Eisenhower's presidency, after he was discovered to have accepted gifts from a wealthy businessman.

Eisenhower's consistent inclination was to limit federal activities and encourage private enterprise. He opposed the Democrats in their bid to ensure

EISENHOWER AND DULLES. Although Eisenhower's likeable personality did not come across fully on television, his was the first administration to make extensive use of the new medium to promote its policies and dramatize its actions. The president's press conferences were frequently televised, and on several occasions Secretary of State John Foster Dulles reported to the president in front of the cameras. Dulles is shown in the Oval Office on May 17, 1955, reporting on a nine-day trip through western Europe, where he had signed a treaty restoring sovereignty to Austria.

federal control of atomic energy. Instead, Eisenhower approved legislation that allowed private companies to manufacture, own, and operate atomic power plants under the supervision of the Atomic Energy Commission. Soon after, the first private nuclear power plant in America was constructed in Pennsylvania. Eisenhower also supported the private rather than public development of natural resources (and once talked about selling the Tennessee Valley Authority to a private company). To the chagrin of farmers, he lowered federal support for farm prices. He also removed the last limited wage and price controls maintained by the Truman administration. He opposed the creation of new social welfare programs such as national health insurance. He strove constantly to reduce federal expenditures (even during the recession of 1958) and balance the budget. He ended 1960, his last full year in office, with a $1 billion budget surplus.

Federal Spending

The president took few new initiatives in domestic policy, but he resisted pressure from the right wing of his party to dismantle those welfare policies of the New Deal that had survived the conservative assaults of the war years and after. "Any political party" that tried to "abolish social security and eliminate labor laws and farm programs," he once told his brother, would not be heard from "again in our political history." While acknowledging that some extremist businessmen and politicians advocated such drastic measures, Eisenhower explained, "their number is negligible and they are stupid." Indeed, during his first term, Eisenhower agreed to extend the Social Security system to an additional 10 million people and unemployment compensation to an additional 4 million people. He also agreed to increase the minimum hourly wage from 75 cents to one dollar.

Perhaps the most significant legislative accomplishment of the Eisenhower administration was the Federal Highway Act of 1956, which authorized $25 billion for a ten-year effort to construct over 40,000 miles of interstate highways. It was the biggest public works project in American history. The program was to be funded through a highway "trust fund," whose revenues would come from new taxes on the purchase of fuel, automobiles, trucks, and tires. Highways were the one federal project Eisenhower seemed enthusiastic about funding throughout his presidency. He viewed their construction as a way of employing Americans, improving internal transportation, and strengthening national defense.

HIGHWAY CONSTRUCTION. In the 1950s massive outlays of federal funds for interstate highway construction began, resulting in the building of thousands of miles of new roadways. Here workmen in Topeka, Kansas spread wet burlap over newly poured concrete. After two days, the burlap would be removed and expansion joints would be sawed into the concrete.

Improved federal highways were important not only for travel and commerce. They would also be crucial, in the event of a nuclear war, for evacuating cities and moving military equipment.

Eisenhower displayed more fiscal conservatism in his attitude toward housing policies. In response to an enormous need for housing among the rapidly growing families of the postwar period, Democrats favored an expansive federal role in building and financing new homes. Republicans, however, believed such projects should be undertaken privately by the construction industry. Eisenhower, characteristically, attempted to forge a compromise. His Housing Act of 1954 established a four-year schedule for federal construction of some 140,000 homes, a number far smaller than that advocated by many Democrats. The time limit was designed to ensure that the federal government would gradually ease its way out of housing construction in favor of providing low-cost mortgages to new home owners.

In 1956, Eisenhower ran for a second term, even though he had suffered a serious heart attack the previous year. With Adlai Stevenson opposing him once again, he won by another, even greater landslide, receiving nearly fifty-seven percent of the popular vote and 442 electoral votes to Stevenson's eighty-nine. Still, Democrats retained the control of both houses of Congress they had won in 1954. And in 1958—during a serious recession—they increased that control by substantial margins.

Eisenhower and the Crusade Against Subversion

The Eisenhower administration did little in its first years in office to discourage the anticommunist furor that had gripped the nation. Indeed, in many ways it helped sustain it. The president intensified the search for subversives in the government, which Truman had begun several years earlier. More than 2,220 federal employees resigned or were dismissed as a result of security investigations. Among them were most of the leading Asian experts in the State Department, many of whom were harried from office because they had shown inadequate enthusiasm for the now exiled regime of Chiang Kai-shek.

Eisenhower also advanced legislation to increase federal control of the American Communist party. The Communist Control Act of 1954 cracked down hard on the party, stipulating, among other things, that citizens who advocated overthrow of the government by force be stripped of their citizenship and that labor organizations infiltrated by communists lose rights provided to them by the National Labor Relations Act.

Among the most celebrated controversies of the first year of the new administration was the case of J. Robert Oppenheimer, director of the Manhattan Project during the war and one of the nation's most distinguished and admired physicists. Although Oppenheimer was now out of government service, he continued as a consultant to the Atomic Energy Commission. But he had angered some officials by his public opposition to development of the new, more powerful hydrogen bomb, which Truman had launched toward the end of his presidency.

In 1953, the FBI distributed a dossier within the administration detailing Oppenheimer's prewar association with various left-wing groups. There was, in fact, nothing new about the information it contained. What was new was that Joseph McCarthy had acquired it. Fearful that McCarthy would exploit the issue, Eisenhower's advisers urged the president to act quickly to address the matter. Eisenhower privately expressed skepticism about the disloyalty charges. Even if the physicist had passed secrets to the Soviets, Eisenhower noted, ousting him now "would not be a case of merely locking the stable door after the horse is gone; it would be more like trying to find a door for a burned-down stable." Nonetheless the president ordered that a "blank wall" be placed between Oppenheimer and government secrets pending further official investigation. A federal inquiry, requested by Oppenheimer himself and conducted in an inflamed and confused atmosphere, confirmed the decision to deny him a security clearance not because he was disloyal but because he had "fundamental defects of character."

By 1954, however, such policies were beginning to produce significant popular opposition—an indication that the anticommunist passions of several years earlier were beginning to subside. The clearest signal of that change was the political demise of Senator McCarthy.

The Army-McCarthy Hearings

During the first year of the Eisenhower administration, McCarthy continued to operate with impunity. The president, who privately loathed him, nevertheless refused to speak out against him in public. Relatively few others—in the political world or in the press—were any more courageous. But McCarthy finally overreached himself in January 1954 when he attacked Secretary of the Army Robert Stevens and the armed services in general.

McCarthy spent much of the month of February 1954 hounding a decorated general, Ralph Zwicker, who had served with great valor in World War II. Among the things McCarthy was ostensibly attempting to learn was why a dentist who had been drafted into the army and who was alleged to be a communist had been promoted. When Zwicker disclaimed any knowledge of the event, McCarthy alternately ridiculed the general, whom the senator said did not possess "the brains of a five-year-old child," or vilified him as a man "unfit to wear that uniform." Army Secretary Stevens was outraged and instructed Zwicker not to reappear before McCarthy's committee. Now McCarthy demanded that Stevens himself appear to answer the charges.

At a private lunch, Stevens and McCarthy then worked out a compromise. Zwicker would return for testimony, Stevens would investigate further the promotion in question, and McCarthy would suspend his harassment of the army witness. Almost instantly, however, McCarthy turned the compromise to his ad-

THE ARMY-MCCARTHY HEARINGS. Senator Joseph McCarthy accuses Joseph Welch, chief counsel for the army, of a "smear" against members of McCarthy's office. Welch appears nonplussed. The televised hearings were called to mediate the dispute between McCarthy and the U.S. Army. They gave many Americans their first glimpse of McCarthy in action and contributed to McCarthy's 1954 censure by the Senate.

vantage by suggesting that Stevens and the Eisenhower administration had been bested. Eisenhower was furious and heatedly told an aide: "This guy McCarthy is going to get into trouble over this. I'm not going to take this lying down." Still, when a special congressional investigation of some of McCarthy's charges, known as the Army-McCarthy hearings got underway, Eisenhower continued to remain aloof. He believed that acting presidential and refusing to even address the "sideshow" was the best defense against McCarthy.

Meanwhile, however, McCarthy continued his attack on the army. He insisted upon playing a role in the Army-McCarthy hearings even though he and his own staff were now being investigated. The hearings were designed to explore the charge that McCarthy and Roy Cohn, counsel to McCarthy's subcommittee, had attempted to use their influence to procure special treatment for G. David Schine, another committee staffer who had been drafted into the army. McCarthy countercharged that the army was trying to stall his investigations of communist influence in the military.

The Army-McCarthy hearings, which began in late April 1954, were among the first congressional hearings to be nationally televised. For two months, much of the nation watched the spectacle with rapt attention. Eisenhower himself was riveted, although, he said, he found the events "close to disgusting. It saddens me that I must feel ashamed for the United States Senate." But it was less the Senate that reaped the popular disgust with the spectacle than McCarthy himself. The hearings had devastating results on the senator and his crusade against alleged communists in government. As the nation witnessed McCarthy in action—bullying witnesses, hurling groundless (and often cruel) accusations, evading issues—much of the public began to see him as a villain, and even a buffoon.

During the hearings, McCarthy met more than his match in Boston lawyer Joseph Welch, chief counsel for the army. With rapier wit and keen intelligence, Welch managed to turn the tables on McCarthy and expose his "cruelty," his "recklessness," and his ignorance. "Have you no sense of decency, sir, at long last?" Welch asked McCarthy in one of the most dramatic moments in the hearings. "Have you left no sense of decency?" McCarthy seemed unable to provide an answer. When the hearings came to a close, McCarthy had been badly discredited. In December 1954, the Senate voted sixty-seven to twenty-two to condemn him for "conduct unbecoming a senator." Three years later, with little public support left, he died—a victim, apparently, of complications arising from alcoholism.

In the midst of the hearings, Eisenhower made a crucial decision freighted with great future significance. In an effort to limit McCarthy's ability to subpoena military and personnel records and even officials from the executive branch to give testimony, Eisenhower invoked the doctrine of "executive privilege." Discussions among advisers to the president, Eisenhower asserted, were privileged. "It is not in the public interest," the president maintained, "that any of their conversations or communications, or any documents or reproductions, concerning such advice be disclosed." The president made it clear that his advisers should not offer any testimony before McCarthy's committee. Such a broad assertion of presidential power to withhold information from Congress was virtually unprecedented.

COLD WAR TENSIONS

The diminishing credibility of domestic anticommunist crusades occurred in the midst of continuing anxiety about American national security and the conflict with the Soviet Union. The threat of nuclear war with the Soviet Union, in particular, created a sense of real tension in international relations during the 1950s.

But the nuclear threat had another effect as well. With the potential costs of war now so enormous, both superpowers began to edge away from direct confrontations. Instead, the attention of both the United States and the Soviet Union gradually turned to the rapidly escalating instability in Third World nations. This would become the stage on which the superpowers would increasingly clash for the remainder of the Cold War.

"Massive Retaliation"

Among those who helped to define American foreign policy in the Eisenhower years was Secretary of State John Foster Dulles, an aristocratic corporate lawyer with a stern moral revulsion to communism. Second only to the president himself, Dulles was the dominant figure in the nation's foreign policy establishment in the 1950s. He entered office denouncing the containment policies of the Truman years as excessively passive, arguing that the United States should pursue an active program of "liberation," which would lead to a "rollback" of communist expansion. Once in power, however, he had to defer to the far more moderate views of the president, and he began to develop a new set of doctrines that reflected the impact of nuclear weapons on the world.

The most prominent of those doctrines was the policy of "massive retaliation," which Dulles announced early in 1954. The United States would, he explained, respond to communist threats to its allies not by using conventional forces in local conflicts (a policy that had led to so much frustration in Korea) but by relying on "the deterrent of massive retaliatory power" (by which he clearly meant nuclear weapons).

In part, the new doctrine reflected Dulles's inclination for tense confrontations, an approach he once defined as "brinksmanship"—pushing the Soviet Union to the brink of war in order to exact concessions. But the real force behind the massive retaliation policy was economics. With pressure growing both in and out of government for a reduction in American military expenditures, an increasing reliance on atomic weapons seemed to promise, as some advocates put it, "more bang for the buck."

At the same time, Dulles intensified the efforts of Truman and Acheson to "integrate" the entire noncommunist world into a system of mutual defense pacts modeled on NATO—but, without exception, far weaker than the European pact. By the end of the decade, the United States had become a party to almost a dozen such treaties in all areas of the world.

Korea and Vietnam

What had been the most troubling foreign policy concern of the Truman years—the war in Korea—plagued the Eisenhower administration only briefly. On July 27, 1953, negotiators at Panmunjom finally signed an agreement ending the hostilities. Each antagonist was to withdraw its troops a mile and a half from the existing battle line, which ran roughly along the thirty-eighth parallel, the prewar border between North and South Korea. A conference in Geneva was to consider means by which to reunite the nation peacefully—although, in fact, the 1954 meeting produced no agreement and left the cease-fire line as the apparently permanent border between the two countries.

Almost simultaneously, however, the United States faced a difficult choice in Southeast Asia where France was fighting to retain control of its one-time

THE FRENCH INDOCHINA WAR. These French soldiers keep watch for the enemy—the Vietminh—at their fortress in Dienbienphu as others remain in their trenches, visible only by their helmets. The disastrous battle of Dienbienphu marked the end of the French war effort.

colony, Vietnam. Opposing the French, however, were the powerful nationalist forces of Ho Chi Minh (who was both a committed nationalist and a committed communist), determined to win independence for their nation. Concerned about the potential for communist expansionism into Indochina, the Truman administration had supported the French, one of America's most important Cold War allies, and the Eisenhower administration at first did the same.

Early in 1954, however, 12,000 French troops became surrounded in a disastrous siege in the valley of Dienbienphu. Only direct American military intervention, it was clear, could prevent the total collapse of the French war effort. Yet despite the urging of Secretary of State Dulles, Vice President Nixon, and others, Eisenhower refused to permit direct American military intervention in Vietnam, claiming that neither Congress nor America's other allies would support such action. Without American aid, the French defense of Dienbienphu finally collapsed on May 7, 1954; and France quickly agreed to a settlement of the conflict at the same conference in Geneva that summer that was considering the

Korean settlement. The agreement marked the end of the French commitment to Vietnam and the beginning of an expanded American presence there.

Israel and the Crises of the Middle East

The 1950s also produced critical changes in America's relationship with the Middle East. Especially important to the future were the ties between the United States and the young nation of Israel. For more than half a century before World War II, the establishment of a Jewish state in Palestine had been the dream of a powerful international Zionist movement. The plight of the homeless Jews uprooted by the war, and the international horror at revelations of the Holocaust gave new strength to Zionist demands in the late 1940s. So did the enormous immigration of European Jews into Palestine after 1945, despite the efforts of Britain (which had governed the region since World War I) to limit them.

Finally, Britain brought the problem to the United Nations, which responded by recommending the partition of Palestine into a Jewish and an Arab state. On May 14, 1948, British rule ended, and Jews proclaimed the existence of the nation of Israel. President Truman recognized the new government the following day. But the creation of Israel, while it resolved some conflicts, produced others. Palestinian Arabs, unwilling to accept being displaced from what they considered their own country, fought determinedly against the new state in 1948—the first of several Arab–Israeli wars.

America was also concerned about the stability and friendliness of the Arab regimes in the area. The reason was simple: The region contained the richest oil reserves in the world, reserves in which American companies had already invested heavily, reserves on which the health of the American (and world) economy would ultimately come to depend. Thus the United States reacted with alarm as it watched Mohammed Mossadegh, the nationalist prime minister of Iran, begin to resist the presence of western corporations in his nation in the early 1950s. In 1953, the American CIA joined forces with conservative Iranian military leaders to engineer a coup that drove Mossadegh from office. To replace him, the CIA helped elevate the young Shah of Iran, Mohammed Reza Pahlevi, from his position as a token constitutional monarch to that of a virtually absolute ruler. The Shah remained closely tied to the United States for the next twenty-five years.

American policy was less effective in dealing with the nationalist government of Egypt, under the leadership of General Gamal Abdel Nasser, which began to develop a trade relationship with the Soviet Union in the early 1950s. In 1956, to punish Nasser for his friendliness toward the communists, Dulles withdrew American offers to assist in building the great Aswan Dam across the Nile. A week later, Nasser retaliated by seizing control of the Suez Canal from the British, saying that he would use the income from it to build the dam himself. The repercussions of that seizure were quick and profound.

On October 29, 1956, Israeli forces struck a pre-emptive blow against Egypt. The next day the British and French landed troops in the Suez to drive the Egyptians from the canal. Dulles and Eisenhower feared that the Suez crisis would drive the Arab states toward the Soviet Union and precipitate a new world war. By refusing to support the invasion, and by joining in a United Nations denunciation of it, the United States helped pressure the French and British to withdraw and helped persuade Israel to agree to a truce with Egypt.

Nasser's continuing flirtation with the Soviet Union strengthened American resolve to resist the growth of communist influence in the Middle East. It also increased the tendency of American officials to equate Arab nationalism with communism. In 1958, as pan-Arab forces loyal to Nasser challenged the government of Lebanon, Eisenhower ordered 5,000 American Marines to land on the beaches of Beirut to protect the existing regime; British troops entered Jordan at about the same time to resist a similar threat there. The effect of the interventions was negligible. The governments of both countries managed to stabilize their positions on their own, and within months both the American and British forces withdrew.

Latin America and "Yankee Imperialism"

World War II and the Cold War had eroded the limited initiatives of the Good Neighbor Policy toward Latin America, as American economic aid now flowed increasingly to Europe. Latin American animosity toward the United States grew steadily during the 1950s, as more people in the region came to view the expanding influence of American corporations in their countries as a form of imperialism. Such concerns deepened in 1954, when the Eisenhower administration ordered the CIA to help topple the new, leftist government of Jacobo Arbenz Guzman in Guatemala, a regime that Dulles (responding to the entreaties of the United Fruit Company, a major investor in Guatemala fearful of Arbenz) argued was potentially communist. Four years later, the depths of anti-American sentiment became clear when Vice President Richard Nixon visited the region, to be greeted in city after city by angry, hostile, occasionally dangerous mobs.

No nation in the region had been more closely tied to America than Cuba. Its leader, Fulgencio Batista y Saldivar, had ruled as a military dictator since 1952, when with American assistance he had toppled a more moderate government. Cuba's relatively prosperous economy had become a virtual fiefdom of American corporations, which controlled almost all the island's natural resources and had cornered over half the vital sugar crop. American organized crime controlled much of the lucrative tourist industry. Beginning in 1957, a popular movement of resistance to the Batista regime began to gather power under the leadership of Fidel Castro. By late 1958, the Batista forces were in almost total disarray. And on January 1, 1959, with Batista now in exile in Spain, Castro marched into Havana and established a new regime.

At first, the American government reacted warmly to Castro, relieved to be rid of the corrupt and ineffective Batista, hopeful that Castro would be a mod-

FIDEL CASTRO. After a long struggle in the Cuban countryside, Castro's rebel forces marched toward Havana in the last days of 1958 and, as the government of Fulgencio Batista y Zaldivar fled the country, seized control of Havana on New Year's Day, 1959. Here Castro addresses some of his supporters as he makes his way to Havana.

erate, democratic reformer who would allow American economic activity to continue in Cuba unchallenged. But once Castro began implementing significant land reforms and expropriating foreign-owned businesses and resources, Cuban-American relations rapidly deteriorated. Of particular concern to Eisenhower and Dulles was the Cuban regime's growing interest in communist ideas and tactics. When Castro began accepting assistance from the Soviet Union in 1960, the United States cut back the "quota" by which Cuba could export sugar to America at a favored price. Early in 1961, as one of its last acts, the Eisenhower administration severed diplomatic relations with Castro. The American CIA had already begun secretly training Cuban expatriates for an invasion of the island to topple the new regime. Isolated by the United States, Castro soon cemented an alliance with the Soviet Union.

Europe and the Soviet Union

Although the problems of the Third World were moving slowly to the center of American foreign policy, the direct relationship with the Soviet Union and the effort to resist communist expansion in Europe remained the principal concerns of the Eisenhower administration.

Even as the United States was strengthening NATO and rearming West Germany, however, many Americans continued to hope for negotiated solutions to some of the remaining problems dividing the superpowers. Such hopes grew after the death of Stalin in 1953, especially when the Soviet Union extended a peace overture to the rebellious Tito government in Yugoslavia, returned a military base to Finland, signed a peace treaty with Japan, and ended its long military occupation of Austria by allowing that nation to become an independent, neutral state. In 1955, Eisenhower and other NATO leaders met with the Soviet premier, Nikolai Bulganin, at a cordial summit conference in Geneva. But when a subsequent conference of foreign ministers met to try to resolve specific issues, they could find no basis for agreement.

Relations between the Soviet Union and the West soured further in 1956 in response to the Hungarian Revolution. Inspired by riots in Poland a year earlier, Hungarian dissidents launched a popular uprising in November 1956 to demand democratic reforms. For several days, they had control of the Hungarian government. But before the month was out, Soviet tanks and troops entered Budapest to crush the uprising and restore an orthodox, pro-Soviet regime. The Eisenhower administration refused to intervene. But the suppression of the uprising convinced many American leaders that Soviet policies had not softened as much as the events of the previous two years had suggested.

HUNGARIAN REVOLUTION. In 1956, a popular uprising in Hungary threatened the pro-Soviet regime. Anti-Russian demonstrations swept the city of Budapest leaving bricks and other debris, as depicted in this photograph, in the streets. The rebellion prompted an invasion of Soviet troops and tanks and the restoration of rule by forces that answered to the Soviet Union.

The failure of conciliation brought renewed vigor to the Cold War and, among other things, greatly intensified the Soviet-American arms race. Both nations engaged in extensive nuclear testing. Both nations redoubled efforts to develop effective intercontinental ballistic missiles, which could deliver atomic warheads directly from one continent to another. The American military, in the meantime, developed a new breed of atomic-powered submarines, capable of launching missiles from under water anywhere in the world. Later, the Soviet Union did the same.

The arms race not only increased tensions between the United States and Russia; it increased tensions within each nation as well. In America, public concern about nuclear war was becoming a pervasive national nightmare, a preoccupation never far from popular thought. Movies, television programs, books, and popular songs all expressed the concern. Fear of communism, therefore, combined with fear of atomic war to create a persistent national anxiety.

The U-2 Crisis

In this tense and fearful atmosphere, the Soviet Union raised new challenges to the West in 1958, in Berlin. The continuing existence of an anticommunist West Berlin inside communist East Germany remained an irritant and embarrassment to the Soviets. In November 1958, Nikita Khrushchev, who had succeeded Bulganin as Soviet premier and Communist party chief earlier that year, renewed the demands of his predecessors that the NATO powers abandon the city. The United States and its allies refused.

Khrushchev declined to force the issue. Instead, he suggested that he and Eisenhower discuss the issue personally, both in visits to each other's countries and at a summit meeting in Paris in 1960. The United States agreed. Khrushchev's 1959 visit to America produced a cool but polite response, and plans proceeded for the summit conference and for Eisenhower's visit to Moscow shortly thereafter. Only days before the scheduled beginning of the Paris meeting, however, the Soviet Union announced that it had shot down an American U-2, a high-altitude spy plane, over Russian territory. Its pilot, Francis Gary Powers, was in captivity. The Eisenhower administration responded clumsily, at first denying the allegations and then, when confronted with proof of them, awkwardly admitting that they were true. Khrushchev lashed back angrily, breaking up the Paris summit almost before it could begin and withdrawing his invitation to Eisenhower to visit the Soviet Union. But the U-2 incident was probably only a pretext. By the spring of 1960, Khrushchev—under heavy pressure from hardliners within his own government—knew that no agreement was possible on the Berlin issue; the U-2 incident may have become an excuse to avoid what he believed would be fruitless negotiations.

The events of 1960 provided a somber backdrop for the end of the Eisenhower administration. After eight years in office, Eisenhower had failed to eliminate the tensions between the United States and the Soviet Union. He had failed to end the costly and dangerous armaments race. And he had presided over a transformation of the Cold War from a relatively limited confrontation with the Soviet Union in Europe to a global effort to resist communist subversion. Yet Eisenhower had brought to these matters his own sense of the limits of American power. He had resisted military intervention in Vietnam. And he had placed a measure of restraint on those who urged the creation of an enormous American military establishment, warning in his farewell address in January 1961 of the "unwarranted influence" of a vast "military-industrial complex." His caution, in both domestic and international affairs, stood in marked contrast to the attitudes of his successors, who argued that the United States must act more boldly and aggressively on behalf of its goals at home and abroad.

CHAPTER TWENTY-THREE

The Resurgence of Liberalism

~

B y the late 1950s, a growing restlessness was becoming visible beneath the apparently placid surface of American society. Anxiety about America's position in the world, growing pressures from African Americans and other minorities, the increasing visibility of poverty, the rising frustrations of women, and other problems were beginning to unsettle the nation's public life. Ultimately, that restlessness would make the 1960s one of the most turbulent eras of the twentieth century. But at first, it contributed to a bold and confident effort by political leaders to attack social and international problems within the framework of conventional liberal politics.

THE TRIUMPH OF LIBERAL IDEALS

Those who yearned for a more active government in the late 1950s, and who accused the Eisenhower administration of allowing the nation to "drift," looked above all to the presidency for leadership. The political scientist Richard Neustadt, for example, published an influential book in 1960 entitled *Presidential Power*, which stressed the importance of presidential action in confronting national problems. Presidents faced many constraints, he argued, but effective presidents must learn to break free of them. The two men who served in the White House through most of the 1960s—John Kennedy and Lyndon Johnson—seemed for a time to be the embodiment of these liberal ideals.

The Election of 1960

The campaign of 1960 produced two young candidates who claimed to offer the nation active leadership. The Republican nomination went almost uncontested to Vice President Richard Nixon, who abandoned the strident anticommunism that had characterized his earlier career and adopted a centrist position in favor of moderate reform. The Democrats, in the meantime, emerged from a hotly contested primary campaign united, somewhat uneasily, behind John Fitzgerald Kennedy, an attractive and articulate young senator from Massachusetts who had narrowly missed being the party's vice presidential candidate in 1956.

John Kennedy grew up in a world of ease and privilege, although he himself suffered from a series of grave physical ailments throughout his life. He was the son of the wealthy and powerful Joseph P. Kennedy, controversial American ambassador to Britain at the beginning of World War II. After graduating from Harvard, he served in the navy during World War II, was decorated for bravery, and returned to Massachusetts in 1946 to run for office. Making liberal use of his war record, his father's money, and his family's connections to Boston Irish politics that reached back to the nineteenth century, he won a seat in Congress. Six years later, he was elected to the United States Senate and, in 1958, reelected by a record margin. Within days of his triumph, he was planning a presidential campaign. He premised his candidacy, he said, "on the single assumption that the American people are uneasy at the present drift in our national course."

Three themes dominated his campaign. Kennedy stressed, first, (erroneously as it turned out) that the Soviet Union enjoyed an advantage over the

KENNEDY-NIXON DEBATES. The first televised presidential debates in American history took place during the campaign of 1960. Kennedy made masterful use of television, and the debates helped persuade many that the young candidate could be a forceful and effective president.

Election of 1960   (64% of electorate voting)

	ELECTORAL VOTE	POPULAR VOTE (%)
John F. Kennedy (Democratic)	303	34,227,096 (49.9)
Richard M. Nixon (Republican)	219	34,108,546 (49.6)
Harry F. Byrd (Dixiecrat)	15	501,643 (0.7)
Other candidates (Socialist Labor; Prohibition; National States Rights, Socialist Workers, Constitution)	—	197,029

United States in military power. He argued, as well, that the level of growth in the American economy had begun to compare unfavorably to that of other leading western industrial nations. Finally, the Democratic candidate charged that the United States was "failing to modernize itself." Its cities, schools, and various other public services no longer met the needs of the nation's growing population. In the end, however, Kennedy's youthful, appealing, and carefully crafted public image would prove to be at least as important as his political positions in attracting popular support.

Kennedy also had significant liabilities. He was a Roman Catholic in a nation that had never elected a Catholic president, and that indeed had a long history of religious bigotry toward and suspicion of Roman Catholicism. Kennedy's age (he turned forty-three in 1960), while attractive to many, suggested to some a callow youth who lacked the statesmanlike qualities necessary for the presidency. In addition, his opponent was an experienced and widely known political figure. In the closing days of the campaign, President Eisenhower, who had earlier endorsed his vice president rather tepidly, mounted a vigorous effort on behalf of Nixon. That support, combined with continuing doubts about Kennedy's youth and religion, almost enabled the Republicans to overcome what had been a sizable Democratic lead.

Kennedy's strong performance in a series of televised presidential debates assisted his campaign greatly. Already skilled at dealing with the media, Kennedy proved especially adept in front of the camera as he managed to address most of his remarks to the public rather than to Nixon. Many who heard the debates on radio believed the two candidates had come out relatively evenly. But those who watched them on TV—as millions had—were impressed by Kennedy. In demonstrating the enormous importance of mass media, the first televised presidential debates left a mark on American politics that would be felt for the rest of the century. More immediately, they helped deliver the American presidency to John F. Kennedy, even if by an extraordinarily narrow margin. Kennedy won by only a tiny plurality—49.9 percent of the popular vote to Nixon's 49.6 percent—and only a slightly more comfortable electoral majority of 303 to 219.

If a few thousand voters in a few strategic states had voted differently, Nixon would have won the presidency in 1960.

The New Frontier

Kennedy had campaigned promising a program of domestic legislation more ambitious than any since the New Deal, a program he described as the "New Frontier." But the narrowness of his victory limited his political effectiveness, and throughout his brief presidency he had serious problems with Congress. Although Democrats remained in control of both houses, the party's majorities were heavily dependent on conservative southerners, who were far more likely to vote with the Republicans than with Kennedy. Many of those same southerners occupied powerful committee chairmanships. One after another of Kennedy's legislative proposals found themselves hopelessly stalled.

As a result, the president had to look elsewhere for opportunities to display positive leadership. One area where he believed he could do that was the economy. Economic growth was sluggish in 1961 when Kennedy entered the White House, with unemployment hovering at about six percent of the work force. Kennedy initiated a series of tariff negotiations with foreign governments—the "Kennedy Round"—in an effort to stimulate American exports. He began to consider an expanded use of Keynesian fiscal and monetary tools— culminating in his 1962 proposal for a substantial federal tax cut to stimulate the economy.

He also used his personal prestige to battle inflation. In 1962, several steel companies, led by U.S. Steel, announced that they were raising their prices by six dollars a ton, a move certain to trigger similar action by the rest of the steel industry. When U.S. Steel president Roger Blough appeared in the Oval Office to inform Kennedy, the president reacted with fury. "You have made a terrible mistake," Kennedy warned Blough, "You have double-crossed me." Kennedy then put heavy pressure on Blough and other steel executives to rescind the increase, in part by taking his case to the American people. How, Kennedy asked, could "a tiny handful of steel executives whose pursuit of private power and profit exceeds their sense of public responsibility . . . show such utter contempt for the interests of one hundred eighty-five million Americans." The steel companies soon relented. But it was a fleeting victory. Kennedy's relationship with the corporate community was now permanently strained.

The Charismatic President

More than any other president of the century (except perhaps the two Roosevelts and, later, Ronald Reagan), Kennedy made his own personality an integral part of his presidency and a central focus of national attention. His press conferences demonstrated Kennedy's quick wit and self-deprecating humor, and he relished them. His wife, Jacqueline, brought her natural beauty and her affinity for haute couture to drab political gatherings. His two young children enlivened the White House, where they played on the grounds and visited with their father in the Oval Office. Even the young president's emphasis on physical fitness suggested that a new kind of "vigor" had been brought, not just to the Washington, but to the nation. Although Kennedy in fact suffered from a serious chronic illness for much of his adult life—Addison's disease (a disorder of the adrenal glands)—his good looks and youth seemed to radiate health and energy.

Nothing illustrated Kennedy's impact on the nation more clearly than the popular reaction to the tragedy of November 22, 1963. Kennedy had traveled to Texas with his wife and Vice President Lyndon Johnson for a series of political appearances. While the presidential motorcade rode slowly through the streets of Dallas, shots rang out. Two bullets struck the president—one in the throat, the other in the head. He was sped to a nearby hospital, where minutes later he was pronounced dead. Lee Harvey Oswald, who appeared to be a confused and embittered Marxist, was arrested for the crime later that day. But within another two days he himself was mysteriously murdered by a Dallas nightclub owner, Jack Ruby, as police moved Oswald from one jail to another.

The popular assumption at the time was that both Oswald and Ruby had acted alone, assumptions endorsed by a federal commission, chaired by Chief Justice Earl Warren, that was appointed to investigate the assassination. In later years, however, many Americans—and in 1978 a congressional subcommittee—claimed that the Warren Commission report had not revealed the full story. *JFK*, a popular 1991 film by director Oliver Stone, endorsed one of the many conspiracy theories advanced over the previous decades to explain the assassination. But no solid evidence has ever appeared to confirm any such theories; and many informed observers continue to believe that the Warren Commission (hasty and sloppy as it undoubtedly was) had the story essentially right.

The enormous appeal of conspiracy theories in the more than thirty years after the Kennedy assassination reflected not just the reasonable doubts many Americans harbored about the official explanation of the tragedy. It reflected as well an unwillingness to accept that such a terrible event could have been as random an occurrence as the Warren Commission suggested it was. To many Americans it was almost unthinkable that a vital young president, who appeared in many ways larger than life, could have been felled by such an insignificant person.

In fact, whatever lay behind President Kennedy's murder in Dallas, there can be no question that the event itself left a deep mark on millions of Americans. Kennedy's assassination, like only a few other public events in national history, left most who experienced it with an indelible memory of where they were and how they felt when they heard the news on November 22. Over the next four days—as much of the nation suspended normal activity to watch the

THE DEATH OF KENNEDY. The assassination of President Kennedy on November 22, 1963 was a tragedy that profoundly touched millions of Americans. The elaborate state funeral, planned by his widow, was modeled on accounts of Lincoln's funeral in 1865. For days after the president's death, time seemed to stand still as Americans gathered around their televisions to watch as Kennedy was eulogized and finally brought to rest in Arlington Cemetery.

televised events surrounding the presidential funeral—images of Kennedy's widow, his small children, his funeral procession, his grave site at Arlington Cemetery with its symbolic eternal flame—all became deeply embedded in the public mind. In later years, when Americans looked back at the optimistic days of the 1950s and early 1960s and wondered how everything had subsequently seemed to unravel, many would think of November 22, 1963, as the beginning of the change.

President Johnson

At the time, however, much of the nation took comfort in the personality and performance of Kennedy's successor in the White House, Lyndon Baines Johnson. Johnson was a native of the poor "hill country" of west Texas and had risen to eminence by dint of extraordinary, even obsessive effort and ambition. He entered public life in the 1930s as an aide to a Texas congressman, then as the Texas director of the New Deal's National Youth Administration, and then, after 1937, as a young member of Congress fervently committed to Franklin Roosevelt. He rose steadily in Congress by working extraordinarily hard and by cultivating the favor of party leaders. In 1948, he narrowly won election to the United States Senate; a few years later he became the Senate Majority Leader, a job in which he displayed a legendary ability to persuade and cajole his colleagues into following his lead. Having failed to win the Democratic nomination for president in 1960, he surprised many who knew him—including it appears John F. Kennedy—by agreeing to accept the second position on the ticket. The events in Dallas thrust him into the presidency.

Johnson's rough-edged, even crude personality could hardly have been more different from Kennedy's. But like Kennedy, Johnson was a man who believed in the active use of power. And he proved, in the end, more effective than his predecessor in translating his goals into reality. Between 1963 and 1966, he compiled the most impressive legislative record of any president since Franklin Roosevelt. He was aided by the tidal wave of emotion that followed the Kennedy assassination, which helped win support for many New Frontier proposals. But Johnson also constructed a remarkable reform program of his own, one that he ultimately labeled the "Great Society." And he won approval of much of it through the same sort of skillful lobbying of Congress that had made him an effective majority leader.

Johnson envisioned himself, as well, as a great "coalition builder." He wanted the support of everyone, and for a time he very nearly got it. His first year in office was, by necessity, dominated by the campaign for reelection. There was little doubt that he would win—particularly after the Republican party fell under the sway of its right wing and nominated the conservative Senator Barry Goldwater of Arizona. Liberal Republicans abandoned Goldwater and openly supported Johnson. In the November election, the president received a larger plurality, over sixty-one percent, than any candidate before or since. Goldwater managed to carry only his home state of Arizona and five states in the deep South. Record Democratic majorities in both houses of Congress, many of whose members had been swept into office only because of the margin of Johnson's victory, ensured that the president would be able to fulfill many of his goals. Johnson seemed well on his way to achieving his cherished aim: becoming the most successful reform president of the century.

Health Care

The domestic programs of the Kennedy and Johnson administrations had two basic goals: maintaining the strength of the American economy and expanding the responsibilities of the federal government for social welfare. In the first, the two presidents were largely continuing a commitment that had been central to virtually every administration since early in the century. In the second, however, they were responding to a marked (and temporary) change in public attitudes. In particular, they were responding to what some described as the "discovery of poverty" in the late 1950s and early 1960s—the realization by Americans who had been glorying in prosperity that there were substantial portions of the population that remained destitute.

For the first time since the 1930s, the federal government took steps to create important new social welfare programs. The largest and most important of these was Medicare: a program to provide federal aid to the elderly for medical expenses. Kennedy initially proposed legislation to give Americans over sixty-five years old ninety days of hospital care and 180 days of nursing home assistance. But Kennedy's bill went down to defeat in the Senate in 1962. The president lambasted the Congress for delivering "a most serious defeat for every American family."

Lyndon Johnson finally made Medicare possible in 1965 bringing a temporary end to a bitter, twenty-year debate between those who believed in the concept of national health assistance and those who denounced it as "socialized medicine." The program, as crafted by the Kennedy and Johnson administrations, removed many objections. For one thing, it avoided the stigma of "welfare" by making Medicare benefits available to all elderly Americans, regardless of need (just as Social Security had done with pensions). That created a large middle-class constituency for the program. The legislation also defused the opposition of the medical community by allowing doctors serving Medicare patients to practice privately and to charge their normal fees; Medicare simply shifted responsibility for paying those fees from the patient to the government. In 1966, Johnson won passage as well of the Medicaid program, which extended federal medical assistance to welfare recipients of all ages. Criticism of both programs grew in subsequent years, both from those who thought Medicare and Medicaid were inadequate and from those who thought they were too expensive. But broad public support ensured their survival, and many liberals continued to hope for genuinely universal national health insurance.

The War on Poverty

Medicare and Medicaid were the first steps in a much larger assault on poverty—one that Kennedy had been contemplating in the last months of his life, and one that Johnson launched only weeks after taking office. It emerged out of a long debate within the administration, and within Congress, about the nature

ENACTING MEDICARE. With former President Harry Truman and Vice President Hubert Humphrey standing by, President Johnson signs legislation creating Medicare. Decades earlier, Truman had proposed national health insurance but had been unsuccessful in advancing that goal.

of poverty and the best way to fight it. And it reflected the views of those who believed that poverty was a result of more than lack of money; it was a product of institutional and cultural deficiencies that must be addressed to allow the poor to help themselves. That, in the end, was the key to the effort to end poverty: the effort to train the poor, to help the indigent climb the ladder of opportunity out of poverty. It was, as Johnson once put it, a "hand up, not a handout."

The centerpiece of this "war on poverty," as Johnson called it, was the Office of Economic Opportunity (OEO), which created an array of new educational, employment, housing, and health care programs. But the OEO was controversial from the start, in part because of its commitment to the idea of "Community Action." Community Action was an effort to involve members of poor communities themselves in the planning and administration of the programs designed to help them, to promote what some of its advocates called "maximum feasible participation." The Community Action programs provided some important benefits. In particular, they gave jobs to many poor people and gave them important experience in administrative and political work. Many men and women who went on to important careers in politics or community organizing, including many black and Hispanic politicians who would rise to prominence in the 1970s and 1980s, got their start in Community Action programs.

The programs were also important to Native Americans. They allowed tribal leaders to design and run programs for themselves and to apply for funds from the federal government on an equal basis with state and municipal authorities. Administering these programs helped produce a new generation of tribal leaders who learned much about political and bureaucratic power from the experience.

But despite its achievements, the Community Action approach proved impossible to sustain. Many programs fell victim to mismanagement or to powerful opposition from the local governments with which they were at times competing. Some activists in Community Action agencies employed tactics that mainstream politicians considered frighteningly radical. The apparent excesses of a few agencies damaged the popular image of the Community Action program as a whole. And even though Community Action was a relatively small part of the war on poverty, its growing unpopularity undermined support for the larger program as well.

The OEO spent nearly $3 billion during its first two years of existence, and it helped alleviate poverty in many ways. But it fell far short of eliminating poverty altogether. That was in part because of the weaknesses of the programs themselves and in part because funding for them, inadequate from the beginning, dwindled as the years passed and a costly war in Southeast Asia became the nation's first priority.

Still, the war on poverty left a number of significant legacies. A generation of minority men and women became politically active in the Community Action programs and continued to play a major role in public life for many years after. A series of programs—Head Start, a preschool program to help the children of poor families prepare for their educations; Food Stamps, which provided cash assistance to allow poor families to buy food; and others—were genuinely successful and had a permanent impact on poverty. Medicare and Medicaid, costly as they became, made major contributions to a long-term improvement in health care for the elderly and the poor.

Revitalizing American Cities and Schools

Closely tied to the antipoverty program were federal efforts to revitalize decaying cities and to strengthen the nation's schools. The Housing Act of 1961 offered $4.9 billion in federal grants to cities for the preservation of open spaces, the development of mass-transit systems, and the subsidization of middle-income housing. In 1966, Johnson established a new cabinet agency, the Department of Housing and Urban Development (led by Robert Weaver, the first African American ever to serve in a cabinet). Johnson also inaugurated the Model Cities program, which offered federal subsidies for urban redevelopment.

Kennedy had fought long and hard for federal aid to public education, but he had failed to overcome two important obstacles. Many Americans feared aid to education as the first step toward federal control of the schools. Many Catholics insisted federal assistance must extend to the parochial as well as public schools, a demand that raised serious constitutional issues and one that Kennedy (a Catholic himself) refused to consider. Johnson managed to circumvent both objections with the Elementary and Secondary Education Act of 1965 and a se-ries of subsequent measures. The bills extended aid to both private and parochial schools and based the aid on the economic conditions of their students, not the needs of the schools themselves. Total federal expenditures for education and technical training rose from $5 billion to $12 billion between 1964 and 1967.

The Johnson administration also supported the Immigration Act of 1965, one of the most important pieces of legislation of the 1960s, even if largely un-noticed at the time. The law maintained a strict limit on the number of newcom-ers admitted to the country each year (170,000), but it eliminated the "national origins" system established in the 1920s, which gave preference to immigrants from northern Europe over those from other parts of the world. It continued to restrict immigration from some parts of Latin America, but it allowed people from all parts of Europe, Asia, and Africa to enter the United States on an equal basis. It meant that large new categories of immigrants—and especially large numbers of Asians—would begin entering the United States by the early 1970s and changing the character of the American population. Prior to the 1965 act, ninety percent of immigrants to the United States each year came from European countries. For more than twenty years after the act, only ten percent did.

The Impact of the Great Society

The great surge of reform during the Kennedy-Johnson years reflected a new awareness of social problems in America. It also reflected the confidence of many liberals that America's resources were virtually limitless and that purposeful pub-lic effort could surmount almost any obstacle—that it was possible, as Lyndon Johnson insisted, to create a "Great Society" through purposeful public action. By the time Johnson left office, legislation had been either enacted or initiated to deal with a remarkable number of social issues: poverty, health care, educa-tion, cities, transportation, the environment, consumer protection, agriculture, science, the arts.

Taken together, the Great Society reforms meant a significant increase in federal spending. For a time, rising tax revenues from the growing economy nearly compensated for the new expenditures. In 1964, Johnson managed to win passage of the $11.5 billion tax cut that Kennedy had first proposed in 1962. The cut increased the federal deficit, but it helped produce substantial economic growth over the next several years that made up for much of the revenue initially lost. As Great Society programs began to multiply, however, and particularly as they began to compete with the escalating costs of America's military ventures, the federal budget rapidly outpaced increases in revenues. In 1961, the federal government had spent just under $98 billion and had carried a deficit of $3.3 billion. By 1968, that sum had risen to $153 billion, with a $25 billion deficit.

The high costs of the Great Society programs, and the inability of the government to find the revenues to pay for them, contributed to a growing disillusionment in later years with the idea of federal efforts to solve social problems. By the 1980s, many Americans had become convinced that the Great Society efforts had not worked and that, indeed, government programs to solve social problems could not work. Others, however, argued equally fervently that social programs had made important contributions both to the welfare of the groups they were designed to help and to the health of the economy as a whole.

Whether because of economic growth or because of government antipoverty efforts—or, as seems most likely, because of both—the decade of the 1960s saw the most substantial decrease in poverty in the United States of any period in the nation's history. In 1959, according to the most widely accepted estimates, twenty-one percent of the American people lived below the officially established poverty line. By 1969, only twelve percent remained below that line. The improvements affected blacks and whites in about the same proportion: fifty-six percent of the black population had lived in poverty in 1959, while only thirty-two percent did so ten years later—a forty-two percent reduction; eighteen percent of all whites had been poverty-stricken in 1959, but only ten percent were living below the poverty line a decade later—a forty-four percent reduction.

THE CIVIL RIGHTS MOVEMENT
IN TRIUMPH AND CRISIS

The nation's most important domestic initiative in the 1960s was the continuing struggle to address racial injustice and inequality. It was not an easy project, and it produced severe strains in American society. Although the initial aims of the civil rights movement fit comfortably with the ideals of American liberalism, tensions deepened as the movement advanced. There were important victories in the struggle to dismantle segregation in the South. But when the movement's attention turned to the racial problems in northern society, many of whose roots lay less in law than in economics, conflict between the moderate stance of most liberals and the growing impatience of many African Americans quickly grew.

Striking Down Segregation

John Kennedy had long been vaguely sympathetic to the cause of racial justice, but he was hardly a committed crusader. His intervention during the 1960 campaign to help win the release of Martin Luther King, Jr. from a Georgia prison won him a large plurality of the black vote. But like many presidents before him, he feared alienating southern Democratic voters and powerful southern Democrats in Congress. His administration set out to contain the racial problem by expanding enforcement of existing laws and supporting litigation to overturn existing segregation statutes. He hoped to make modest progress without creating politically damaging divisions.

But the pressure for more fundamental change was not so easy to resist in the 1960s. In February 1960, black college students in Greensboro, North Carolina staged a sit-in at a segregated Woolworth's lunch counter; and in the following months, similar demonstrations spread throughout the South, forcing many merchants to integrate their facilities. In the spring of 1960, some of those who had participated in the sit-ins formed the Student Nonviolent Coordinating Committee (SNCC), which worked to keep the spirit of resistance alive. Uneasy with the power of single charismatic individuals within the civil rights movement, and determined to marshall the commitment and daring of a younger generation, SNCC soon set off on its own course. It embraced participatory democracy as its model for decision making. And it set voter registration drives and citizen education as its priorities.

At the same time, other challenges to segregation continued and accelerated. In 1961, an interracial group of students, working with the Congress of Racial Equality (CORE), began what they called "freedom rides" (reviving a tactic CORE had tried, without much success, in the 1940s). Traveling by bus throughout the South, the freedom riders tried to force the desegregation of bus stations. In some places, they met with such savage violence at the hands of enraged whites that the president finally dispatched federal marshals to help keep the peace and ordered the integration of all bus and train stations. "Where are they getting these ideas?" Kennedy asked one African-American adviser with frustration as he observed the persistence of civil rights activists. "From you," came the answer.

In the meantime, SNCC workers began fanning out through African-American communities and even into remote rural areas to encourage blacks to challenge the obstacles to voting that white society had created. The Southern Christian Leadership Conference (SCLC) also created citizen education and other programs—many of them organized by the remarkable Ella Baker, one of the great grass-roots leaders of the movement—to mobilize black workers, farmers, housewives, and others to challenge segregation, disenfranchisement, and discrimination.

Continuing judicial efforts to enforce the integration of public education increased the pressure on national leaders to respond to the civil rights movement. In October 1962, a federal court ordered the University of Mississippi to enroll its first black student, James Meredith; Governor Ross Barnett, a strident segregationist, refused to enforce the order. When angry whites in Oxford, Mississippi, began rioting to protest the court decree, President Kennedy sent federal troops to the city to restore order and protect Meredith's right to attend the university.

BIRMINGHAM, ALABAMA IN 1963. During the spring of 1963, a series of peaceful civil rights demonstrations in Birmingham led to violence as Police Commissioner Eugene "Bull" Connor attempted to repress the protests. Here firemen direct their hoses on demonstrators who are attempting to protect themselves from the enormous pressure of the water.

Events in Alabama in 1963 helped bring the growing movement to something of a climax. In April, Martin Luther King, Jr. helped launch a series of nonviolent demonstrations in Birmingham, Alabama, a city unsurpassed in the strength of its commitment to segregation. Police Commissioner Eugene "Bull" Connor personally supervised a brutal effort to break up the peaceful marches, arresting hundreds of demonstrators and using attack dogs, tear gas, electric cattle prods, and fire hoses—at times even against small children— as much of the nation watched televised reports in horror. Two months later, Governor George Wallace—who had won election in 1962 promising staunch resistance to integration—pledged to stand in the doorway of a building at the University of Alabama to prevent the court-ordered enrollment of several black students. Only after the arrival of federal marshals and a visit from Attorney General Robert Kennedy did he give way. Even though the standoff with the federal government was a victory for integration, tensions remained high, as did the threat of violence. In fact, the night of the University of Alabama confrontation, NAACP official Medgar Evers was murdered in Mississippi.

Civil Rights Legislation

The events in Alabama and Mississippi were a warning to the president that he could no longer contain or avoid the issue of racism. In an important television address on June 12 during the University of Alabama confrontation, Kennedy spoke eloquently of the "moral issue" facing the nation. "If an American," he asked, "because his skin is dark, . . . cannot enjoy the full and free life which all of us want, then who among us would be content to have the color of his skin changed and stand in his place? Who among us would then be content with the counsels of patience and delay?" Days later, he introduced a series of new legislative proposals prohibiting segregation in "public accommodations" (stores, restaurants, theaters, hotels), barring discrimination in employment, and increasing the power of the government to file suits on behalf of school integration.

MARTIN LUTHER KING, JR., IN 1963. On August 28, 1963 the greatest civil rights demonstration in American history was held in Washington, D.C. During the "March on Washington," as the event was known, over 200,000 people gathered in front of the Lincoln Memorial. Among the addresses they heard was the Reverend Martin Luther King, Jr.'s famous "I Have A Dream" speech—perhaps the most memorable oration in twentieth-century American history. King described his vision of a future in which racial harmony would prevail and all Americans would unite around the principle and practice of racial equality.

To generate support for the legislation, and to dramatize the power of the growing movement, more than 200,000 demonstrators marched down the Mall in Washington, D.C., in August 1963 and gathered before the Lincoln Memorial for the greatest civil rights demonstration in the nation's history. President Kennedy, who had at first opposed the idea of the march, in the end gave it his open support after receiving pledges from organizers that speakers would not criticize the administration. Martin Luther King, Jr., in one of the greatest speeches of his remarkable oratorical career, aroused the crowd with a litany of images prefaced again and again by the phrase "I have a dream." The march was the high-water mark of the peaceful, inter-racial civil rights movement—and one of the last moments of real harmony within it.

The assassination of President Kennedy three months later gave new impetus to the battle for civil rights legislation. The ambitious measure that Kennedy had proposed in June 1963 was stalled in the Senate after having passed through the House of Representatives with relative ease. Early in 1964, after Johnson applied both public and private pressure, supporters of the measure finally mustered the two-thirds majority necessary to close debate and end a filibuster by southern senators. The Senate then passed the most comprehensive civil rights bill in the history of the nation.

The Battle for Voting Rights

Having won a significant victory in one area, the civil rights movement shifted its focus to another: voting rights. During the summer of 1964, thousands of civil rights workers, black and white, northern and southern, spread out through the South, but primarily in Mississippi, to work on behalf of black voter registration and participation. The campaign was known as "Freedom Summer," and it produced a violent response from some southern whites. Before it had even begun, three participants—two whites, Andrew Goodman and Michael Schwerner, and one black, James Chaney—disappeared after traveling to Mississippi to investigate a church bombing. Their bodies were found later buried in an earthen dam. They had been murdered, an informant later revealed, by local police and Ku Klux Klansmen. This chilling event, and numerous other bombings during Freedom Summer, did much to transform the perspective of many civil rights activists, especially in SNCC. Although civil rights activists continued their efforts, many began to doubt the philosophy of passive resistance and nonviolence.

Freedom Summer also produced the Mississippi Freedom Democratic party (MFDP), an integrated alternative to the regular all-white state party organization. Under the leadership of Fannie Lou Hamer and others, the MFDP challenged the regular party's right to its seats at the Democratic National Convention that summer. President Johnson, eager to avoid antagonizing anyone (even southern white Democrats who seemed likely to support his Republican opponent) attempted to broker a compromise. The Democratic party leadership offered to seat two MFDP delegates along with the regular slate, with promises of party reforms later on. But the MFDP rejected the compromise measure, and many MFDP delegates walked out of the convention in protest.

A year later, in March 1965, King helped organize a major demonstration in Selma, Alabama to press the demand for the right of blacks to register to vote. Selma sheriff Jim Clark led local police in a brutal attack on the demonstrators—which, as in Birmingham, received graphic television coverage and horrified many viewers across the nation. Two northern whites participating in the Selma march were murdered in the course of the effort there—one, a minister, beaten to death in the streets of the town; the other, a Detroit housewife, shot as she drove along a highway at night with a black passenger in her car. The national outrage that followed the events in Alabama helped push Lyndon Johnson to propose and win passage of the Civil Rights Act of 1965, better known as the Voting Rights Act, which provided federal protection to blacks attempting to exercise their right to vote. But important as such gains were, they failed to satisfy the rapidly rising expectations of African Americans as the focus of the movement began to move from political to economic issues.

From De Jure to De Facto Segregation

For decades, the nation's African-American population had been undergoing a major demographic shift; and by the 1960s, the problem of race was no longer primarily southern or rural, as it had been earlier in the century. By 1966, sixty-nine percent of American blacks were living in metropolitan areas and forty-five percent outside the South. Although the economic condition of much of American society was improving, in the poor urban communities in which the black population was concentrated, things were getting significantly worse. Well over half of all American nonwhites lived in poverty at the beginning of the 1960s; black unemployment was twice that of whites.

By the mid-1960s, therefore, the issue of race was moving out of the South and into the rest of the nation. The legal battle against school desegregation had moved beyond the initial assault on *de jure* segregation (segregation by law) to an attack on *de facto* segregation (segregation in practice, as through residential patterns), thus carrying the fight into northern cities. Many African-American leaders (and their white supporters) were demanding, similarly, that the battle against job discrimination move to a new level. Employers should not only abandon negative measures to deny jobs to blacks; they should adopt positive measures to recruit minorities, thus compensating for past injustices. Lyndon Johnson gave his tentative support to the concept of "affirmative action" in 1965. Over the next decade, affirmative action guidelines gradually extended to virtually all institutions doing business with or receiving funds from the federal government (including schools and universities)—and to many others as well.

A symbol of the movement's new direction, and of the problems it would cause, was a major campaign in the summer of 1966 in Chicago, in which King played a prominent role. Organizers of the Chicago campaign hoped to direct national attention to housing and employment discrimination in northern industrial cities in much the same way similar campaigns had exposed legal racism in the South. But the Chicago campaign not only evoked vicious and at times violent opposition from white residents of that city; it failed to arouse the national conscience in the way events in the South had done. It did produce a weak agreement with the city government to end housing discrimination, but little changed as a result. The Chicago campaign was, on the whole, an exercise in frustration.

Urban Violence

Well before the Chicago campaign, the problem of urban poverty had thrust itself into the national consciousness when riots broke out in black neighborhoods in major cities. There were a few scattered disturbances in the summer of 1964, most notably in New York City's Harlem. The first large race riot since the end of World War II occurred the following summer in the Watts section of Los Angeles. In the midst of a seemingly routine traffic arrest, a white police officer

RIOT IN WATTS. A fire burns out of control during the 1965 riot in the Los Angeles neighborhood known as Watts. Firefighters, attempting to subdue the blaze, were fired upon by snipers, and National Guardsmen were called out to protect them as they tried to control the conflagration. The riot led to enormous destruction in Watts and the deaths of 34 people, almost all of them African Americans.

struck a protesting black bystander with his club. The incident triggered a storm of anger and a week of violence (and revealed how deeply blacks in Los Angeles, and in other cities, resented their treatment at the hands of local police). As many as 10,000 rioters were estimated to have participated—attacking white motorists, burning buildings, looting stores, and sniping at policemen. Thirty-four people died during the Watts uprising, which was eventually quelled by the National Guard; twenty-eight of the dead were African Americans. In the summer of 1966, there were forty-three additional outbreaks, the most serious of them in Chicago and Cleveland. And in the summer of 1967, there were eight major riots, including the largest of the decade—a racial clash in Detroit in which forty-three people (thirty-three of them black) died.

Televised reports of the violence alarmed millions of Americans and created both a new sense of urgency and a growing sense of doubt among those whites who had embraced the cause of racial justice only a few years before. A special Commission on Civil Disorders created by the president in response to the riots, known as the Kerner Commission, issued a celebrated report in the spring of 1968 recommending massive spending to eliminate the abysmal conditions of the ghettoes. "Only a commitment to national action on an unprecedented scale," the commission concluded, "can shape a future compatible with the historic ideals of American society." To many white Americans, however, the lesson of the riots was the need for stern measures to stop violence and lawlessness.

Black Power

Disillusioned with the ideal of peaceful change in cooperation with whites, an increasing number of African Americans were turning to a new approach to the racial issue: the philosophy of "black power." Black power meant different things to different people. But in all its forms, it suggested a move away from interracial cooperation and toward increased racial self-awareness and independence. It was part of a long nationalist tradition among African Americans that extended back into slavery and that had had its most visible twentieth-century expression in the Garvey movement.

Perhaps the most enduring impact of black-power ideology was a social and psychological one: instilling racial pride in African Americans, who lived in a society whose dominant culture generally portrayed blacks as inferior to whites. It encouraged the growth of black studies in schools and universities. It helped stimulate important black literary and artistic movements. It produced a new interest among many blacks in their African roots. It led to a rejection by some African Americans of certain cultural practices borrowed from white society: "Afro" hair styles began to replace artificially straightened hair; some blacks began to adopt African styles of dress, even to change their names.

But black power took political forms as well, most notably in creating a deep schism within the civil rights movement. Traditional black organizations that had emphasized cooperation with sympathetic whites—groups such as the NAACP, the Urban League, and King's Southern Christian Leadership Conference—now faced competition from more radical groups. The Student Nonviolent Coordinating Committee and the Congress of Racial Equality had both begun as relatively moderate, inter-racial organizations. By the mid-1960s, however, these and other groups were calling for more radical and occasionally even violent action against the racism of white society and were openly rejecting the approaches of older, more established black leaders.

Particularly alarming to many whites were organizations that existed entirely outside the mainstream civil rights movement. In Oakland, California, the Black Panther party (founded by Huey Newton and Bobby Seale) promised to defend African-American rights against oppression even if that required violence. Black Panthers organized along semimilitary lines and wore weapons openly and proudly. They were, in fact, more the victims of violence from the police than they were practitioners of violence themselves. But they created an image, quite deliberately, of militant blacks willing to fight for justice, in Newton's words, "through the barrel of a gun."

In Detroit, a once-obscure separatist group, the Nation of Islam, gained new prominence. Founded in 1931 by Elijah Poole (who converted to Islam and re-

MALCOLM X. Though criticized by many whites for his extremism, Malcolm X, stressed self-help and black independence. An outspoken critic of racism and a charismatic figure among Black Muslims, Malcolm X attracted a large following, especially among young African Americans in the inner-cities. Here he addresses a huge rally in Harlem.

named himself Elijah Mohammed), the movement taught blacks to take responsibility for their own lives, to be disciplined, to live by strict codes of behavior,
and to reject any dependence on whites. The most celebrated of the Black Muslims, as whites often termed them, began his life as Malcolm Little, spent much
of his youth as a drug addict and pimp and served time in prison. He rebuilt his
life after joining the movement. He adopted the name Malcolm X ("X" to denote his lost African surname). And he became one of the movement's most influential spokesmen, particularly among younger blacks, as a result of his intelligence, his oratorical skills, and his harsh, uncompromising opposition to all
forms of racism and oppression. He did not advocate violence, as his critics often claimed; but he insisted that black people had the right to defend themselves,
violently if necessary, from those who assaulted their freedom. Malcolm died in
1965 when black gunmen, presumably under orders from rivals within the Nation of Islam, assassinated him in New York. But a book he had been working on
before his death with the writer Alex Haley (*The Autobiography of Malcolm X*) attracted wide attention after its publication in 1965. Malcolm X remained an influential figure in many black communities long after his death—as important
and revered a symbol to some African Americans as Martin Luther King, Jr., was
to others.

By the mid-1960s, the struggle against racial discrimination and oppression
was challenging many of the assumptions that had formed the core of postwar
American liberalism. The persistent evidence of urban poverty in northern cities
raised questions about the distribution of American abundance and the effectiveness of reform programs. The increasing violence, both among those who
resisted change and those who were impatient to create it, suggested that deep
fissures existed, which could not easily be healed by a common commitment to
liberal ideals. The growing emphasis on self-help and black separatism disturbed
many liberals who continued to emphasize the importance of peaceful integration. These conflicts would only grow deeper as the 1960s wore on.

CHAPTER TWENTY-FOUR

From Flexible Response to Vietnam

∼

I n international as much as in domestic affairs, the optimistic liberalism of the Kennedy and Johnson administrations dictated a positive, active approach to dealing with the nation's problems. And just as the new activism in domestic reform proved more difficult and divisive than liberals had imagined, so too did it create frustrations and failures in foreign policy. Both Kennedy and Johnson shared their predecessors' concern about communist expansionism. During the 1960s, the effort to stop it enmeshed the United States in a disastrous war in Vietnam that shook the nation's confidence in the Cold War and strained its social fabric.

COLD WAR CONFRONTATIONS

John Kennedy's inaugural address was a clear indication of how central opposition to communism was to his and the nation's thinking. "In the long history of the world," he proclaimed, "only a few generations have been granted the role of defending freedom in its hour of maximum danger. I do not shrink from this responsibility; I welcome it." Yet the speech—which, significantly, made no mention whatsoever of domestic affairs—was also an indication of Kennedy's belief that the United States was not doing enough to counter the communist threat; that it needed to be able to resist aggression in more flexible ways than the atomic weapons–oriented defense strategy of the Eisenhower years permitted.

Diversifying American Foreign Policy

Kennedy remained committed to the nation's atomic weapons program. Indeed, he ran for president criticizing the Eisenhower administration for allowing an imbalance of nuclear weapons (a "missile gap") to develop between the

United States and the Soviet Union. In fact, as Kennedy discovered even before the election, whatever missile gap there was favored the United States. But Kennedy insisted on proceeding with an expansion of the nation's atomic arsenal nevertheless—and the Soviet Union, which several years earlier had slowed the growth of its own nuclear weapons stockpile, responded in kind.

Kennedy's unhappiness with the Eisenhower foreign policy was not simply that it relied too heavily on nuclear weapons; it was also that it developed too few other tools for countering aggression. Kennedy argued for a new and more versatile approach to containment that became known as "flexible response." He claimed that the United States lacked the capacity to respond quickly to problems for which nuclear weapons were inappropriate solutions. In particular, he was not satisfied with the nation's ability to meet the communist threat in "emerging areas" of the Third World where the Soviet Union was supporting wars of national liberation. In 1959, the Soviet Union endorsed such wars as a means of achieving global communism. Kennedy, likewise, concluded that the Third World would be the arena in which the real struggle against communism would be waged in the future. He gave enthusiastic support to the expansion of "counterinsurgency" training, and took a great interest in the Special Forces, a small branch of the army created in the 1950s to wage guerrilla warfare in limited conflicts. Kennedy expanded the unit, allowed its members to wear distinctive headgear (from which the Special Forces drew the informal name "the Green Berets"), and gave them an elite status within the military they had never had before.

Kennedy also favored expanding American influence through peaceful means. To repair the badly deteriorating relationship with Latin America, he proposed an "Alliance for Progress": a series of projects undertaken cooperatively by the United States and Latin American governments for peaceful development and stabilization of the nations of that region. Its purpose was both to spur social and economic development and to inhibit the rise of Castro-like movements in other Central or South American countries. Kennedy also inaugurated the Agency for International Development (AID) to coordinate foreign aid. And he established what became one of his most popular innovations: the Peace Corps, which sent young American volunteers abroad to work in developing areas.

The Bay of Pigs Invasion

Among the first foreign policy ventures of the Kennedy administration was a disastrous assault on the Castro government in Cuba. The Eisenhower administration had launched the project; and by the time Kennedy took office, the CIA had been working for months in Central America to train a small army of anti-Castro Cuban exiles to invade Cuba and overthrow the Castro regime. The operation proceeded under an assumed veil of secrecy, although news leaks compromised the planned invasion almost from its beginning. Kennedy had misgivings about the project, but in one of his first actions as president he decided to proceed.

PEACE CORPS. Among the many young Americans who responded to President Kennedy's call to devote their energy and talent to service in the developing world was this Peace Corps volunteer. He is instructing children in a school in Africa. The Peace Corps was one of the most popular programs undertaken during the Kennedy administration. It seemed to many to encapsulate the youthful idealism of the early 1960s.

Kennedy had warned that "communist domination in this hemisphere can never be negotiated." He believed that Castro represented a threat to the stability of other Latin American nations. For these reasons, and others, he accepted the CIA's optimistic assessments of the chances for success and approved the invasion.

On April 17, 1961, 2,000 of the armed exiles landed at the Bay of Pigs in Cuba, expecting first American air support and than a spontaneous uprising by the Cuban people on their behalf. They received neither. An initial bombing raid, flown by a Cuban exile who was a CIA operative in a plane painted with Cuban insignia, tried but failed to cripple the Cuban air force. As the exiles landed at the Bay of Pigs, the CIA requested that American planes cover the invading forces. Here Kennedy held the line—he was adamant that U.S. forces not be involved directly in the invasion. (Air support would not likely have changed the result in any case.) Not only did the expected uprising not occur, but well-armed Castro forces easily surrounded and crushed the invaders. Near the final moment, Kennedy permitted a few navy jets, with their markings blacked out, to fly cover but it was too late. Within two days the entire mission had collapsed.

Kennedy somberly took public responsibility for the fiasco. "How could I have been so stupid?" Kennedy rhetorically asked more than one of his confidantes. The president vowed privately never again to accept at face value the reassurances of the Joint Chiefs of Staff when they reported on planned military operations. But he refused to rule out further measures against the Castro regime. "We do not intend to abandon Cuba to the communists," he said only three days after the Bay of Pigs. In fact, after the failed invasion, the Kennedy administration redoubled its efforts to develop a strategy for removing Castro from power. Among the ideas being discussed within the government were various plans for assassinating Castro.

Confrontations with Khrushchev

In the grim aftermath of the Bay of Pigs, Kennedy traveled to Vienna in June 1961 for his first meeting with Soviet Premier Nikita Khrushchev. Their frosty exchange of views did little to reduce tensions between the two nations, nor did Khrushchev's continuing irritation over the existence of a noncommunist West Berlin in the heart of East Germany. The two men talked openly about each nation's ability to destroy the other. Kennedy appeared stunned by Khrushchev's belligerence and what he believed was a dismissive attitude toward him personally. When asked later how the summit went, Kennedy replied dejectedly, "worst thing in my life. He savaged me." Kennedy took away from the summit a nagging worry that Khrushchev had sized him up as a man who did not have the "guts" to stand up to the Soviet Union. "We have to see what we can do that will restore a feeling in Moscow that we will defend our national interest," Kennedy confessed to a reporter after the summit. "I'll have to increase the defense budget. And we will have to confront them. The only place we can do that is in Vietnam. We have to send more people there."

For the moment, however, the focus was Berlin. In Vienna, Khrushchev had threatened war if the West did not abandon its defense of Berlin. Later in the summer, however, he settled on a less dangerous—but still highly provocative—approach to the problem. Particularly embarrassing to the communists was the mass exodus of residents of East Germany to the West through the easily traversed border in the center of Berlin. Before dawn on August 13, 1961, the Soviet Union stopped the exodus by directing East Germany to construct a wall between East and West Berlin. Guards fired on those who continued to try to escape. For nearly thirty years, the Berlin Wall stood as the most potent physical symbol of the conflict between the communist and non-communist worlds. Although American troops were deployed to West Berlin to show American determination to protect its freedom, and although Kennedy himself paid a dramatic and supportive visit to the city, there was little the United States could do to change the Soviet determination to wall off West Berlin.

Rising tensions with the Soviet Union culminated the following October in the most dangerous and dramatic crisis of the Cold War. During the summer of 1962, American intelligence agencies had become aware of the arrival of a new wave of Soviet technicians and equipment in Cuba and of military construction in progress. On October 14, aerial reconnaissance photos produced

THE BERLIN WALL–1961. Constructed to prevent the exodus of refugees from East Germany to the West, the Berlin Wall served for nearly thirty years as a symbol of political repression. In this photograph, taken in September 1961, an East German policeman helps build the wall even higher to prevent Germans on either side from glimpsing those in the opposite sector.

clear evidence that the Soviets were constructing sites on the island for offensive nuclear weapons. To the Soviets, placing missiles in Cuba probably seemed a reasonable, and relatively inexpensive, way to counter the presence of American missiles in Turkey (and a way to deter any future American invasion of Cuba). But to Kennedy and most other Americans, the missile sites represented an act of aggression by the Soviets toward the United States. Almost immediately, the president decided that the weapons could not be allowed to remain.

On October 22, after nearly a week of tense deliberations by a special task force in the White House, Kennedy ordered a naval and air blockade around Cuba, a "quarantine" against all offensive weapons. Soviet ships bound for the island slowed down or stopped before reaching the point of confrontation. But work on the missile sites continued. Preparations were under way for an American air attack on Cuba when, late in the evening of October 26, Kennedy received a message from Khrushchev implying that the Soviet Union would remove the missile bases in exchange for an American pledge not to invade Cuba. Ignoring other, tougher Soviet messages, the president agreed. Privately, he also promised to remove American missiles from Turkey, a decision he had reached months earlier but had not yet implemented. The crisis was over.

The Cuban missile crisis brought the world closer to nuclear war than at any time since World War II. Both the United States and the Soviet Union had been forced to confront the momentous potential consequences of their rivalry. In the following months, both seemed ready to move toward a new accommodation. In June 1963, President Kennedy spoke at American University in Washington, D.C., and seemed for the first time to offer hope for a peaceful rapprochement with the Soviet Union. The United States did not seek, Kennedy said, a "Pax Americana enforced on the world by American weapons of war." He went on to strike an unusual conciliatory cord. "If we cannot end now all our differences, at least we can help make the world safe for diversity." That same summer, the United States and the Soviet Union concluded years of negotiation by agreeing to a treaty to ban the testing of nuclear weapons in the atmosphere—the first step toward de-escalating the arms race since the beginning of the Cold War.

In the longer run, however, the missile crisis had more ominous consequences. The humiliating retreat the United States forced upon the Soviet leadership undermined the position of Nikita Khrushchev and contributed to his fall from power a year later. His replacement, Leonid Brezhnev, was a much more orthodox party figure, less interested in reform than Khrushchev had been. Perhaps more important, the graphic evidence the crisis gave the Soviets of their military inferiority helped produce a dramatic Soviet arms buildup over the next two decades, a buildup that contributed to a comparable increase in the United States in the early 1980s and that for a time undermined American support for a policy of rapprochement.

Johnson and Containment

Lyndon Johnson entered the presidency lacking even John Kennedy's limited prior experience with international affairs. He was eager, therefore, not only to continue the policies of his predecessor but to prove quickly that he, too, was a strong and forceful world leader. Johnson relied upon many of Kennedy's foreign policy advisers as he worked to put together his own administration. He strongly shared his predecessor's belief that it was imperative to prevent communist aggression.

An internal rebellion in the Dominican Republic gave Johnson an early opportunity to demonstrate his anticommunist convictions. A 1961 assassination had toppled the repressive dictatorship of General Rafael Trujillo Molina, and for the next four years various factions in the country had struggled for dominance. In the spring of 1965, a conservative military regime began to collapse in the face of a revolt by a broad range of groups on behalf of the nationalist reformer Juan Bosch, who had been elected president in 1962 and deposed by the military after only seven months in office. Arguing (without any evidence) that Bosch planned to establish a pro-Castro, communist regime, Johnson dispatched 30,000 American troops to quell the disorder. Only after a conservative candidate defeated Bosch in a 1966 election were the forces withdrawn.

From Johnson's first moments in office, however, his foreign policy was almost totally dominated by the bitter civil war in Vietnam and by the expanding involvement of the United States there. In many respects, Johnson was on this issue simply the unfortunate legatee of commitments initiated by his predecessors. But the determination of the new president and of others within his administration to prove their resolve in the battle against communism helped produce the final, decisive steps toward a full-scale commitment.

THE WARS FOR INDOCHINA

George Kennan, who helped devise the containment doctrine in whose name the United States went to war in Vietnam, once called the conflict "the most disastrous of all America's undertakings over the whole 200 years of its history." In retrospect, few would now disagree. Yet at first, the Vietnam War seemed simply one more Third World struggle on the periphery of the Cold War, a struggle in which the United States would try to tip the balance against communism without becoming too deeply or directly engaged. No president really decided to go to war in Vietnam. The American involvement there emerged, rather, from years of slowly increasing commitments that gradually and imperceptibly expanded.

The First Indochina War

Vietnam had a long history both as an independent kingdom and a major power in its region, and as a subjugated province of China; its people were both proud of their past glory and painfully aware of their many years of foreign domination. In the mid-nineteenth century, Vietnam became a colony of France. And, like other European possessions in Asia, it fell under the control of Japan during World War II. After the defeat of Japan, the question arose of what was to happen to Vietnam in the postwar world.

There were two opposing forces attempting to answer that question, both of them appealing to the United States for help. The French were seeking to reassert their control over Vietnam. Challenging them was a powerful nationalist movement within Vietnam committed to creating an independent nation. The nationalists were organized into a political party, the Vietminh, which had been created in 1941 and led ever since by Ho Chi Minh, a communist educated in Paris and Moscow, and a fervent Vietnamese nationalist.

The Vietminh had fought against Japan throughout World War II (unlike the French colonial officials, who had remained in Vietnam during the war as representatives of the Vichy regime and had collaborated with the Japanese). In the fall of 1945, after the collapse of Japan and before the western powers had time to return, the Vietminh declared Vietnam an independent nation and set up a nationalist government under Ho Chi Minh in Hanoi.

Ho had worked closely during the war with American intelligence forces in Indochina in fighting the Japanese; he apparently considered the United States something of an ally. When the war ended in 1945, he began writing President Truman asking for support in his struggle against the French. He received no reply to his letters, probably because no one in the State Department had heard of him. At the same time, Truman was under heavy pressure from both the British and the French to support France in its effort to reassert control over Vietnam. The French argued that without Vietnam, their domestic economy would collapse. Since the economic revival of western Europe was quickly becoming one of the Truman administration's top priorities, the United States did nothing to stop (although, at first, also relatively little to encourage) the French as they moved back into Vietnam in 1946 and began a struggle with the Vietminh to reestablish control over the country.

At first, the French had little difficulty reestablishing control. They drove Ho Chi Minh out of Hanoi and into hiding in the countryside; and in 1949, they established a nominally independent national government under the leadership of the former emperor, Bao Dai—an ineffectual, westernized playboy unable to assert any real independent authority. The real power remained in the hands of the French. But the Vietminh continued to challenge the French-dominated regime and slowly increased its control over large areas of the countryside. The French appealed to the United States for support; and in February 1950, the Truman administration formally recognized the Bao Dai regime and agreed to provide it with direct military and economic aid.

For the next four years, during what has become known as the First Indochina War, Truman and then Eisenhower continued to support the French military campaign against the Vietminh; by 1954, according to some calculations, the United States was paying eighty percent of France's war costs. But the war went badly for the French anyway. Finally, late in 1953, Vietminh forces engaged the French in a major battle in the far northwest corner of the country, in a valley at Dienbienphu, an isolated and almost indefensible site. The Vietminh succeeded in seizing the hills around a garrison the French had established in the valley in a futile effort to lure the Vietminh into the open. The French wound up surrounded and unable to resupply their forces. The battle turned into a prolonged and horrible siege, with the French position steadily deteriorating. It was at this point that the Eisenhower administration decided not to intervene to save the French. The defense of Dienbienphu collapsed and the French government decided the time had come to get out. The First Indochina War had come to an end.

Geneva and the Two Vietnams

An international conference at Geneva, planned many months before to settle the Korean dispute and other controversies, now took up the fate of Vietnam as well. The United States was only indirectly involved in this part of the Geneva Conference. Secretary of State Dulles, who did not really believe in negotiating with communists, reluctantly attended (described by one observer as a "puritan in a house of ill repute") but left early; the United States never signed the accords. Even so, the Geneva Conference produced an agreement to end the Vietnam conflict. There would be an immediate cease-fire in the war; Vietnam would be temporarily partitioned along the seventeenth parallel, with the Vietminh in control of North Vietnam, and a pro-western regime in control of the South. In 1956, there would be elections to reunite the country under a single government. In the interim, no new military forces were to be introduced into Vietnam; nor was either section of the country to form any military alliances.

The partition of Vietnam was, essentially, an artificial one. But there were important differences between North and South Vietnam. North Vietnam, the area now to be controlled by the Vietminh, was the heart of traditional Vietnamese society, the area where French influence had been the weakest. Hence the North had remained a reasonably stable, reasonably homogeneous culture, most of whose people lived in very close-knit, traditional villages. Northern Vietnam was also the poorest region of the country: overpopulated, plagued by serious maldistribution of scarce land, and hit by a serious famine at the end of the war. The Vietminh had worked effectively to alleviate the great famine and had won strong popular allegiance to the regime as a result. (Later, in the early 1950s, it launched a disastrous land reform policy, which it soon repudiated.) The Hanoi government was also strengthened by the mass exodus, in 1954, at the time of the partition, of many of the Catholics and others in the North who might have opposed them had they stayed. The North Vietnamese were passionately committed to the unification of the nation, a commitment that had deep roots in Vietnamese history.

South Vietnam, by contrast, was a much more recently settled area. Until the early nineteenth century, in fact, very few Vietnamese had lived there. Even in the 1950s, most of its people had been there only three generations or less. It had for many years been something like the American West in the nineteenth century—the place where adventurous, opportunistic, or disenchanted people from the poor, overpopulated North would move in search of a new beginning, and in search of land (which was scarce in the North but plentiful in the South). It was a looser, more heterogeneous, more individualistic society. It was highly factionalized—religiously, politically, and ethnically—with powerful sects (and even a powerful mafia) all competing for power. It was also more prosperous and fertile than the North. It was not overpopulated. It had experienced no famine. It was the only region of the country producing a surplus for export.

South Vietnam had no legacy of strong commitment to the Vietminh and a much less fervent commitment to national unification. It was the area where the influence of the French (their language, culture, and values) had been strongest and where there was a substantial, westernized middle class. It was, in other words, a society much more difficult to unite and to govern than the society of the North.

America and Diem

As soon as the Geneva Accords established the partition, the French finally left Vietnam altogether. The United States almost immediately stepped into the vacuum and became the principal benefactor of the new government in the South, led by Ngo Dinh Diem.

Diem was an aristocratic Catholic from central Vietnam, an outsider in the South. But he was also a nationalist, uncontaminated by collaboration with the French. And he was, for a time, successful. With the help of the American CIA, Diem waged a successful campaign against some of the powerful religious sects and the South Vietnamese mafia, which had challenged the authority of the central government. As a result, the United States came to regard Diem as a powerful and impressive alternative to Ho Chi Minh. Lyndon Johnson once called him the "Churchill of Southeast Asia."

The American government supported Diem's refusal in 1956 to permit the elections called for by the Geneva Accords, reasoning, almost certainly correctly, that Ho Chi Minh would easily win any such election. Ho could count on the entire vote of the North, with its much larger population, and at least some support in the South. The United States, in the meantime, poured military and economic aid into South Vietnam. By 1956, it was the second largest recipient of American military aid in the world, after Korea.

Diem's early successes in suppressing the sects in Vietnam led him in 1959 to begin a similar campaign to eliminate the Vietminh supporters who had stayed behind in the South after the partition. He was quite successful for a time, so successful in fact that the North Vietnamese found it necessary to respond. A new policy emanating from Moscow beginning in 1959, emphasizing wars of national liberation (as opposed to direct confrontations in Europe), also encouraged Ho Chi Minh to resume his armed struggle for national unification. In 1959, the Vietminh cadres in the South reorganized and created the National

Liberation Front (NLF), known to many Americans as the Viet Cong (a derogatory shorthand for Vietnamese Communists). The National Liberation Front was closely allied from the start with the North Vietnam government who, of course, supported its goals to overthrow the "puppet regime" of Diem and reunite the nation. In 1960, under orders from Hanoi, and with both material and manpower support from North Vietnam, the NLF began military operations in the South. This marked the beginning of the Second Indochina War.

By 1961, NLF forces were very successfully destabilizing the Diem regime. They were killing over 4,000 government officials a year (mostly village leaders) and establishing effective control over many areas of the countryside. Diem was also by now losing the support of many other groups in South Vietnam, and he was even losing support within his own military. In 1963, the Diem regime precipitated a major crisis by trying to discipline and repress the South Vietnamese Buddhists in an effort to make Catholicism the dominant religion of

BUDDHIST PROTESTS. To protest the repression of their religion by the Diem regime, Buddhist monks staged a series of demonstrations in South Vietnam. Here a Buddhist monk has immolated himself in the streets of downtown Saigon in June 1963—the first in a series of such self-immolations. Photographs and videotape of these gruesome protests were disseminated around the world and only sharpened the Kennedy administration's growing conviction that Diem could no longer be trusted to lead South Vietnam.

the country. The Buddhists began to stage enormous antigovernment demonstrations; and after Diem launched a series of heavy-handed military and police actions against them—which included several massacres of demonstrators and violent government raids on their sacred pagodas—the demonstrations grew much larger. Several Buddhist monks doused themselves with gasoline, sat cross-legged in the streets of downtown Saigon, and set themselves on fire—in view of photographers and television cameras.

The Buddhist crisis was alarming and embarrassing to the Kennedy administration and caused the American government to reconsider its commitment to Diem—although not to the survival of South Vietnam; Kennedy had greatly increased the number of American personnel and the level of American assistance to the anticommunist regime. American officials pressured Diem to reform his government, but Diem made no significant concessions. As a result, in the fall of 1963, Kennedy gave his tacit approval to a plot hatched by a group of South Vietnamese generals, with CIA encouragement, to topple Diem. In early November 1963, the generals staged the coup, assassinated Diem and his brother and principal advisor, Ngo Dinh Nhu (something the United States had not wanted or expected), and established the first of a series of new governments. But these regimes, were, for over three years, even less stable than Diem's. A few weeks after the coup, John Kennedy, too, was dead.

Intervention

Lyndon Johnson, therefore, inherited what was already a substantial American commitment to the survival of an anticommunist South Vietnam. During his first two years in office, he expanded that commitment into a full-scale American war. Why he did so has long been a subject of debate.

Many factors played a role in Johnson's fateful decision. But the most obvious explanation is that the new president faced many pressures to expand the American involvement and only a very few to limit it. As the untested successor to a revered and martyred president, he felt obliged to prove his worthiness for the office by continuing the policies of his predecessor. Aid to South Vietnam had been one of the most prominent of those policies. Johnson also felt it necessary to retain in his administration many of the important figures of the Kennedy years. In doing so, he surrounded himself with a group of foreign policy advisers—Secretary of State Dean Rusk, Secretary of Defense Robert McNamara, National Security Adviser McGeorge Bundy, and others—who believed not only that the United States had an obligation to resist communism in Vietnam but that it possessed the ability and resources to make that resistance successful. A compliant Congress raised little protest to, and indeed at one point openly endorsed, Johnson's use of executive powers to lead the nation into war. And for several years at least, public opinion remained firmly behind him—in part because Barry Goldwater's bellicose remarks about the war during the 1964 campaign made Johnson seem by comparison to be a moderate on the issue.

THE WAR IN VIETNAM AND INDOCHINA, 1964–1975

CHINA

Lao Cai

Than Uyen

Red River

Yen Bay

Dienbienphu

NORTH VIETNAM

BURMA

Hanoi

Red River Delta

Haiphong

Pak Seng

Luang Prabang

Ban Ban

Plain of Jars

Vang Vieng

Gulf of Tonkin

Hainan

Vinh

Vientiane

Mekong River

L A O S

Udon Thani

Phanom

Dong Hoi

Partition Line 1954

Vinh Linh

DMZ (Demilitarized Zone)

QUANG TRI PROVINCE

Khesanh

Hue

Phu Bai

Da Nang

Hoi An

THAILAND

FRIENDSHIP HIGHWAY

Tamky

Takhli

Don Muang

Lop Buri

Ratchasima

Udon Ratchathani

Chulai

My Lai

Quang Ngai

Dak To

Kontum

Pleiku

Ankhe

Quinhon

Plateau of Kontum

South China Sea

Bangkok

Angkor Wat

Tonle

Sap

CAMBODIA

Mekong River

Plateau of Darlac

Ban Me Thout

Sattahip

Battambang

Nhatrang

Da Lat

Camranh Bay

Kompong Cham

Bo Duc

Phnom Penh

Prey Veng

1970: U.S. and South Vietnam troops entered Viet Cong strongholds inside Cambodia

Tay Ninh

Ben Cat

SOUTH VIETNAM

Phanrang

Gulf of Thailand

Sihanoukville

Tan Son Nhut Airbase

Bienhua

Saigon

Vung Tau

Rach Gia

Cantho

Mekong Delta

Quan Long

Ca Mau Peninsula

Con Son

0   150 Miles
0   150 Kilometers

■ U.S. bases

← U.S. and South Vietnam invasion of Cambodia

← Ho Chi Minh Trail (communist supply route)

LYNDON JOHNSON AND ROBERT MCNAMARA. LBJ inherited the Vietnam War from his predecessors, and he relied especially upon advice from former Kennedy advisers such as Robert McNamara in determining how to proceed. As secretary of defense, McNamara played an important role in shaping the military effort in Vietnam. Here the strain shows in Johnson's face as he is briefed by McNamara in 1964.

Above all, intervention in South Vietnam was fully consistent with nearly twenty years of American foreign policy. An anticommunist ally was appealing to the United States for assistance; all the assumptions of the containment doctrine, as it had come to be defined by the 1960s, seemed to require the nation to oblige. Vietnam, Johnson believed, was a test of American willingness to fight communist aggression, a test he was determined not to fail. He was also acutely aware of the political costs a president who wavered in the face of communism might sustain. He was determined to ensure that his domestic agenda would not be jeopardized by critics who might pounce upon any show of weakness, particularly in the contested sphere of anticommunism.

During his first months in office, Johnson expanded the American involvement in Vietnam only slightly, sending an additional 5,000 military advisers there and preparing to send 5,000 more. Then, early in August 1964, the president announced that American destroyers on patrol in international waters in the Gulf of Tonkin had been attacked without provocation by North Vietnamese torpedo boats. Later information raised serious doubts as to whether the administration reported the attacks accurately. At the time, however, virtually no one questioned Johnson's portrayal of the incident as a serious act of aggression or his insistence that the United States must respond. By a vote of 416 to zero in the House and eighty-eight to two in the Senate, Congress hurriedly passed the Gulf of Tonkin Resolution, which authorized the president to "take all necessary measures" to protect American forces and "prevent further aggression" in Southeast Asia. The resolution became, in Johnson's view at least, an open-ended legal authorization for escalation of the conflict.

With the South Vietnamese leadership still in disarray, more and more of the burden of opposing the Viet Cong fell on the United States. In February 1965, seven marines died when communist forces attacked an American military base at Pleiku. Johnson retaliated by ordering American bombings of the North, which attempted to destroy the depots and transportation lines responsible for the flow of North Vietnamese soldiers and supplies into South Vietnam. The bombing continued intermittently until 1972. These bombing raids provided the rationale for introducing American ground forces into Vietnam. Military advisers warned the president that the bombing raids might well lead the Viet Cong to retaliate against the air bases from which the missions were flown. For this reason, initially, Johnson approved the introduction of troops to Vietnam. And in March 1965, two battalions of American marines landed at Da Nang in South Vietnam. There were now more than 100,000 American troops in Vietnam.

Four months later, the president finally admitted that the character of the war had changed. American soldiers would now, he announced, begin playing an active combat role in the conflict. By the end of the year, there were more than 180,000 American combat troops in Vietnam; in 1966, that number doubled; and by the end of 1967, there were over 500,000 American soldiers there—along with considerable civilian personnel working in various capacities and many American women (some enlisted, some not) who worked as nurses in military hospitals. In the meantime, the air war had intensified until the tonnage of bombs dropped on North Vietnam ultimately exceeded that in all theaters during World War II. And American casualties were mounting. In 1961, fourteen Americans had died in Vietnam. By the spring of 1966, more than 4,000 Americans had been killed.

Yet the gains resulting from the carnage were negligible. The United States had finally succeeded in 1965 in creating a reasonably stable government in the South under General Nguyen Van Thieu. But the new regime was hardly less corrupt or brutal than its predecessors, and no more able than they to establish its authority in its own countryside. The Viet Cong, not the Thieu regime, controlled the majority of South Vietnam's villages and hamlets.

The Quagmire

For more than seven years, American combat forces remained bogged down in a war that the United States was never able either to win or fully to understand. Combating a foe whose strength lay less in weaponry than in its infiltration of the population, the United States responded with heavy-handed technological warfare designed for conventional battles against conventional armies. American forces succeeded in winning most of the major battles in which they became engaged. Astounding (if not always reliable) casualty figures showed that far more communists than Americans were dying in combat. A continuous stream of optimistic reports poured forth from American military commanders, government officials, and others—including the famous statement of Secretary of Defense McNamara that he could see "the light at the end of the tunnel." But if the war was not actually being lost, neither was it being won.

Central to the American war effort was a commitment to what the military called "attrition," a strategy premised on the belief that the United States could inflict so many casualties and so much damage on the enemy that eventually they would be unable and unwilling to continue the struggle. But the attrition strategy failed because the North Vietnamese proved willing to commit many more

BOMBING CAMPAIGNS. Phantom jets drop a rain of bombs on North Vietnam in an effort to cripple Hanoi's capacity to wage war, prevent the movement of enemy supplies into South Vietnam along the Ho Chi Minh Trail, and persuade North Vietnam it could not win against the United States' superior military hardware and technology. In the end, although the bombing inflicted extensive damage, it did not succeed in defeating or demoralizing the North Vietnamese.

soldiers to the conflict than the United States had expected (and many more than America was willing to send).

It failed, too, because the United States relied heavily on its bombing of the North to eliminate the communists' warmaking capacity. American bombers struck at strategic targets in North Vietnam to weaken the material capacity of the communists to continue the war (factories, bridges, railroads, shipyards, oil storage facilities, depots, etc.); and they bombed jungle areas of Vietnam, Laos, and Cambodia to cut off the "Ho Chi Minh Trail," the infiltration routes by which Hanoi sent troops and supplies into the South. In addition, the Americans hoped bombing would weaken the will of North Vietnam to continue the war.

By the end of 1967, virtually every identifiable target of any strategic importance in North Vietnam had been destroyed. The bombing badly damaged the North Vietnamese economy, killed many soldiers and civilians, and made life difficult for those who survived. But it produced few of the effects that the United States had intended. North Vietnam was not a modern, industrial society; it did not have many of the sorts of targets that bombing is effective against. And in any case, the North Vietnamese responded to the air raids with enormous ingenuity: they created a great network of underground tunnels, shops, and factories. They also secured increased aid from the Soviet Union and China. Infiltration of the South was unaffected; the North Vietnamese just kept moving the Ho Chi Minh Trail. Nor did the bombing weaken North Vietnam's will to continue fighting. On the contrary, it seemed to increase the nation's resolve and strengthen its hatred of the United States. As one North Vietnamese leader later explained: "There was extraordinary fervor then. The Americans thought that the more bombs they dropped, the quicker we would fall to our knees and surrender. But the bombs heightened rather than dampened our spirit."

Another crucial part of the American strategy was the "pacification" program, whose purpose was to push the Viet Cong from particular regions and then "pacify" those regions by winning the "hearts and minds" of the people. Routing the Viet Cong was often possible, but the subsequent pacification proved more difficult. American forces appeared unable to establish the same kind of rapport with provincial Vietnamese that the Viet Cong had created; and the American military never gave that part of the program a very high priority in any case. Gradually, the pacification program gave way to the more heavy-handed relocation strategy, through which American troops uprooted villagers from their homes, sent them fleeing to refugee camps or into the cities (producing by 1967 more than 3 million refugees), and then destroyed the vacated villages and surrounding countryside. Saturation bombings (using conventional weapons), bulldozing settlements, chemically defoliating fields and jungles, and burning areas with napalm—were all tactics designed to eliminate possible Viet Cong sanctuaries. But the Viet Cong responded by moving to new sanctuaries elsewhere. The futility of the United States' effort was suggested by the statement of an American officer after flattening one such hamlet: it had been "necessary to destroy [the village] in order to save it."

As the war dragged on and victory remained elusive, some American officers and officials began to urge the president to expand the military efforts. Some argued for heavier bombing and increased troop strength; others insisted that the United States attack communist enclaves in surrounding countries; a few began to urge the use of nuclear weapons. The Johnson administration, however, resisted. Unwilling to abandon its commitment to South Vietnam for fear of destroying American "credibility" in the world, the government was also unwilling to expand the war too far, for fear of provoking direct intervention by the Chinese, the Soviets, or both. In the meantime, the president began to encounter additional obstacles and frustrations at home.

The Antiwar Movement

Few Americans, and even fewer influential ones, protested American involvement in Vietnam as late as the end of 1965. But as the war dragged on and its futility began to become apparent, political support for it began to erode. A series of "teach-ins" on university campuses, beginning at the University of Michigan in 1965, sparked a national debate over the war before such debate developed inside the government itself. Such pacifist organizations as the American Friends Service Committee and the Women's International League for Peace and Free-

ANTIWAR MARCH–1967. By 1967, protests against American involvement in the Vietnam War were growing. This demonstrator taunts a military policeman who is guarding the Pentagon during a massive antiwar march in Washington.

dom organized early protests. By the end of 1967, American students opposed to the war had become a significant political force. Enormous peace marches in New York, Washington, D.C., and other cities drew broad public attention to the antiwar movement. In the meantime, a growing number of journalists, particularly reporters who had spent time in Vietnam, helped sustain the movement with their frank revelations about the brutality and apparent futility of the war.

The growing chorus of popular protest soon was joined by opposition to the war from within the government. Senator J. William Fulbright of Arkansas, chairman of the powerful Senate Foreign Relations Committee, turned against the war and in January 1966 began to stage highly publicized and occasionally televised congressional hearings to air criticisms of it. Distinguished figures such as George F. Kennan and retired general James Gavin testified against the conflict, giving opposition to the war respectability in the minds of many Americans generally unwilling to question the government or the military. Other members of Congress joined Fulbright in opposing Johnson's policies—including, in 1967, Robert F. Kennedy, brother of the slain president, now a senator from New York. Even within the administration, the consensus seemed to be crumbling. Robert McNamara, who had done much to help extend the American involvement in Vietnam, quietly left the government, disillusioned, in 1968. His successor as secretary of defense, Clark Clifford, became a quiet but powerful voice within the administration on behalf of a cautious scaling down of the commitment.

In the meantime, the American economy began to suffer. Johnson's commitment to fighting the war while continuing his Great Society reforms—his promise of "guns and butter"—proved impossible to maintain. The inflation rate, which had remained at two percent through most of the early 1960s, rose to three percent in 1967, four percent in 1968, and six percent in 1969. In August 1967, Johnson asked Congress for a tax increase—a ten percent surcharge, widely labeled a "war tax"—which he knew was necessary if the nation was to avoid even more ruinous inflation. In return, congressional conservatives demanded and received a $6 billion reduction in the funding for Great Society programs.

By now it had become apparent that Vietnam was proving to be far costlier—in dollars, lives, and political capital—than anyone had anticipated. At home, dissent frayed the shared values so critical to the triumph of American liberalism. Even vociferous defenders of the president watched with dismay as his political support crumbled. The growing militancy of the antiwar movement created deep divisions, often generational, among many groups of Americans. In 1968, these divisions, and others, would erupt.

CHAPTER TWENTY-FIVE

Cultural Revolutions

~

The liberalism of the early 1960s rested on a series of optimistic assumptions about America's resources and about the essential stability of its society. The architects of the New Frontier and the Great Society, and the millions of Americans who supported their work, believed that rapid economic growth was now the normal condition of society. They believed that purposeful government action could erase poverty and solve social problems without creating serious conflict or requiring substantial sacrifice. They believed that most Americans embraced a shared set of social and cultural values, and that extending rights and freedoms to previously excluded groups would bring those groups into the national consensus.

By the late 1960s, all of those assumptions were in disarray. The American people were entering a period of profound change and unprecedented turmoil, and it may not be too much to say that the United States was in the throes of a series of cultural revolutions. The nation's political and economic institutions survived the turbulence of these years relatively unscathed. But American society and American culture were transformed.

THE TRAUMAS OF 1968

By the end of 1967, the twin crises of the war in Vietnam and the deteriorating racial situation at home, crises that fed upon and inflamed each other, had already unsettled American life. In the course of 1968, the tensions they had created suddenly burst to the surface and threatened the nation with chaos. Not since World War II had the United States experienced so profound a sense of crisis.

The Tet Offensive

On January 31, 1968, the first day of the Vietnamese New Year (Tet), communist forces launched an enormous, concerted attack on American strongholds throughout South Vietnam. A few cities, most notably Hue, fell to the communists. Others suffered major disruptions. But in the end, the communists suffered serious defeats in most of their engagements with the Americans. What made the Tet Offensive so shocking to the American people, however, was the fierce fighting of an enemy the American military command had said was weakening.

TET OFFENSIVE. Two American soldiers lie dead under a tarp in the U.S. Embassy compound in Saigon on January 31, 1968. For several hours, the Embassy itself became a battleground when Viet Cong guerrillas attacked the most visible symbol of the American presence in South Vietnam as well as outlying cities and towns. Although American military forces eventually subdued the enemy, the surprise attack by the Viet Cong undermined confidence among Americans that the U.S. was really winning the war.

Through much of the Tet Offensive the nation witnessed on television the jarring sight of communist forces in the heart of Saigon, setting off bombs, shooting South Vietnamese officials and troops, and holding down fortified areas (including, briefly, the grounds of the American embassy).

The Tet Offensive also dramatized for the American public the brutality of the war in Vietnam. In the midst of the fighting, television cameras recorded the sight of a captured Viet Cong soldier being led up to a South Vietnamese officer in the streets of Saigon. Without a word, the officer pulled out his pistol and shot the young man in the head at point blank range, leaving him lying dead in the street, his blood pouring onto the pavement. It may be that no single event did more to undermine support for the war in the United States.

American forces soon dislodged the Viet Cong from most of the positions they had seized. Indeed, the Tet Offensive cost the communists such appalling casualties that they were significantly weakened for months to come. Tet would permanently deplete the ranks of the NLF and force North Vietnamese troops to take on a much larger share of the subsequent fighting. But all that had little impact on American opinion. Tet may have been a military victory for the United States; but it was a political defeat for the administration, a defeat from which it would never fully recover.

In the following weeks, opposition to the war grew substantially. Leading newspapers and magazines, television commentators, and mainstream politicians began taking public stands in favor of de-escalation of the conflict. Within weeks of the Tet Offensive, public opposition to the war had almost doubled. And Johnson's personal popularity rating slid to thirty-five percent, the lowest of any president since Harry Truman.

"Dumping" Johnson

Beginning in the summer of 1967, dissident Democrats (led by the talented activist Allard Lowenstein) tried to mobilize support behind an antiwar candidate who would challenge Lyndon Johnson in the 1968 primaries. When Robert Kennedy declined their invitation, they turned to Senator Eugene McCarthy of Minnesota. A brilliantly orchestrated campaign by Lowenstein and thousands of young volunteers in the New Hampshire primary produced a startling showing by McCarthy in March; he nearly defeated the president.

A few days later, Robert Kennedy finally entered the campaign, embittering many McCarthy supporters, but bringing his own substantial strength among African Americans, poor people, and workers to the antiwar cause. Polls showed the president trailing badly in Wisconsin, the next scheduled primary. Indeed, public animosity toward the president was now so intense that Johnson did not even dare to leave the White House to campaign. On March 31, he went on television to announce a limited halt in the bombing of North Vietnam—his first major concession to the antiwar forces—and, much more surprising, his withdrawal from the presidential contest.

For a moment, it seemed as though the antiwar forces had won. Robert Kennedy quickly established himself as the champion of the Democratic primaries, winning one election after another. In the meantime, however, Vice President Hubert Humphrey, with the support of President Johnson, entered the contest and began to attract the support of party leaders and of the many delegations that were selected not by popular primaries but by state party organizations. He soon appeared to be the front runner in the race.

The King and Kennedy Assassinations

In the midst of this bitter political battle, in which the war had been the dominant issue, attention turned suddenly back to the nation's enduring racial conflicts. On April 4, Martin Luther King, Jr., who had traveled to Memphis, Tennessee, to lend his support to striking black sanitation workers in the city, was shot and killed while standing on the balcony of his motel. The assassin, James Earl Ray, who was captured days later in London, had no apparent motive. Later evidence suggested that he had been hired by others to do the killing, but he never revealed the identity of his employers.

King's tragic death produced an outpouring of grief matched in recent memory only by the reaction to the death of John Kennedy. Among many African Americans, it also produced anger. In the days after the assassination, major riots broke out in more than sixty American cities. Forty-three people died; more than 3,000 suffered injuries; as many as 27,000 people were arrested.

In the midst of grief and turmoil, Robert Kennedy continued his campaign for the presidential nomination, raising the hopes of the many who believed he could heal some of the divisions in the nation. Late on the night of June 6, he appeared in the ballroom of a Los Angeles hotel to acknowledge his victory in that day's California primary. As he left the ballroom after his victory statement, Sirhan Sirhan, a young Palestinian apparently enraged by Kennedy's pro-Israel views, emerged from a crowd and shot him in the head. Early the next morning, Kennedy died.

By the time of his death, Robert Kennedy—who earlier in his career had been widely considered a cold, ruthless agent of his more attractive brother—had emerged as a figure of enormous popular appeal. More than John Kennedy, Robert identified his hopes with the American "dispossessed"—with African Americans, Hispanics, Native Americans, the poor—and with the many American liberals who were coming to believe that the problems of such groups demanded attention. Indeed, Robert Kennedy, much more than John, shaped what some would later call the "Kennedy legacy," a set of ideas that would for a time become central to American liberalism: the fervent commitment to using government to help the powerless. In addition, Robert had an impassioned following among many people who saw in him (and his family) the kind of glamour and hopefulness they had come, at least in retrospect, to identify with the martyred president. His campaign appearances inspired outbursts of public enthusiasm rarely seen in political life. The passions Kennedy aroused made his violent

ROBERT KENNEDY. Two weeks before his assassination, Robert Kennedy campaigns in California. The New York senator, and brother of the slain president, attracted adoring crowds throughout this last campaign. As he stood in this open car, he was virtually unprotected from potential assailants. Shortly after declaring his victory in the primary, Senator Kennedy was shot in the head by Sirhan Sirhan, a Palestinian enraged by Kennedy's pro-Israeli views on foreign policy. He died the following day.

death a particularly shattering experience for many Americans. The assassination helped spark a searching debate about violence in American society—why it occurred, how it could be stopped, what it said about the nation.

Chicago

Meanwhile, the presidential campaign continued gloomily during the last weeks before the convention. Hubert Humphrey, who had seemed likely to win the nomination even before Robert Kennedy's death, now faced only minor opposition—despite the embittered claims of many Democrats that Humphrey would simply continue the bankrupt policies of the Johnson administration. The approaching Democratic Convention, therefore, began to take on the appearance of an exercise in futility; and antiwar activists, despairing of winning any victories within the convention, began to plan major demonstrations outside it.

When the Democrats finally gathered in Chicago in August, even the most optimistic observers predicted a turbulent convention. Inside the hall, delegates bitterly debated an antiwar plank in the party platform that both Kennedy and

McCarthy supporters favored. Miles away, in a downtown park, thousands of antiwar protesters staged demonstrations. On the third night of the convention, as the delegates began their balloting on the now virtually inevitable nomination of Hubert Humphrey, demonstrators and police clashed in a bloody riot in the streets of Chicago. Hundreds of protesters were injured as police attempted to disperse them with tear gas and billy clubs. Aware that the violence was being televised to the nation, the demonstrators taunted the authorities with the chant, "The whole world is watching!" And Hubert Humphrey, who had spent years dreaming of becoming his party's candidate for president, received a nomination that appeared at the time to be almost worthless.

The Conservative Reaction

The turbulent events of 1968 persuaded many observers that American society was in the throes of revolutionary change. In fact, however, the response of most Americans to the turmoil was a conservative one.

The most visible sign of the conservative backlash was the surprising success of the campaign of George Wallace for the presidency. Wallace had established himself in 1963 as one of the nation's leading spokesmen for the defense of segregation when, as governor of Alabama, he had attempted to block the admission of black students to the University of Alabama. In 1964, he had run in a few Democratic presidential primaries and had done surprisingly well, even in several states outside the South. In 1968, after again running in several Democratic primaries and again showing striking strength, he became a third party candidate for president, basing his campaign on a host of conservative grievances, only some connected to race. He denounced the forced busing of students, the proliferation of government regulations and social programs, and the permissiveness of authorities toward race riots and antiwar demonstrations. There was never any serious chance that Wallace would win the election; but his standing in the polls rose at times to over twenty percent.

A more effective effort to mobilize the "silent majority" in favor of order and stability was under way within the Republican party. Richard Nixon, whose political career had seemed at an end after his losses in the presidential race of 1960 and a California gubernatorial campaign two years later, re-emerged as the preeminent spokesman for what he called "Middle America." Nixon recognized that many Americans were tired of hearing about their obligations to the poor, tired of hearing about the sacrifices necessary to achieve racial justice, tired of judicial reforms that seemed designed to help criminals. By offering a vision of stability, law and order, government retrenchment, and "peace with honor" in Vietnam, he easily captured the nomination of his party for the presidency. And after the spectacle of the Democratic Convention, he enjoyed a commanding lead in the polls as the November election approached.

That lead diminished greatly in the last weeks before the voting. Old doubts about Nixon's character continued to haunt the Republican candidate. A skillful

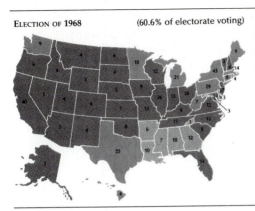

ELECTION OF 1968	(60.6% of electorate voting)			
Richard M. Nixon (Republican)		301	31,770,237 (43.4)	
Hubert H. Humphrey (Democratic)		191	31,270,533 (42.7)	
George C. Wallace (American Independence)		46	9,906,141 (13.5)	
Other candidates (Socialist Labor; D. Gregory; Socialist Workers; Peace and Freedom; McCarthy; Prohibition)		—	218,347	

last-minute surge by Hubert Humphrey, who managed to restore a tenuous unity to the Democratic party, narrowed the gap further. And the Wallace campaign appeared to be hurting the Republicans more than the Democrats. In the end, however, Nixon eked out a victory almost as narrow as his defeat in 1960. He received 43.4 percent of the popular vote to Humphrey's 42.7 percent (a margin of only about 500,000 votes), and 301 electoral votes to Humphrey's 191. George Wallace, who like most third-party candidates faded in the last weeks of the campaign, still managed to poll 13.5 percent of the popular vote and to carry five southern states with a total of forty-six electoral ballots—the best showing by a third party candidate since the 1920s. Nixon had hardly won a decisive personal mandate. But the election made clear that a majority of the American electorate was more interested in restoring stability than in promoting social change.

THE CRISIS OF AUTHORITY

The election of Richard Nixon in 1968 was the result of more than the unpopularity of Lyndon Johnson and the war. It was the result, too, of a strong public reaction against what many Americans considered a frontal assault on the foundations of their culture. Throughout the late 1960s and early 1970s, new interest groups were mobilizing to demand protections and benefits. New values and assumptions were emerging to challenge traditional patterns of thought and behavior. The United States was in the throes, some believed, of a genuine cultural revolution.

Some Americans welcomed the changes. But many—a clear majority, it seemed, on the basis of the 1968 election returns—feared them. There was growing resentment of the attention directed toward minorities and the poor, of the federal social programs that were funneling billions of dollars into the inner cities, of the increasing tax burden on the middle class, and of the "hippies" and radicals who were dominating public discourse with their bitter critiques of middle-class values. It was time, many men and women believed, for a restoration of stability and a relegitimization of traditional centers of authority.

In Richard Nixon, many Americans found a man who seemed perfectly to match their mood. Himself a product of a hard-working, middle-class family, Nixon had risen to prominence on the basis of his own unrelenting efforts; he projected an image of stern dedication to traditional values. Yet the presidency of Richard Nixon, far from returning calm and stability to American politics, coincided with, and in many ways helped to produce, more years of crisis.

What was perhaps most alarming to conservative Americans in the 1960s and 1970s was a pattern of social and cultural protest that was emerging from people, especially in the younger generation, who gave vent to two related impulses. One impulse, emerging from the political left, sought to create a new active community of the people that would rise up to break the power of elites—the "establishment"—and force the nation to end the war, pursue racial and economic justice, and transform its political life. The other, at least equally powerful, impulse appeared related to, but not entirely compatible with, the first: the vision of individual "liberation." It found expression in part through the efforts of particular groups—African Americans, Native Americans, Hispanics, women, homosexuals, and others—to define a place for themselves within the larger society. It also found expression through attempts to create a new culture—one that would permit escape from what some considered the dehumanizing pressures of modern "technocracy."

The New Left

In retrospect, it seems unsurprising that young Americans became so assertive and powerful in American culture and politics in the 1960s. The postwar baby-boom generation, the unprecedented number of people born in a few years during and just after World War II, was growing up. By 1970, more than half the American population was under thirty years old, and over eight million Americans (eight times the number in 1950) were attending college. This was the largest generation of youth in American history, one that came of age in a time of unprecedented affluence and opportunity. Young people are always more likely than their elders to challenge the existing order. And while relatively few young Americans embraced radical political causes or rebelled in any fundamental way against their culture in the 1960s, those who did were numerous enough, and assertive enough, to have a powerful impact on the nation's cultural and political climate.

The radicalization of many American young people was apparent in the rise of the New Left—a large, diverse group of men and women (many, but not all, of whom were students) energized by the polarizing developments of their time to challenge the political system. The New Left embraced the cause of African Americans and other minorities, but its own ranks consisted overwhelmingly of white Americans.

The New Left emerged from many sources. Some of its members were the children of radical parents (members of the so-called "Old Left" of the 1930s and 1940s) and grew up with an activist perspective on society and politics. Indeed, the New Left drew considerable support, and guidance, from groups and individuals from the Old Left; it was not as entirely "new" as its champions liked to claim. The New Left drew as well from the writings of some of the important social critics of the 1950s—among them C. Wright Mills, a sociologist at Columbia University who wrote a series of scathing and brilliant critiques of modern bureaucracies. And while relatively few members of the New Left were communists, many were drawn to the writings of Karl Marx and such other Marxist theorists as Antonio Gramsci and Herbert Marcuse. Some came to revere Third World Marxists such as Che Guevara, Mao Zedong, and Ho Chi Minh. For a while, left-leaning figures in the labor movement helped nurture the New Left—although relations between the two movements soon deteriorated.

But the New Left drew from nothing so much as the civil rights movement, in which many idealistic young white Americans had become involved in the early 1960s. Racism, oppression, and violence were nothing new to the many African Americans fighting for civil rights. But to white college students from middle-class backgrounds, the exposure to social injustice (and personal danger) in the South was shocking and disillusioning. It led many of them to question their assumptions about the basic values and institutions of American life. Within a few years, some white civil rights activists were beginning to consider broader political commitments.

In 1962, a group of college students gathered in Michigan (at a conference center owned by the United Auto Workers) to form an organization to give voice to their demands: Students for a Democratic Society (SDS). Their declaration of beliefs, the Port Huron Statement, expressed their disillusionment with the society they had inherited and their determination to build a new politics. "Many of us began maturing in complacency," the statement (most of it the work of student activist Tom Hayden) declared. "As we grew, however, our comfort was penetrated by events too troubling to dismiss." In the following years, SDS became the principal organization of student radicalism.

Some members of SDS moved into inner-city neighborhoods and tried for a time to mobilize poor and working-class people politically. But most members of the New Left were students, and over time they came to focus their radicalism on the modern university. One early indication of this emphasis was a 1964 dispute at the University of California at Berkeley over the rights of students to engage in political activities on campus. The Free Speech Movement, as it called itself, created turmoil at Berkeley, as students challenged campus police, occupied administrative offices, and produced a strike in which nearly three quarters of Berkeley students participated. The immediate issue focused on the right of students to pass out literature and recruit volunteers for political causes on campus. But the protest quickly evolved into a more basic critique of the university, and the society it seemed to represent. Mario Savio, a Berkeley graduate student and one of the leaders of the Free Speech Movement, captured something of the political anguish in a famous speech on campus, in which he said:

> There is a time when the operation of the machine becomes so odious, makes you so sick at heart, that you can't take part; you can't even passively take part, and you've got to put your bodies upon the gears and upon the wheels, upon the levers, upon all the apparatus and you've got to make it stop. And you've got to indicate to the people who run it, to the people who own it, that unless you're free, the machine will be prevented from working at all.

The revolt at Berkeley was the first outburst of what was to be nearly a decade of campus turmoil.

Students at Berkeley and elsewhere protested the impersonal character of the modern university. But their criticism also sought to expose the connections between academic institutions and the federal government. In particular, the university became for many activists a microcosm of many of the ills that existed in American society, most notably what they considered its corrupt and immoral public policies. The antiwar movement greatly inflamed the challenge to the universities and turned its focus to the ways in which they were complicit in the war in Vietnam: by having Reserve Officer Training Corps (ROTC) programs, by conducting research for the Defense Department, by facilitating the recruitment of students to work after graduation for companies engaged in producing arms and napalm.

Beginning in 1968, campus demonstrations, riots, and building seizures became almost commonplace. At Columbia University in New York, students seized the offices of the president and other members of the administration and faculty and occupied them for several days until local police forcibly (and violently) ejected them. Harvard University had a similarly violent experience a year later. Also in 1969, Berkeley became the scene of perhaps the most prolonged and traumatic conflict of any American college campus in the 1960s: a battle over the efforts of a few students to build a "People's Park" on land the university planned to use to build a parking garage.

This seemingly minor event precipitated weeks of impassioned and often violent conflicts between the university administration and its students and between students and police. By the end of the People's Park battle, which lasted for more than a week, the Berkeley campus was completely polarized; even students who had not initially supported or even noticed the People's Park (the great majority) were by the end committed to its defense; eighty-five percent of the 15,000 students who participated in a referendum voted to leave the park alone. Student radicals, for the first time, won large audiences for their heated rhetoric linking together university administrators, the police, and the larger political and economic system, describing them all as part of one, united, oppressive force. As one Berkeley activist said in the midst of the battle: "You've pushed us to the end of your civilization here, against the sea in Berkeley. Then you pushed us into a square-block area called People's Park. It was the last thing we had to defend, this square block of sanity amid all your madness. . . . We are now homeless in your civilized world. We have become the great American gypsies, with only our mythology for a culture." Over the next several years, hardly any major university was immune to some level of disruption. Small groups of especially dogmatic radicals—among them the "Weathermen," a violent offshoot of SDS—were responsible for a few cases of arson and bombing that destroyed campus buildings and claimed several lives.

Not many people ever accepted the radical political views that lay at the heart of the New Left. But many supported the position of SDS and other groups on particular issues, and above all on the Vietnam War. Between 1967 and 1969, student radicals organized some of the largest political demonstrations in American history. The march on the Pentagon of October 1967, where demonstrators were met by a solid line of armed troops; the "spring mobilization" of April 1968, which attracted hundreds of thousands of demonstrators in cities around the country; the Vietnam "moratorium" of the fall of 1969, during which millions of opponents of the war gathered in major rallies across the nation; and countless other demonstrations, large and small—all helped thrust the issue of the war into the center of American politics.

Closely related to opposition to the war—and another issue that helped fuel the New Left—was opposition to the military draft. The gradual abolition of many traditional deferments—for graduate students, teachers, husbands, fathers, and others—swelled the ranks of those faced with conscription (and thus likely to oppose it). Draft card burnings became common features of antiwar rallies on college campuses. Many draft-age Americans simply refused induction, accepting what were occasionally long terms in jail as a result. Thousands of others fled to Canada, Sweden, and elsewhere (where they were joined by many deserters from the armed forces) to escape conscription. Not until 1977, when President Jimmy Carter issued a general pardon to draft resisters and a far more limited amnesty for deserters, did the Vietnam exiles begin to return to the country in substantial numbers.

The Counterculture

Closely related to the New Left was a youth culture openly scornful of the values and conventions of middle-class society. The most visible characteristic of the counterculture, as it became known, was a change in lifestyle. As if to display their contempt for conventional standards, young Americans wore long hair and distinctive clothing (ragged or flamboyant by turns) and indicated a rebellious disdain for traditional speech and decorum. Central to the counterculture were drugs: marijuana smoking—which after 1966 became almost as common a youthful diversion as beer drinking—and the less widespread but still substantial use of other drugs, including potent hallucinogens such as LSD.

There was also a new, more permissive view of sexual behavior—the beginnings of what some called the "sexual revolution." To some degree, the emergence of more relaxed approaches to sexuality was a result less of the counterculture than of the new accessibility of effective contraceptives. The introduction of the birth control pill in 1960 and, a decade later, legalized abortion did much to diminish fear of unwanted pregnancy, a powerful force inhibiting female sexuality. But the new sexuality also reflected the counterculture's belief that individuals should strive for release from inhibitions and should give vent to their instincts—including the instinct for sensual pleasure.

The counterculture's iconoclasm and hedonism sometimes masked its implicit philosophy, which offered a fundamental challenge to the American middle-class mainstream. Like the New Left, with which it in many ways overlapped, the counterculture challenged the structure of modern American society, attacking its banality, its consumerism, its hollowness, its artificiality, and its isolation from nature. The most committed adherents of the counterculture—the hippies, who came to dominate the Haight-Ashbury neighborhood of San Francisco and other places, and social dropouts, many of whom retreated to rural communes—rejected modern society altogether and attempted to find refuge in a simpler, more "natural" existence. But even those whose commitment to the counterculture was less dramatic were attracted to the idea of personal fulfillment through rejecting the inhibitions and conventions of middle-class culture. In a corrupt and alienating society, the new creed seemed to suggest, the first responsibility of the individual was cultivation of the self, the unleashing of one's own full potential for pleasure and fulfillment.

Theodore Roszak, whose book *The Making of a Counter Culture* (1969) became a central document of the era, captured much of the spirit of the movement in his frank admission that "the primary project of our counter culture is to proclaim a new heaven and a new earth so vast, so marvelous that the inordinate claims of technical expertise must of necessity withdraw to a subordinate and marginal status in the lives of men." Charles Reich's *The Greening of America* (1970) created a short-lived sensation with its argument that the individual should strive for a new form of consciousness—"Consciousness III," as he called it—in which the self would be the only reality.

The effects of the counterculture reached out to the larger society and helped create a new set of social norms that many young people (and some adults) chose to imitate. Long hair and bohemian clothing became the badge not only of hippies and radicals but of an entire generation. The use of marijuana, the freer attitudes toward sex, the iconoclastic (and sometimes obscene) language—all spread far beyond the realm of the true devotees of the counterculture.

Perhaps the most pervasive element of the new youth society was one that even the least radical members of the generation embraced: rock music. Rock-'n'-roll first achieved wide popularity in the 1950s, on the strength of such early performers as Buddy Holly and, above all, Elvis Presley. Early in the 1960s, its influence began to spread, a result in large part of the phenomenal popularity of the Beatles, the English group whose first visit to the United States in 1964 created a remarkable sensation known at the time as "Beatlemania." For a time, most rock musicians—like most popular musicians before them—concentrated largely on romantic themes. One of the first great hits of the Beatles was a song with the innocuous title "I Want to Hold Your Hand." By the late 1960s, however, rock music had begun to reflect many of the new iconoclastic values of its time. The Beatles, for example, abandoned their once simple and seemingly innocent style for a new, experimental, even mystical approach that reflected their own growing fascination with drugs and Eastern religions. Other groups, such as the Rolling Stones, turned even more openly to themes of anger, frustration, and rebelliousness. Many popular musicians used their music to express explicit political radicalism as well—especially some of the leading folk singers of the era, such as Bob Dylan and Joan Baez. Rock's driving rhythms, its undisguised sensuality, and its sometimes harsh and angry tone all made it a compelling vehicle for expressing the unrest of the late 1960s.

A powerful symbol of the fusion of rock music and the counterculture was the great music festival at Woodstock, New York, in the summer of 1969, where 400,000 people gathered on a farm for nearly a week. Despite heavy rain, mud, inadequate facilities, and impossible crowding, the audience remained peaceful and harmonious. Champions of the counterculture spoke rhapsodically at the time of how Woodstock represented the birth of a new youth nation, the "Woodstock nation." The Beat poet Allen Ginsberg, revered by many enthusiasts of the counterculture and himself a champion of the "new consciousness," wrote an ecstatic poem proclaiming that at Woodstock "a new kind of man has come to his bliss/to end the cold war he has borne/against his own kind of flesh."

Virtually no Americans could avoid evidence of how rapidly the norms of their society were changing in the late 1960s. Those who attended movies saw a gradual disappearance of the banal, conventional messages that had dominated films since the 1920s. Instead, they saw explorations of political issues, of new sexual mores, of violence, and of social conflict. Television also began to turn (even if more slowly than the other media) to programming that reflected social and cultural conflict—as exemplified by the enormously popular *All in the Family*, whose working-class protagonist, Archie Bunker, displayed both obvious prejudice and, by episode's end, often some simple wisdom.

THE MOBILIZATION OF MINORITIES

The growth of black protest, and of a significant white response to it, both preceded the political and cultural upheavals of the 1960s and helped to produce them. It also encouraged other minorities to assert themselves and demand redress of their grievances. For Native Americans, Hispanic Americans, gay men and women, and others, the late 1960s and 1970s were a time of growing self-expression and political activism.

Seeds of Indian Militancy

Few minorities had deeper or more justifiable grievances against the prevailing culture than American Indians—or Native Americans, as many began to call themselves in the 1960s. Native Americans suffered enormous social and economic deprivations in American society. Average annual family income for Indians was 1,000 dollars less than that for blacks . The Native American unemployment rate was ten times the national rate. Joblessness was particularly high on the reservations, where nearly half of all Native Americans lived. But even most Native Americans living in cities suffered from their limited education and training and could find only menial jobs. Life expectancy among Indians fell twenty years below the national average. Suicides among Indian youths were a hundred times more frequent than among white youths. And while African Americans attracted the attention (for good or for ill) of many whites, Native Americans for many years remained largely ignored.

For much of the postwar era, and particularly after the resignation of John Collier as Commissioner of Indian Affairs in 1946, federal policy toward the tribes had been shaped by a determination to incorporate Indians into mainstream American society whether Indians wanted to assimilate or not. Two laws passed in 1953 established the basis of a new policy, which became known as "termination." Through termination, the federal government withdrew all official recognition of the tribes as legal entities, administratively separate from state governments, and made them subject to the same local jurisdictions as white residents. At the same time, the government encouraged Indians to assimilate into the larger society and worked to funnel Native Americans into cities, where, presumably, they would adapt themselves to the white world and lose their cultural distinctiveness.

To some degree, the termination and assimilation policies achieved their objectives. The tribes grew weaker as legal and political entities. Many Native Americans adapted to life in the cities, at least to a degree. On the whole, however, the new policies were a disaster for the tribes and a failure for the reformers who had promoted them. Termination led to widespread corruption and abuse. And the Indians themselves fought so bitterly against it that in 1958 the Eisenhower administration barred further "terminations" without the consent of the affected tribes. In the meantime, the struggle against termination had mobilized a new generation of Indian militants and had breathed life into the principal Native American organization, the National Congress of American Indians (NCAI), which had been created in 1944.

The Democratic administrations of the 1960s did not disavow the termination policy, but neither did they make any effort to revive it. Instead, they made modest efforts to restore at least some degree of tribal autonomy. The funneling of OEO money to tribal organizations through the Community Action program was one prominent example. In the meantime, the tribes themselves were beginning to fight for self-determination—partly in response to the black civil rights movement and partly in response to other social and cultural changes (among them, the expanding mobility and rising educational levels of younger Indians who refused to defer to the status quo and who fought inequalities aggressively.) The new militancy also benefited from the rapid increase in the Indian population, which was growing much faster than that of the rest of the nation (nearly doubling between 1950 and 1970 to a total of about 800,000).

The Indian Civil Rights Movement

In 1961, more than 400 members of sixty-seven tribes gathered in Chicago to discuss ways of bringing all Indians together in an effort to redress common wrongs. The manifesto they issued, the Declaration of Indian Purpose, stressed the "right to choose our own way of life" and the "responsibility of preserving our precious heritage."

The 1961 meeting was only one example of a growing Indian self-consciousness. Indians and others began writing books (for example, Vine Deloria, Jr.'s *Custer Died for Your Sins* and Dee Brown's *Bury My Heart at Wounded Knee*) and otherwise drawing renewed attention to the wrongs inflicted on the tribes by white people in past generations. One result was a gradual change in the way popular culture depicted Native Americans. By the 1970s, almost no films or television programs portrayed Indians as brutal savages attacking peaceful white people (as had been the norm for much of the 1950s). And Native American activists even persuaded some white institutions to abandon what they considered demeaning references to them, including some colleges who agreed to cease referring to their athletic teams as the "Indians." The National Indian Youth Council, created in the aftermath of the 1961 Chicago meeting, promoted the idea of Indian nationalism and intertribal unity. In 1968, a group of young, militant Indians established the American Indian Movement (AIM), which drew its greatest support from those Native Americans who lived in urban areas but soon established a significant presence on the reservations as well.

The new activism had some immediate political results. In 1968, Congress passed the Indian Civil Rights Act, which guaranteed reservation Native Americans many of the protections accorded other citizens by the Bill of Rights, but which also recognized the legitimacy of tribal laws within the reservations. But leaders of AIM and other insurgent groups were not satisfied and turned increasingly to direct action. In 1968, Native American fishermen, citing old treaty rights, clashed with Washington state officials on the Columbia River and in Puget Sound. The following year, members of several tribes occupied the abandoned federal prison on Alcatraz Island in San Francisco Bay, claiming the site "by right of discovery."

In response to the growing pressure, the new Nixon administration appointed a Mohawk-Sioux to the position of Commissioner of Indian Affairs in 1969; and in 1970, the president promised both increased tribal self-determination and an increase in federal aid. But the protests continued. In November 1972, nearly a thousand demonstrators, most of them Sioux Indians, forcibly occupied the building of the Bureau of Indian Affairs in Washington for six days. A more celebrated protest occurred later that winter at Wounded Knee, South Dakota, the site of the 1890 massacre of Sioux by federal troops.

In the early 1970s, Wounded Knee was part of a large Sioux reservation, two-thirds of which had been leased to white ranchers for generations as an outgrowth of the Dawes Act. Conditions for the Native-American residents were desperate, and passions grew quickly in 1972 in response to the murder of a Sioux by a group of whites, who were not, many Native Americans believed, adequately punished. In February 1973, members of AIM seized and occupied the town of Wounded Knee for two months, demanding radical changes in the administration of the reservation and insisting that the government honor its long-forgotten treaty obligations. A brief clash between the occupiers and federal

WOUNDED KNEE–1973. Oscar Running Bear, a member of the American Indian Movement, strikes a defiant stance during the confrontation between militant Native Americans and the federal government in Wounded Knee, South Dakota. For two months, members of AIM occupied the town of Wounded Knee to protest conditions on the large Sioux reservation and their unequal treatment in the larger society.

forces left one Native American dead and another wounded. Shortly thereafter the siege came to an end.

More immediately effective than these militant protests were the victories that various tribes were achieving in the 1970s in the federal courts. In *United States v. Wheeler* (1978), the Supreme Court confirmed that tribes had independent legal standing and could not be "terminated" by Congress. Other decisions ratified the authority of tribes to impose taxes on businesses within their reservations and perform other sovereign functions. In 1985, the U.S. Supreme Court, in *County of Oneida v. Oneida Indian Nation* supported Native American claims to 100,000 acres in upstate New York that the Oneida tribe claimed by virtue of treaty rights long forgotten by whites.

The Indian civil rights movement, like other civil rights movements of the same time, fell far short of winning full justice and equality for Native Americans. Nor did it ever resolve its own internal conflicts—conflicts similar to those facing other minority groups at the same time. To some Native Americans, the principal goal was to defend tribal autonomy, to protect the rights of Indians (and, more to the point, individual tribal groups) to remain separate and distinct. To others, the goal was equality—to win for Indians a place in society equal to that of other groups of Americans. This latter goal helped produce a new spirit of "pan-Indianism," an effort to persuade Native Americans to transcend tribal divisions and work together as "a Greater Indian America." But because there was no single Native American culture or tradition in America, pan-Indianism operated within strict limits.

For all its limits, however, the Indian civil rights movement helped the tribes win a series of new legal rights and protections that, together, gave them a stronger position than they had enjoyed at any previous time in the twentieth century. It helped many Native Americans gain a renewed awareness of and pride in their identity as Indians and as part of distinct communities within the larger United States. And it challenged patterns of discrimination that had prevented many Native Americans from advancing in the world outside the tribes.

Hispanic-American Activism

More numerous and more visible than Native Americans were Hispanic Americans (also known as Latinos), the fastest growing minority group in the United States. No more than Native Americans are they a single, cohesive group. Some—including the descendants of early Spanish settlers in New Mexico— have roots as deep in American history as those of any other group. Most are men and women who have immigrated since World War II. Nor are Latinos racially distinct. They can be descendants of Europeans, Africans, or Indians— or in most cases, some combination of all three.

Large numbers of Puerto Ricans had migrated to eastern cities, particularly New York. South Florida's substantial Cuban population began with a wave of middle-class refugees fleeing the Castro regime in the early 1960s. These first

Cuban migrants quickly established themselves as a successful and increasingly assimilated part of Miami's middle class. In 1980, a second, much poorer wave of Cuban immigrants—the so-called Marielistas, named for the port from which they left Cuba—arrived in Florida when Castro temporarily relaxed exit restrictions. (This group included a large number of criminals, whom Castro had, in effect, expelled from the country.) This second wave was less easily assimilated. Later in the 1980s, large numbers of immigrants (both legal and illegal) began to arrive from the troubled nations of Central and South America—from Guatemala, Nicaragua, El Salvador, Peru, and others. But the most numerous and important Hispanic group in the United States was Mexican Americans.

There had been a significant Mexican-American population in the West throughout the nineteenth and early twentieth centuries—descendants of Spanish and Mexican people who had settled in lands that once belonged to the Spanish empire and the Republic of Mexico. But the number grew rapidly and substantially during and after World War II. Large numbers of Mexican Americans entered the country during the war in response to the labor shortage, and many remained in the cities of the Southwest and the Pacific Coast. After the war, when legal agreements that had allowed Mexican contract workers to enter the country expired, large numbers of immigrants continued to move to the United States illegally. In 1953, the government launched what it called Operation Wetback to deport the illegals, but the effort failed to stem the flow of new arrivals. By 1960, there were substantial Mexican-American neighborhoods (or *barrios*) in American cities from El Paso to Detroit. The largest (with more than 500,000 people, according to census figures) was in Los Angeles, which by then had a bigger Mexican population than anyplace except Mexico City, Mexico.

But the greatest expansion in the Mexican-American population was yet to come. In 1960, the census reported slightly more than 3 million Hispanics (the great majority of them Mexican Americans) living in the United States. In 1970, that number had grown to 9 million and by 1990 to 20 million. Hispanics constituted more than a third of all legal immigrants to the United States after 1960. Since there was also an uncounted but very large number of illegal immigrants in those years (estimates ranged from 7 million to 12 million), the real percentage of Hispanic immigrants was undoubtedly much larger.

By the late 1960s, therefore, Mexican Americans were one of the largest population groups in the West (outnumbering African Americans) and had established communities in most other parts of the nation as well. They were also among the most urbanized groups in the population; almost ninety percent of them lived and worked in cities. Many of them (particularly members of the oldest and most assimilated families of Mexican descent) were wealthy and successful people. Affluent Cubans in Miami filled important positions in the professions and local government; in the Southwest, Mexican Americans elected their own leaders to seats in Congress and to governorships.

But most newly arrived Mexican Americans and others were less well educated than either "Anglos" or African Americans and hence found it difficult to secure high-paying jobs. The fact that some spoke little or no English further limited their employment prospects. Some found good industrial jobs in unionized industries, and some Mexican Americans became important labor organizers in the AFL-CIO. But many more (including the great majority of illegal immigrants) worked in low-paying service jobs with few if any benefits and no job security. And, like African Americans and other minorities, Mexican Americans encountered almost impossible obstacles when they attempted to move out of blue-collar or low-status service jobs. Almost nowhere were they able to establish themselves as managers or executives in the companies in which they worked; few were able to pursue successful professional careers.

Partly because of language barriers, partly because the family-centered culture of many Hispanic communities discouraged effective organization, and partly because of discrimination, Mexican Americans and others were slower to mobilize politically than were some other minorities. But many Latinos did respond to the highly charged climate of the 1960s by strengthening their ethnic identification and organizing. Young Mexican-American activists began to call themselves "Chicanos" (once a term of derision used by whites) as a way of emphasizing the shared culture of Spanish-speaking Americans; and the term quickly moved into widespread (although never universal) use among Mexican Americans. Some Chicanos advocated a form of nationalism not unlike the ideas of black power advocates. The Texas leaders of *La Raza Unida*, a Chicano political party in the Southwest, called for the creation of something like an autonomous Mexican-American state within a state; it demonstrated significant strength at the polls in the 1970s.

One of the most visible efforts to organize Mexican Americans occurred in California, where an Arizona-born Chicano farm worker, Cesar Chavez, created an effective union of itinerant farm workers. His United Farm Workers (UFW), a largely Mexican-American organization, launched a prolonged strike in 1965 against growers to demand, first, recognition of their union and, second, increased wages and benefits. When employers resisted, Chavez enlisted the cooperation of college students, churches, and civil rights groups (including CORE and SNCC) and organized a nationwide boycott, first of table grapes and then of lettuce. In 1968, Chavez campaigned openly for Robert Kennedy. Two years later, he won a substantial victory when the growers of half of California's table grapes signed contracts with his union.

Hispanic Americans were at the center of another controversy of the 1970s and beyond: the issue of bilingualism. It was a question that aroused the opposition not only of many whites but of some Hispanics too. Supporters of bilingualism in education (which included Hispanics, Asians, and others) argued that non–English speaking Americans were entitled to at least some schooling in their own language, that otherwise they would be at a grave disadvantage in comparison with native English speakers. Bilingualism, they argued, was the

CESAR CHAVEZ. By the early 1970s, when this photo was taken, Cesar Chavez (at left, wearing a white short-sleeved shirt) was a nationally known champion of farm workers. His United Farm Workers (UFW) provided a voice, especially for Chicano migrant workers who picked crops under harsh conditions in California and had little power over the conditions of their labor. Chavez's national grape and lettuce boycotts succeeded in winning concessions from some employers, including recognition of the UFW by half the growers of California table grapes in 1970.

only way to overcome the language barrier that kept many students from making even minimal academic progress and the best way to move students into the English-speaking educational system. The United States Supreme Court confirmed the right of non–English speaking students to schooling in their native language in 1974. Opponents cited not only the cost and difficulty of bilingualism but the dangers they claimed it posed to the ability of students to become assimilated into the mainstream of American culture. Even many Hispanics feared that bilingualism might isolate their communities further from the rest of America and increase resentments toward them.

Challenging the "Melting Pot" Ideal

The efforts of blacks, Hispanics, Indians, Asians, and others to forge a clearer group identity seemed to challenge a long-standing premise of American political thought—the idea of the "melting pot." Older, European immigrant groups liked to believe that they had advanced in American society by adopting the values and accepting the rules of the world to which they had moved, by advancing within it on its own terms. The newly assertive ethnic groups of the 1960s and after were less willing to accept the standards of the larger society and more likely to demand recognition of their own ethnic identities. Many (although not all) African Americans, Indians, Hispanics, and Asians challenged the assimilationist idea and advocated instead a culturally pluralistic society, in which racial and ethnic groups would preserve not only a sense of their own heritage (which older, more "assimilationist" ethnic groups did as well) but also their own social and cultural norms.

To a large degree, the advocates of cultural pluralism succeeded. Recognition of the special character of particular groups was embedded in federal law through a wide range of affirmative action programs, which extended not only to blacks, but to Indians, Hispanics, Asians, and others. Ethnic studies programs proliferated in schools and universities. Eventually, this impulse led to an even more assertive (and highly controversial) cultural movement that in the 1980s and 1990s became known as "multiculturalism," which challenged the "Eurocentric" basis of American education and culture and demanded that non-European civilizations be accorded equal attention.

Gay Liberation

The last important liberation movement to emerge in the 1960s was the effort by homosexuals and lesbians to win political and economic rights and, equally important, social acceptance. Homosexuality had been an unacknowledged reality throughout American history; not until many years after their deaths did many Americans know, for example, that revered cultural figures such as Walt Whitman and Horatio Alger were homosexuals. Nonheterosexual men and women had long been forced either to suppress their sexual preferences, to exercise them surreptitiously, or to live within isolated and often persecuted communities. But by the late 1960s, the liberating impulses that had affected other groups helped mobilize gay men and women (as homosexuals and lesbians came to call themselves) to fight for their own rights.

On June 27, 1969, police officers raided the Stonewall Inn, a gay nightclub in New York City's Greenwich Village, and began arresting patrons simply for frequenting the place. The raid was not unusual; police had been harassing gay bars (and homosexual men and women) for years. It was, in fact, the accumulated resentment of this long history of assaults and humiliations that caused the extraordinary response that summer night. Gay onlookers taunted the police, then attacked them. Someone started a blaze in the Stonewall Inn itself, almost trapping the policemen inside. Rioting continued throughout Greenwich Village (the center of New York's gay community) through much of the night.

The "Stonewall Riot" marked the beginning of the gay liberation movement—one of the most controversial challenges to traditional values and assumptions of its time. New organizations—among them the Gay Liberation Front, founded in New York in 1969—sprang up around the country. Public discussion and media coverage of homosexuality, long subject to an unofficial taboo, quickly and dramatically increased. Gay activists had some success in challenging the long-standing assumption that homosexuality was "aberrant" behavior and argued that no sexual preference was any more "normal" than another.

Most of all, however, the gay liberation movement transformed the outlook of gay men and women themselves. It helped them to "come out," to express their preferences openly and unapologetically, and to demand from society a recognition that gay relationships were as significant and worthy of respect as heterosexual ones. Some gays advocated not only an acceptance of homosexuality as a valid and "normal" preference, but a change in the larger society as well: a redefinition of personal identity to give much greater importance to erotic impulses. Those changes did not quickly occur. But by the early 1980s, the gay liberation movement had made remarkable strides. Even the ravages of the AIDS epidemic, which in America affected the gay community first and for a time more disastrously than it affected any other group, failed to halt the growth of gay liberation. In many ways, it strengthened it.

By the early 1990s, homosexuals and lesbians were achieving some of the same milestones that other oppressed minorities had attained in earlier decades. Some openly gay politicians won election to public office. Universities established gay and lesbian studies programs. And laws prohibiting discrimination on the basis of sexual preference made slow, halting progress at the local level. But gay liberation produced a powerful backlash as well, as became evident when President Bill Clinton's 1993 effort to lift the ban on gays serving in the military fell victim to a storm of criticism from members of Congress and from within the military itself.

THE REVIVAL OF AMERICAN FEMINISM

Given the relative quiescence of the 1950s and its emphasis on domesticity, few would have predicted that the 1960s would give rise to a new, powerful wave of American feminism. But this was precisely what happened. At first haltingly, and then with increasing militancy, feminists began to direct attention to the place of women within American society and to attract millions of converts to their cause.

Sexual discrimination was deeply embedded in the fabric of society, and women faced many obstacles to equality. During the early 1960s, female professionals especially mobilized to improve the economic status of women in American society. As the decade wore on, however, a growing feminist movement expanded its agenda to attack deeper manifestations of "sexism"—as bias against women was increasingly known. Private life—woman's place within the family, her relationships to men, her sexuality—became especially important issues to those who advanced the "women's liberation movement" of the late 1960s and early 1970s. American women constituted fifty-one percent of the population and for that reason, among others, feminists succeeded in sparking a major debate and much legislative reform by the early 1970s. Public awareness of women's issues increased dramatically, and in many respects, the roles of women in American society—or at least prevailing conceptions of them—also changed fundamentally.

Rejecting the Feminine Mystique

Feminism had been a weak and often embattled force in American life for more than forty years after the adoption of the woman suffrage amendment in 1920. A few determined women kept feminist political demands alive in the National Woman's party and other organizations. Many more women expanded the acceptable bounds of female activity by entering new areas of the workplace or engaging in political activities. Nevertheless, through the 1950s active feminism seemed in retreat. That changed very dramatically in the early 1960s.

The 1963 publication of Betty Friedan's *The Feminine Mystique* is often cited as the first event of contemporary women's liberation. Friedan had traveled around the country interviewing the women who had graduated with her from Smith College in 1947. Most of these women were living out the dream that postwar American society had created for them; they were affluent wives and mothers living in comfortable suburbs. And yet many of them were deeply frustrated and unhappy. The suburbs, Friedan claimed, had become a "comfortable concentration camp," providing the women who inhabited them with no outlets for their intelligence, talent, and education. The "feminine mystique" was responsible for "burying millions of women alive." The only escape was for them to begin to fulfill "their unique possibilities as separate human beings." By chronicling their unhappiness and frustration, Friedan's book had a powerful impact. But it did not so much cause the revival of feminism as help give voice to a movement that was already stirring.

By the time *The Feminine Mystique* appeared, John Kennedy had established the President's Commission on the Status of Women. The president's motives in creating it probably had more to do with deflecting more substantive feminist demands than with real commitment to women's goals. Nonetheless, its creation reflected a growing recognition that a "problem" existed regarding women in American society. Furthermore, the commission brought national attention to sexual discrimination and helped create important networks of feminist activists who would lobby for legislative redress. Also in 1963, the Kennedy administration helped win passage of the Equal Pay Act, which barred the pervasive practice of paying women less than men for equal work. A year later, Congress incorporated into the Civil Rights Act of 1964 an amendment—Title VII—that extended to women many of the same legal protections against discrimination that were being extended to blacks.

The events of the early 1960s helped expose a contradiction that had been developing for decades between the image and the reality of women's roles in America. The image was what Friedan had called the "feminine mystique"—the ideal of women living happy, fulfilled lives in purely domestic roles. The reality was that increasing numbers of women (including, by 1963, over a third of all married women) had already entered the workplace and were encountering widespread discrimination there; and the reality was, too, that many other women were finding their domestic lives less than completely fulfilling. The conflict between the ideal and the reality was crucial to the rebirth of feminism.

In 1966, Friedan joined with other feminists to create the National Organization for Women (NOW), which was to become the nation's largest and most influential feminist organization. "The time has come," the founders of NOW maintained, "to confront with concrete action the conditions which now prevent women from enjoying the equality of opportunity and freedom of choice which is their right as individual Americans and as human beings." Like other movements for liberation, feminism drew much of its inspiration from the black struggle for freedom. "There is no civil rights movement to speak for women," the NOW organizers claimed, "as there has been for Negroes and other victims of discrimination."

The new organization reflected the varying constituencies of the emerging feminist movement. It responded to the complaints of the women Friedan's book had examined—affluent suburbanites with no outlet for their interests—by demanding greater educational opportunities for women and denouncing the ten-

BETTY FRIEDAN. At an April, 1975 rally in Chicago, feminist Betty Friedan exhorts her listeners to support the Equal Rights Amendment. One of the founders of the modern women's movement, Friedan helped provide intellectual and organizational leadership to the growing feminist movement.

dency to uphold the domestic ideal and the traditional concept of marriage as the singular goals of all women. But the heart of the movement, at least in the beginning, was directed toward the needs of women in the workplace. NOW denounced the exclusion of women from professions, from politics, and from countless other areas of American life. It decried legal and economic discrimination, including the practice of paying women less than men for equal work (a practice the Equal Pay Act had not eliminated). The organization called for "a fully equal partnership of the sexes, as part of the worldwide revolution of human rights." By the end of the decade, its membership had expanded to 15,000.

Women's Liberation

By the late 1960s, new and more radical feminist demands were also attracting a large following, especially among younger, affluent, white, educated women—although generally not among the older women whose lives Friedan had studied. The new feminists were mostly younger, the vanguard of the baby-boom generation. Many of them arrived at their commitment to feminism through their experience in the New Left and the civil rights movement. Even within those movements, dedicated as they claimed to be to freedom and equality, women faced discrimination and exclusion by male leaders. Indeed, in 1964 one of the first protests against sex discrimination within the civil rights movement came from African-American women in SNCC, who decried the automatic assignment of clerical duties to women. In SDS, women activists split off from the organization at one national conference to form small groups where they could openly discuss discrimination against women in "the movement." Soon what had begun as a growing awareness of gender discrimination gained coherence and emerged as a full-fledged drive to address the persistent inequality facing many American women.

Indeed, by the early 1970s, a significant change was visible in the tone and direction of the organization, and of the women's movement as a whole. New books by younger feminists expressed a harsher critique of American society than Friedan had offered. Kate Millett's *Sexual Politics* (1969) signaled the new direction by complaining that "every avenue of power within the society is entirely within male hands." The answer to women's problems, in other words, was not, as Friedan had suggested, for individual women to search for greater personal fulfillment; it was for women to band together to assault the male power structure. Shulamith Firestone's *The Dialectic of Sex* (1970) was subtitled "The Case for Feminist Revolution."

In its most radical form, the new feminism rejected the whole notion of marriage, family, and even heterosexual intercourse (a vehicle, some women claimed, of male domination). Not many women, not even many feminists, embraced such ideas. But by the early 1970s large numbers of women were coming to see themselves as an exploited group banding together against oppression and developing cultures and communities of their own. The women's liberation movement inspired the creation of grass-roots organizations and activities through which women not only challenged sexism and discrimination but created communities of their own. In cities and towns across the country, feminists opened women's bookstores, bars, and coffee shops. They founded feminist newspapers and magazines. They created centers to assist victims of rape and abuse, women's health clinics (and, particularly after 1973, abortion clinics), and daycare centers. These women-centered activities were crucial to the modern women's movement.

Expanding Achievements

By the early 1970s, the public and private achievements of the women's movement were already substantial. In 1971, the government extended its affirmative action guidelines to include women—linking sexism with racism as an officially acknowledged social problem. Women were making rapid progress, in the meantime, in their efforts to move into the economic and political mainstream. The nation's major all-male educational institutions began to open their doors to women. (Princeton and Yale did so in 1969, and most other once all-male colleges and universities soon did the same.) Some women's colleges, in the meantime, began accepting male students—although many remained committed to single-sex education, arguing for the value of the women's communities their campuses created. Passage of Title IX of the Higher Education Act in 1972 mandated that any co-educational college or university receiving federal funds could not discriminate against women in hiring, wages, admissions, access to instruction, or rules governing behavior, among other provisions.

Women were also becoming an important force in business and the professions. Nearly half of all married women held jobs by the mid-1970s, and almost nine-tenths of all women with college degrees worked. The two-career family, in which both the husband and the wife maintained active professional lives, was becoming a widely accepted norm; many women were postponing marriage or motherhood for the sake of their careers. There were also important symbolic changes, such as the refusal of many women to adopt their husbands' names when they married and the use of the term "Ms." in place of "Mrs." or "Miss" to denote the irrelevance of a woman's marital status in the professional world.

In politics, women were beginning to compete effectively with men by the early 1970s for both elected and appointive positions. By the early 1990s, women were serving in both houses of Congress, in numerous federal cabinet positions, as governors of several states, and in many other positions. Ronald Reagan named the first female Supreme Court Justice, Sandra Day O'Connor, in 1981; and Bill Clinton named the second, a self-proclaimed feminist, Ruth Bader Ginsburg, in 1993. In 1984, the Democratic party chose a woman, Representative Geraldine Ferraro of New York, as its vice presidential candidate. In academia, women were expanding their presence in traditional scholarly fields; they were also creating a field of their own—women's studies, which in the 1980s and early 1990s was the fastest growing area of American scholarship.

In professional athletics, in the meantime, women began to compete with men both for attention and for an equal share of prize money. Billie Jean King spearheaded the most effective female challenge to male domination of sports. Under her leadership, professional woman tennis players established their own successful tours and demanded equal financial incentives when they played in the same tournaments as men. By the late 1970s, the federal government was pressuring colleges and universities to provide women with athletic programs equal to those available to men. Women even joined what had previously been the most celebrated all-male fraternity in American culture: the space program. Sally Ride became the first woman astronaut to travel in space in 1983.

In 1972, Congress approved the Equal Rights Amendment to the Constitution, which some feminists had been promoting since the 1920s, and sent it to the states. For a while ratification seemed almost certain. By the late 1970s, however, the momentum behind the amendment had died. The ERA was in trouble not because of indifference but because of a rising chorus of objections to it from people (including many antifeminist women), who feared it would disrupt traditional social patterns. In 1982, the amendment finally died when the time allotted for ratification expired.

The Abortion Question

A vital element of American feminism since the 1920s has been the effort by women to win greater control of their own sexual and reproductive lives. This impulse helped produce an increasing awareness in the 1960s and 1970s of the problems of rape, sexual abuse, and wife beating. There continued to be some controversy over the dissemination of contraceptives and birth-control information; but that issue, at least, seemed to have lost much of the explosive character it had possessed in the 1920s, when Margaret Sanger had become a figure of public scorn for her efforts on its behalf. A related issue, however, stimulated as much popular passion as any question of its time: abortion.

Abortion had once been legal in much of the United States, but by the beginning of the twentieth century it was banned by statute in most of the country and remained so into the 1960s (although many abortions continued to be performed quietly, and often dangerously, out of sight of the law). But the women's movement created strong new pressures to legalize abortion and to give to women alone the right to choose whether or not to carry a pregnancy to term. Several states had abandoned restrictions on abortion by the end of the 1960s.

In 1973, the Supreme Court handed down a decision in *Roe* v. *Wade* based on a relatively new theory of a constitutional "right to privacy," first recognized by the Court only a few years earlier in *Griswold* v. *Connecticut* (1965). The Roe decision invalidated all laws prohibiting abortion during the first trimester—the first three months of pregnancy. Further, it supported the notion that the decision whether or not to have an abortion fell within the constitutional right of privacy. *Roe* v. *Wade* did not uphold the right to "abortion on demand." But it did stress that until a fetus was viable outside the womb, the abortion decision belonged to a woman and her physician; the state's interest in regulating abortion was restricted to protecting the health or life of the woman. The issue, it seemed, had been settled. But it soon became clear that it had not.

In many ways, feminism was much like other "liberation" movements of the 1960s and 1970s. But it differed in one fundamental respect: its success. The women's movement may not have fulfilled all its goals. But it achieved fundamental and permanent changes in the position of women in American life and promised to do much more.

CHAPTER TWENTY-SIX

The Imperial Presidency

he troubled social and cultural landscape of the late 1960s, and the powerful political reaction it created, shaped the presidency of Richard Nixon—one of the boldest and most divisive presidencies in American history. Nixon had been a familiar figure in American politics for more than a generation when he entered the White House in 1969. But nothing in his, or the nation's, past prepared him for the difficulties he would encounter in the turbulent years of the late 1960s and early 1970s.

The great majority of the voters had made clear in the 1968 election that they wanted a restoration of stability and order to American domestic life and to the nation's tortured adventures abroad. Nixon set out to provide both. He wanted to rebuild the legitimacy of traditional values and institutions at home. He wanted to bring "peace with honor" to Vietnam. And he wanted to build a new "structure of peace" in the world. In pursuing these bold goals, he took many risks and achieved many things. He also adopted a style of governance, rooted in his belief in the illegitimacy of the forces opposing him, that eventually led him to disaster.

THE VIETNAM WAR IN THE NIXON YEARS

Of all the ambitious goals Nixon carried with him into the White House, none was more important to him than creating a new and more stable international order. He knew from his long career in politics that the electorate cared first and foremost about domestic issues, and he was careful not to neglect them. But Nixon himself was most comfortable in the larger world, and foreign policy always remained his first and primary interest.

Central to his hopes for international stability was resolving the stalemate in Vietnam. Yet the new president felt no freer than his predecessor to abandon the

American commitment there. He realized that the endless war was undermining both the nation's domestic stability and its position in the world. But he feared that a precipitous retreat would destroy American honor and "credibility."

During the 1968 campaign, Nixon claimed to have formulated a plan to bring "peace with honor" in Vietnam, but he had refused to disclose its details. Once in office, however, he soon made clear that the plan consisted of little more than a vague set of general principles, not of any concrete measures to extricate the United States from the quagmire. American involvement in Indochina continued for four more years. And when a settlement finally emerged early in 1973, it produced neither peace nor honor. It succeeded only in removing the United States from the wreckage.

Vietnamization

Despite Nixon's own passionate interest in international affairs, he brought with him into government a man who often seemed to overshadow the president in the conduct of diplomacy: Henry Kissinger, a Harvard professor whom Nixon appointed as his special assistant for national security affairs. Kissinger quickly established dominance over both the Secretary of State, William Rogers, and the Secretary of Defense, Melvin Laird, although both were more experienced than he in public life. That was in part a result of Nixon's passion for concentrating decision making in the White House. But Kissinger's keen intelligence, his bureaucratic skills, and his success in handling the press were at least equally important. Together, Nixon and Kissinger set out to find an acceptable solution to the stalemate in Vietnam.

The new Vietnam policy moved along several fronts. One was an effort to limit domestic opposition to the war so as to permit the administration more political space in which to maneuver. Aware that the military draft was one of the most visible targets of dissent, the administration devised a new "lottery" system, through which only a limited group—those nineteen year olds with low lottery numbers—would be subject to conscription. Later, the president urged the creation of an all-volunteer army. By 1973, the Selective Service System was on its way to at least temporary extinction.

More important in stifling dissent, however, was the new policy of "Vietnamization" of the war—that is, the training and equipping of the South Vietnamese military to assume the burden of combat in place of American forces. In the fall of 1969, Nixon announced the withdrawal of 60,000 American ground troops from Vietnam, the first reduction in U.S. troop strength since the beginning of the war. The withdrawals continued steadily for more than three years, so that by the fall of 1972 relatively few American soldiers remained in Indochina. From a peak of more than 540,000 in 1969, the number had dwindled to about 60,000.

Vietnamization did help quiet domestic opposition to the war. It did nothing, however, to break the stalemate in the negotiations with the North Vietnamese in Paris. The new administration quickly decided that new military pressures would be necessary to do that.

Escalation

By the end of their first year in office, Nixon and Kissinger had concluded that the most effective way to tip the military balance in America's favor was to destroy the bases in Cambodia from which the American military believed the North Vietnamese were launching many of their attacks. Very early in his presidency, Nixon ordered the air force to begin bombing Cambodian territory to destroy the enemy sanctuaries. He kept the raids secret from Congress and the public. In the spring of 1970, possibly with American encouragement and support, conservative military leaders overthrew the neutral government of Cambodia and established a new, pro-American regime under General Lon Nol. Lon Nol quickly gave his approval to American incursions into his territory; and on

KENT STATE. The horrified expression on this young woman's face as she kneels over a slain student became a symbol of the tragedy of Kent State. Four students were killed at the university in May of 1970, when Ohio National Guardsmen fired into a crowd of anti-war demonstrators. Two days later, violence also broke out at Jackson State University in Mississippi when police fired on students during a demonstration, leaving two dead.

April 30, Nixon went on national television to announce that he was ordering American troops across the border into Cambodia to "clean out" the bases that the enemy had been using for its "increased military aggression."

Literally overnight, the Cambodian invasion restored the dwindling antiwar movement to vigorous life. The first days of May saw the most widespread and vocal antiwar demonstrations ever. Hundreds of thousands of protesters gathered in Washington to denounce the president's policies. Millions participated in countless smaller demonstrations on campuses and other sites nationwide. Antiwar frenzy was reaching so high a level that it was briefly possible for some Americans to believe (incorrectly) that a genuine revolution was imminent. The mood of crisis intensified greatly on May 4, when four college students were killed and nine others injured after members of the National Guard opened fire on antiwar demonstrators at Kent State University in Ohio. Ten days later, police killed two black students at Jackson State University in Mississippi during a demonstration there.

The clamor against the war quickly spread into the government and the press. Congress angrily repealed the Gulf of Tonkin Resolution in December, stripping the president of what had long served as the legal basis for the war. Nixon ignored the action. Then, in June 1971, first the *New York Times* and later other newspapers began publishing excerpts from a secret study of the war prepared by the Defense Department during the Johnson administration. The so-called Pentagon Papers, leaked to the press by former Pentagon official Daniel Ellsberg, provided confirmation of what many had long believed: that the government had been dishonest, both in reporting the military progress of the war and in explaining its own motives for American involvement. The administration went to court to suppress the documents, but the Supreme Court finally ruled that the press had the right to publish them.

Particularly troubling, both to the public and to the government itself, were signs of decay within the American military. Morale and discipline among U.S. troops in Vietnam, who had been fighting a savage and inconclusive war for more than five years, was rapidly deteriorating. The trial and conviction in 1971 of Lieutenant William Calley, who was charged with overseeing a massacre of more than 100 unarmed South Vietnamese civilians, attracted wide public attention to the dehumanizing impact of the war on those who fought it—and to the terrible consequences for the Vietnamese people of that dehumanization. Less publicized were other, more widespread problems among American troops in Vietnam: desertion, drug addiction, racial hostilities, refusal to obey orders, even the killing of unpopular officers by enlisted men.

The continuing carnage, the increasing savagery, and the social distress at home had largely destroyed public support for the war. By 1971, nearly two-thirds of those interviewed in public-opinion polls were urging American withdrawal from Vietnam. From Richard Nixon, however, there came no sign of retreat. On the contrary, the events of the spring of 1970 left him more convinced than ever of the importance of resisting what he once called the "bums" who opposed his military policies. With the approval of the White House, both the FBI and the CIA intensified their surveillance and infiltration of antiwar and radical groups, often resorting to blatant illegalities in the process. Administration officials sought to discredit prominent critics of the war by leaking damaging personal information about them. At one point, White House agents broke into the office of a psychiatrist in an unsuccessful effort to steal files on Daniel Ellsberg. During the congressional campaign of 1970, Vice President Spiro Agnew, using the acid rhetoric that had already made him the hero of many conservatives, stepped up his attack on the "effete" and "impudent" critics of the administration. The president himself once climbed on top of an automobile to taunt a crowd of angry demonstrators.

In Indochina, meanwhile, the fighting raged on. In February 1971, the president ordered the air force to assist the South Vietnamese army in an invasion of Laos—a test, as he saw it, of his Vietnamization program. Within weeks, the South Vietnamese scrambled back across the border in defeat. American bombing in Vietnam and Cambodia increased, despite its apparent ineffectiveness. In March 1972, the North Vietnamese mounted their biggest offensive since 1968 (the so-called "Easter Offensive"). American and South Vietnamese forces managed to halt the communist advance, but it was clear that without American support the offensive would have succeeded. At the same time, Nixon ordered American planes to bomb targets near Hanoi, the capital of North Vietnam, and Haiphong, its principal port, and called for the mining of seven North Vietnamese harbors (including Haiphong) to stop the flow of supplies from China and the Soviet Union.

"Peace with Honor"

As the 1972 presidential election approached, the administration stepped up its effort to produce a breakthrough in negotiations with the North Vietnamese. In April 1972, the president dropped his longtime insistence on a removal of North Vietnamese troops from the South before any American withdrawal. Meanwhile, Henry Kissinger was meeting privately in Paris with the North Vietnamese foreign secretary, Le Duc Tho, to work out terms for a cease-fire. On October 26, only days before the presidential election, Kissinger announced that "peace is at hand."

Several weeks later (after the election), negotiations broke down once again. Although both the American and the North Vietnamese governments were ready to accept the Kissinger-Tho plan for a cease-fire, the Thieu regime balked, still insisting on a full withdrawal of North Vietnamese forces from the South. Kissinger tried to win additional concessions from the communists to meet Thieu's objections; but on December 16, talks broke off.

The next day, December 17, American B52s began the heaviest and most destructive air raids of the entire war on Hanoi, Haiphong, and other North Vietnamese targets. Civilian casualties were high. And fifteen American B52s were shot down by the North Vietnamese; in the entire war to that point, the United

States had lost only one of the giant bombers. On December 30, Nixon terminated the "Christmas bombing." The United States and the North Vietnamese returned to the conference table. And on January 27, 1973, they signed an "agreement on ending the war and restoring peace in Vietnam." Nixon claimed that the Christmas bombing had forced the North Vietnamese to relent. At least equally important, however, was the enormous American pressure on Thieu to accept the cease-fire.

The terms of the Paris accords were little different from those Kissinger and Tho had accepted in principle a few months before. There would be an immediate cease-fire. The North Vietnamese would release several hundred American prisoners of war, whose fate had become an emotional issue of great importance within the United States. After that the agreement descended quickly into murky, unworkable arrangements. The Thieu regime would survive for the moment—the principal North Vietnamese concession to the United States—but North Vietnamese forces already in the South would remain there. An undefined committee would work out a permanent settlement.

PARIS ACCORDS–1973. Barely visible in this crowded room are representatives of the United States, North Vietnam, South Vietnam, and the Viet Cong as they sign the Paris accords officially ending the Vietnam War. Although the agreement created the outlines for a permanent settlement of the war and mandated a cease-fire, it broke down within months. It did, however, permit the United States to extricate itself from Vietnam after the long and bloody conflict.

Defeat in Indochina

American forces were hardly out of Indochina before the Paris accords collapsed. During the first year after the cease-fire, the contending Vietnamese armies suffered greater battle losses than the Americans had absorbed during ten years of fighting. In March 1975, finally, the North Vietnamese launched a full-scale offensive against the now greatly weakened forces of the South. Thieu appealed to Washington for assistance; the president (now Gerald Ford) appealed to Congress for additional funding; Congress refused. Late in April 1975, communist forces marched into Saigon, shortly after officials of the Thieu regime and the staff of the American embassy had fled the country in humiliating disarray. Communist forces quickly occupied the capital, renamed it Ho Chi Minh City, and began the process of reuniting Vietnam under the harsh rule of Hanoi. At about the same time, the Lon Nol regime in Cambodia fell to the murderous communists of the Khmer Rouge—whose genocidal policies led to the deaths of more than a third of the country's people over the next several years.

Such were the dismal results of more than a decade of direct American military involvement in Vietnam. More than 1.2 million Vietnamese soldiers had died in combat, along with countless civilians throughout the region. A beautiful land had been ravaged, its agrarian economy left in ruins; for many years after, Vietnam remained one of the poorest and most politically oppressive nations in the world. The United States had paid a heavy price as well. The war had cost the nation almost $150 billion in direct costs and much more indirectly. It had resulted in the deaths of 58,000 young Americans and the injury of 300,000 more. And the nation had suffered a blow to its confidence and self-esteem from which it would not soon recover.

NIXON, KISSINGER, AND THE WORLD

The continuing war in Vietnam provided a dismal backdrop to what Nixon considered his larger mission in world affairs: the construction of a new international order. The president had become convinced that old assumptions of a "bipolar" world—in which the United States and the Soviet Union were the only truly great powers—were now obsolete. America must adapt to the new "multipolar" international structure, in which China, Japan, and western Europe were becoming major, independent forces. "It will be a safer world and a better world," he said in 1971, "if we have a strong, healthy United States, Europe, Soviet Union, China, Japan—each balancing the other, not playing one against the other, an even balance."

Nixon and Kissinger believed it was possible to construct something like the "balance of power" that had permitted nineteenth-century Europe to experience nearly a century of relative stability. To do so, however, required a major change in several long-standing assumptions of American foreign policy.

China and the Soviet Union

For more than twenty years, ever since the fall of Chiang Kai-shek in 1949, the United States had treated China, the second largest nation on earth, as if it did not exist. Instead, America recognized the forlorn regime-in-exile on Taiwan as the legitimate government of mainland China. Nixon and Kissinger wanted to forge a new relationship with the Chinese communists—in part to strengthen them as a counterbalance to the Soviet Union. The Chinese, for their part, were eager to forestall the possibility of a Soviet-American alliance against China and to end China's own isolation from the international arena.

In July 1971, Nixon sent Henry Kissinger on a secret mission to Beijing. When Kissinger returned, the president made the startling announcement that

NIXON IN CHINA. President Nixon and Chou En-Lai review troops during Nixon's historic visit to China. A determined anticommunist for much of his political career, Nixon took bold steps as president toward normalizing U.S. relations in China.

he would visit China himself within the next few months. That fall, with American approval, the United Nations admitted the communist government of China and expelled the representatives of the Taiwan regime. Finally, in February 1972, Nixon paid a formal visit to China and, in a single stroke, erased much of the deep American animosity toward the Chinese communists. Nixon did not yet formally recognize the communist regime, but in 1972 the United States and China began low-level diplomatic relations.

The initiatives in China coincided with (and probably assisted) an effort by the Nixon administration to improve relations with the Soviet Union. In 1969, American and Soviet diplomats met in Helsinki, Finland to begin talks on limiting nuclear weapons. In 1972, they produced the first Strategic Arms Limitation Treaty (SALT I), which froze the nuclear missiles (ICBMs) of both sides at present levels. In May of that year, the president traveled to Moscow to sign the agreement. The next year, the Soviet premier, Leonid Brezhnev, visited Washington; and the two leaders pledged renewed efforts to speed the next phase of arms control negotiations.

The Problems of Multipolarity

The policies of rapprochement with communist China and detente with the Soviet Union reflected Nixon's and Kissinger's belief in the importance of stable relationships among the great powers. But great-power relationships could not alone ensure international stability, for the Third World remained the most volatile and dangerous source of international tension.

Central to the Nixon-Kissinger policy toward the Third World was the effort to maintain a stable status quo without involving the United States too deeply in local disputes. In 1969 and 1970, the president described what became known as the Nixon Doctrine, by which the United States would "participate in the defense and development of allies and friends" but would leave the "basic responsibility" for the future of those "friends" to the nations themselves. In practice, the Nixon Doctrine meant a declining American interest in contributing to Third World development; a growing contempt for the United Nations, where underdeveloped nations were gaining influence through their sheer numbers; and increasing support to authoritarian regimes attempting to withstand radical challenges from within.

In 1970, for example, the CIA poured substantial funds into Chile to help support the established government against a communist challenge. When the Marxist candidate for president, Salvador Allende, came to power through an honest election, the United States began funneling more money to opposition forces in Chile to help "destabilize" the new government. In 1973, a military junta seized power from Allende, who was subsequently murdered. The United States developed a friendly relationship with the new, repressive military government of General Augusto Pinochet.

CRISES IN THE MIDDLE EAST

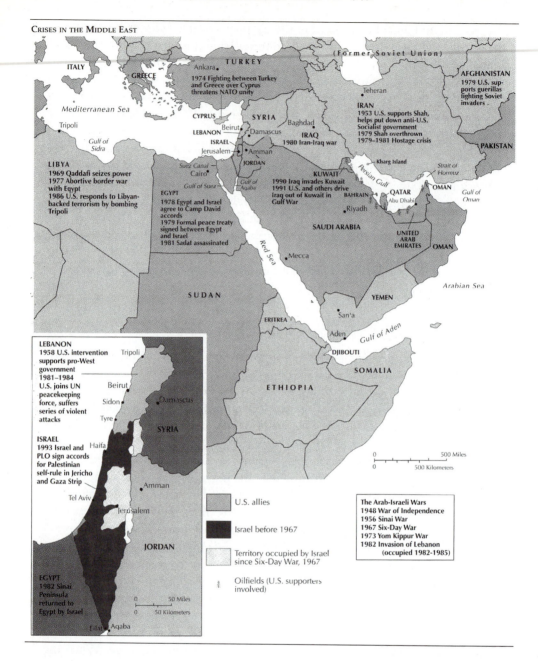

LEBANON
1958 U.S. intervention supports pro-West government
1981–1984 U.S. joins UN peacekeeping force, suffers series of violent attacks

ISRAEL
1993 Israel and PLO sign accords for Palestinian self-rule in Jericho and Gaza Strip

EGYPT
1982 Sinai Peninsula returned to Egypt by Israel

U.S. allies

Israel before 1967

Territory occupied by Israel since Six-Day War, 1967

Oilfields (U.S. supporters involved)

The Arab-Israeli Wars
1948 War of Independence
1956 Sinai War
1967 Six-Day War
1973 Yom Kippur War
1982 Invasion of Lebanon
    (occupied 1982-1985)

In the Middle East, conditions were growing more volatile in the aftermath of the 1967 "Six-Day War," in which Israel routed Egyptian, Syrian, and Jordanian forces and occupied substantial new territories: on the west bank of the Jordan River, the Gaza Strip, and elsewhere. The war also increased the number of refugee Palestinians—Arabs who claimed the lands now controlled by Israel and who, dislodged from their homes, became a source of considerable instability in

Jordan, Lebanon, and the other surrounding countries into which they now moved. Jordan's ruler, King Hussein, was particularly alarmed by the influx of Palestinians and by the activities of the Palestinian Liberation Organization (PLO) and other radical groups, which he feared would threaten Jordan's important relationship with the United States. After a series of uprisings in 1970, Hussein ordered the Jordanian army to expel the Palestinians. Many of them moved to Lebanon, where they became part of many years of instability and civil war.

In October 1973, on the Jewish high holy day of Yom Kippur, Egyptian and Syrian forces attacked Israel. For ten days, the Israelis struggled to recover from the surprise attack; finally, they launched an effective counteroffensive against Egyptian forces in the Sinai. At that point, the United States intervened, placing heavy pressure on Israel to accept a cease-fire rather than press its advantage.

The imposed settlement of the Yom Kippur War demonstrated the growing dependence of the United States and its allies on Arab oil. Permitting Israel to continue its drive into Egypt might have jeopardized the ability of the United States to purchase needed petroleum from the Arab states. A brief but painful embargo by the Arab governments on the sale of oil to supporters of Israel (including America) in 1973 provided an ominous warning of the costs of losing access to the region's resources. The lesson of the Yom Kippur War, therefore, was that the United States could no longer ignore the interests of the Arab nations in its efforts on behalf of Israel.

A larger lesson of 1973 was that the nations of the Third World could no longer be expected to act as passive, cooperative "client states." The United States could no longer depend on cheap, easy access to raw materials as it had in the past.

POLITICS AND ECONOMICS UNDER NIXON

For a time in the late 1960s, it had seemed to many Americans that the forces of chaos and radicalism were taking control of the nation. The domestic policy of the Nixon administration was an attempt to restore balance between the needs of the poor and the desires of the middle class, and between the power of the federal government and the interests of local communities. In the end, however, economic and political crises—some beyond the administration's control, some of its own making—sharply limited Nixon's ability to fulfill his domestic goals.

Domestic Initiatives

Many of Nixon's domestic policies were a response to what he believed to be the demands of his constituency—conservative, middle-class people whom he liked to call the "silent majority" and who wanted to reduce federal "interference" in local affairs. He tried, unsuccessfully, to persuade Congress to pass legislation prohibiting the use of forced busing to achieve school desegregation. He forbade the

Department of Health, Education, and Welfare to cut off federal funds from school districts that had failed to comply with court orders to integrate. At the same time, he began to reduce or dismantle many of the social programs of the Great Society and the New Frontier. In 1973, he abolished the Office of Economic Opportunity, the centerpiece of the antipoverty program of the Johnson years.

Yet Nixon's domestic efforts were also strikingly innovative. One of the administration's boldest efforts was an attempt to overhaul the nation's welfare system. Nixon proposed replacing the existing system, which almost everyone agreed was cumbersome, expensive, and inefficient, with what he called the Family Assistance Plan (FAP). It would in effect have created a guaranteed annual income for all Americans: $1,600 in federal grants, which could be supplemented by outside earnings up to $4,000. Even many liberals applauded the proposal as an important step toward expanding federal responsibility for the poor. Nixon, however, presented the plan in conservative terms: as something that would reduce the supervisory functions of the federal government and transfer to welfare recipients themselves daily responsibility for their own lives. Although the FAP won approval in the House in 1970, concerted attacks by welfare recipients (who considered the benefits inadequate), members of the welfare bureaucracy (whose own influence stood to be sharply diminished by the bill), and conservatives (who opposed a guaranteed income on principle) helped kill it in the Senate.

The Nixon Court

Of all the liberal institutions that had aroused the enmity of the "silent majority" in the 1950s and 1960s, none had evoked more anger and bitterness than the Supreme Court. Not only had its rulings on racial matters disrupted traditional social patterns in both the North and the South, but its staunch defense of civil liberties had, in the eyes of many Americans, contributed directly to the increase in crime, disorder, and moral decay. In *Engel* v. *Vitale* (1962), the Court had ruled that prayers in public schools were unconstitutional, sparking outrage among religious fundamentalists and others. In *Roth* v. *United States* (1957), the Court had sharply limited the authority of local governments to curb pornography. In a series of other decisions, the Court had greatly strengthened the civil rights of criminal defendants and had, in the eyes of many Americans, greatly weakened the power of law-enforcement officials to do their jobs. For example, in *Gideon* v. *Wainwright* (1963), the Court had ruled that every felony defendant was entitled to a lawyer regardless of his or her ability to pay. In *Escobedo* v. *Illinois* (1964), it had ruled that a defendant must be allowed access to a lawyer before questioning by police. In *Miranda* v. *Arizona* (1966), the Court had confirmed the obligation of authorities to inform a criminal suspect of his or her rights. By 1968, the Warren Court had become the target of Americans of all kinds who felt the balance of power in the United States had shifted too far toward the poor and dispossessed at the expense of the middle class, too far toward the rights of criminals at the expense of their victims.

Perhaps the most important decision of the Warren Court in the 1960s was *Baker* v. *Carr* (1962), which required state legislatures to apportion electoral districts so that the votes of all citizens would have equal weight. In dozens of states, systems of legislative districting had given disproportionate representation to sparsely populated rural areas, hence diminishing the voting power of urban residents. The reapportionment that the decision required greatly strengthened the voting power of African Americans, Hispanics, and other groups concentrated in cities.

Nixon was determined to use his judicial appointments to give the Court a more conservative cast. His first opportunity came almost as soon as he entered office. When Chief Justice Earl Warren resigned early in 1969, Nixon replaced him with a federal appeals court judge of known conservative leanings, Warren Burger. A few months later, Associate Justice Abe Fortas resigned his seat after the disclosure of a series of alleged financial improprieties. To replace him, Nixon named Clement F. Haynsworth, a respected federal circuit court judge from South Carolina. But Haynsworth came under fire from Senate liberals, African-American organizations, and labor unions for his conservative record on civil rights and for what some claimed was a conflict of interest in several of the cases on which he had sat. The Senate rejected him. Nixon's next choice was G. Harold Carswell, a judge of the Florida federal appeals court almost entirely lacking in distinction and widely considered unfit for the Supreme Court. The Senate rejected his nomination, too.

Nixon angrily denounced the votes, calling them expressions of prejudice against the South. But he was careful thereafter to choose men of standing within the legal community to fill vacancies on the Supreme Court: Harry Blackmun, a moderate jurist from Minnesota; Lewis F. Powell, Jr., a respected judge from Virginia; and William Rehnquist, a member of the Nixon Justice Department. In the process, he transformed the Warren Court into what some called the "Nixon Court" and others the "Burger Court."

The new Court, however, fell short of what the president and many conservatives had expected. Rather than retreating from its commitment to social reform, the Court in many areas actually moved further. In *Swann* v. *Charlotte-Mecklenburg Board of Education* (1971), it ruled in favor of the use of forced busing to achieve racial balance in schools. Not even the intense and occasionally violent opposition of local communities as diverse as Boston and Louisville, Kentucky, was able to weaken the judicial commitment to integration. In *Furman* v. *Georgia* (1972), the Court overturned existing capital punishment statutes and established strict new guidelines for such laws in the future. In *Roe* v. *Wade* (1973), it struck down laws forbidding abortions.

In other decisions, however, the Burger Court was more moderate. Although the justices approved busing as a tool for achieving integration, they rejected, in *Milliken* v. *Bradley* (1974), a plan to transfer students across district lines (in this case, between Detroit and its suburbs) to achieve racial balance. While the Court upheld the principle of affirmative action in its celebrated 1978 decision *Bakke v. Board of Regents of California*, it established restrictive new guidelines for such programs in the future. In *Stone v. Powell* (1976), the Court agreed to certain limits on the right of a defendant to appeal a state conviction to the federal judiciary.

The Election of 1972

However unsuccessful the Nixon administration may have been in achieving some of its goals, Nixon entered the presidential race in 1972 with a substantial reserve of strength. The events of that year improved his position immeasurably. His energetic re-election committee collected enormous sums of money to support the campaign. The president himself used the powers of incumbency, refraining from campaigning and concentrating on highly publicized international decisions and state visits. Agencies of the federal government dispensed funds and favors to strengthen Nixon's political standing in questionable areas.

Nixon was most fortunate in 1972, however, in his opposition. The return of George Wallace to the presidential fray caused some early concern. Nixon was delighted to see Wallace run in the Democratic primaries and had quietly encouraged him to do so. But he feared that Wallace would again launch a third party campaign; Nixon's own re-election strategy rested on the same appeals to the troubled middle class that Wallace was expressing. The possibility of such a campaign vanished in May, when a would-be assassin shot the Alabama governor during a rally at a Maryland shopping center. Paralyzed from the waist down, Wallace was unable to continue campaigning.

The Democrats, in the meantime, were making their own contributions to the Nixon cause by nominating for president a representative of their most liberal wing: Senator George S. McGovern of South Dakota. An outspoken critic of the war, a forceful advocate of advanced liberal positions on virtually every social and economic issue, McGovern seemed to embody those aspects of the turbulent 1960s that middle-class Americans were most eager to reject. McGovern profited greatly from party reforms (which he himself had helped to draft) that gave increased influence to women, blacks, and young people in the selection of the Democratic ticket. But those same reforms helped make the Democratic Convention of 1972 an unappealing spectacle to much of the public. The candidate then disillusioned even some of his own supporters by his indecisive reaction to revelations that his running mate, Senator Thomas Eagleton of Missouri, had undergone treatment for an emotional disturbance. Eagleton finally withdrew from the ticket. The remainder of the Democratic presidential campaign was an exercise in futility.

On election day, Nixon won re-election by one of the largest margins in history: 60.7 percent of the popular vote compared with 37.5 percent for the forlorn McGovern, and an electoral margin of 520 to 17. The Democratic candidate had carried only Massachusetts and the District of Columbia. The new commitments that Nixon had so effectively expressed—to restraint in social reform, to decentralization of political power, to the defense of traditional values, and to a new balance in international relations—had clearly won the approval of the American people. But other problems were already lurking in the wings.

The Troubled Economy

Although it was political scandal that would ultimately destroy the Nixon presidency, the most important national crisis of the early 1970s was the decline of the American economy. For three decades, the economic might of the United States had been the envy of the world. America had produced as much as a third of the world's industrial goods and had dominated international trade. The American dollar had been the strongest currency in the world, and the American standard of living had risen steadily from its already substantial heights. Most Americans assumed that this remarkable prosperity was the normal condition of their society. In fact, however, it rested in part on several artificial conditions that were rapidly disappearing by the late 1960s: the absence of significant foreign competition and easy access to raw materials in the Third World.

The most disturbing economic problem of the 1970s was inflation, which had been creeping upward for several years when Richard Nixon took office and which soon began to soar. Its most visible cause was a significant increase in federal deficit spending in the 1960s, when the Johnson administration tried to fund the war in Vietnam and its ambitious social programs without raising taxes. But there were other, equally important causes of the inflation and of the economic problems that lay behind it. No more did the United States have exclusive access to cheap raw materials around the globe; not only were other industrial nations now competing for increasingly scarce raw materials, but Third World suppliers of those materials were beginning to realize their value and demand higher prices for them.

The greatest immediate blow to the American economy was the increasing cost of energy. More than any nation on earth, the United States based its economy on the easy availability of cheap and plentiful fuels. No society was more dependent on the automobile; none was more wasteful in its use of oil and gas in its homes, schools, and factories. Domestic petroleum reserves were no longer sufficient to meet this demand, and the nation was heavily dependent on imports from the Middle East and Africa.

For many years, the Organization of Petroleum Exporting Countries (OPEC) had operated as an informal bargaining unit for the sale of oil by Third World (mostly Middle Eastern) nations but had seldom managed to exercise any real strength. But in the early 1970s, OPEC began to assert itself, to use its oil both as an economic tool and as a political weapon. In 1973, in the midst of the Yom Kippur War, Arab members of OPEC announced that they would no longer ship petroleum to nations supporting Israel—that is, to the United States and its allies in western Europe. At about the same time, the OPEC nations agreed to raise their prices 400 percent. These twin shocks produced momentary economic chaos in the West. The United States suffered its first fuel shortage since World War II. And although the crisis eased a few months later, the price of energy continued to skyrocket both because of OPEC's newly militant policies and because of the weakening competitive position of the dollar in world markets. No single factor did more to produce the soaring inflation of the 1970s.

But inflation was only one of the new problems facing the American economy. Another was the decline of the nation's manufacturing sector. American industry had flourished in the immediate aftermath of World War II, in part because of the new plant capacity the war had created, in part because it faced almost no competition from other industrial nations, all of them ravaged by war. American workers in unionized industries had profited from this postwar success by winning some of the most generous wage and benefits packages in the world.

By the 1970s, however, the climate for American manufacturing had changed significantly. Many of the great industrial plants were now many decades old, much less efficient than the newer plants that Japan and European industrial nations had constructed after the war. In some industries (notably steel and automobiles), management had become complacent and stultifyingly bureaucratic. Most importantly, U.S. manufacturing now faced major competition from abroad—not only in world trade (which still constituted only a small part of the American economy) but also at home. Automobiles, steel, and many other manufactured goods from Japan and Europe established major footholds in the United States markets. Some of America's new competitors benefited from lower labor costs than their U.S. counterparts; but that was only one of many reasons for their successes.

The 1970s marked the beginning, therefore, of a long, painful process of deindustrialization, during which thousands of factories across the country closed their gates and millions of workers lost their jobs. New employment opportunities were becoming available in other, growing areas of the economy: technology, information systems, and many other more "knowledge-based" industries. But many industrial workers were poorly equipped to move into those jobs. The result was a growing pool of unemployed and underemployed workers; the virtual disappearance of industrial jobs from many inner cities, where large numbers of minorities lived; and the impoverishment of communities dependent on particular industries. Some of the nation's manufacturing sectors ultimately revived, but few regained the size and dominance they had enjoyed in the 1950s and 1960s; and few employed a work force as large or as relatively well paid as they once had.

The Nixon Response

The Nixon administration responded to these mounting economic problems by focusing on the one thing it thought it could control: inflation. The government moved first to reduce spending and raise taxes. But those policies produced both congressional and popular protest, and Nixon turned increasingly to an economic tool more readily available to him: control of the currency. Placing conservative economists at the head of the Federal Reserve Board, he ensured sharply higher interest rates and a contraction of the money supply. But the tight money policy did little to curb inflation. The cost of living rose a cumulative fifteen percent during Nixon's first two and a half years in office. Economic growth, in the meantime, declined. The United States was encountering a new and puzzling dilemma: "stagflation," a combination of rising prices and general economic stagnation.

In the summer of 1971, Nixon imposed a ninety-day freeze on all wages and prices at their existing levels. Then, in November, he launched Phase II of his economic plan: mandatory guidelines for wage and price increases, to be administered by a federal agency. Inflation subsided temporarily, but the recession continued. Fearful that the recession would be more damaging than inflation in an election year, the administration reversed itself late in 1971: Interest rates dropped sharply, and government spending increased—producing the largest budget deficit since World War II. The new tactics helped revive the economy in the short term, but inflation rose substantially—particularly after the administration abandoned the strict Phase II controls and replaced them with a set of voluntary, and almost entirely ineffective, guidelines. In 1973, prices rose nine percent; in 1974, after the Arab oil embargo and the OPEC price increases, they rose twelve percent—the highest rate since the relaxation of price controls shortly after World War II. The value of the dollar continued to slide, and the nation's international trade continued to decline. The energy crisis, in the meantime, was quickly becoming a national preoccupation. But while Nixon talked often about the need to achieve "energy independence," he offered few concrete proposals.

The erratic economic programs of the Nixon administration were a sign of a broader national confusion about the prospects for American prosperity. The Nixon pattern—of lurching from a tight money policy to curb inflation at one moment to a spending policy to cure recession at the next—repeated itself during the two administrations that followed.

THE WATERGATE CRISIS

Although economic problems greatly concerned the American people in the 1970s, another stunning development almost entirely preoccupied the nation beginning early in 1973: the fall of Richard Nixon. The president's demise was a result in part of his own personality. Defensive, secretive, resentful of his critics, he brought to his office an element of mean-spiritedness that helped undermine even his most important accomplishments. But the larger explanation lay in Nixon's view of American society and the world, and of his own role in both. The president believed the United States faced grave dangers from the radicals and dissidents who were challenging his policies. He came increasingly to consider any challenge to his power a threat to "national security." By identifying his own political fortunes with those of the nation, Nixon was creating a climate in which he and those who served him could justify almost any tactics to stifle dissent and undermine opposition.

The Break-In

Nixon's outlook was in part a culmination of long-term changes in the presidency. Public expectations of the president had increased dramatically in the years since World War II; yet the constraints on the authority of the office had grown as well. In response, a succession of presidents had sought new methods for the exercise of power, often stretching the law, occasionally breaking it.

Nixon not only continued but greatly accelerated these trends. Facing a Democratic Congress hostile to his goals, he attempted to find ways to circumvent the legislature whenever possible. Saddled with a federal bureaucracy unresponsive to his wishes, he constructed a hierarchy of command in which virtually all executive power became concentrated in the White House. Operating within a rigid, even autocratic staff structure, the president became a solitary, at times brooding, figure whose contempt for his opponents and impatience with obstacles to his policies festered and grew. Unknown to all but a few intimates, the White House also became mired in a pattern of illegalities and abuses of power that late in 1972 began to break through to the surface.

Early on the morning of June 17, 1972, police arrested five men who had broken into the offices of the Democratic National Committee in the Watergate office building in Washington, D.C. Two others were seized a short time later and charged with supervising the break-in. When reporters for the *Washington Post* began researching the backgrounds of the culprits, they discovered that among those involved in the burglary were former employees of the Committee for the Re-Election of the President (CRP). One of them had worked in the White House itself. They had, moreover, been paid for the break-in from a secret fund of the re-election committee, a fund controlled by members of the White House staff.

Public interest in the disclosures grew slowly in the last months of 1972. Few Americans questioned the president's assurances that neither he nor his staff had any connection with what he called "this bizarre incident." Early in 1973, however, the Watergate burglars went on trial; and under relentless prodding from federal judge John J. Sirica, one of the defendants, James W. McCord, agreed to cooperate both with the grand jury and with a special Senate investigating committee recently established under Senator Sam J. Ervin of North Carolina. McCord's testimony opened a floodgate of confessions, and for months a parade of White House and campaign officials exposed one illegality after another. Foremost among them was a member of the inner circle of the White House, Counsel to the President John Dean, who leveled allegations against Nixon himself.

Two different sets of scandals emerged from the investigations. One was a general pattern of abuses of power involving both the White House and the Nixon campaign committee, which included, but was not limited to, the Watergate break-in. The other scandal, and the one that became the major focus of public attention for nearly two years, was the way in which the administration tried to manage the investigations of the Watergate break-in and other abuses— a pattern of behavior that became known as the "cover-up." There was never any conclusive evidence that the president had planned or approved the burglary in advance. But there was mounting evidence that he had been involved in illegal efforts to obstruct investigations of and withhold information about the episode. Testimony before the Ervin committee provided evidence of the complicity of Dean, Attorney General John Mitchell, top White House assistants H. R. Haldeman and John Ehrlichman, and others. As interest in the case grew to something approaching a national obsession, the investigation focused increasingly on a single question: In the words of Senator Howard Baker of Tennessee, a member of the Ervin committee, "What did the President know and when did he know it?"

Nixon accepted the departure of those members of his administration implicated in the scandals. But he continued to insist that he himself was innocent. There the matter might have rested had it not been for the disclosure during the Senate hearings of a White House taping system that had recorded virtually

WATERGATE HEARINGS. The testimony of White House advisers and officials during special Senate investigative hearings into the Watergate break-in proved devastating to President Nixon. Among those who inflicted the greatest damage was John Dean, counsel to the president, who testified that he believed President Nixon was involved in the cover-up of the break-in into the offices of the Democratic National Committee.

every conversation in the president's office during the period in question. All those investigating the scandals sought access to the tapes; Nixon, pleading "executive privilege," refused to release them. A special prosecutor appointed by the president to handle the Watergate cases, Harvard law professor Archibald Cox, took Nixon to court in October 1973 in an effort to force him to relinquish the recordings. Nixon, now clearly growing desperate, fired Cox and suffered the humiliation of watching both Attorney General Elliot Richardson and his deputy resign in protest. This "Saturday night massacre" made the president's predicament infinitely worse. Not only did public pressure force him to appoint a new special prosecutor, Texas attorney Leon Jaworski, who proved just as determined as Cox to subpoena the tapes; but the episode precipitated an investigation by the House of Representatives into the possibility of impeachment.

Nixon's Resignation

Nixon's situation deteriorated further in the following months. Late in 1973, Vice President Spiro Agnew became embroiled in a scandal of his own when evidence surfaced that he had accepted bribes and kickbacks while serving as governor of Maryland and even as vice president. In return for a Justice Department agreement not to press the case, Agnew pleaded no contest to a lesser charge of income-tax evasion and resigned from the government. With the controversial Agnew no longer in line to succeed to the presidency, the prospect of removing Nixon from the White House became less worrisome to his opponents. The new vice president (the first appointed under the terms of the Twenty-fifth Amendment, which had been adopted in 1967) was House Minority Leader Gerald Ford, an amiable and popular Michigan congressman.

The impeachment investigation quickly gathered pace. In April 1974, in an effort to head off further subpoenas of the tapes, the president released transcripts of a number of relevant conversations, claiming that they proved his innocence. Investigators and much of the public felt otherwise. Even these edited tapes seemed to suggest Nixon's complicity in the cover-up. In July, the crisis reached a climax. First the Supreme Court ruled unanimously, in *United States* v. *Richard M. Nixon*, that the president must relinquish the tapes to Special Prosecutor Jaworski. Days later, the House Judiciary Committee voted to recommend three articles of impeachment, charging that Nixon had, first, obstructed justice in the Watergate cover-up; second, misused federal agencies to violate the rights of citizens; and third, defied the authority of Congress by refusing to deliver tapes and other materials subpoenaed by the committee.

Even without additional evidence, Nixon might well have been impeached by the full House and convicted by the Senate. Early in August, however, he provided at last what some called the "smoking gun"—the concrete proof of his guilt that his defenders had long contended was missing from the case against him. Among the tapes that the Supreme Court compelled Nixon to relinquish were several that offered apparently incontrovertible evidence of his involve-

NIXON'S RESIGNATION. The President and
First Lady say goodbye to their successors,
Gerald and Betty Ford, on August 8, 1974, as
they board a helicopter on the White House
lawn moments after Richard Nixon's
unprecedented resignation from office.

ment in the Watergate cover-up. Only days after the burglary, the recordings
disclosed, the president had ordered the FBI to stop investigating the break-in.
Impeachment and conviction now seemed inevitable.

For several days, Nixon brooded in the White House, on the verge,
some claimed, of a breakdown. Finally, on August 8, 1974, he announced his
resignation—the first president in American history ever to do so. At noon the
next day, while Nixon and his family were flying west to their home in California, Gerald Ford took the oath of office as president.

Many Americans expressed relief and exhilaration that, as the new president
put it, "Our long national nightmare is over." Many were relieved to be rid of
Richard Nixon, who had lost virtually all of the wide popularity that had won
him his landslide re-election victory only two years before. And many were also
exhilarated that, as some boasted, "the system had worked." But the wave of
good feeling could not obscure the deeper and more lasting damage the Watergate crisis had done. In a society in which distrust of leaders and institutions of
authority was already widespread, the fall of Richard Nixon seemed to confirm
the most cynical assumptions about the character of American public life.

CHAPTER TWENTY-SEVEN

The Rise of American Conservatism

~

The frustrations of the early 1970s—the defeat in Vietnam, the Watergate crisis, the decay of the American economy—inflicted damaging blows to the confident, optimistic nationalism that had characterized so much of the postwar era. At first, many Americans responded to these problems by announcing the arrival of an "age of limits," in which America would have to learn to live with increasingly constricted expectations. By the end of the decade, however, the contours of another response to the challenges had become visible in both American culture and American politics. It was a response that combined a conservative retreat from some of the heady liberal visions of the 1960s with a reinforced commitment to the idea of economic growth, international power, and American exceptionalism.

POLITICS AND DIPLOMACY AFTER WATERGATE

In the aftermath of Richard Nixon's ignominious departure from office, many wondered whether faith in the presidency, and in the government as a whole, could easily be restored. The administrations of the two presidents who succeeded Nixon did little to answer those questions.

The Ford Presidency

Gerald Ford inherited the presidency under unenviable circumstances. He had to try to rebuild confidence in government in the face of the widespread cynicism the Watergate scandals had produced. And he had to try to restore prosperity in the face of major domestic and international challenges to the American economy. He enjoyed some success in the first of these efforts but very little in the second.

The new president's effort to establish himself as a symbol of political integrity suffered a setback only a month after he took office, when he granted Richard Nixon "a full, free, and absolute pardon" for any crimes he may have committed during his presidency. Ford explained that he was attempting to spare the nation the ordeal of years of litigation and to spare Nixon himself any further suffering. But much of the public suspected a secret deal with the former president. The pardon caused a decline in his popularity from which he never fully recovered. Nevertheless, most Americans considered Ford a decent man; his honesty and amiability did much to reduce the bitterness and acrimony of the Watergate years.

The Ford administration enjoyed less success in its effort to solve the problems of the American economy. In his efforts to curb inflation, the president rejected the idea of wage and price controls and called instead for largely ineffective voluntary efforts. After supporting high interest rates, opposing increased federal spending (through liberal use of his veto power), and resisting pressures for a tax reduction, Ford had to deal with a serious recession in 1974 and 1975. Central to the economic problems was the continuing energy crisis. In the aftermath of the Arab oil embargo of 1973, the OPEC cartel began to raise the price of oil—by 400 percent in 1974 alone. Even so, American dependence on OPEC supplies continued to grow—one of the principal reasons why inflation reached eleven percent in 1976.

At first it seemed that the foreign policy of the new administration would differ little from that of its predecessor. The new president retained Henry Kissinger as secretary of state and continued the general policies of the Nixon years. Late in 1974, Ford met with Leonid Brezhnev at Vladivostok in Siberia and signed an arms control accord that was to serve as the basis for SALT II, thus achieving a goal the Nixon administration had long sought. The following summer, after a European security conference in Helsinki, Finland, the Soviet Union and western nations agreed to ratify the borders that had divided Europe since 1945; and the Soviets pledged to increase respect for human rights within their own country. In the Middle East, in the meantime, Henry Kissinger helped produce a new accord by which Israel agreed to return large portions of the occupied Sinai to Egypt, and the two nations pledged not to resolve future differences by force. In China, finally, the death of Mao Zedong in 1976 brought to power a new, apparently more moderate government, eager to expand its ties with the United States.

Nevertheless, as the 1976 presidential election approached, Ford's policies were coming under attack from both the right and the left. In the Republican primary campaign, the president faced a powerful challenge from former California governor Ronald Reagan, leader of the party's conservative wing, who spoke for many on the right unhappy with any conciliation of communists.

The president only barely survived the assault to win his party's nomination. The Democrats, in the meantime, were gradually uniting behind a new and, before 1976, almost entirely unknown candidate: Jimmy Carter, a former governor of Georgia who organized a brilliant primary campaign and appealed to the general unhappiness with Washington by offering honesty, piety, and an outsider's skepticism of the federal government. And while Carter's once-mammoth lead in opinion polls dwindled to almost nothing by election day, unhappiness with the economy and a general disenchantment with Ford enabled the Democrat to hold on for a narrow victory. Carter emerged with 50 percent of the popular vote to Ford's 47.9 percent and 297 electoral votes to Ford's 240.

JIMMY CARTER.   Jimmy Carter campaigned for president by stressing that he was a Washington "outsider"—a message that appealed to many Americans after the political crisis of Watergate and the paralysis that seemed to grip government in its aftermath. The public image of a simple "peanut farmer" from Plains, Georgia did little to reveal, however, the depth of experience Carter brought to the White House. A graduate of the Naval Academy, a millionaire agricultural businessman, an engineer, and the reform governor of Georgia, Carter won admiration for his sincerity, intelligence, and informality. But he faced formidable challenges as president, including reversals in foreign policy, that would ultimately undermine public faith in him and lose him the presidency.

Jimmy Carter's Ordeal

Like Ford, Jimmy Carter assumed the presidency at a moment when the nation faced problems of staggering complexity and difficulty. Perhaps no leader could have thrived in such inhospitable circumstances. But Carter seemed at times to make his predicament worse by a style of leadership that many considered self-righteous and inflexible. He left office in 1981 one of the least popular presidents of the century.

Carter had campaigned for the presidency as an "outsider," representing Americans suspicious of entrenched bureaucracies and complacent public officials. He carried much of that suspiciousness with him to Washington. He surrounded himself in the White House with a group of close-knit associates from Georgia; and in the beginning, at least, he seemed deliberately to spurn assistance from more experienced political figures. Carter was among the most intelligent men ever to serve in the White House, but his critics charged that he provided no overall vision or direction to his government. His ambitious legislative agenda included major reforms of the tax and welfare systems; Congress passed virtually none of it.

Carter devoted much of his time to the problems of energy and the economy. Entering office in the midst of a recession, he moved first to reduce unemployment by raising public spending and cutting federal taxes. Unemployment declined, but inflation soared—less because of the fiscal policies he implemented than because of the continuing, sharp increases in energy prices imposed on the West by OPEC. During Carter's last two years in office, prices rose at well over a ten-percent annual rate. Like Nixon and Ford before him, Carter responded with a combination of tight money and calls for voluntary restraint. He appointed first G. William Miller and then Paul Volcker, conservative economists, to head the Federal Reserve Board, thus ensuring a policy of high interest rates and reduced currency supplies. By 1980, interest rates had risen to the highest levels in American history; at times, they exceeded twenty percent.

The problem of energy also grew steadily more troublesome in the Carter years. In the summer of 1979, instability in the Middle East produced a second major fuel shortage in the United States. In the midst of the crisis, OPEC announced another large price increase, clouding the economic picture still further. Faced with increasing pressure to act (and with public-opinion polls showing his approval rating at a dismal twenty-six percent, lower than Richard Nixon's lowest figures), Carter withdrew to Camp David, the presidential retreat in the Maryland mountains. Ten days later, he emerged to deliver a remarkable television address. It included a series of proposals for resolving the energy crisis. But it was most notable for Carter's bleak assessment of the national condition. Speaking with unusual fervor, he complained of a "crisis of confidence" that had struck "at the very heart and soul of our national will." The address became known as the "malaise" speech (although Carter himself had never used that word), and it helped fuel charges that the president was trying to blame his own problems on the American people. Carter's sudden firing of several members of his cabinet a few days later deepened his political problems.

Human Rights and National Interests

Among Jimmy Carter's most frequent campaign promises was a pledge to build a new basis for American foreign policy, one in which the defense of "human rights" would replace the pursuit of "selfish interests." Carter spoke out sharply and often about violations of human rights in many countries (including, most prominently, the Soviet Union). Beyond that general commitment, the Carter administration focused on several more traditional concerns. The president completed negotiations begun several years earlier on a pair of treaties to turn over control of the Panama Canal to the government of Panama. Domestic opposition to the treaties was intense, especially among conservatives who viewed the new arrangements as part of a general American retreat from international power. But the administration argued that relinquishing the canal was the best way to improve relations with Latin America and avoid violence in Panama. After an acrimonious debate, the Senate ratified the treaties by sixty-eight to thirty-two, only one vote more than the necessary two-thirds.

Less controversial, within the United States at least, was Carter's stunning success in arranging a peace treaty between Egypt and Israel—the crowning accomplishment of his presidency. Middle East negotiations had seemed hopelessly stalled when a dramatic breakthrough occurred in November 1977. The Egyptian president, Anwar Sadat, accepted an invitation from Prime Minister Menachem Begin to visit Israel. In Tel Aviv, he announced that Egypt was now willing to accept the state of Israel as a legitimate political entity. But translating these good feelings into an actual peace treaty proved more difficult.

When talks between Israeli and Egyptian negotiators stalled, Carter invited Sadat and Begin to a summit conference at Camp David in September 1978, holding them there for two weeks while he and others helped mediate the disputes between them. On September 17, Carter escorted the two leaders into the White House to announce agreement on a "framework" for an Egyptian-Israeli peace treaty. Carter intervened again several months later, when talks stalled once more and helped produce a vague compromise on the most sensitive issue between the two parties: the Palestinian refugee issue. On March 26, 1979, Begin and Sadat returned together to the White House to sign a formal peace treaty between their two nations.

In the meantime, Carter continued trying to improve relations with China and the Soviet Union and to complete a new arms agreement. He responded eagerly to the overtures of Deng Xiaoping, the new Chinese leader, who was attempting to open his nation to the outside world. On December 15, 1978, Washington and Beijing announced the resumption of formal diplomatic relations between the two nations. A few months later, Carter traveled to Vienna to meet with the aging and visibly ailing Brezhnev to finish drafting the new SALT

CAMP DAVID ACCORDS. Jimmy Carter gathered Egyptian President Anwar Sadat and Israeli Prime Minister Menachem Begin for a summit in September 1978 in the hopes of advancing peace in the Middle East. After two weeks of intense negotiation, a "framework" for peace between Israel and Egypt was agreed upon. Though further obstacles remained, in March 1979 Begin and Sadat came to the White House to sign a formal peace treaty. Carter considered the treaty one of the greatest achievements of his presidency.

II arms control agreement. The treaty set limits on the number of long-range missiles, bombers, and nuclear warheads on each side. Almost immediately, however, SALT II met with fierce conservative opposition in the United States. Central to the arguments was a fundamental distrust of the Soviet Union that nearly a decade of détente had failed to destroy; but specific provisions of the treaty—which even some supporters of détente felt were too favorable to the Soviets—also fueled the opposition. By the fall of 1979, with the Senate scheduled to begin debate over the treaty shortly, ratification was already in jeopardy. Events in the following months would provide a final blow, both to the treaty and to the larger framework of détente.

The Hostage Crisis

Ever since the early 1950s, the United States had provided political support and, more recently, massive military assistance to the government of the Shah of Iran, hoping to make his nation a bulwark against Soviet expansion in the Middle East. By 1979, however, the Shah was in deep trouble with his own people. Many Iranians resented the repressive, authoritarian tactics through which the Shah had maintained his autocratic rule. At the same time, Islamic clergy (and much of the fiercely religious majority of the populace) opposed his efforts to modernize and westernize a fundamentalist society. The combination of resentments produced a powerful revolutionary movement. In January 1979, the Shah fled the country.

The United States made cautious efforts in the first months after the Shah's abdication to establish cordial relations with the succession of increasingly militant regimes that followed. By late 1979, however, revolutionary chaos in Iran was making any normal relationships impossible. What power there was resided with a zealous religious leader, the Ayatollah Ruhollah Khomeini, whose hatred of the West in general and the United States in particular was intense.

In late October 1979, the deposed Shah arrived in New York to be treated for cancer. Days later, on November 4, an armed mob invaded the American embassy in Teheran, seized the diplomats and military personnel inside, and demanded the return of the Shah to Iran in exchange for their freedom. Fifty-three Americans remained hostages in the embassy for over a year. Coming after years of other international humiliations and defeats, the hostage seizure released a deep well of anger and emotion in the United States.

Only weeks after the hostage seizure, on December 27, 1979, Soviet troops invaded Afghanistan, the mountainous, Islamic nation lying between the USSR and Iran. The Soviet Union had, in fact, been a power in Afghanistan for years, and the dominant force since April 1978, when a coup had established a Marxist government there with close ties to the Kremlin. Challenges to that regime had sparked the Soviet intervention. But while some observers claimed that the Soviet invasion was a Russian attempt to secure the status quo, others—most notably the president—considered it a Russian "stepping stone to their possible control over much of the world's oil supplies." It was also, Carter claimed, the "gravest threat to world peace since World War II." Carter angrily imposed a series of economic sanctions on the Russians, canceled American participation in the 1980 summer Olympic Games in Moscow, and announced the withdrawal of SALT II from Senate consideration.

The combination of domestic economic troubles and international crises created widespread anxiety, frustration, and anger in the United States—damaging President Carter's already low standing with the public, and giving added strength to an alternative political force that had already made great strides.

THE RISE OF THE RIGHT

Much of the anxiety that pervaded American life in the 1970s was a result of jarring public events that left many men and women shaken and uncertain about their leaders and their government. But much of it was a result, too, of significant changes in the character of America's economy, society, and culture. Together these changes disillusioned many liberals, perplexed the already weak-

AMERICANS HELD HOSTAGE.   On November 4, 1979, Iranian militants overran the American Embassy in Teheran, took American personnel there hostage, and then paraded their captives in the streets while taunting and threatening them. Though a few hostages were subsequently released, fifty-five others were held captive for more than a year before they gained their freedom. This humiliating crisis put Jimmy Carter and his administration in an impossible position where the desire to gain the safe release of the Americans had to be weighed against the costs of negotiating with Iran's revolutionary regime. The crisis ended with the hostages' release on the last day of Carter's presidency.

ened left, and provided the right with its most important opportunity in generations to seize a position of authority in American life.

Sunbelt Politics

The most widely discussed demographic phenomenon of the 1970s was the rise of what became known as the "Sunbelt"—a term coined by the political analyst Kevin Phillips to describe a collection of regions that emerged together in the postwar era to become the most dynamically growing parts of the country. The Sunbelt included the Southeast (particularly Florida), the Southwest (particularly Texas), and above all, California, which became the nation's most populous state, surpassing New York, in 1964 and continued to grow in the years that followed. By 1980, the population of the Sunbelt had risen to exceed that of the industrial regions of the North and East, which were experiencing not only a relative, but in some cases an absolute, decline in population.

In addition to shifting the nation's economic focus from one region to another, the rise of the Sunbelt helped produce a change in the political climate. The strong populist traditions in the South and West were capable of producing progressive and even radical politics; but more often in the late twentieth century, they produced a strong opposition to the growth of government and a resentment of the proliferating regulations and restrictions that the liberal state were producing. Many of those regulations and restrictions—environmental laws, land-use restrictions, even the fifty-five-mile-per-hour speed limit created during the energy crisis to force motorists to conserve fuel—affected the West more than any other region. Both the South and the West, moreover, embraced myths about their own pasts that reinforced hostility to the liberal government of the mid- and late-twentieth century. White southerners equated the federal government's effort to change racial norms in the region with what they believed was the tyranny of Reconstruction. Westerners embraced an image of their region as a refuge of "rugged individualism" and resisted what they considered efforts by the government to impose new standards of behavior on them. Thus, the same impulses and rhetoric that populists had once used to denounce banks and corporations, the new conservative populists of the postwar era used to attack the government—and the liberals, radicals, and minorities whom they believed were driving its growth.

The so-called Sagebrush Rebellion, which emerged in parts of the West in the late 1970s, mobilized conservative opposition to environmental laws and restrictions on development. It also sought to portray the West (which had probably benefited more than any other region from federal investment) as a victim of government control. Its members complained about the very large amounts of land the federal government owned in many western states and demanded that they be opened for development.

The South as a whole was considerably more conservative than other parts of the nation, and its growth served to increase the power of the right in the 1960s and 1970s. The West was not, on the whole, a notably more conservative region than others; but its rise in the postwar period did help produce some of the most numerous and powerful conservative movements in the nation—particularly in southern California, where Orange County (a large suburban area south of Los Angeles) emerged as one of the most important centers of right-wing politics in the country. When the right rose to power in the 1970s and 1980s, westerners were among its most important leaders and constituents.

Religious Revivalism

In the 1960s, many social critics had predicted the virtual extinction of extensive religious influence in American life. *Time* magazine had reported such assumptions in 1966 with a celebrated cover emblazoned with the question, "Is God

Dead?" But religion in America was far from dead. Indeed, in the 1970s the United States experienced the beginning of a major religious revival, perhaps the most powerful since the second Great Awakening of the early nineteenth century. It continued in various forms into the 1990s.

Some of the new religious enthusiasm found expression in the rise of various cults and pseudo-faiths: the Church of Scientology; the Unification Church of the Reverend Sun Myung Moon; even the tragic People's Temple, whose members committed mass suicide in their jungle retreat in Guyana in 1978. But the most important impulse of the religious revival was the rise of evangelical Christianity.

Evangelicism is the basis of many forms of Christian faith. But evangelicals have in common a belief in personal conversion through direct communication with God. Evangelical religion had been the dominant form of Christianity in America through much of its history, and a substantial subculture since the late nineteenth century. In its modern form, it had been increasingly visible since at least the early 1950s, when fundamentalists such as Billy Graham and pentecostals such as Oral Roberts had begun to attract huge national (and international) followings for their energetic revivalism.

For many years, the evangelicals had gone largely unnoted by much of the media and the secular public, which had dismissed them as a limited, provincial phenomenon. By the early 1980s, it was no longer possible to do so. Earlier in the century, many (although never all) evangelicals had been relatively poor rural people, largely isolated from the mainstream of American culture. But the great capitalist expansion after World War II had lifted many of these people out of poverty and into the middle class, where they were more visible and more assertive. More than 70 million Americans now described themselves as "born-again" Christians—men and women who had established a "direct personal relationship with Jesus." Christian evangelicals owned their own newspapers, magazines, radio stations, and television networks. They operated their own schools and universities. They occupied positions of eminence in the worlds of entertainment and professional sports. And one of their number ultimately occupied the White House itself—Jimmy Carter, who during the 1976 campaign had spoken proudly of his own "conversion experience" and who continued openly to proclaim his "born-again" Christian faith during his years in office.

For Jimmy Carter and for some others, evangelical Christianity was the basis of a commitment to racial and economic justice and to world peace. For many evangelicals, however, the message of the new religion was very different—but no less political. In the 1970s, some Christian evangelicals became active on the political and cultural right. They were alarmed by what they considered the spread of immorality and disorder in American life; and they were concerned about the way a secular and, as they saw it, godless culture was intruding into their communities and families—through popular culture, through the schools, and through government policies. Many evangelical men and women feared the growth of feminism and the threat they believed it posed to the traditional family; and they resented the way in which government policies advanced the goals of the women's movement. Particularly alarming to them were Supreme Court decisions eliminating all religious observance from schools and, later, the decision guaranteeing women the right to an abortion.

By the late 1970s the "Christian right" had become a powerful and highly visible political force. Jerry Falwell, a fundamentalist minister in Virginia with a substantial television audience, launched a movement he called the Moral Majority, which attacked the rise of "secular humanism" in American culture. The Moral Majority and other organizations of similar inclination opposed federal interference in local affairs, denounced abortion, divorce, feminism, and homosexuality, defended unrestricted free enterprise, and supported a strong American posture in the world. Some evangelicals reopened issues that had long seemed closed. For example, many fundamentalist Christians questioned the scientific doctrine of evolution and urged the teaching in schools of the biblical story of the Creation instead. Others demanded various forms of censorship or control of television, movies, rock music, books, magazines, and newspapers. Their goal was a new era in which Christian values once again dominated American life.

The Emergence of the New Right

Evangelical Christians were an important part, but only a part, of what became known as the New Right—a diverse but powerful movement that enjoyed rapid growth in the 1970s and early 1980s. It had begun to take shape after the 1964 election, in which Barry Goldwater had suffered his shattering defeat. It was then that Richard Viguerie, a remarkable conservative activist and organizer, took a list of 12,000 contributors to the Goldwater campaign and used it to develop a formidable conservative communications and fund-raising organization. By the mid-1970s, he had gathered a list of 4 million contributors and 15 million supporters. Conservative campaigns had for many years been less well funded and organized than those of their rivals. Beginning in the 1970s, largely because of these and other organizational advances, conservatives found themselves almost always better funded and organized than their opponents. Gradually these direct-mail operations helped create a much larger conservative infrastructure, designed to match and even exceed what the right saw as the powerful liberal infrastructure. By the late 1970s, there were right-wing think tanks, consulting firms, lobbyists, foundations, and scholarly centers.

Another factor in the revival of the right was the emergence of a credible right-wing leadership in the late 1960s and early 1970s to replace the discredited (and somewhat erratic) conservative hero of the 1950s, Barry Goldwater. Chief among this new generation of conservative leaders was Ronald Reagan. Reagan had grown up in modest circumstances in the Midwest and attended a small college in Illinois. In 1937, at the age of twenty-six, he went to Hollywood and became a moderately successful actor, in westerns at times, but mostly in light romantic comedies. A liberal and a fervent admirer of Franklin Roosevelt as a young man, he later moved decisively to the right, especially when, as president of the Screen Actors Guild, he became embroiled in battles with communists in the union. In the early 1950s, he became a corporate spokesman for General Electric and won a wide following on the right with his smooth, eloquent speeches in defense of individual freedom and private enterprise.

In 1964, he delivered a memorable television address on behalf of Goldwater. After the Republican defeat that year, he worked quickly not only to seize the leadership of the conservative wing of the party but to denounce those Republicans who had repudiated Goldwater. "I don't think we should turn the high command over to leaders who were traitors during the battle just ended," Reagan said in 1965, when other Republicans were trying to push anti-Goldwater moderates into positions of leadership in the party. In 1966, with the support of a group of wealthy conservatives, he won the first of two terms as governor of California—which gave him a much more visible platform for promoting himself and his ideas.

The presidency of Gerald Ford also played an important role in the rise of the right by destroying the fragile equilibrium that had enabled the right wing and the moderate wing of the Republican party to coexist. Ford, probably without realizing it, touched on some of the right's rawest nerves. He appointed as vice president Nelson Rockefeller, the liberal Republican governor of New York and an heir to one of America's great fortunes; many conservatives had been demonizing Rockefeller and his family for more than twenty years. (Viguerie attributed the birth of the new right to this event alone.) Ford proposed an amnesty program for draft resisters, embraced and even extended the hated Nixon-Kissinger policies of détente, presided over the fall of Vietnam, and agreed to cede the Panama Canal to Panama. When Reagan challenged Ford in the 1976 Republican primaries, the president survived, barely, only by dumping Nelson Rockefeller from the ticket and replacing him with the more reliably conservative Robert Dole, a senator from Kansas, and by agreeing to a platform largely written by one of Reagan's principal allies, Jesse Helms. Reagan hailed that platform by saying that the party "must raise a banner of no pale pastels, but bold colors which make it unmistakably clear where we stand on all the issues troubling the people."

The Tax Revolt

At least equally important to the success of the new right was a new and potent conservative issue: the tax revolt. It had its public beginnings in 1978, when Howard Jarvis, a conservative activist, launched a major and successful citizens' tax revolt in California with Proposition 13, a referendum question on the state ballot rolling back property tax rates. Similar antitax movements soon began in other states and eventually spread to national politics.

The tax revolt became the solution to one of the right's biggest problems. For more than thirty years after the New Deal, Republican conservatives had struggled to halt and even reverse the growth of the federal government. Most of those efforts had ended in futility. Attacking government programs directly, as right-wing politicians from Robert Taft to Barry Goldwater discovered, was not the way to attract majority support. Every federal program had a political constituency. The biggest and most expensive programs had the broadest support. (Goldwater was plagued throughout the 1964 campaign by fears he would dismantle Social Security.)

In Proposition 13 and similar initiatives, members of the right found a better way to undermine government than by attacking specific programs: attacking taxes. By separating the issue of taxes from the issue of what taxes supported, the right found a way to achieve the most controversial elements of its own agenda (eroding the government's ability to expand and launch new programs) without openly antagonizing the millions of voters who supported specific programs. Virtually no one liked to pay taxes; and as the economy grew weaker and the relative burden of paying taxes grew heavier, that resentment naturally rose. The right exploited that resentment and, in the process, expanded its constituency far beyond anything it had known before. The 1980 presidential election propelled it to a historic victory.

The Campaign of 1980

By the time of the crises in Iran and Afghanistan, Jimmy Carter was in desperate political trouble—his standing in popularity polls lower than that of any president in history. Senator Edward Kennedy, younger brother of John and Robert Kennedy and one of the most magnetic figures in the Democratic party, was preparing to challenge him in the primaries. For a short while, the seizure of the hostages and the stern American response to the Soviet invasion revived Carter's candidacy. But as the hostage crisis dragged on, public impatience grew. Kennedy won a series of victories over the president in the later primaries. Carter managed in the end to stave off Kennedy's challenge and win his party's nomination. But it was an unhappy convention that heard the president's listless call to arms, and Carter's campaign aroused little popular enthusiasm as he prepared to face a powerful challenge.

The Republican party, in the meantime, had rallied enthusiastically behind the man who, four years earlier, had nearly stolen the nomination from Gerald Ford. Ronald Reagan was a sharp critic of the excesses of the federal government. He linked his campaign to the spreading tax revolt (something to which he had paid relatively little attention in the past) by promising substantial tax cuts. Equally important, he championed a restoration of American "strength" and "pride" in the world. Although he refrained from discussing the issue of the hostages, Reagan clearly benefited from the continuing popular frustration at Carter's inability to resolve the crisis. In a larger sense, he benefited as well from the accumulated frustrations of more than a decade of domestic and international disappointments.

On election day 1980, the anniversary of the seizure of the hostages in Iran, Reagan swept to victory with fifty-one percent of the vote to forty-one percent for Jimmy Carter, and seven percent for John Anderson—a moderate Republican congressman from Illinois who had mounted an independent campaign. Carter carried only five states and the District of Columbia, for a total of forty-nine electoral votes to Reagan's 489. The Republican party won control of the Senate for the first time since 1952; and although the Democrats retained a modest majority in the House, the lower chamber, too, seemed firmly in the hands of conservatives.

On the day of Reagan's inauguration, the American hostages in Iran were released after their 444-day ordeal. Jimmy Carter, in the last hours of his presidency, had concluded months of negotiations by agreeing to release several billion dollars in Iranian assets that he had frozen in American banks shortly after the seizure of the embassy. The government of Iran, desperate for funds to support its floundering war against neighboring Iraq, had ordered the hostages freed in return. Americans welcomed the hostages home with demonstrations of joy and patriotism not seen since the end of World War II. But while the celebration in 1945 had marked a great American triumph, the euphoria in 1981 marked something quite different—a troubled nation grasping for reassurance. Ronald Reagan set out to provide it.

THE "REAGAN REVOLUTION"

Ronald Reagan assumed the presidency in January 1981 promising a change in government more fundamental than any since the New Deal of fifty years before. While his eight years in office produced a significant shift in public policy, they brought nothing so radical as many of his supporters had hoped or his opponents had feared. But there was no ambiguity about the Reagan presidency's purely political achievements. Reagan succeeded brilliantly in making his own engaging personality the central fact of American politics in the 1980s.

The Reagan Coalition

Reagan owed his election to widespread disillusionment with Carter and to the crises and disappointments that many voters, perhaps unfairly, associated with him. But he owed it as well to the emergence of a powerful coalition of conservative groups. That coalition was not a single, cohesive movement. It was an uneasy and generally temporary alliance among several very different movements.

The Reagan coalition included a small but highly influential group of wealthy Americans associated with the corporate and financial world—the kind of people who had dominated American politics and government through much of the nation's history until the New Deal began to challenge their pre-eminence. What united this group was a firm commitment to capitalism and to unfettered economic growth; a deep hostility to most (although not all) government interference in markets; and a belief that most of what is valuable in American life depended on the health and strength of the corporate world, and thus that the corporate world was entitled to a special position of influence and privilege in society. Central to this group's agenda in the 1980s was opposition to what it considered the "redistributive" politics of the federal government (and especially its highly progressive tax structure) and hostility to the rise of what they believed were "antibusiness" government regulations. Reagan courted them carefully and effectively.

A second element of the Reagan coalition was even smaller, but also disproportionately influential: a group of intellectuals commonly known as "neoconservatives," who gave to the right something it had not had in many years—a firm base among "opinion leaders," people with access to the most influential public forums for ideas. Many of these people had once been liberals and, before that, socialists. But during the turmoil of the 1960s, they had become alarmed by what they considered a dangerous and destructive radicalism that they feared was destabilizing American life, and by the weakening of liberal ardor in the battle against communism. Neoconservatives were sympathetic to the complaints and demands of capitalists; but their principal concern was to reassert legitimate authority and reaffirm western democratic, anticommunist values and commitments. They considered themselves engaged in a battle to regain control of the marketplace of ideas—to "win back the culture"—from the crass, radical ideas that had polluted it. Some neoconservative intellectuals eventually became important figures in the battle against multiculturalism and "political correctness" within academia.

These two groups joined in an uneasy alliance in 1980 with the vast and growing movement known as the "new right" (or, to some, the populist right). Several things differentiated the new right from the corporate conservatives and the neoconservatives. Perhaps the most important was a fundamental distrust of the "eastern establishment": a suspicion of its motives and goals; a sense that it exercised a dangerous, secret power in American life; a fear of the hidden influence of such establishment institutions and people as the Council on Foreign Relations, the Trilateral Commission, Henry Kissinger, or the Rockefellers. These "populist" conservatives expressed the kinds of concerns that outsiders, non-elites, have traditionally voiced in American society: an opposition to centralized power and influence; a fear of living in a world where distant, hostile forces are controlling society and threatening individual freedom and community autonomy. It was a testament to Ronald Reagan's political skills and personal charm that he was able to generate enthusiastic support from these populist conservatives while at the same time appealing to more elite conservative groups whose concerns were in many ways antithetical to those of the new right.

RONALD REAGAN.   Ronald Reagan at his ranch in Santa Barbara, displaying the informal geniality that accounted for much of his remarkable popularity.

Reagan in the White House

Even many people who disagreed with Reagan's policies found themselves drawn to his attractive and carefully honed public image. Reagan was a master of television, a gifted public speaker, and—in public at least—rugged, fearless, and seemingly impervious to danger or misfortune. He turned seventy-years-old weeks after taking office and was the oldest man ever to serve in the White House. But through most of his presidency, he seemed vigorous, resilient, even youthful. He spent his many vacations on a California ranch, where he chopped wood and rode horses. When he was wounded in an assassination attempt in 1981, he joked with doctors on his way into surgery and appeared to bounce back from the ordeal with remarkable speed. Four years later, he seemed to rebound from cancer surgery with similar zest. He had few visible insecurities. Even when things went wrong, as they often did, the blame seldom seemed to attach for long to Reagan himself (inspiring some Democrats to begin referring to him as "the Teflon president").

Reagan was not much involved in the day-to-day affairs of running the government; he surrounded himself with tough, energetic administrators who insulated him from many of the pressures of the office and apparently relied on him largely for general guidance, not specific decisions. At times, the president revealed a startling ignorance about the nature of his own policies or the actions of his subordinates. But Reagan did make active use of his office to generate support for his administration's programs, by appealing repeatedly to the public over television and by fusing his proposals with a highly nationalistic rhetoric.

"Supply-Side" Economics

Reagan's 1980 campaign for the presidency had promised, among other things, to restore the economy to health by a bold experiment that became known as "supply-side" economics or, to some, "Reaganomics." Supply-side economics operated from the assumption that the woes of the American economy were in large part a result of excessive taxation, which left inadequate capital available to investors to stimulate growth. The solution, therefore, was to reduce taxes, with particularly generous benefits to corporations and wealthy individuals, in order to encourage new investments. The result would be a general economic revival that would help everyone. Because a tax cut would reduce government revenues (at least at first), it would also be necessary to reduce government expenses. A cornerstone of the Reagan economic program, therefore, was a series of dramatic cuts in federal spending.

In its first months in office, accordingly, the new administration hastily assembled a legislative program based on the supply-side idea. It proposed $40 billion in budget reductions and managed to win congressional approval of almost all of them. In addition, the president proposed a bold, three-year rate reduction of thirty percent on both individual and corporate taxes. In the summer of 1981, Congress passed it too, after lowering the reductions slightly, to twenty-five percent. Not since Lyndon Johnson had a president compiled so impressive a legislative record in his first months in office. Reagan was successful because he had a disciplined Republican majority in the Senate, and because the Democratic majority in the House was weak and riddled with defectors. Shaken by the results of the 1980 election, dozens of Democrats from relatively conservative districts (mostly in the South) deserted the party's leadership; the defectors became known as "boll weevils."

Men and women appointed by Reagan fanned out through the executive branch of government committed to reducing the role of government in American economic life. "Deregulation," an idea many Democrats had begun to embrace in the Carter years, became the religion of the Reagan administration. Secretary of the Interior James Watt, who had been a major figure in the Sagebrush Rebellion, opened up public lands and water to development. The Environmental Protection Agency (before its directors were indicted for corruption) relaxed or entirely eliminated enforcement of critical environmental laws and regulations. The Civil Rights Division of the Justice Department eased enforcement of civil-rights laws. The Department of Transportation slowed implementation of new rules limiting automobile emissions and imposing new safety standards on cars and trucks. By getting government "out of the way," Reagan officials promised, they were ensuring economic revival.

By early 1982, however, the nation had sunk into the most severe recession since the 1930s. The Reagan economic program was not directly to blame for the problems. The recession was more a result of the high interest rates the Federal Reserve Board (run by Carter appointee William Volcker) had maintained since the late 1970s. The high rates made it difficult for businesses and individuals to borrow money for investment or consumer purchases. They also made the dollar attractive to overseas investors and significantly raised its value—thus making American products more expensive abroad and significantly reducing exports. By 1984, the U.S. trade deficit was $111 billion; in 1980, there had been a $25 billion surplus. The recession had particularly devastating effects on American industry, which had already been experiencing serious problems for a decade. Industrialists closed some plants, reduced the labor force in others, and eliminated millions of manufacturing jobs. In 1982, unemployment reached eleven percent, its highest level in over forty years. Farmers, even more dependent than manufacturers on the export trade, fared even worse. Hundreds of thousands of farmers lost so much money in the early 1980s that they could not keep their farms.

The recession convinced many people, including some conservatives, that the Reagan economic program (and thus the Reagan presidency) had failed. In fact, however, the economy recovered more rapidly and impressively than almost anyone had expected. By late 1983, unemployment had fallen to 8.2 percent, and it declined steadily for several years after that. The gross national product had grown 3.6 percent in a year, the largest increase since the mid-1970s. Inflation had fallen below five percent. The economy continued to grow, and both inflation and unemployment remained low (at least by the new and more pessimistic standards the nation seemed now to have accepted) through most of the decade.

The recovery was a result of many things. The years of tight-money policies by the Federal Reserve Board, however painful and destructive they may have been in other ways, had helped lower inflation; and equally important, the Board had lowered interest rates early in 1983 in response to the recession. A worldwide "energy glut" and the virtual collapse of the OPEC cartel had produced at least a temporary end to the inflationary pressures of spiraling fuel costs. And staggering federal budget deficits were pumping billions of dollars into the flagging economy. As a result, consumer spending and business investment both increased. And the stock market rose up from the doldrums of the late 1970s and began a sustained and historic boom. In August 1982, the Dow Jones Industrial Average stood at 777. Five years later, it had passed 2,000. Despite a frightening crash in the fall of 1987, the market continued to grow. In late 1996, the Dow Jones average was nearing 6,000.

The Fiscal Crisis

The economic revival did little, however, to reduce the staggering, and to many Americans alarming, deficits in the federal budget. By the mid-1980s, this growing fiscal crisis had become one of the central issues in American politics. Having entered office promising a balanced budget within four years, Reagan presided over record budget deficits and accumulated more debt in his eight years in office than the American government had accumulated in its entire

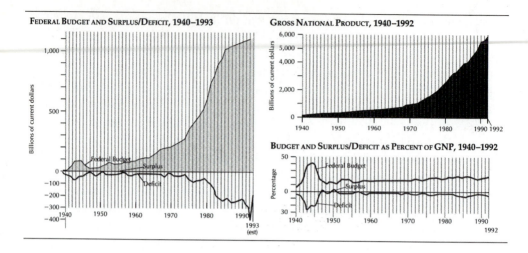

previous history. Before the 1980s, the highest single-year budget deficit in American history had been $66 billion (in 1976). Throughout the 1980s, the annual budget deficit consistently exceeded $100 billion (and in 1991 peaked at $268 billion). The national debt rose from $907 billion in 1980 to nearly $3.5 trillion by 1991.

The enormous deficits had many causes, some of them stretching back over decades of American public policy decisions. In particular, the budget suffered from enormous increases in the costs of "entitlement" programs (especially Social Security and Medicare), a product of the aging of the population and the dramatic increase in the cost of health care. But some of the causes of the deficit lay in the policies of the Reagan administration. The 1981 tax cuts, the largest in American history, eroded the revenue base of the federal government and accounted for a significant percentage of the deficit. The massive increase in military spending (a proposed $1.6 trillion over five years) on which the Reagan administration insisted added more to the federal budget than its cuts in domestic spending removed.

In the face of these deficits, the administration refused to consider raising income taxes (although it did agree to a major increase in the Social Security tax). It would not agree to reductions in military spending. It could not much reduce the costs of entitlement programs, and it could do nothing to reduce interest payments on the massive (and growing) debt. Its answer to the fiscal crisis, therefore, was further cuts in "discretionary" domestic spending, which included many programs aimed at the poorest (and politically weakest) Americans. There were reductions in funding for food stamps; a major cut in federal subsidies for low-income housing (which contributed to the radical increase in homelessness that by the late 1980s was plaguing virtually all American cities); strict new limitations on Medicare and Medicaid payments; reductions in student loans, school lunches, and other educational programs; and an end to many forms of federal assistance to the states and cities—which helped precipitate years of local fiscal crises as well.

By the end of Reagan's third year in office, funding for domestic programs had been cut nearly as far as Congress (and, apparently, the public) was willing to tolerate; and still no end was in sight to the rising deficits. Congress responded with the so-called Gramm-Rudman bill, passed late in 1985, which mandated major deficit reductions over five years and provided for automatic budget cuts in all areas of government spending should the president and Congress fail to agree on an alternative solution. Under Gramm-Rudman, the budget deficit did decline for several years from its 1983 high. But much of that decline was a result of a substantial surplus in the Social Security trust fund (which the sharply increased Social Security taxes had produced), not of the provisions of the law. By the late 1980s, some fiscal conservatives were calling for a constitutional amendment mandating a balanced budget—a provision the president himself claimed to support but did little to promote.

Reagan and the World

Reagan encountered a similar combination of triumphs and difficulties in international affairs. Determined to restore American pride and prestige in the world, he argued that the United States should once again become active and assertive in opposing communism and supporting friendly governments whatever their internal policies.

Relations with the Soviet Union, which had been steadily deteriorating in the last years of the Carter administration, grew still more chilly in the first years of the Reagan presidency. The president spoke harshly of the Soviet regime (which he once called the "evil empire"), accusing it of sponsoring world terrorism and declaring that any armaments negotiations must be "linked" to negotiations about Soviet behavior in other areas. Relations with the Russians deteriorated further after the government of Poland (under strong pressure from Moscow) imposed martial law on the country in the winter of 1981 to crush a growing challenge from an independent labor organization, Solidarity.

Although the president had long denounced the SALT II arms control treaty as unfavorable to the United States, he continued to honor its provisions. But the Reagan administration at first made little progress toward arms control in other areas. In fact, the president proposed the most ambitious new military program in many years: the so-called Strategic Defense Initiative (SDI), widely known as "Star Wars" (after a popular movie by that name). Reagan claimed that SDI, through the use of lasers and satellites, could provide an effective shield against incoming missiles and thus make nuclear war obsolete. The Soviet Union claimed that the new program would elevate the arms race to new and more dangerous levels and insisted that any arms control agreement begin with an American abandonment of SDI.

The escalation of Cold War tensions and the slowing of arms control initiatives helped produce an important popular movement in Europe and the United States calling for an end to nuclear weapons buildups. In America, the principal goal of the movement was a "nuclear freeze," an agreement between the two superpowers not to expand their atomic arsenals. In what many believed was the largest mass demonstration in American history, nearly a million people rallied in New York City's Central Park in 1982 to support the freeze. Perhaps in response to this growing pressure, the administration began tentative efforts to revive arms control negotiations in 1983.

It also began, rhetorically at least, to support opponents of communism anywhere in the world, whether or not the regimes or movements they were challenging had any direct connection to the Soviet Union. This new policy became known as the Reagan Doctrine, and it meant, above all, a new American activism in the Third World. The most conspicuous examples of the new activism came in Latin America. In October 1982, the administration sent American soldiers and Marines into the tiny Caribbean island of Grenada to oust an anti-American Marxist regime that showed signs of forging a relationship with Moscow. In El Salvador, where first a repressive military regime and later a moderate civilian one were engaged in murderous struggles with left-wing revolutionaries (who were supported, according to the Reagan administration, by Cuba and the Soviet Union), the president provided increased military and economic assistance. In neighboring Nicaragua, a pro-American dictatorship had fallen to the revolutionary "Sandinistas" in 1979; the new government had grown increasingly anti-American (and increasingly Marxist) throughout the early 1980s. The administration gave both rhetorical and material support to the so-called *contras*, a guerrilla movement drawn from several antigovernment groups and fighting (without great success) to topple the Sandinista regime. Indeed, support of the *contras* became a mission of special importance to the president, and later the source of some of his greatest difficulties.

In other parts of the world, the administration's bellicose rhetoric seemed to hide an instinctive restraint. In June 1982, the Israeli army launched an invasion of Lebanon in an effort to drive guerrillas of the Palestinian Liberation Organization from the country. The United States supported the Israelis rhetorically but also worked to permit PLO forces to leave Lebanon peacefully. An American peacekeeping force entered Beirut to supervise the evacuation. American Marines then remained in the city, apparently to protect the fragile Lebanese government, which was embroiled in a vicious civil war. Now identified with one faction in the struggle, Americans became the targets of a terrorist bombing of a U.S. military barracks in Beirut in 1983 that left 241 marines dead. Rather than become more deeply involved in the Lebanese struggle, Reagan withdrew American forces.

The tragedy in Lebanon was an example of the changing character of Third World struggles: an increasing reliance on terrorism by otherwise relatively powerless groups to advance their political aims. A series of terrorist acts in the 1980s—attacks on airplanes, cruise ships, commercial and diplomatic posts; the seizing of American and other western hostages—alarmed and frightened much of the western world. The Reagan administration spoke bravely about its resolve to punish terrorism; and at one point in 1986, the president ordered American planes to bomb sites in Tripoli, the capital of Libya, whose controversial leader Muammar al-Qaddafi was widely believed to be a leading sponsor of terrorism. In general, however, terrorists remained difficult to identify or control; and policymakers, in their frustration, began to search for new ways to deal with them.

The Election of 1984

Reagan approached the campaign of 1984 at the head of a united Republican party firmly committed to his candidacy. The Democrats, as had become their custom, followed a more fractious course. Former Vice President Walter

MONDALE-FERRARO.   Walter Mondale made history when he selected Geraldine Ferraro, a member of the House of the Representatives from New York, as his running mate in 1984. Ms. Ferraro was the first woman nominated by a major political party for national office. Her historic selection, however, did not persuade voters to choose Mondale over Reagan, who won the election in a landslide.

Mondale established an early and commanding lead in the race by soliciting support from a wide range of traditional Democratic interest groups and survived challenges from Senator Gary Hart of Colorado (who claimed to represent a "new generation" of leadership) and the magnetic Jesse Jackson, a charismatic African-American leader who had established himself as the nation's most prominent spokesman for minorities and the poor. Mondale captured the nomination and brought momentary excitement to the Democratic campaign by selecting a woman, Representative Geraldine Ferraro of New York, to be his running mate and the first female candidate ever to appear on a national ticket.

The Republican party rallied comfortably behind its revered leader, who in his triumphant campaign that fall scarcely took note of his opponents and spoke instead of what he claimed was the remarkable revival of American fortunes and spirits under his leadership. His campaign emphasized such phrases as "It's Morning in America" and "America is Back." Reagan's victory in 1984 was decisive. He won approximately fifty-nine percent of the vote, and he carried every state but Mondale's native Minnesota and the District of Columbia. But Reagan was much stronger than his party. Democrats gained a seat in the Senate and maintained only slightly reduced control of the House of Representatives.

The triumphant re-election of Ronald Reagan was the high watermark of conservative, and Republican, fortunes in the postwar era to that point. It reflected satisfaction with the impressive performance of the economy under the Republican economic program and pride in the new assertiveness the United States was showing in the world. To many Reagan supporters, the 1984 election seemed to be the dawn of a new conservative era. But almost no one anticipated the revolutionary changes that would transform the world, and the United States's place in it, within a very few years. The election of 1984 was, therefore, not so much the first of a new era as it was the last of an old one. It was the final campaign of the Cold War.

CHAPTER TWENTY-EIGHT

Modern Times

~

On November 8, 1989, East German soldiers stood guard at the Berlin Wall—keeping westerners out and easterners in—as they had done every day for more than twenty-eight years. The next day they were gone. Within hours, thousands of citizens of both sides of the divided city were swarming over the wall in celebration. Within weeks, bulldozers were tearing it down. Within a year, East and West Germany—divided by the Cold War for forty-five years—had reunited.

The breaching of the Berlin Wall and the reunification of Germany were among the most dramatic of a series of changes between 1986 and 1991 that radically transformed the world. The Cold War, which as late as 1985 had seemed a permanent fact of international life, came to an end. A new world order, the outlines of which were still only dimly visible, was in the process of being born.

The Cold War had shaped the foreign policy and much of the domestic life of the United States for nearly half a century. Its sudden end changed the character of national politics, economics, and culture. But America in the late 1980s and early 1990s was also encountering a series of other important social and economic changes, many of them unrelated to the Cold War. As the end of the twentieth century approached, most Americans were uncertain whether the changes would bring a better, safer world or a harsher and more dangerous one.

THE END OF THE COLD WAR

Many factors contributed to the collapse of the Soviet empire. The long, stalemated war in Afghanistan proved at least as disastrous to the Soviet Union as the Vietnam War had been to America. The government in Moscow had failed to address a long-term economic decline in the Soviet republics and the eastern-bloc nations. Restiveness with the heavy-handed policies of communist police states was growing throughout much of the Soviet empire. But the most visible factor at the time was the emergence of a single man: Mikhail Gorbachev, who succeeded to the leadership of the Soviet Union in 1985 and, to the surprise of almost everyone, very quickly became the most revolutionary figure in world politics in at least four decades.

The Fall of the Soviet Union

Gorbachev quickly transformed Soviet politics with two dramatic new initiatives. The first he called *glasnost* (openness): the dismantling of many of the repressive mechanisms that had been conspicuous features of Soviet life for over half a century. The other policy Gorbachev called *perestroika* (reform): an effort to restructure the rigid and unproductive Soviet economy by introducing, among other things, such elements of capitalism as private ownership and the profit motive. He also began to transform Soviet foreign policy.

The severe economic problems at home evidently convinced Gorbachev that the Soviet Union could no longer sustain its extended commitments around the world. As early as 1987, he began reducing Soviet influence in eastern Europe. And in 1989, in the space of a few months, every communist state in Europe—Poland, Hungary, Czechoslovakia, Bulgaria, Romania, East Germany, Yugoslavia, and Albania—either overthrew its government or forced it to transform itself into an essentially noncommunist (and in some cases, actively anticommunist) regime. The communist parties of eastern Europe all but collapsed (although some of them later revived in altered form). Gorbachev and the Soviet Union actively encouraged the changes.

The challenges to communism were not successful everywhere. In May 1989, students in China launched a mass movement calling for greater democratization. But in June, hardline leaders seized control of the government and sent military forces to crush the uprising. The result was a bloody massacre on June 3, 1989, in Tiananmen Square in Beijing, in which a still-unknown number of demonstrators died. The assault crushed the democracy movement and restored the hardliners to power. It did not, however, stop China's efforts to modernize and even westernize its economy.

But China was an exception to the worldwide movement toward democratization, which even extended to parts of the world far removed from the Soviet empire. Early in 1990, the government of South Africa, long an international pariah for its rigid enforcement of "apartheid" (a system of legalized segregation of the races designed to protect white supremacy) began a cautious retreat from its traditional policies. Among other things, it legalized the chief black party in the nation, the African National Congress, which had been banned for decades, and on February 11, 1990, it released from prison the leader of the ANC, and a revered hero to black South Africans, Nelson Mandela, who had been in jail for twenty-seven years. Over the next several years, the South African government repealed its apartheid laws. And in 1994, there were national elections in which all South Africans could participate. As a result, Nelson Mandela became the first black president of South Africa.

In 1991, communism began to collapse at the site of its birth: the Soviet Union itself. An unsuccessful coup by hardline Soviet leaders on August 19 precipitated a dramatic unraveling of communist power. Within days, the coup itself collapsed in the face of resistance from the public and, more important, crucial elements within the military. Mikhail Gorbachev returned to power; but it soon became evident that the legitimacy of both the Communist party and the central Soviet government had been fatally injured. By the end of August, almost every republic in the Soviet Union had declared independence; the Soviet government was clearly powerless to stop the fragmentation. Gorbachev himself finally resigned as leader of the now virtually powerless Communist party and Soviet government, and the Soviet Union ceased to exist. Boris Yeltsin, the president of the Russian Republic who had led popular opposition to the coup, now emerged as the leader of the largest and most powerful part of the former Soviet empire. (In 1996, he staved off a strong challenge from unrepentant communists and won re-election.)

Reagan and Gorbachev

The last years of the Reagan administration coincided with the first years of the Gorbachev regime; and while Reagan was skeptical of Gorbachev at first, he gradually became convinced that the Soviet leader was sincere in his desire for reform. At a summit meeting with Reagan in Reykjavik, Iceland, in 1986,

THREE PRESIDENTS, 1988   President-elect George Bush and President Ronald Reagan stand with Soviet President Mikhail Gorbachev before the Statue of Liberty on December 7, 1988, during a visit by Gorbachev to the United Nations.

Gorbachev proposed reducing the nuclear arsenals of both sides by fifty percent or more, although continuing disputes over Reagan's commitment to the SDI program derailed agreements. But in 1988, after Reagan and Gorbachev exchanged cordial visits to each other's capitals, the two superpowers signed a treaty eliminating American and Soviet intermediate-range nuclear forces (INF) from Europe—the most significant arms control agreement of the nuclear age. At about the same time, Gorbachev ended the Soviet Union's long and frustrating military involvement in Afghanistan, removing one of the principal irritants in the relationship between Washington and Moscow.

DOMESTIC POLITICS
IN THE POST–COLD WAR PERIOD

As the Cold War came to an end, American political life also seemed to move toward a complex, ambiguous, and unpredictable stage in which neither of the major political parties appeared to provide a vision adequate for the new world. Americans remained preoccupied with the economy, less than confident in their future, and skeptical about the direction of change. In this context, political leaders had a difficult time maintaining power for long. The voters seemed to choose change whenever they had the opportunity.

The Fading of the Reagan Revolution

For a time, the dramatic changes around the world and Reagan's personal popularity deflected attention from a series of scandals that might well have destroyed another administration. There were revelations of illegality, corruption, and ethical lapses in the Environmental Protection Agency, the CIA, the Department of Defense, the Department of Labor, the Department of Justice, and the Department of Housing and Urban Development. A more serious scandal emerged within the savings and loan industry, which the Reagan administration had helped deregulate in the early 1980s. Many savings banks had responded by rapidly, often recklessly, and sometimes corruptly, expanding. By the end of the decade the industry was in chaos, and the government was forced to step in to prevent a complete collapse. Government insurance covered the assets of most savings and loan depositors; but the cost to the public of the debacle eventually ran to more than half a trillion dollars.

The most politically damaging scandal of the Reagan years came to light in November 1986, when the White House conceded it had sold weapons to the revolutionary government of Iran as part of a largely unsuccessful effort to secure the release of several Americans being held hostage by radical Islamic groups in the Middle East. Even more damaging was the revelation that some of the money from the arms deal with Iran had been covertly and illegally funneled into a fund to aid the *contras* in Nicaragua.

In the months that followed, aggressive reporting and a highly publicized series of congressional hearings exposed a widespread pattern of covert activities orchestrated by the White House and dedicated to advancing the administration's foreign policy aims through secret and at times illegal means. The principal figure in this covert world appeared at first to be an obscure marine lieutenant colonel assigned to the staff of the National Security Council, Oliver North. But gradually it became clear that North was acting in concert with other, more powerful figures in the administration. The Iran-contra scandal, as it became known, did serious damage to the Reagan presidency—even though the investigations were never able decisively to tie the president himself to the most serious violations of the law. A blue ribbon commission appointed to explore Iran-contra painted a devastating picture of Reagan in its report. The president, the commission concluded, seemed detached, disinterested, and even unaware of events occurring in his own administration.

The Election of 1988

The fraying of the Reagan administration helped the Democrats regain control of the United States Senate in 1986 and fueled hopes in the party for a presidential victory in 1988. Even so, several of the most popular figures in the Democratic party refused to run. The nomination finally went to a previously little-known figure: Michael Dukakis, a three-term governor of Massachusetts. Dukakis was a dry, even dull campaigner with a reputation for honesty and competence and for presiding over an impressive economic revival in his home state, often called the "Massachusetts Miracle." Democrats were optimistic about their prospects in 1988, however, less because of Dukakis than because of the identity of their opponent, Vice President George Bush, who had captured the Republican nomination without great difficulty, but who had failed to spark any real public enthusiasm. He entered the last months of the campaign well behind Dukakis.

Beginning at the Republican convention, however, Bush staged a remarkable turnaround by transforming his campaign into a long, relentless attack on Dukakis, tying him to all the unpopular social and cultural stances Americans had come to identify with "liberals." Indeed, the Bush campaign was almost certainly the most savage of the twentieth century. It was also, apparently, one of the most effective, although the listless, indecisive character of the Dukakis effort contributed to the Republican cause as well. Bush won a substantial victory in November: fifty-four percent of the popular vote to Dukakis's forty-six, and 426 electoral votes to Dukakis's 112. But Bush carried few Republicans into office with him; the Democrats retained secure majorities in both houses of Congress.

The Bush Presidency

The Bush presidency was notable for a series of dramatic developments in international affairs and an almost complete absence of initiatives or ideas on domestic issues. For a time, Bush's achievements in foreign policy managed to obscure the absence of a domestic agenda. By early 1992, however, with the nation in the second year of a serious recession, the president's popularity had begun to fray.

The broad popularity Bush enjoyed during much of his first three years in office was partly because of his subdued, unthreatening public image. But it was primarily because of the wonder and excitement with which Americans viewed the dramatic events in the rest of the world. Bush moved cautiously at first in dealing with the changes in the Soviet Union. But like Reagan, he eventually embraced Gorbachev and reached a series of significant agreements with the Soviet Union in its waning years. In the three years after the INF agreement in 1988, the United States and the Soviet Union moved rapidly toward even more far-reaching arms reduction agreements, including major troop reductions in Europe and the dismantling of new categories of strategic weapons.

On domestic issues, the Bush administration was less successful—partly because the president himself seemed to have little interest in promoting a domestic agenda and partly because he faced serious obstacles. His administration inherited a staggering burden of debt and a federal deficit that had been out of control for nearly a decade. Any domestic agenda that required significant federal spending was, therefore, incompatible with the president's pledge to reduce the deficit and his 1988 campaign promise of "no new taxes." Bush faced a Democratic Congress with an agenda very different from his own. And he was constantly concerned about the right wing of his own party. In his eagerness to ingratiate himself with them, the president took divisive positions on such cultural issues as abortion and affirmative action that further damaged his ability to work with Congress.

Despite this political stalemate, Congress and the White House managed on occasion to agree on significant measures. They cooperated in producing a plan to salvage the floundering savings and loan industry. In 1990, the president bowed to congressional pressure and agreed to a large tax increase as part of a multiyear "budget package" designed to reduce the deficit. In 1991, after almost two years of acrimonious debate, the president and Congress agreed on a civil rights bill to combat job discrimination.

But the most politically damaging domestic problem facing the Bush administration was one to which neither the president nor Congress had any answer: a recession that began late in 1990 and slowly increased its grip on the national economy in 1991 and 1992. Because of the enormous level of debt that corporations (and individuals) had accumulated in the 1980s, the recession caused an unusual number of bankruptcies. It also created growing fear and frustration among middle- and working-class Americans and increasing pressure on the government to address such problems as the rising cost of health care.

The Gulf War

The events of 1989–1991 had left the United States in the unanticipated position of being the only real superpower in the world. The Bush administration, therefore, had to consider what to do with America's formidable political and military power in a world in which the major justification for that power—the Soviet threat—was now gone.

The events of 1989–1991 suggested two possible answers, both of which had some effect on policy. One was that the United States would reduce its military strength dramatically and concentrate its energies and resources on pressing domestic problems. And, indeed, there was considerable movement in that direction both in Congress and within the administration. The other was that America would continue to use its power actively, not to fight communism but to defend its regional and economic interests. In 1989, that impulse led the administration to order an invasion of Panama, which overthrew the unpopular military leader Mañuel Noriega (under indictment in the United States for drug trafficking) and replaced him with an elected, pro-American regime. And in 1991, that same impulse drew the United States into the turbulent politics of the Middle East.

On August 2, 1990, the armed forces of Iraq invaded and quickly overwhelmed their small, oil-rich neighbor, the emirate of Kuwait. Saddam Hussein, the militaristic leader of Iraq, soon announced that he was annexing Kuwait and set out to entrench his forces there. After some initial indecision, the Bush administration agreed to join with other nations to force Iraq out of Kuwait—through the pressure of economic sanctions if possible, through military force if necessary. Within a few weeks, Bush had persuaded virtually every important government in the world, including the Soviet Union and almost all the Arab and Islamic states, to join in a United Nations–sanctioned trade embargo of Iraq.

At the same time, the United States and its allies (including the British, French, Egyptians, and Saudis) began deploying a massive military force along the border between Kuwait and Saudi Arabia, a force that ultimately reached 690,000 troops (425,000 of them American) and that assembled the largest and most sophisticated collection of military technology ever used in warfare. On November 29, the United Nations, at the request of the United States, voted to authorize military action to expel Iraq from Kuwait if Iraq did not leave by January 15, 1991. On January 12, both houses of Congress voted to authorize the use of force against Iraq, although many Democrats opposed the resolution, arguing that sanctions should be given more time to work. And on January 16, American and allied air forces began a massive bombardment of Iraqi forces in Kuwait and of military and industrial installations in Iraq itself.

The allied bombing continued for six weeks, meeting only token resistance from the small Iraqi air force and ground defenses. And on February 23, allied (mostly American) forces under the command of General Norman Schwarzkopf began a major ground offensive—not primarily against the heavily entrenched Iraqi forces along the Kuwait border, as expected, but into Iraq itself. The allied armies encountered almost no resistance and suffered only light casualties (141 fatalities). There were no reliable figures for the number of Iraqi military casualties, but some estimated the deaths (most as a result of the bombing) to be 100,000 or more. There were also a significant, if unverifiable, number of civilian casualties. On February 28, Iraq announced its acceptance of allied terms for a cease-fire, and the brief war came to an end.

The quick and (for America) relatively painless victory over Iraq was highly popular in the United States. But the longer range results of the Gulf War were more difficult to assess. The tyrannical regime of Saddam Hussein survived, in a weakened form but showing few signs of retreat from its militaristic ambitions. And Kuwait returned to the control of its prewar government, an undemocratic monarchy increasingly unpopular with its own people.

The Election of 1992

President Bush's popularity reached a record high in the immediate aftermath of the Gulf War. But the glow of the Gulf War victory faded quickly as the recession worsened in late 1991, and as the administration declined to propose any policies for combatting it. The president's standing soon eroded.

Because the early maneuvering for the 1992 presidential election occurred when President Bush's popularity remained high, many leading Democrats declined to run. That gave Bill Clinton, the young five-term governor of Arkansas, the opportunity to emerge early as the front-runner, as a result of a skillful campaign that emphasized broad economic issues over the racial and cultural questions that had so divided the Democrats in the past. Clinton survived a bruising primary campaign and a series of damaging personal controversies to win his party's nomination. And George Bush withstood an embarrassing primary challenge from the conservative journalist Pat Buchanan to become the Republican nominee again.

Complicating the campaign was the emergence of Ross Perot, a blunt, forthright Texas billionaire who became an independent candidate by tapping popular resentment of the federal bureaucracy and by promising tough, uncompromising leadership to deal with the fiscal crisis and other problems of government. Particularly appealing to many voters were Perot's attacks on corruption in the political system and his insistence that his own campaign (funded by his personal fortune, not by special-interest lobbies) was a pure reflection of the will of the people. At several moments in the spring, Perot led both Bush and Clinton in public opinion polls. In July, as he began to face hostile scrutiny from the media, he abruptly withdrew from the race. But early in October, he re-entered and soon regained much (although never all) of his early support.

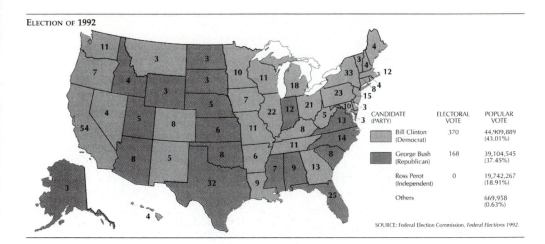

ELECTION OF 1992

CANDIDATE (PARTY)	ELECTORAL VOTE	POPULAR VOTE
Bill Clinton (Democrat)	370	44,909,889 (43.01%)
George Bush (Republican)	168	39,104,545 (37.45%)
Ross Perot (Independent)	0	19,742,267 (18.91%)
Others		669,958 (0.63%)

SOURCE: Federal Election Commission, *Federal Elections 1992*.

After a campaign in which the economy and the president's unpopularity were the principal issues, Clinton won a clear, but hardly overwhelming, victory over Bush and Perot. He received forty-three percent of the vote in the three-way race, to the president's thirty-eight percent and Perot's nineteen percent (the best showing for a third party or independent candidate since Theodore Roosevelt in 1912). Clinton won 370 electoral votes to Bush's 168; Perot won none. Democrats retained control of both houses of Congress.

Launching the Clinton Presidency

Bill Clinton was the first Democratic president since Jimmy Carter, and the first liberal activist to be president since Lyndon Johnson. He entered office carrying the extravagant expectations of liberals who had spent a generation in exile and with a domestic agenda more ambitious than that of any president since Lyndon Johnson. But Clinton also had significant political weaknesses. Having won the votes of well under half the electorate, he enjoyed no powerful mandate. Democratic majorities in Congress were frail, and Democrats in any case had grown unaccustomed to bowing to presidential leadership. The Republican leadership in Congress was highly adversarial and opposed the president with unusual unanimity on many issues.

The new administration compounded its problems with a series of missteps and misfortunes in its first months. The president's effort to end the longtime ban on gay men and women serving in the military met with ferocious resistance from the armed forces themselves and from many conservatives in both parties. He was forced to settle for a pallid compromise. Several of his early appointments—to the Justice Department, in particular—became so controversial he had to withdraw them. A longtime friend of the president from Arkansas serving in the office of the White House counsel committed suicide in

BILL CLINTON.   After a difficult campaign for the
Democratic nomination in which he was almost derailed
more than once in the primaries, Bill Clinton secured the
nomination and went on to defeat incumbent George Bush
in a harshly fought battle for the presidency. A member of
the "baby boom" generation, Clinton brought a youthful
energy to the presidency not seen since John F. Kennedy.
But, he soon learned how difficult advancing a
liberal reform agenda was in the political context
of the late twentieth century.

the summer of 1993. His death helped spark an escalating inquiry into some
banking and real estate ventures involving the president and his wife in the early
1980s; and the clumsy actions of some administration officials raised suspicions
that the White House was attempting to interfere with the investigation into
what became known as the Whitewater affair. A special prosecutor began exam-
ining these issues in 1993, and several congressional committees began hearings
that continued into 1996.

Despite its many problems, the Clinton administration could boast of some
significant achievements in its first year. The president narrowly (by a single vote
in the Senate) won approval of a budget that marked a significant turn away from
the policies of the Reagan-Bush years. It included a substantial tax increase on the
wealthiest Americans, a significant reduction in many areas of government spending, and a major expansion of tax credits to low-income working people, designed
to help lift many struggling families out of poverty. And after a long and difficult
battle against, among others, Ross Perot, the AFL-CIO, and most Democrats in
Congress, he won approval of the North American Free Trade Agreement, which
eliminated most trade barriers among the United States, Canada, and Mexico.

But the administration's substantial achievements were overshadowed by
a large failure. The president's most important and ambitious initiative—the

project that he hoped would define his presidency—was a major reform of the nation's health care system. Early in 1993, he appointed a task force chaired by his wife, Hillary Rodham Clinton, which proposed a sweeping reform designed to guarantee coverage to every American and hold down the costs of medical care. (In the process of heading the task force, Mrs. Clinton emerged as the most powerful First Lady in American history). The Clinton plan relied heavily on existing institutions, most notably private insurance companies; some critics from the left complained that the new system would be too closely tied to an unreliable market. But the most substantial opposition came from those who believed the reform would transfer too much power to the government; and that opposition—combined with the determination of Republican leaders to deny the president any kind of victory on this potent issue—doomed the plan. There was particular opposition to the proposed tax on employers to finance the plan, a tax that small businesses claimed would be too burdensome for them. But there were complaints, too, from doctors, drug companies, insurance companies, and many people who were content with their existing insurance plans and who feared the new system would treat them less favorably. In September 1994, after a series of compromises failed to attract majorities, Congress abandoned the health reform effort.

The foreign policy of the Clinton administration was at first cautious and even tentative—a reflection, perhaps, of the president's relative inexperience in international affairs, but also of the rapidly changing character of the world order. Gradually, however, the president seemed to gain assurance and secured a number of notable achievements. Clinton presided over (although his administration had played only a small role in creating) a historic agreement between Israel and the Palestinian Liberation Organization to end their long struggle over the lands Israel had occupied in 1967. His administration reached an agreement with Ukraine for an elimination of the nuclear weapons that had been positioned there when the republic had been part of the Soviet Union. And the president helped broker an agreement that led to the departure of a brutal military government from Haiti; American troops arrived to help preserve order as the elected president of Haiti returned from exile and established a new civilian regime.

The most troubling international question of the early 1990s emerged in eastern Europe. Yugoslavia, a nation created after World War I out of a group of small Balkan countries formerly part of the Austro-Hungarian empire, dissolved into several new nations in the wake of the collapse of European communism after 1989. Bosnia was among the new nations, and it quickly became embroiled in a bloody civil war between its two major ethnic groups: one Muslim, the other Serbian and Christian. All efforts by the other European nations and the United States to negotiate an end to the struggle failed until 1995, when the American negotiator Richard Holbrooke finally brought the warring parties together and crafted an agreement to partition Bosnia. The United States was among the nations to send peacekeeping troops to Bosnia to police the fragile settlement.

The Republican Resurgence

The trials of the Clinton administration, and the failure of the health care reform in particular, proved enormously damaging to the Democratic party as it faced the congressional elections of 1994. Few doubted that the Republicans would make significant gains that year, but almost everyone was surprised by the dimensions of their victory. Every Republican incumbent won re-election. Democrats lost in droves. For the first time in forty years, Republicans seized control of both houses of Congress.

Several months before the election, Representative Newt Gingrich of Georgia released a set of campaign promises signed by almost all Republican candidates for the House and labeled the "Contract With America." It called for dramatic changes in federal spending to produce a balanced budget, tax reductions, and a host of other promises consistent with the long-time goals of the Republican party's conservative wing. Opinion polls suggested that few voters in 1994 were aware of the "Contract" at the time they voted. But Gingrich and the new Republican congressional leadership nevertheless interpreted the election results as a mandate for their program.

Throughout 1995, the Republican Congress worked at a sometimes feverish pace to construct one of the most ambitious and even radical legislative programs in modern times. They proposed a series of measures to transfer important powers from the federal government to the states (including a proposal to abolish welfare as it had existed since the 1930s and replace it with block grants to state governments). They proposed dramatic reductions in federal spending, including a major restructuring of the once-sacrosanct Medicare program, to reduce costs. They attempted to scale back a wide range of federal regulatory functions. In all these efforts, they could count on an unprecedentedly disciplined Republican majority in the House and an only slightly less united Republican majority in the Senate. The Republican agenda, if successfully enacted, would have represented the most substantial shift in the distribution of public authority in at least fifty years.

President Clinton responded to the 1994 election results by shifting his own agenda conspicuously to the center and calling for his own plan to cut taxes and balance the budget. Indeed, the gap between the Democratic White House and the Republican Congress on most major issues was relatively small. But because the legislative politics of 1995 was becoming part of the presidential politics of 1996, compromise between the president and Congress became very difficult. At one point in November 1995, the federal government literally shut down for nearly a week because the president and Congress could not agree on a budget. There was another shutdown, for the same reason, in January. By the beginning of 1996, public opinion was turning against much of the Republican agenda— and against the man most clearly identified with it. Gingrich was one of the most unpopular political leaders in the nation, while Clinton was slowly improving his standing in the polls.

The 1996 Campaign

The 1996 campaign began with the president unopposed within his own party (the first Democratic incumbent to run for re-nomination unchallenged since Franklin Roosevelt) and holding a substantial lead in public opinion polls against most of his likely Republican opponents. The former chairman of the Joint Chiefs of Staff, Colin Powell, a widely revered man—all the more so, it seemed, because he was an African American— flirted for a time with running for president as a Republican but ultimately decided to stay out of the race. The remaining Republican candidates were far less popular. After some early setbacks that almost destroyed his candidacy, Robert Dole of Kansas, the Senate Majority Leader, emerged to secure his party's nomination. He approached his party's convention trailing the president in most polls by more than 20 points.

In the meantime, the 104th Congress was making its own bid for re-election. In the summer of 1996, after nearly two years of stalemate, it finally produced several significant measures—some through negotiations with the White House, some through an alliance of Democrats and moderate Republicans. They raised the minimum wage for the first time in more than a decade. They passed legislation, jointly sponsored by Senator Edward Kennedy of Massachusetts (a Democrat) and Senator Nancy Kassebaum of Kansas (a Republican), to ensure that laid-off workers could keep their health insurance after leaving their jobs. Most significantly, they passed a dramatic reform of the nation's welfare system that effectively ended the sixty-year federal entitlement, Aid to Families with Dependent Children. Instead, the new law provided for federal "block grants" to the states to use for welfare programs as they thought best; it denied benefits to illegal immigrants; it called for most welfare recipients to lose their benefits after two years; and it established a five-year lifetime maximum for benefits for the majority of the poor. Despite strong opposition from many Democrats, President Clinton agreed to sign the bill, even while expressing reservations about some of its harsher provisions. The flurry of legislation gave Republicans in Congress a list of accomplishments to take home as they campaigned for re-election. But it also permitted the president to take credit for some important legislative achievements.

As the party conventions approached in the summer of 1996, the Dole campaign—having failed to make any headway against the president— announced a bold proposal for a fifteen percent income tax cut. To burnish his previously weak credentials as a tax cutter, Dole chose as his running mate former congressman and cabinet secretary Jack Kemp, a leading advocate of "supply-side economics." Democrats ridiculed the Republican proposal as an election-year gamble that would increase deficits and raise interest rates, while President Clinton proposed a series of much more modest tax cuts, targeted at middle-class families. Republicans insisted their plan would restore dynamic growth to what they claimed was a sluggish economy. But as the last weeks of the campaign began, President Clinton remained comfortably in the lead.

AMERICAN SOCIETY AT THE CLOSE OF THE CENTURY

The widespread popular suspicion of politics and government that characterized American life in the 1980s and 1990s was in part a result of decades of crises and scandals in public life. But it reflected, too, a series of major changes in the character and behavior of the American economy and American society, changes more rapid—and more jarring—than those of any since at least the 1930s. As the United States approached the end of the twentieth century, formidable challenges remained.

The Two-Tiered Economy

Foremost among these changes was the dramatic transformation of the American economy, a transformation that had begun in earnest in the early 1970s and that continued unabated in the mid-1990s. The new economy created dazzling new miracles of technology that transformed the lives of almost everyone. It created enormous new wealth that enriched those talented, or lucky, enough to profit from the areas of growth. And it produced tremendous disparities in income, wealth, and opportunity that contributed to deep and increasingly corrosive divisions in American society.

The jarring changes in America's relationship to the world economy that had begun in the 1970s—the loss of cheap and easy access to raw materials, the penetration of the American market by foreign competitors, the restructuring of American heavy industry so that it produced fewer jobs and paid lower wages—continued and in some respects accelerated through the last decades of the century. Economic growth continued, but at a slower rate than before. In the twenty years after World War II, the gross national product grew, on average, by 3.8 percent a year. In the 1970s, 1980s, and 1990s, the GNP grew by an average of under 2.6 percent. Productivity grew 2.6 percent a year in the 1950s and 1960s; in the 1970s, 1980s, and 1990s, it grew by less than one percent. The national savings rate—the rate at which individuals and institutions saved income, which then became available for investment—peaked at around ten percent between 1948 and 1973. The highest single-year rate after that was 3.2 percent.

For many families and individuals, the results of these contractions were jarring. In the first twenty years after World War II, it was possible for many, perhaps most, Americans to sustain themselves on a single income. In later years, more and more families required two incomes to sustain their standards of living, and even that was often not enough. In the 1950s and 1960s, most Americans could expect to live more comfortably as adults than their parents had; in the 1980s and 1990s, increasing numbers of Americans were finding it impossible even to live as well as the generation before them. From 1973 to 1989, median family income increased under two percent after inflation (from

33,656 dollars a year to 34,213 in constant dollars), even though many families added a second income in those years. Incomes increased somewhat more rapidly in the 1990s, as the economy experienced a period of sustained, if less than robust, growth. But the problem of wage stagnation for most working people remained.

Poverty in America had declined steadily and at times dramatically in the years after World War II, so that by the end of the 1970s the percentage of people living in poverty had dropped to 12.3 percent (from 22.2 percent in 1960). By the early 1980s, the poverty rate was on the rise. It reached fifteen percent in 1993. As always, this increase in poverty affected women, children, and minorities more than any other groups.

The increasingly unequal distribution of wealth and income in the United States accentuated these changes. Between 1968 and 1994, the share of national income going to the wealthiest twenty percent of American households rose from 40.5 percent to 46.9 percent. That represented an average increase in income for this top group of forty-four percent after inflation. The poorest twenty percent of households in the same period saw their postinflation income rise by only seven percent during the same period. The vast majority of the new wealth the American economy created over this nearly thirty-year period went, in other words, to the most affluent fifth of the population. It was little wonder that the economic anxieties of the working and middle classes became one of the central issues in American politics in the late 1980s and 1990s.

The new economy caused a real decline in the standard of living of most working-class Americans and even of many members of the middle class. But it created enormous rewards for others. The most dramatic area of growth in the 1980s and 1990s was in technology, a field in which the United States continued to be highly competitive internationally. Biotechnology—which included pioneering new areas of medical research—was one sector of the economy that produced a bonanza. Even more important were computers, whose impact on American life exploded beginning in the 1980s and showed no signs of slowing as the century neared its close. Many of the greatest fortunes of the late twentieth century went to those men and women who capitalized on the growing market for computers and the services they provided. The wealthiest man in America in the mid-1990s was William Gates, the founder and president of Microsoft—the software company whose operating systems served the vast majority of the world's computers. But Gates was only the most fabulously successful of large numbers of people who earned great wealth through technology and, in the process, created flourishing new areas of the national and international economies.

It became a cliché of public rhetoric that the new economy rewarded education, skills, and knowledge; like many clichés, this one was largely true. Older sectors that relied on heavy machinery, large labor forces, and big corporate organizations did not disappear; in many cases, they restructured themselves and became more profitable—although often at the expense of their workers. But the "knowledge-based economy" was creating a disproportionate amount of wealth and the bulk of the highly paid jobs of the 1990s.

The result was what many began to call a "two-tiered economy"—an increasingly affluent group at the top, constituting a quarter of the population or less; a struggling middle class faced with stagnating incomes and increasing insecurity; and an impoverished bottom, at times approaching a quarter of the population, with decreasing prospects for advancement in a world in which unskilled and semiskilled labor had much less value than in the past.

"Globalization"

Perhaps the most important change, and certainly the one whose impact was the most difficult to gauge, was what became known as the "globalization" of the economy. The great prosperity of the 1950s and 1960s had rested on, among other things, the relative insulation of the United States from the pressures of international competition. As late as 1970, only nine percent of the goods made in America were exported. More importantly, less than a third of the goods produced in America faced competition from abroad for the domestic market. The United States was an important participant in international trade. But in 1970, international trade still played a relatively small role in the American economy as a whole, which thrived on the basis of the huge domestic market in North America.

By the end of the 1970s, the world had intruded into the American economy in profound ways, and that intrusion increased unabated for the next twenty years. Exports rose, both in absolute numbers and as a percentage of goods produced: from just under $43 billion in 1970 to nearly $513 billion in 1994. But imports rose even more dramatically: from just over $40 billion in 1970 to over $663 billion in 1994. As early as 1980, over seventy percent of American products faced foreign competition inside the United States, most notably some of the products whose role in creating and sustaining prosperity was especially important: steel and automobiles. America had made seventy-six percent of the world's automobiles in 1950 and forty-eight percent in 1960. By 1990, that share had dropped to twenty percent; and in 1994, even after a substantial revival of the automobile industry, the American share had risen only to twenty-five percent.

America was the largest exporter in the world in the 1980s and 1990s, and yet it had a huge trade imbalance (meaning it was importing much more than it was exporting). That was a reflection of how many competitors it faced and how deeply they had penetrated the U.S. market. The first American trade imbalance in the postwar era occurred in 1971; only twice since then, in 1973 and 1975, has the balance been favorable.

Globalization brought many benefits for the American consumer: new and more varied products, and lower prices for many of them. Most economists, and most national leaders, welcomed the process and worked to encourage it through lowering trade barriers. The North American Free Trade Agreement (NAFTA), ratified by the U.S. Senate in 1993, and the General Agreement on Trade and Tariffs (GATT), ratified a year later, were the boldest of a long series of treaties to lower trade barriers stretching back to the 1960s.

But globalization was also enormously destabilizing. It was particularly hard on industrial workers, who were affected in two important ways. First, American workers lost industrial jobs as American companies lost market share. As foreign, especially Japanese, competition cut into steel, automobiles, and other heavy industries in the 1970s and beyond, the work forces in those industries declined. Second, American workers lost jobs as American companies began exporting work: building plants in Mexico, Asia, and other lower wage countries to avoid having to pay the high wages workers had won in America. More than half of the production costs of making American cars were spent outside the United States by the 1990s. That was one reason for the rising unpopularity of free trade among many working-class people—an unpopularity effectively exploited by such self-proclaimed "populist" politicians as Ross Perot and Pat Buchanan, the conservative Republican who ran for president for the second time in 1996 and scored a startling victory in the New Hampshire primary that year but faded later on.

But it was not just the loss of market share or jobs to other countries that plagued industrial workers. It was also the downward pressure on wages and benefits that globalization imposed on those who remained employed in American factories. In almost every major industry, there was increasing pressure on workers and their unions to accept lower wage increases (or actual wage cuts); to contribute more to the cost of their health insurance; and to give up other economic benefits they had won earlier in the postwar era. Unions almost everywhere found themselves on the defensive, and union membership continued its fifty-year decline as a percentage of the work force. In 1945, 35.5 percent of the labor force had consisted of union members. By 1980, that figure had declined to 21.9 percent, and by 1994 to 15.5. The American work force grew from 90.6 million in 1980 to 108 million in 1994; the number of union members in the same period declined from just under 20 million to below 17 million. In 1995, Lane Kirkland, the long-time president of the AFL-CIO and a symbol to many of the complacent union leadership of much of the postwar era, resigned under pressure from his membership. His replacement, John Sweeney, was a much more aggressive figure determined to restore a sense of activism and even militancy to the union movement in an effort to help it regain its lost influence.

Globalization was also visible in the increasing presence of non-American investors and corporations within the American economy. Japanese and German automobile companies built new plants in the United States. European and Asian corporations established large presences in America and sometimes bought up major American companies. A group of Japanese investors bought the Columbia motion picture studio in 1989, and foreign companies purchased American corporations as large and visible as RCA, Goodyear, and Pillsbury.

The Graying of America

The new profile of the American population was also having profound effects on the economy and politics. After decades of steady growth, the nation's birth rate began to decline in the 1970s and remained low through the 1980s and early 1990s. In 1970, there were 18.4 births for every 1,000 people in the population. By 1975, the rate had declined to 14.6, the lowest in the twentieth century. And despite a modest increase in the 1980s, the rate remained below sixteen in the mid-1990s. The declining birth rate and a significant rise in life expectancy produced a substantial increase in the proportion of elderly citizens. There were 17 million Americans over sixty-five-years old in 1960 and 33 million in 1994. Over twelve percent of the population was more than sixty-five-years old by 1990, as compared with eight percent in 1970. That figure was projected to rise to over twenty percent by the end of the century as the members of the postwar baby boom began to enter old age. In 1994 the median age was 34 years, as compared with 28 in 1970.

The aging of the population had important political and economic implications. It was a cause of the increasing costliness of Social Security pensions, and of steadily rising payroll taxes to sustain the system. It helped cause dramatic increases in health costs, both for the federal Medicare and Medicaid systems and for private hospitals and insurance companies. One of the reasons for the enormous federal deficits that came to dominate American political life in the late twentieth century was the rapidly rising cost of these pensions and medical programs for the elderly. But the changing demography also ensured that the aged, who already formed one of the most powerful interest groups in America, would remain politically formidable well into the twenty-first century.

The Changing Profile of Immigration

Perhaps the most striking demographic change in America in the 1980s and 1990s, and one of those likely to have the farthest reaching consequences, was the enormous change in both the extent and the character of immigration. Immigration had steadily declined for sixty years until the 1970s, when it began sharply to increase. In the 1970s, more than 4 million legal immigrants entered the United States. In the 1980s and early 1990s, that number rose to more than 6 million. (In 1994 alone, over 800,000 legal immigrants entered the United States.) When the uncounted but very large numbers of illegal immigrants in those years are included, the wave of immigration in the quarter century after 1970 is the largest of the twentieth century. In 1994, 8.7 percent of the American population was foreign born—the largest percentage since 1940 and an eighty percent increase from 1970.

Equally striking was the character of the new immigration. The Immigration Reform Act of 1965 had eliminated quotas based on national origin; from then on, newcomers from regions other than Latin America were generally admitted on a first-come, first-served basis. In 1965, ninety percent of the immigrants to the United States came from Europe. Twenty years later, only ten percent of the new arrivals were Europeans, although that number began to rise slowly in the 1990s after the collapse of the Soviet empire, as increasing numbers of eastern Europeans began to move to America. The three largest groups of foreign-born Americans in 1994 were, in order, Mexicans, Filipinos, and Cubans. The extent and character of the new immigration was causing a dramatic change in the composition of the American population. Already by the early 1990s, people of white European background constituted under eighty percent of the population (as opposed to ninety percent a half century before). Some predicted that by the middle of the twenty-first century, whites of European heritage would constitute less than fifty percent of the population.

Hispanics and Asian Americans

Particularly important to the new immigration were two groups: Hispanics and Asians. Both had been significant segments of the American population for many decades—Hispanics since the very beginning of the nation's history, Asians since the waves of Chinese and Japanese immigration in the nineteenth century. But both groups experienced enormous, indeed unprecedented, growth after 1965.

People from Latin America—from Cuba, El Salvador, the Dominican Republic, and above all Mexico—constituted more than a third of the total number of legal immigrants to the United States in every year after 1965—and a much larger proportion of the total number of illegal immigrants. In California and the Southwest, in particular, they became an increasingly important presence. There were also substantial Hispanic populations in Illinois, New York, and Florida. High birth rates among Hispanic communities already in the United States further increased their numbers. In the 1980 census, six percent of the population was listed as being of Hispanic origin. The 1990 census showed an increase to nine percent—or 20 million people. (Twenty years earlier, the number had been 7 million.) Economic problems and political repression in Mexico and other Latin American and Caribbean nations propelled the new immigrants to move north; but in most of the areas of the United States to which they moved, opportunities were also hard to find. Mexican Americans had an official poverty rate of twenty percent in 1990 (and a real poverty rate that was probably much higher, given the number of illegal immigrants who evaded official statistics). The poverty rate among Puerto Ricans was thirty percent. For illegal immigrants, conditions were particularly dire. Because they were subject to deportation if they came to the attention of the government, they had no legal recourse when they were exploited by employers. Most worked for subsistence wages in menial jobs, constantly fearful of exposure. And both federal and state governments in the 1990s placed increasingly rigid restrictions on the public benefits they (and their children) received and the services they could use.

The growing Hispanic presence became a political issue of increasing importance in the 1980s and 1990s, both to "Anglos" and, of course, to Hispanics themselves. The Immigration Reform and Control (or Simpson-Mazzoli) Act of 1987 reflected the political power of both groups. Its principal goal was to respond to the demands of whites in the Southwest and California by stemming the flow of illegal immigrants (mostly from Mexico). To that end, it placed the burden on employers for the first time to confirm the legal status of their employees. Those who failed to do so faced economic and even criminal penalties. Hispanics charged that the bill would increase discrimination in hiring, and in the first years after its passage there was considerable evidence that such charges were well founded. At the same time, the act responded to the growing political influence of Hispanics by offering amnesty to all undocumented workers who had entered the country before 1982. By the early 1990s, however, it seemed clear that the law was failing. Illegal immigration from Mexico and elsewhere was continuing at near record levels.

White residents of areas in which the Hispanic populations were growing rapidly often reacted with alarm, fearing that they would soon become a minority in what they considered their own cities. Such fears lay behind efforts to bar the use of the Spanish language in public schools and other measures to force Hispanic immigrants to assimilate more quickly and completely.

In the 1980s and early 1990s, Asian immigrants arrived in numbers almost equal to those of Hispanics. Over six million of the foreign born in America in 1994 were from Asian nations (most notably the Philippines, China, Korea, Vietnam, and India). They swelled the already substantial Chinese communities in California and elsewhere. And they created substantial new communities of immigrants from other areas of Asia. By 1990, there were more than 7 million Asian Americans in the United States, more than twice the number of ten years before. Like Hispanics, they were concentrated mainly in large cities and in the West.

Like most new immigrant groups, Asian Americans found adjustment to the very different culture of the United States difficult and disorienting. They also experienced resentment and discrimination. Whites feared Asian competition in economic activities that they had been accustomed to controlling. For example, there were heated disputes between white and Vietnamese shrimpers on the Gulf Coast in Texas, Mississippi, and Louisiana. Some African Americans resented the success of Asian merchants in black neighborhoods (as the black filmmaker Spike Lee noted in his 1989 film *Do the Right Thing*). In New York, racial tensions led to a black boycott of some Korean grocery stores in African American neighborhoods in 1990.

VIETNAMESE REFUGEES. Nearly 500,000 Vietnamese refugees came to the United States after the fall of South Vietnam. Many quickly applied themselves with extraordinary determination to mastering the intricacies of their new country. These two immigrants stand in front of their grocery store in Arlington, Virginia, where they routinely spent thirteen hours a day meeting the needs of shoppers—especially those in the local Vietnamese community.

Resentment of Asian Americans may have been a result, in part, of their remarkable success. Indeed, some Asian groups (most notably Indians, Japanese, and Chinese) were by the 1980s earning larger average annual incomes than whites. Chinese and Japanese Americans consistently ranked at or near the top of high school and college classes in the 1980s. That was in part because Asian-American communities contained significant numbers of people who had been involved in business and the professions before coming to America and had arrived with a high degree of expertise. Many Asian families also placed an unusually high value on education.

African Americans in the Post-Liberal Era

The civil rights movement and the other liberal efforts of the 1960s had two very different effects on African Americans. On the one hand, there were increased opportunities for advancement available to those in a position to profit from them. On the other hand, as the industrial economy declined and government services dwindled, there was a growing sense of helplessness and despair among the large groups of nonwhites who continued to find themselves barred from upward mobility.

For the black middle class, which by the late 1970s constituted nearly a third of the entire black population of America, the progress was at times astonishing. Economic disparities between black and white professionals did not vanish, but they diminished substantially. Black families moved into more affluent urban communities and suburbs—at times as neighbors of whites, often into predominantly black communities. The number of African Americans attending college rose by 350 percent in the decade following the passage of the civil rights acts (in contrast to a 150 percent increase among whites); African Americans made up twelve percent of the college population in 1990 (up from five percent twenty-five years earlier), although by 1994 that figure had declined to just over ten percent. The percentage of black high-school graduates going on to college was by then virtually the same as that of white high-school graduates (although a far smaller proportion of blacks than whites completed high school). And African Americans were making rapid strides in many professions from which, a generation earlier, they had been barred or within which they had been segregated. They were becoming partners in major law firms and joining the staffs of major hospitals and the faculties of major universities. Nearly half of all employed blacks in the United States had white-collar jobs. There were few areas of American life from which blacks were any longer entirely excluded. Middle-class blacks, in other words, had realized great gains from the legislation of the 1960s, from a softening of many of the worst barriers imposed by racial discrimination, and from the creation of affirmative action programs.

But the rise of a black middle class also accentuated the increasingly desperate plight of other African Americans, whom many of the liberal programs of the 1960s had never reached. This growing "underclass" made up about a third of the nation's black population. It felt the impact of the economic troubles of the 1970s and 1980s with special force. As more successful blacks moved out of the inner cities, the poor were left virtually alone in decaying neighborhoods from which most jobs had disappeared. A third of all black families lived in poverty in 1993; at the same time, just over twelve percent of white families could be officially classified as poor. Less than half of young inner-city blacks finished high school; more than sixty percent were unemployed.

Exacerbating the problems imposed by urban poverty were the number of single-parent, female-headed black households in the 1970s and 1980s. In the early 1990s, over sixty percent of all black children were born into single-parent families, as opposed to only fifteen percent of white children (also a substantial increase over earlier eras). In 1960, only twenty percent of black children had lived in single-parent homes. In a society in which women continued to earn significantly lower wages than men, in which gender segregation in the labor market remained widespread, and in which many working mothers needed daycare many of them could not afford, families led by women were often poor families.

Nonwhites faced many disadvantages in the changing social and economic climate of the 1980s. Among them was a growing impatience with affirmative action and other programs designed to advance their fortunes, as symbolized by the Bakke case in 1978 and by a growing reluctance among federal officials after 1980 to move aggressively to enforce affirmative action guidelines. By the mid-1990s, the white assault on affirmative action had gained so much momentum that there was real doubt as to whether very much of it would survive. Nonwhites suffered as well from a steady decline in the number of unskilled jobs in the economy. They suffered from the long, steady deterioration of urban public education and of other social services, which made it more difficult for them to find opportunities for advancement. And they suffered, in some cases, from a sense of futility and despair, born of years of entrapment in poverty.

By the early 1990s, whole generations of nonwhites had grown to maturity living in destitute neighborhoods where welfare, drug dealing, and other crimes were virtually the only means of support for some. Violence was increasingly a part of daily life. While rates of violent crime were declining nationally in the late 1980s and early 1990s, violence (much of it entirely random) was escalating in many inner-city communities—a result of the drug trade, gang wars, and the proliferation of guns.

The anger and despair such conditions were creating among inner-city residents became clear in the summer of 1992 in Los Angeles. The previous year, a bystander had videotaped several Los Angeles police officers beating an apparently helpless black man whom they had captured after an auto chase. Broadcast repeatedly around the country, the tape evoked outrage among whites and blacks alike. But an all-white jury in a suburban community just outside Los Angeles acquitted the officers when they were tried for assault. African-American residents of South Central Los Angeles, one of the poorest communities in the city, erupted in anger—precipitating the largest racial disturbance of the twentieth century. There was widespread looting and arson. More than fifty people died. In the 1960s, urban uprisings had helped produce a major (if ultimately inadequate) government effort to deal with the problems of the inner city. But in the fiscally starved 1990s, the Los Angeles riot produced no such response.

What Americans had long called "race relations," the way in which white and black Americans viewed each other, grew increasingly sour in these difficult years. White impatience with black demands grew, as did a willingness to listen to old and long-discredited arguments about genetic differences between the races. A controversial book by two social scientists, *The Bell Curve*, published in 1994, helped reopen this bitter debate about the innate capacities of members of different races. Many African Americans, for their part, felt an intensified mistrust of the institutions of white society—of the government, the corporations, the universities, and perhaps above all the system of law enforcement.

Nowhere was this mutual suspicion more evident than in the celebrated trial of the former football star O. J. Simpson, who was accused of murdering his former wife and a young man in Los Angeles in 1994. The long and costly "O. J. trial" was an enormous media sensation for over a year; and throughout the proceedings, opinions about Simpson's guilt broke down along strikingly racial lines. A vast majority of whites believed that he was guilty, and a vast majority of blacks believed he was innocent. Simpson's defense focused on the issue of police corruption and succeeded, it appeared, in deflecting attention away from (or casting doubt upon) the defendant's record of domestic violence and the extensive DNA evidence tying him to the crime. Simpson's acquittal in the fall of 1995 caused great celebrations in many African-American communities and a quiet disgust among many whites.

Modern Plagues: Drugs, AIDS, and Homelessness

Poor African Americans and new immigrants found themselves clustered, often trapped, in cities being ravaged not just by economic decline but by two new and deadly epidemics. One was a dramatic increase in drug use, which penetrated nearly every community in the nation. The enormous demand for drugs, and particularly for "crack" cocaine, spawned what was in effect a multibillion dollar industry; and those reaping the enormous profits of the illegal trade fought strenuously and often savagely to protect their positions.

Political figures of both parties spoke heatedly about the need for a "war on drugs"; but in the absence of significant funding for such programs, government efforts appeared to be having little effect. Drug use declined significantly among middle-class people beginning in the late 1980s, but the epidemic showed no signs of abating in the poor urban neighborhoods, where it was doing the most severe damage.

The drug epidemic was directly related to another scourge of the 1980s and 1990s: the epidemic spread of a new and lethal disease first documented in 1981 and soon named AIDS (acquired immune deficiency syndrome). AIDS is the product of the human immunodeficiency virus (HIV), which is transmitted by the exchange of bodily fluids (blood or semen). The virus gradually destroys the body's immune system and makes its victims highly vulnerable to a number of diseases (particularly to various forms of cancer and pneumonia) to which they would otherwise have a natural resistance. Although many of those infected with the virus (i.e., people who are "HIV positive") lived for many years without developing AIDS, once they did become ill they were, until the mid-1990s at least, virtually certain to die—although new treatments for the disease were extending the life expectancy of many of the infected and showing some promise of giving them a relatively normal lifespan. The first American victims of AIDS (and in

The other night Charlie brought home a quart of milk, a loaf of bread and a case of AIDS.

Charlie always felt his bisexual affairs were harmless enough.

But Charlie did catch the AIDS virus. That's why his family's at risk. His wife risks losing her husband, and when she has sex with him, her own life. If she becomes pregnant she can pass the AIDS virus to her baby.

Charlie could have protected himself. Saying "No" could have done it, or using a condom.

Right now there's no vaccine for AIDS, and no cure in sight. With what we know today, and with the precautions that can be taken, no

AIDS
one has to come home with a story like Charlie's.

If you think you can't get it, you're dead wrong.

AIDS EDUCATION.   This poster was prepared by the AIDS Action Committee of Massachusetts to educate the public about transmission and prevention of the disease. Many Americans mistakenly believed only those in the gay community, where the disease first appeared, were vulnerable to the disease. This poster stresses the threat to women and children through heterosexual transmission of the disease.

the early 1990s the group among whom cases remained the most numerous) were homosexual men. But by the late 1980s, as the gay community began to take preventive measures, the most rapid increase in the spread of the disease occurred among heterosexuals, many of them intravenous drug users, who spread the virus by sharing contaminated hypodermic needles. By the mid-1990s, U.S. government agencies were estimating that between 1 and 1.5 million Americans were infected with HIV. (Worldwide, the figure was over 18 million.) Over 400,000 Americans had actually contracted AIDS, and over 280,000 had died by the mid-1990s.

A large research effort produced a wealth of new knowledge about the virus and developed the drugs that were succeeding in delaying or limiting the effects of AIDS. But neither a cure nor a vaccine seemed imminent. Governments and private groups, in the meantime, began promoting AIDS awareness in increasingly visible and graphic ways—urging young people, in particular, to avoid "unsafe sex" through abstinence or the use of latex condoms. The spread of AIDS had a chilling effect on the sexual revolution that had transformed behavior beginning in the 1960s. Fear of infection caused many people to avoid casual sexual relations; but the more puritanical sexual standards against which many Americans had rebelled in the 1960s—and that some conservative Americans hoped to restore—did not return.

The increasing scarcity of housing for low-income people contributed to another urban crisis of the 1980s and 1990s: homelessness. There had always been homeless men and women in most major cities; but their numbers were clearly growing at an alarming rate in the face of rising housing costs, severe cutbacks in federal support for public housing, reduced welfare assistance, deinstitutionalization of the mentally ill, and the declining availability of unskilled jobs. An accurate number of the total homeless population was virtually impossible to determine. Still, the phenomenon of tens of thousands of homeless people at large in the cities put pressure on municipal governments to provide shelter and assistance for the indigent; but in an age of fiscal stringency and greatly reduced federal aid, cities found it difficult to respond adequately to the dimensions of the crisis.

Battles Against Feminism and Abortion

Among the principal goals of the New Right, as it became more powerful and assertive in the 1980s and 1990s, was to challenge feminism and its achievements. Leaders of the New Right had campaigned successfully against the proposed Equal Rights Amendment to the Constitution. And they played a central role in the most divisive issue of the late 1980s and early 1990s: the controversy over abortion rights.

For those who favored allowing women to choose to terminate unwanted pregnancies, the Supreme Court's decision in *Roe* v. *Wade* (1973) had seemed to settle the question. By the 1980s, abortion was the most commonly performed surgical procedure in the country. But at the same time, opposition to abortion was creating a powerful grassroots movement. The right-to-life movement, as it called itself, found its most fervent supporters among Catholics; and indeed, the Catholic church itself lent its institutional authority to the battle against legalized abortion. Religious doctrine also motivated the antiabortion stance of Mormons, fundamentalist Christians, and other groups. The opposition of some other antiabortion activists had less to do with religion than with their commitment to traditional notions of family and gender relations. To them, abortion was a particularly offensive part of a much larger assault by feminists on the role of women as wives and mothers. It was also, many foes contended, a form of murder. Fetuses, they claimed, were human beings who had a "right to life" from the moment of conception.

Although the right-to-life movement was persistent in its demand for a reversal of *Roe* v. *Wade* or, barring that, a constitutional amendment banning the procedure, it also attacked abortion in more limited ways, at its most vulnerable points. In the 1970s, Congress and many state legislatures began barring the use of public funds to pay for abortions, thus making them almost inaccessible for many poor women. The Reagan and Bush administrations imposed further restrictions on federal funding and even on the right of doctors in federally funded clinics to give patients any information on abortion. (President Clinton eliminated many of those restrictions in 1993.) Extremists in the right-to-life movement began picketing, occupying, and at times bombing abortion clinics. One antiabortion activist murdered a doctor in Florida who performed abortions; other physicians were subject to campaigns of terrorism and harassment—part of an effort to force them to abandon serving women who wanted abortions.

The changing composition of the Supreme Court in the 1980s to early 1990s (when five new conservative justices were named by Presidents Reagan and Bush) renewed the right-to-life movement's hopes for a reversal of *Roe* v. *Wade*. In *Webster* v. *Reproductive Health Services* (1989), the Court upheld a Missouri law that forbade any institution receiving state funds from performing abortions, whether or not those funds were used to finance the abortions. But the Court stopped short of overturning the 1973 *Roe* v. *Wade* decision.

Through much of the 1970s and much of the 1980s, defenders of abortion had remained confident that *Roe* v. *Wade* protected women's right to choose abortion and that the antiabortion movement was unlikely to prevail. But the changing judicial climate of the late 1980s and early 1990s mobilized defenders of abortion as never before. They called themselves the "pro-choice" movement, because they were defending not so much abortion itself as every woman's right to choose whether and when to bear a child. It quickly became clear that the pro-choice movement was in many parts of the country at least as strong as, and in some areas much stronger than, the right-to-life movement. With the election of President Clinton in 1992, the immediate threat to *Roe* v. *Wade* seemed to fade. In his first two years in office, Clinton named two pro-choice justices to the Court—Ruth Bader Ginsburg and Stephen Breyer. But the increasing strength of the Republican right, as demonstrated in the 1994 congressional elections, suggested that the issue was far from closed.

At times the pro-choice campaign overshadowed other efforts by feminists to protect and expand the rights of women. But such efforts continued. Women's organizations and many individual women worked strenuously in the 1980s and 1990s to improve access to childcare for poor women, and to win the right to caregiver leaves for parents. They also worked to raise awareness of sexual harassment in the workplace, with considerable success. Colleges, universities, government agencies, even many corporations established strict new standards of behavior for their employees in dealing with members of the opposite sex and created grievance procedures for those who believed they had been harassed.

Both the achievements and the limits of their progress on this issue were evident in the sensational controversy in 1991 over Judge Clarence Thomas, President Bush's nominee for a seat on the Supreme Court. Late in the confirmation proceedings, accusations of sexual harassment from Anita Hill, a law professor and former employee of Thomas, became public. Hill's testimony before the Senate Judiciary Committee dramatically polarized both the Senate and the nation. Feminists and others tended to believe the accusations, based in part upon their own experience in the labor force. They hailed Anita Hill for drawing national attention to the issue of harassment. But many other Americans (and most members of the virtually all-male Senate) apparently did not believe Hill—or at least concluded that the alleged activities should not disqualify Thomas from serving on the Court. Thomas was ultimately confirmed by a narrow margin. But the issue of sexual harassment remained a matter of debate and discussion, one that many American women especially believed deserved far more attention than it had heretofore received.

The Changing Left and the New Environmentalism

The New Left of the 1960s and early 1970s did not disappear after the end of the war in Vietnam, but it faded rapidly. Many of the students who had fought in its battles grew up, left school, and entered conventional careers. Some radical leaders, disillusioned by the unresponsiveness of American society to their demands, resignedly gave up the struggle and chose instead to work "within the system." Radical ideas continued to flourish in some academic circles, but to much of the public they came to appear dated and irrelevant— particularly as, beginning in 1989, Marxist governments collapsed in disrepute around the world.

ANITA HILL.   University of Oklahoma law professor Anita
Hill testifies before the Senate Judiciary Committee in
1991 about what she claimed was Supreme Court nominee
Clarence Thomas's sexual harassment of her when they
both worked at the EEOC (Equal Employment
Opportunities Commission). Thomas vigorously denied
the charges and was later confirmed by the Senate.

Yet a left of sorts did survive, giving evidence in the process of how greatly the nation's political climate had changed. Where 1960s activists had rallied to protest racism, poverty, and war, their counterparts in the 1980s and 1990s more often fought to stop the proliferation of nuclear weapons and power plants, to save the wilderness, to protect endangered species, to limit reckless economic development, and otherwise to protect the environment.

Public concerns about the environment had arisen intermittently since the beginning of the industrial era and had been growing in intensity since 1962, when the publication of Rachel Carson's *Silent Spring* aroused widespread public concern about the effect of insecticides on the natural world. Several highly visible environmental catastrophes in the 1960s and 1970s greatly increased that concern. Among them were a major oil spill off Santa Barbara, California, in 1969; the discovery of large deposits of improperly disposed toxic wastes in a residential community in upstate New York in 1978; and a frightening accident at the nuclear power plant on Three Mile Island, Pennsylvania in 1979. These and other revelations of the extent to which human progress threatened the natural world helped produce a major popular movement.

In the spring of 1970, a nationwide "Earth Day" signaled the beginning of the modern environmental movement. It differed markedly from the "conservation" movements of earlier years. Modern environmentalists shared the concerns of such earlier figures as John Muir and Gifford Pinchot about preserving some areas of the wilderness and carefully managing the exploitation of resources. But the new activists went much further, basing their positions on the developing field of ecology, the study of the interconnections among all components of an environment. Toxic wastes, air and water pollution, the destruction of forests, the extinction of species—these were not separate, isolated problems, the new environmentalists claimed. All elements of the earth's environment were intimately and delicately linked. According to ecologists, damaging any one of those elements risked damaging all the others. Only by adopting a new social ethic, in which economic growth became less important than ecological health, or a new economics, in which environmental costs were factored into economic analyses, could humans hope to preserve a healthy world for themselves and their children.

In the twenty-five years after the first Earth Day, environmental issues gained increasing attention and support. The federal government passed important legislation in the early 1970s requiring measures to clean up the nation's environment, and over time these new requirements contributed to a dramatic improvement in the quality of the air and water in much of the country. The Environmental Protection Agency, a new federal bureau established in 1971, gave the federal government far more authority than it had ever had before to police the environment and force remedies to ecologically dangerous practices—although the vigor with which the EPA pursued its goals varied greatly from one administration to another. Other legislation gave the government the power to protect endangered species and to limit development in other ways—powers that became increasingly controversial in an age of slow economic growth and that helped spawn the powerful antienvironmental movements of the 1980s and 1990s. Environmentalists won significant victories in blocking the construction of roads, airports, and other projects (including American development of the supersonic transport airplane, or SST) that they believed would be ecologically dangerous. And they created wide alarm with their warnings that the release into the atmosphere of certain industrial pollutants (most notably chlorofluorocarbons) was depleting the ozone layer of the earth's atmosphere, which protects the globe from the most dangerous rays of the sun. They warned, too, of the related danger of global warming, a rise in the earth's temperature as a result of emissions from the burning of coal, oil, and other fossil fuels.

The concern for the environment, the opposition to nuclear power, the resistance to economic development—all were reflections of a more fundamental characteristic of the post-Vietnam left. In a sharp break from the nation's long commitment to growth and progress, many dissidents argued that only by limiting growth and curbing traditional forms of progress could society hope to survive. Some of these critics of the "idea of progress" expressed a gloomy resignation, urging a lowering of social expectations and predicting an inevitable deterioration in the quality of life. Other advocates of restraint believed that change did not require decline: human beings could live more comfortably and more happily if they learned to respect the limits imposed on them by their environment. But in either case, such arguments evoked strong opposition from conservatives and others, who ridiculed the no-growth ideology as an expression of defeatism and despair. Ronald Reagan, in particular, made an attack on the idea of "limits" central to his political success.

The rising popularity of environmental issues reflected another important shift both in the character of the American left and in the tone of American public life generally. Through much of the first half of the twentieth century, American politics had been preoccupied with debates over economic power and disparities of wealth. In the late twentieth century, with concentrations of wealth and power reaching unprecedented levels, such debates had largely ceased. There were, of course, economic implications to environmentalism and other no-growth efforts. But what drove such movements was less a concern about power and wealth than a concern about the quality of individual and community life.

The "Culture Wars"

As class-based controversies ceased to shape American public life, cultural battles took their place. Indeed, few issues attracted more attention in the 1990s than the battle over what became known as "multiculturalism." Multiculturalism meant different things to different people, but at its core was an effort to legitimize the cultural pluralism of the rapidly diversifying American population. That meant acknowledging that "American culture," which had long been defined primarily by white males of European descent, also included other traditions: female, African-American, Native American, and increasingly in the late twentieth century, Hispanic and Asian. Although such demands were often controversial, especially when they became the basis of assaults on traditional academic curricula, much greater acrimony emerged out of efforts by some revisionists to portray traditional western culture as inherently racist and imperialistic. A prolonged, if somewhat muted, dispute over how to commemorate the 500th anniversary of Columbus's first voyage to the "New World" illustrated how sharply ideas of multiculturalism had changed the way Americans discussed their past. In 1892, the Columbian anniversary had been the occasion of a boisterous national celebration—and a great world's fair in Chicago. In 1992, it produced agonizing debates over the impact of the European discovery on native peoples; and the only world's fairs were in Italy and Spain.

Debates over multiculturalism and related issues helped produce an increasingly strained climate in academia and in the larger American intellectual world. People on the left complained that the ascendancy of conservative politics placed new and intolerable limits on freedom of expression, as efforts to restrict grants by the National Endowment for the Arts to controversial artists suggested. Many on the right complained equally vigorously of a tyranny of "political correctness," by which feminists, cultural radicals, and others introduced a new form of intolerance to public discourse in the name of defending the rights of women and minorities.

The controversies surrounding multiculturalism and "political correctness" were illustrations of a painful change in the character of American society. Traditional patterns of authority faced challenges from women, minorities, and others. The liberal belief in tolerance and assimilation was fraying in the face of the growing cultural separatism of some ethnic and racial groups. Confidence in the nation's future was declining, and with it confidence in the capacity of American society to provide justice and opportunity to all its citizens.

Facing the New Century

The American people approached the end of the twentieth century filled with anxieties, doubts, and resentments. Faith in the nation's institutions—most notably government—was at its lowest point in many decades. Confidence in the nation's leaders had badly eroded. Economic resentments, which few Americans seemed able to translate into a coherent economic agenda, increased the nation's growing discontent.

And yet the United States in the 1990s, despite its many problems, remained a remarkably successful society—and one that had made dramatic strides in improving the lives of its citizens and dealing with many of its social problems since the end of World War II. The crisis of confidence that darkened the nation's public life in the waning years of the century was not irrational to be sure. There were many reasons for concern, even alarm, about the national condition. But the problems facing the United States as the twentieth century drew to a close were not unprecedented. Many Americans like to believe that the crises of our own time mark a sharp departure from the normal condition of our national life. But in reality, conflict and uncertainty are much more the normal condition of American history than the stability and consensus many critics of our present condition seek to restore. In the twentieth century alone, the United States has experienced two world wars and two agonizing conflicts in Asia. It has struggled through a decade of the worst economic depression in its history. It has survived revolutionary changes in the structure of international relations. It has experienced repeated racial and cultural conflict. It has seen dramatic increases, and then significant declines, in poverty, crime, and disease. It has worked repeatedly to protect the environment from the effects of economic growth. The nation's record in solving such problems has been decidedly mixed, to be sure. But the effort to confront seemingly insuperable obstacles has been a central part of American history.

The American people have never been wholly content about the condition of their nation. But they have also been extraordinarily resilient—and through much of their history they have clung resolutely to the belief that if they tried hard enough, they could, if not perfect, then at least improve their world. Strengthening the nation's waning faith in the possibility of progress—a faith at the heart of most of the many traditions that have shaped American history—is one of the great challenges of our time.

Suggested Readings

16: FIGHTING A GLOBAL WAR

Wartime Military and Diplomatic Experiences. Stephen Ambrose, *The Supreme Commander* (1970); *Eisenhower: Soldier, General of the Army, President-Elect* (1983); *D-Day: June 6, 1944* (1994). Albert Russell Buchanan, *The United States and World War II*, 2 vols. (1962). James MacGregor Burns, *Roosevelt: The Soldier of Freedom* (1970). Winston S. Churchill, *The Second World War*, 6 vols. (1948–1953). Robert Divine, *Second Chance* (1967); *Roosevelt and World War II* (1969). Dwight D. Eisenhower, *Crusade in Europe* (1948). John S. D. Eisenhower, *Allies: Pearl Harbor to D-Day* (1982). Kenneth Greenfield, *American Strategy in World War II* (1963). Max Hastings, *Overlord: D-Day and the Battle for Normandy* (1984). Patrick Heardon, *Roosevelt Confronts Hitler: American Entry into World War II* (1987). Godfrey Hodgson, *The Colonel: The Life and Wars of Henry Stimson, 1867–1950* (1990). Michael Howard, *The Mediterranean Strategy in World War II* (1968). Margaret Hoyle, *A World in Flames* (1970). D. Clayton James, *A Time for Giants: Politics of the American High Command in World War II* (1987). John Keegan, *Six Armies in Normandy: From D-Day to the Liberation of Paris, June 6–August 25, 1944* (1982). Warren Kimball, *The Juggler: Franklin Roosevelt as Wartime Statesman* (1991). E. J. Kind and W. M. Whitehill, *Fleet Admiral King* (1952). Charles B. McDonald, *The Mighty Endeavor* (1969). William Manchester, *American Caesar* (1979). Samuel Eliot Morison, *Strategy and Compromise* (1958); *History of United States Naval Operations in World War II*, 14 vols. (1947–1960); *The Two Ocean War* (1963). Geoffrey Perret, *There's a War to Be Won: The United States Army in World War II* (1991). Forrest Pogue, *George C. Marshall*, 2 vols. (1963–1966). Gordon W. Prange, *At Dawn We Slept: The Untold Story of Pearl Harbor* (1981). Fletcher Pratt, *War for the World* (1951). Cornelius Ryan, *The Longest Day* (1959); *The Last Battle* (1966). Ronald Schaffer, *Wings of Judgment: American Bombing in World War II* (1985). Michael Schaller, *The United States Crusade in China, 1938–1945* (1979). Michael Sherry, *Preparing for the Next War: American Plans for Postwar Defense, 1941–1945* (1977); *The Rise of American Air Power* (1987). Louis Simpson, "A Deadly Welcome", *New York Times Magazine*, 7 May 1995, pp. 75–77. Gaddis Smith, *American Diplomacy During the Second World War* (1964). Ronald H. Spector, *Eagle Against the Sun: The American War with Japan* (1985). James L. Stokesbury, *A Short History of World War II* (1980). Mark A. Stoler, *The Politics of the Second Front: Planning and Diplomacy in Coalition Warfare, 1941–1945* (1977). Studs Terkel, *The Great War* (1984). Christopher Thorne, *Allies of a Kind: The United States, Britain and the War Against Japan, 1941–1945* (1978). John Toland, *The Last Hundred Days* (1966); *The Rising Sun* (1970). Barbara Tuchman, *Stilwell and the American Experience in China* (1971). Russell Weigley, *The American Way of War* (1973); *Eisenhower's Lieutenants: The Campaign of France and Germany, 1944–1945* (1981). Gerhard Weinberg, *A World At Arms: A Global History of World War II* (1994). Chester Wilmot, *The Struggle for Europe* (1952). David S. Wyman, *The Abandonment of the Jews: America and the Holocaust, 1941–1945* (1984).

Atomic Warfare. Gar Alperovitz, *Atomic Diplomacy* (1965). Nuel Davis, *Lawrence and Oppenheimer* (1969). Robert Donovan, *Conflict and Crisis* (1977). Herbert Feis, *The Atomic Bomb and the End of World War II* (1966). Gregg Herken, *The Winning Weapon: The Atomic Bomb in the Cold War* (1980). John Hersey, *Hiroshima* (1946). Robert Jungk, *Brighter Than a Thousand Suns* (1958). Richard Rhodes, *The Making of the Atomic Bomb* (1987). W. S. Schoenberger, *Decision of Destiny* (1969). Martin Sherwin, *A World Destroyed* (1975). Leon V. Sigal, *Fighting to a Finish* (1988).

17: WARTIME SOCIETY AND CULTURE

War and American Society. John Morton Blum, *V Was for Victory* (1976). Lewis A. Erenberg and Susan E. Hirsch, *The War in American Culture: Society and Consciousness during World War II* (1996). Mark J. Harris et al., *The Homefront* (1984). Glen Jeansonne, *Women of the Far Right: The Mothers' Movement and World War II* (1996). Richard R. Lingeman, *Don't You Know There's a War On?* (1970). Gerald D. Nash, *The American West Transformed: The Impact of the Second World War* (1985). Geoffrey Perrett, *Days of Sadness, Years of Triumph: The American People, 1939–1945* (1974). Richard Polenberg, *War and Society* (1972). Studs Terkel, *"The Good War" An Oral History of World War II* (1984).

War Mobilization. Oscar E. Anderson, Jr., *The New World* (1962). Ellsworth Barnard, *Wendell Willkie* (1966). Chester Bowles, *Promises to Keep* (1971). Alan Brinkley, *The End of Reform: New Deal Liberalism in Recession and War* (1995). David Brinkley, *Washington Goes to War* (1987). James MacGregor Burns, *Roosevelt: The Soldier of Freedom* (1970). Bruce Catton, *War Lords of Washington* (1946). Lester V. Chandler, *Inflation in the United States, 1940–1948* (1951). Alan Clive, *State of War: Michigan in World War II* (1979). George Q. Flynn, *The Mess in Washington: Manpower Mobilization in World War II* (1979). Doris Kearns Goodwin, *No Ordinary Time: Franklin and Eleanor Roosevelt: The Home Front in World War II* (1994). Leslie R. Groves, *Now It Can Be Told* (1962). Howell John Harris, *The Right to Manage* (1982). Maurice Isserman, *Which Side Were You On? The American Communist Party During World War II* (1982). Eliot Janeway, *Struggle for Survival* (1951). Paul A. C. Koistinen, *The Military-Industrial*

Complex: A Historical Perspective (1980). Philip Knightley, *The First Casualty* (1975). Nelson Lichtenstein, *Labor's War at Home: The CIO in World War II* (1982). Donald Nelson, *Arsenal of Democracy* (1946). Joel Seidman, *American Labor from Defense to Reconversion* (1953). Bradley F. Smith, *The Shadow Warriors: The OSS and the Origins of the CIA* (1983). Richard Steele, *Propaganda in an Open Society* (1985). Patrick S. Washburn, *A Question of Sedition: The Federal Government's Investigation of the Black Press During World War II* (1986). Michi Weglyn, *Years of Infamy: The Untold Story of America's Concentration Camps* (1976). Alan M. Winkler, *The Politics of Propaganda: The Office of War Information, 1942–1945* (1978).

The War and Race. Beth Bailey and David Farber. *The First Strange Place: The Alchemy of Race and Sex in World War II Hawaii* (1993). Domenic J. Capeci, Jr., *The Harlem Riot of 1943* (1977); *Race Relations in Wartime Detroit* (1987). Richard M. Dalfiume, *Desegregation of the U.S. Armed Forces* (1969). Roger Daniels, *The Politics of Prejudice* (1962); *Concentration Camps, USA: Japanese Americans and World War II* (1971); *Prisoners Without Trial: Japanese Americans in World War II* (1993). John W. Dower, *War Without Mercy: Race and Power in the Pacific War* (1986). Mario T. Garcia, *Mexican-Americans: Leadership, Ideology, and Identity, 1930–1960* (1989). Herbert Garfinkel, *When Negroes March* (1959). Audrie Girdner and Anne Loftis, *The Great Betrayal* (1969). Bill Hosokawa, *Nisei* (1969). Peter Irons, *Justice at War* (1983). Thomas James, *Exiles Within: The Schooling of Japanese-Americans, 1942–1945* (1987). Valerie J. Matsumoto, *Farming the Home Place: A Japanese American Community in California, 1919–1982* (1993). Philip McGuire, ed., *Taps for a Jim Crow Army: Letters from Black Soldiers in World War II* (1982). Mauricio Mazon, *The Zoot-Suit Riots* (1984). August Meier and Elliott Rudwick, *CORE* (1973). Louis Ruchames, *Race, Jobs, and Politics* (1953). Holly Cowan Shulman, *The Voice of America* (1991). Neil Wynn, *The Afro-American and the Second World War* (1976).

Women and the War. Karen Anderson, *Wartime Women: Sex Roles, Family Relations, and the Status of Women During World War II* (1981). D'Ann Campbell, *Women at War with America* (1984). Sherna B. Gluck, *Rosie the Riveter Revisited* (1987). Susan Hartmann, *The Homefront and Beyond: American Women in the 1940s* (1982). Margaret R. Higgonet et al., *Behind the Lines: Gender and the Two World Wars* (1987). Maureen Honey, *Creating Rosie the Riveter: Class, Gender, and Propaganda During World War II* (1984). Ruth Milkman, *Gender at Work: The Dynamics of Job Segregation by Sex During World War II* (1987). Susan M. Reverby, *Ordered to Care: The Dilemma of American Nursing, 1850–1945* (1987). Leila Rupp, *Mobilizing Women for War* (1978).

18: WAGING PEACE

Origins of the Cold War. Gar Alperovitz, *Atomic Diplomacy: Hiroshima and Potsdam*, rev. ed. (1985). Stephen Ambrose, *Rise to Globalism*, 5th ed. (1988). Terry H. Anderson, *The United States, Great Britain, and the Cold War, 1944–1947* (1981). H. W. Brands, *Inside the Cold War: Loy Henderson and the Rise of the American Empire, 1918–1961* (1991). Diane Clemens, *Yalta* (1970). Warren I. Cohen, *The Cambridge History of American Foreign Relations, vol. 4: America in the Age of Soviet Power, 1945–1991* (1991). Herbert Feis, *Churchill, Roosevelt, and Stalin* (1957); *Between War and Peace: The Potsdam Conference* (1960). John Lewis Gaddis, *The United States and the Origins of the Cold War, 1941–1947* (1972); *Strategies of Containment* (1982); *The Long Peace* (1987). Lloyd C. Gardner, *Spheres of Influence: The Great Powers Partition Europe, from Munich to Yalta* (1993). Gregg Herken, *The Winning Weapon: Then Atomic Bomb in the Cold War, 1945–1950* (1980). George C. Herring, Jr., *Aid to Russia* (1973). Timothy P. Ireland, *Creating the Entangling Alliance: The Origins of NATO* (1981). Bruce Kuniholm, *The Origins of the Cold War in the Middle East* (1980). Walter LaFeber, *America, Russia, and the Cold War, 1945–1967*, rev. ed. (1980). Melvyn P. Leffler, *A Preponderance of Power:*

National Security, the Truman Administration, and the Cold War (1992). William McNeill, *America, Britain, and Russia* (1953). Wilson D. Miscamble, *George F. Kennan and the Making of American Foreign Policy, 1947–1950* (1992). W. L. Neumann, *After Victory* (1969). Thomas G. Paterson, *Soviet-American Confrontation* (1974); *On Every Front: The Making of the Cold War* (1979); *Meeting the Communist Threat* (1988). Robert A. Pollard, *Economic Security and the Origins of the Cold War* (1985). Martin Sherwin, *A World Destroyed* (1975). Gaddis Smith, *American Diplomacy During the Second World War* (1965); *Dean Acheson* (1972). John L. Snell, *Illusion and Necessity* (1967). William Taubman, *Stalin's American Policy* (1982). Athan G. Theoharis, *The Yalta Myths* (1970). Adam Ulam, *The Rivals: America and Russia Since World War II* (1971). Bernard Weisberger, *Cold War, Cold Peace* (1984). Lawrence Wittner, *American Intervention in Greece, 1943–1949* (1982). Daniel Yergin, *Shattered Peace* (1977).

Truman's Foreign Policy. Dean Acheson, *Present at the Creation* (1970). Hadley Arkes, *Bureaucracy, the Marshall Plan and National Interest* (1973). Richard J. Barnet, *The Alliance* (1983). Robert M. Blum, *Drawing the Line: The Origin of the American Containment Policy in East Asia* (1982). Russell D. Buhite, *Soviet-American Relations in Asia, 1945–1954* (1982). Warren I. Cohen, *America's Response to China*, rev. ed. (1980). Jeffrey Diefendorf, *American Policy and the Reconstruction of West Germany, 1945–1955* (1993). Robert Donovan, *Conflict and Crisis* (1977); *Tumultuous Years* (1982). John King Fairbank, *The United States and China*, rev. ed. (1971). Lloyd Gardner, *Architects of Illusion* (1970). Fraser J. Harbutt, *The Iron Curtain: Churchill, America, and the Origins of the Cold War* (1986). Michael Hogan, *The Marshall Plan* (1987). Akira Iriye, *The Cold War in Asia* (1974). Laurence Kaplan, *The United States and NATO* (1984). George F. Kennan, *American Diplomacy, 1900–1950* (1952); *Memoirs, 1925–1950* (1967). Joyce Kolko and Gabriel Kolko, *The Limits of Power* (1970). Bruce R. Koniholm, *The Origins of the Cold War in the Middle East* (1980).

William R. Louis, *The British Empire in the Middle East* (1984). Gary May, *China Scapegoat* (1979). David Mayer, *George Kennan and the Dilemmas of U.S. Foreign Policy* (1988). Wilson D. Miscamble, *George F. Kennan and the Making of American Foreign Policy, 1947–1950* (1992). Brenda Gayle Plummer, *Black Americans and U.S. Foreign Affairs, 1935–1960* (1996). Edwin O. Reischauer, *The United States and Japan*, rev. ed. (1965). Lisle Rose, *Roots of Tragedy* (1976). Michael Schaller, *Communists* (1971); *The U.S. Crusade in China* (1979); *The American Occupation of Japan: The Origins of the Cold War in Asia* (1985). Howard Schonberger, *Aftermath of War: Americans and the Remaking of Japan* (1989). Anders Stephanson, *Kennan and the Art of Foreign Policy* (1989). Michael B. Stoff, *Oil, War and American Security* (1980). Christopher Thorne, *Allies of a Kind* (1978). Imanuel Wexler, *The Marshall Plan Revisited* (1983).

19: COLD WAR AMERICA

Truman's Domestic Policies. Stephen K. Bailey, *Congress Makes a Law* (1950). Jack S. Ballard, *The Shock of Peace: Military and Economic Demobilization After World War II* (1983). William C. Berman, *The Politics of Civil Rights in the Truman Administration* (1970). Barton J. Bernstein, ed., *Politics and Policies of the Truman Administration* (1970). Allida M. Black, Richard Dalfiume, *Desegregation of the U.S. Armed Forces* (1969); *Casting Her Own Shadow: Eleanor Roosevelt and the Shaping of Postwar Liberalism* (1996). Richard O. Davies, *Housing Reform During the Truman Administration* (1966). John P. Diggins, *The Proud Decades* (1988). Robert Donovan, *Conflict and Crisis* (1977); *Tumultuous Years* (1982). Andrew J. Dunar, *The Truman Scandals and the Politics of Morality* (1984). Robert H. Ferrell, *Harry S. Truman and the Modern American Presidency* (1983). Eric Goldman, *The Crucial Decade—and After: America, 1945–1960* (1961). Alonzo Hamby, *Beyond the New Deal: Harry S. Truman and American Liberalism* (1973). Susan Hartman, *Truman and the 80th Congress* (1971). Roy Jenkins, *Truman* (1986). R. Alton Lee, *Truman and Taft-Hartley* (1967); *Truman and the Steel Seizure Case* (1977). Arthur F. McClure, *The Truman Administration and the Problems of Postwar Labor* (1969). Donald R. McCoy, *The Presidency of Harry S. Truman* (1984). Donald McCoy and Richard Ruetten, *Quest and Response* (1973). David McCullough, *Truman* (1992). Maeva Marcus, *Truman and the Steel Seizure* (1977). Allen J. Matusow, *Farm Policies and Politics in the Truman Years* (1967). Merle Miller, *Plain Speaking* (1980). Richard L. Miller, *Truman: The Rise to Power* (1986). William O'Neill, *American High* (1986). William E. Pemberton, *Harry S. Truman* (1989). Monte S. Poen, *Harry S. Truman Versus the Medical Lobby* (1979). Gary Reichard, *Politics as Usual: The Age of Truman and Eisenhower* (1988). Christopher L. Tomlins, *The State and the Unions* (1985).

Cold War Politics and Culture. H. W. Brands, *The Devil We Knew: Americans and the Cold War* (1993). John P. Diggins, *The Proud Decades, 1941–1960* (1989). Steven M. Gillon, *Politics and Vision: The ADA and American Liberalism, 1947–1985* (1987). David Goldfield, *Black, White, and Southern: Race Relations and Southern Culture* (1990). Maurice Isserman, *If I Had a Hammer . . . : The Death of the Old Left and the Birth of the New Left* (1987). Norman Markowitz, *The Rise and Fall of the People's Century: Henry A. Wallace and American Liberalism, 1941–1948* (1973). James T. Patterson, *Mr. Republican* (1972). Richard Pells, *The Liberal Mind in a Conservative Age: American Intellectuals in the 1940s and 1950s* (1985). Irwin Ross, *The Loneliest Campaign* (1968). Richard Norton Smith, *Thomas E. Dewey and His Times* (1982). Allan M. Winkler, *Life Under a Cloud: American Anxiety about the Atom* (1993). Allen Yarnell, *Democrats and Progressives* (1974).

The Korean War. Carl Berger, *The Korean Knot* (1957). Ronald Caridi, *The Korean War and American Politics* (1969). Bruce Cumings, *The Origins of the Korean War* (1980); Bruce Cumings, ed., *Child of Conflict: The Korean-American Relationship, 1943–1953* (1983).

Charles W. Dobbs, *The Unwanted Symbol* (1981). Joseph C. Goulden, *Korea: The Untold Story of the War* (1982). John Halliday and Bruce Cumings, *Korea: The Unknown War* (1980). Robert Leckie, *Conflict* (1962). Glenn D. Paige, *The Korean Decision* (1968). Michael Schaller, *Douglas MacArthur* (1989). Robert R. Simmons, *The Strained Alliance* (1975). John Spanier, *The Truman–MacArthur Controversy* (1959). Allen Whiting, *China Crosses the Yalu* (1960). *Countersubversion.* Michael R. Belknap, *Cold War Political Justice: The Smith Act, the Communist Party, and American Civil Liberties* (1977). Eric Bentley, ed., *Thirty Years of Treason* (1971). David Caute, *The Great Fear* (1978). Larry Ceplair and Steven Englund, *The Inquisition in Hollywood* (1983). Richard Freeland, *The Truman Doctrine and the Origins of McCarthyism* (1971). Richard Fried, *Men Against McCarthy* (1976); *Nightmare in Red* (1990). Robert Griffith, *The Politics of Fear* (1970). Robert Griffith and Athan Theoharis, eds., *The Specter: Original Essays on the Cold War and the Origins of McCarthyism* (1974). Alan Harper, *The Politics of Loyalty* (1969). Stanley Kutler, *The American Inquisition* (1982). Harvey Levenstein, *Communism, Anticommunism, and the CIO* (1981). Mary Sperling McAuliffe, *Crisis on the Left* (1978). Victor Navasky, *Naming Names* (1980). William O'Neill, *A Better World* (1983). David M. Oshinsky, *A Conspiracy So Immense: The World of Joe McCarthy* (1983). Richard Gid Powers, *Secrecy and Power: The Life of J. Edgar Hoover* (1987). Ronald Radosh and Joyce Milton, *The Rosenberg File* (1983). Thomas C. Reeves, *The Life and Times of Joe McCarthy* (1982). Michael Paul Rogin, *The Intellectuals and McCarthy* (1967). Richard Rovere, *Senator Joe McCarthy* (1959). Walter and Miriam Schneer, *Invitation to an Inquest*, rev. ed. (1983). Ellen Schrecker, *No Ivory Tower* (1986). Edward Shils, *The Torment of Secrecy* (1956). Joseph Starobin, *American Communism in Crisis* (1972). Athan Theoharis, *Seeds of Repression* (1971); *Spying on Americans* (1978). Athan Theoharis and John Stuart Cox, *The Boss: J. Edgar Hoover and the Great American Inquisition* (1988). Allen Weinstein, *Perjury: The Hiss-Chambers Case* (1978). Stephen J. Whitfield, *The Culture of the Cold War* (1991).

20: THE CULTURE OF POSTWAR PROSPERITY

General Studies. Numan V. Bartley, *The New South, 1945–1980* (1995). John Brooks, *The Great Leap* (1966). William Chafe, *The Unfinished Journey* (1986). Carl Degler, *Affluence and Anxiety* (1968). John P. Diggins, *The Proud Decades* (1989). Eric Goldman, *The Crucial Decade and After* (1960). David Halberstam, *The Fifties* (1993). Godfrey Hodgson, *America in Our Time* (1976). William Leuchtenburg, *A Troubled Feast* (1979). Douglas T. Miller and Marion Novak, *The Fifties* (1977). William O'Neill, *American High* (1986). James T. Patterson, *Grand Expectations: Postwar America, 1945–1974* (1996).

Economy and Labor in Postwar America. David P. Calleo, *The Imperious Economy* (1982). Gilbert C. Fite, *American Farmers* (1981). John K. Galbraith, *The Affluent Society* (1958); *The New Industrial State* (1967). Mark I. Gelfand, *A Nation of Cities* (1975). Robert Heilbroner, *The Limits of American Capitalism* (1965). John Hutchinson, *The Imperfect Union* (1970). C. Wright Mills, *The Power Elite* (1956). Loren J. Okroi, *Galbraith, Harrington, Heilbroner* (1986). Joel Seidman, *American Labor from Defense to Reconversion* (1953). David Stebenne, *Arthur J. Goldberg: New Deal Liberal* (1996). Harold G. Vatter, *The U.S. Economy in the 1950s* (1963).

Culture and Ideas. Daniel Bell, *The End of Ideology* (1960); Daniel Bell, ed., *The Radical Right* (1963). Peter Biskind, *Seeing is Believing: How Hollywood Taught Us to Stop Worrying and Love the Fifties* (1983). Paul Boyer, *By the Bomb's Early Light* (1986). Howard Brick, *Daniel Bell and the Decline of Intellectual Radicalism* (1986). James L. Baughman, *The Republic of Mass Culture: Journalism, Filmmaking, and Broadcasting in America since 1941* (1992). Paul A. Carter, *Another Part of the Fifties* (1983). Ann Charters, *Kerouac* (1973). Bruce Cook, *The Beat Generation* (1971). Thomas Cripps, *Making Movies Black: The Hollywood Message Movie from World War II to the Civil Rights Era* (1993). Tom Engelhardt,

The End of Victory Culture: Cold War America and the Disillusioning of a Generation (1995). Edward J. Epstein, *News from Nowhere* (1973). Herbert Gans, *The Levittowners* (1967). William Graebner, *The Age of Doubt: American Thought and Culture in the 1940s* (1991). David Halberstam, *The Powers That Be* (1979). Jeffrey Hart, *When the Going Was Good: American Life in the Fifties* (1982). Dolores Hayden, *Redesigning the American Dream* (1984). Kenneth T. Jackson, *The Crabgrass Frontier: The Suburbanization of the United States* (1985). Marty Jezer, *The Dark Ages: Life in the U.S. 1945–1960* (1982). Landon Y. Jones, *Great Expectations: America and the Baby Boom Generation* (1980). Neil Jumonville, *Critical Crossings: The New York Intellectuals in Postwar America* (1991). George Lipsitz, *Class and Culture in Cold War America* (1981). Roger W. Lotchin, *Fortress California, 1910–1961: From Warfare to Welfare* (1992). Mary Sperling McAuliffe, *Crisis on the Left* (1978). Walter A. McDougall, *The Heavens and the Earth: A Political History of the Space Age* (1985). Dennis McNally, *Desolate Angel* (1979). Margart Marsh, *Suburban Lives* (1990). Douglas T. Miller and Marion Novak, *The Fifties* (1977). Zane L. Miller, *Suburb: Neighborhood and Community in Forest Park, Ohio, 1935–1976* (1981). C. Wright Mills, *White Collar* (1956). Richard H. Pells, *The Liberal Mind in a Conservative Age: American Intellectuals in the 1940s and 1950s* (1985). David Potter, *People of Plenty* (1954). David Riesman, *The Lonely Crowd* (1950). Leila Rupp and Verta Taylor, *Survival in the Doldrums* (1987). Arthur M. Schlesinger, Jr., *The Vital Center* (1949). Lynn Spigel, *Make Room for TV* (1992). Walter Sullivan, ed., *America's Race for the Moon* (1962). John Tytell, *Naked Angels* (1976). Alan M. Wald, *The New York Intellectuals* (1987). Stephen J. Whitfield, *The Culture of the Cold War* (1991). William Whyte, *The Organization Man* (1956). Tom Wolfe, *The Right Stuff* (1979). Gwendolyn Wright, *Building the American Dream: A Social History of Housing in America* (1981).

Women and Families. William Chafe, *The American Woman: Her Changing Social, Economic, and Political Roles, 1920–1970*, rev. ed. (1988). Ruth Cowan, *More Work for Mothers: The Irony of Household Technology* (1983). Eugenia Kaledin, *Mothers and More: American Women in the 1950s* (1984). Susan Estabrook Kennedy, *If All We Did Was to Weep at Home: A History of White Working-Class Women in America* (1979). Alice Kessler-Harris, *Out to Work: A History of Wage-Earning Women in the United States* (1982). Elaine Tyler May, *Homeward Bound: American Families in the Cold War* (1988). Susan Strasser, *Never Done: A History of American Housework* (1982).

Minorities and the Poor. Rodolfo Acuña, *Occupied America: A History of Chicanos* (1981). Larry W. Burt, *Tribalism in Crisis: Federal Indian Policy, 1953–1961* (1982). Donald Fixico, *Termination and Relocation: Federal Indian Policy, 1945–1970* (1986). J. Wayne Flint, *Dixie's Forgotten People: The South's Poor Whites* (1979). Michael Harrington, *The Other America* (1962). Jacqueline Jones, *The Dispossessed: America's Underclasses from the Civil War to the Present* (1992). Nicholas Lemann, *The Promised Land: The Great Black Migration and How It Changed America* (1991). Elena Padilla, *Up from Puerto Rico* (1958). Linda Reed, *Simple Decency and Common Sense* (1992).

21: THE FIGHT FOR RACIAL JUSTICE

Overviews and Early Days. Taylor Branch, *Parting the Waters* (1988). Thomas Brooks, *The Walls Came Tumbling Down* (1974). William Chafe, *Civilities and Civil Rights* (1980). John Egerton, *Speak Now Against the Day: The Generation Before the Civil Rights Movement in the South* (1994). David Garrow, *Bearing the Cross* (1986). Kevin Gaines, *Uplifting the Race: Black Leadership, Politics, and Culture in the Twentieth Century* (1996). Darlene Clark Hine, *Black Victory* (1979). Richard H. King, *Civil Rights and the Idea of Freedom* (1992). Steven Lawson, *Black Ballots* (1976). Steven Lawson, *Running for Freedom* (1991). Nicholas Lehman, *The Promised Land* (1991).

Anthony Lewis, *Portrait of a Decade: The Second American Revolution* (1964). Douglas McAdam, *Political Process and the Development of Black Insurgency* (1982). Benjamin Muse, *The American Negro Revolution* (1970). Manning Marable, *Race, Reform, and Rebellion* (1984). Robert J. Norrell, *Reaping the Whirlwind: The Civil Rights Movement in Tuskegee* (1985). Howell Raines, *My Soul Is Rested* (1977). Harvard Sitkoff, *The Struggle for Black Equality, 1954–1980* (1981). Patricia Sullivan, *Days of Hope: Race and Democracy in the New Deal Era.* Juan Williams, *Eyes on the Prize* (1988).

School Desegregation. John W. Anderson, *Eisenhower, Brownell, and the Congress* (1964). Numan V. Bartley, *The Rise of Massive Resistance* (1969). Jack Bass, *Unlikely Heroes* (1981). Daniel Berman, *It is So Ordered* (1966). Robert F. Burk, *The Eisenhower Administration and Black Civil Rights* (1984). Clarence Clyde Ferguson, Jr., *Desegregation and the Law.* Jack Greenberg, *Race Relations and American Law* (1959). Elizabeth Huckaby, *Crisis at Central High* (1980). Richard Kluger, *Simple Justice* (1976). Melvin Tumin, *Desegregation* (1957).

Montgomery. Taylor Branch, *Parting the Waters* (1988). Virginia Foster Durr, *Outside the Magic Circle* (1985). David Garrow, *Bearing the Cross* (1986). David Garrow, ed., *The Montgomery Bus Boycott and the Women Who Started It: A Memoir of Jo Ann Gibson Robinson* (1987). Martin Luther King, Jr., *Stride Toward Freedom* (1958). David Lewis, *King: A Critical Biography* (1970). Aldon Morris, *The Origins of the Civil Rights Movement* (1984). Stephen B. Oates, *Let the Trumpet Sound* (1982). Earl and Miriam Selby, *Odyssey: Journey Though Black America* (1971).

22: EISENHOWER REPUBLICANISM

Politics in the Eisenhower Years. Sherman Adams, *Firsthand Report* (1961). Charles C. Alexander, *Holding the Line* (1975). Stephen Ambrose, *Eisenhower the President* (1984). John W. Anderson, *Eisenhower, Brownell, and the Congress* (1964). Jean Baker, *The Stevensons: A Biography of an American Family* (1996). Brian Balogh, *Chain Reaction: Expert Debate and Public Participation in American Nuclear Commercial Power, 1945–1975* (1991). Piers Brendon, *Ike* (1986). Jeff Broadwater, *Eisenhower and the Anti-Communist Crusade* (1992). Robert F. Burk, *Dwight D. Eisenhower* (1986). Barbara B. Clowse, *Brainpower for the Cold War: The Sputnik Crisis and the National Defense Education Act of 1958* (1981). Dwight D. Eisenhower, *The White House Years*, 2 vols. *(1963–1965)*. Fred Greenstein, *The Hidden-hand Presidency* (1982). Emmet John Hughes, *The Ordeal of Power* (1963). Peter Lyon, *Eisenhower: Portrait of a Hero* (1974). Richard Nixon, *Six Crises* (1962). Herbert S. Parmet, *Eisenhower and the American Crusades* (1972). Nicol C. Rae, *The Decline and Fall of the Liberal Republicans* (1989). Gary Reichard, *The Reaffirmation of Republicanism* (1975); *Politics as Usual* (1988). David W. Reinhard, *The Republican Right Since 1945* (1983). Elmo Richardson, *The Presidency of Dwight D. Eisenhower* (1979). Mark H. Rose, *Interstate: Express Highway Politics, 1941–1956* (1979). R. L. Rosholt, *An Administrative History of NASA* (1966).

Foreign Policy. Stephen Ambrose, *Ike's Spies* (1981). David L. Anderson, *Trapped by Success: The Eisenhower Administration and Vietnam, 1953–1961* (1991). Howard Ball, *Justice Downwind: America's Nuclear Testing Program in the 1950s* (1986). Michael Beschloss, *MAYDAY* (1986). Henry W. Brands, *Cold Warriors* (1988); *The Spector of Neutralism: The United States and the Emergence of the Third World, 1947–1960* (1989). Blanche W. Cooke, *The Declassified Eisenhower* (1981). Chester Cooper, *Lost Crusade* (1970); *The Lion's Last Roar* (1978). Cecil Currey, *Edward Lansdale: The Unquiet American* (1988). Robert A. Divine, *Foreign Policy and U.S. Presidential Elections*, 2 vols. (1974); *Blowing in the Wind: The Nuclear Test Ban Debate, 1954–1960* (1978); *Eisenhower and the Cold War* (1981). William J. Duiker, *U.S. Containment Policy and the Conflict in Indochina* (1992). Frances Fitzgerald, *Fire in* the Lake (1972). Steven Z. Freiberger, *Dawn over Suez: The Rise of American Power in the Middle East, 1953–1957* (1992). Louis Gerson, *John Foster Dulles* (1967). Gregg Herken, *Counsels of War* (1985). George Herring, *America's Longest War* (1979). Richard G. Hewlett and Jack M. Hall, *Atoms for Peace and War, 1953–1961* (1989). Townsend Hoopes, *The Devil and John Foster Dulles* (1973). Richard Immerman, *The CIA in Guatemala* (1982). Burton Kaufman, *The Oil Cartel Case* (1978). Gabriel Kolko, *Confronting the Third World* (1988). Walter LaFeber, *Inevitable Revolutions* (1983). John T. McAlister, Jr., *Vietnam: The Origins of Revolution* (1969). Richard A. Melanson and David A. Mayers, eds., *Reevaluating Eisenhower* (1986). Stephen G. Rabe, *Eisenhower and Latin America* (1988). Kermit Roosevelt, *Counter-coup* (1980). Andrew Rotter, *The Path to Vietnam* (1987). Richard Smoke, *National Security and the Nuclear Dilemma* (1988). Hugh Thomas, *Suez* (1967). Mira Wilkins, *The Maturing of Multinational Enterprise* (1974).

Legal and Constitutional Issues. Alexander Bickel, *Politics and the Warren Court* (1965); *The Supreme Court and the Idea of Progress* (1970). Phillip Kurland, *Politics, the Constitution, and the Warren Court* (1970). Paul Murphy, *The Constitution in Crisis Times* (1972). Bernard Schwartz, *Super Chief: Earl Warren and His Supreme Court* (1983). Philip Stern, *The Oppenheimer Case* (1969). Michael Straight, *Trial by Television* (1954). John Weaver, *Earl Warren* (1967).

23: THE RESURGENCE OF LIBERALISM

General Studies. William Chafe, *The Unfinished Journey: America Since World War II*, rev. ed. (1991). Godfrey Hodgson, *America in Our Time* (1976). Allen J. Matusow, *The Unraveling of America: A History of Liberalism in the 1960s* (1984). Charles R. Morris, *A Time of Passion* (1984). Theodore H. White, *America in Search of Itself* (1982).

Kennedy and Johnson. Vaughn D. Bornet, *The Presidency of Lyndon B. Johnson* (1983). Thomas Brown, *JFK: The History of an Image* (1988). David Burner, *John F. Kennedy and a New Generation* (1988). Robert Caro, *The Years of Lyndon B. Johnson: The Path to Power* (1982); *Means of Ascent* (1990). Paul K. Conkin, *Big Daddy from the Pedernales* (1986). Robert Dallek, *Lone Star Rising: Lyndon Johnson and His Times, 1908–1960* (1991). Robert A. Divine, *The Johnson Years* (1987). Ronnie Dugger, *The Politician* (1982). Edward J. Epstein, *Inquest* (1966); *Legend* (1978). Henry Fairlie, *The Kennedy Promise: The Politics of Expectation* (1973). Richard Reeves, *President Kennedy: Profile of Power* (1993). Eric Goldman, *The Tragedy of Lyndon Johnson* (1968). Richard N. Goodwin, *Remembering America* (1988). Jim Heath, *Decade of Disillusionment* (1975). Henry Hurt, *Reasonable Doubt* (1985). Lyndon B. Johnson, *Vantage Point* (1971). Doris Kearns, *Lyndon Johnson and the American Dream* (1976). Donald Lord, *John F. Kennedy: The Politics of Confrontation and Conciliation* (1977). William Manchester, *The Death of a President* (1967). Bruce Miroff, *Pragmatic Illusions: The Presidential Politics of JFK* (1976). Lewis Paper, *The Promise and the Performance* (1975). Herbert Parmet, *Jack* (1980); *JFK* (1983). George Reedy, *The Twilight of the Presidency* (1970). Richard Reeves, *President Kennedy* (1992). Thomas Reeves, *A Question of Character: The Life of John F. Kennedy in Image and Reality* (1991). Arthur M. Schlesinger, Jr., *A Thousand Days* (1965). Theodore Sorensen, *Kennedy* (1965). Anthony Summers, *Conspiracy* (1980). Warren Commission, *The Report of the Warren Commission* (1964). Theodore H. White, *The Making of the President, 1960* (1961). Garry Wills, *The Kennedy Imprisonment* (1982).

Domestic Policies and Politics. Henry J. Aaron, *Politics and the Professors* (1978). William H. Chafe, *Never Stop Running: Allard Lowenstein and the Struggle to Save American Liberalism* (1993). Greg J. Duncan, *Years of Poverty, Years of Plenty* (1984). Mark Gelfand, *A Nation of Cities* (1975). James Giglio, *The Presidency of John F. Kennedy*

(1991). Hugh Davis Graham, *Uncertain Trumpet* (1984). Robert H. Haveman, ed., *A Decade of Federal Antipoverty Programs* (1977). Jim Heath, *John F. Kennedy and the Business Community* (1969). Daniel Knapp and Kenneth Polk, *Scouting the War on Poverty* (1971). Sar Levitan, *The Great Society's Poor Law* (1969). Sar Levitan and Robert Taggart, *The Promise of Greatness* (1976). Allen J. Matusow, *The Unraveling of America: A History of Liberalism in the 1960s* (1984). Charles Morris, *A Time of Passion* (1984). Charles Murray, *Losing Ground* (1984). Victor Navasky, *Kennedy Justice* (1971). James T. Patterson, *America's Struggle Against Poverty, 1900–1980* (1981). Frances Fox Piven and Richard Cloward, *Regulating the Poor* (1971). John E. Schwarz, *America's Hidden Success* (1983). James L. Sundquist, *Politics and Policy: The Eisenhower, Kennedy, and Johnson Years* (1968). Tom Wicker, *JFK and LBJ* (1968).

Race Relations and Civil Rights. Taylor Branch, *Parting the Waters: America in the King Years* (1988). Carl Brauer, *John F. Kennedy and the Second Reconstruction* (1977). Paul Burstein, *Discrimination, Jobs, and Politics* (1985). James Button, *Black Violence: Political Impact of the 1960s Race Riots* (1978). Stokely Carmichael and Charles Hamilton, *Black Power* (1967). Clayborne Carson, *In Struggle: SNCC and the Black Awakening of the 1960s* (1981). William Chafe, *Civilities and Civil Rights: Greensboro, North Carolina, and the Black Struggle for Freedom* (1980). Joe R. Feagin and Harlan Hahn, *Ghetto Revolts* (1973). Robert Fogelson, *Violence as Protest* (1971). David Garrow, *Protest at Selma* (1978); *The FBI and Martin Luther King* (1981); *Bearing the Cross* (1986). Hugh Davis Graham, *The Civil Rights Era* (1990). Alex Haley, *The Autobiography of Malcolm X* (1966). Martin Luther King, Jr., *Why We Can't Wait* (1964). Steven Lawson, *Black Ballots: Voting Rights in the South, 1966–1969* (1976). Nicholas Lemann, *The Promised Land: The Great Black Migration and How It Changed America* (1991). David L. Lewis, *King: A Critical Biography* (1970). Doug McAdam, *Freedom Summer* (1988). Benjamin Muse, *The American Negro Revolution* (1969). United States Kerner Commission, *Report of the National Advisory Commission on Civil Disorders* (1968). Stephen Oates, *Let the Trumpet Sound* (1982). Harvard Sitkoff, *The Struggle for Black Equality, 1954–1992* (1992). James R. Ralph Jr., *Northern Protest: Martin Luther King Jr., Chicago, and the Civil Rights Movement* (1993). Mark Stern, *Calculating Visions: Kennedy, Johnson, and Civil Rights* (1992). Abigail Thernstrom, *Whose Votes Count? Affirmative Action and Minority Voting Rights* (1987). Robert Weisbrot, *Freedom Bound: A History of America's Civil Rights Movement* (1990). Nancy J. Weiss, *Whitney M. Young, Jr., and the Struggle for Civil Rights* (1989). Roy Wilkins, *Standing Fast* (1982). Harris Wofford, *Of Kennedy and Kings* (1980). Eugene Wolfenstein, *The Victims of Democracy: Malcolm X and the Black Revolution* (1981). Howard Zinn, *SNCC: The New Abolitionists* (1981).

24: FROM FLEXIBLE RESPONSE TO VIETNAM

Foreign Policy. Elie Abel, *The Missile Crisis* (1966). Graham Allison, *Essence of Decision* (1971). Richard Barnet, *Intervention and Revolution* (1968). Michael Bechloss, *The Crisis Years* (1990). McGeorge Bundy, *Danger and Survival* (1989). Warren Cohen, *Dean Rusk* (1980). Herbert Dinerstein, *The Making of a Missile Crisis* (1976). Bernard Firestone, *The Quest for Nuclear Stability* (1982). Louise Fitzsimmons, *The Kennedy Doctrine* (1972). Philip Geyelin, *Lyndon B. Johnson and the World* (1966). John Girling, *America and the Third World* (1980). Trumball Higgins, *The Perfect Failure: Kennedy, Eisenhower, and the CIA at the Bay of Pigs* (1987). Roger Hilsman, *To Move a Nation* (1965). Haynes Johnson, *The Bay of Pigs* (1964). Robert Kennedy, *Thirteen Days* (1969). Dan Kurzman, *Santo Domingo* (1966). Walter LaFeber, *Inevitable Revolutions: The United States in Central America* (1985). Thomas J. McCormick, *America's Half Century: United States Foreign Policy in the Cold War* (1989). Richard D. Mahoney, *JFK: Ordeal in Africa* (1983). Gerald T.

Rice, *The Bold Experiment: JFK's Peace Corps* (1985). Jerome Slater, *Intervention and Negotiation* (1970). Richard Walton, *Cold War and Counterrevolutions* (1972). Peter Wyden, *Bay of Pigs* (1969).

Vietnam. Mark Baker, Christian G. Appy, *Nam* (1982); *Working-Class War: American Combat Soldiers and Vietnam* (1993). Lawrence Baskir and William Strauss, *Chance and Circumstance* (1978). Larry Berman, *Planning a Tragedy* (1982); *Lyndon Johnson's War* (1989). Peter Braestrup, *Big Story* (1977; abridged ed. 1978). William Broyles, Jr., *Brothers in Arms: A Journey from War to Peace* (1986). Philip Davidson, *Vietnam at War* (1991). Gloria Emerson, *Winners and Losers* (1976). Frances Fitzgerald, *Fire in the Lake* (1972). John Galloway, *The Gulf of Tonkin Resolution* (1970). Leslie Gelb and Richard Betts, *The Irony of Vietnam: The System Worked* (1979). David Halberstam, *The Best and the Brightest* (1972). Michael Herr, *Dispatches* (1977). George C. Herring, *America's Longest War*, rev. ed. (1986). George McT. Kahin, *Intervention* (1986). Stanley Karnow, *Vietnam* (1983). Alexander Kendrick, *The Wound Within* (1974). Gabriel Kolko, *The Anatomy of a War* (1985). Robert W. Komer, *Bureaucracy at War* (1986). David Levy, *The Debate over Vietnam* (1991). Guenter Lewy, *America in Vietnam* (1978). Don Oberdorfer, *Tet* (1971). Bruce C. Palmer, Jr., *The 25-Year War* (1984). *The Pentagon Papers*, Senator Gravel edition (1975). Norman Podhoretz, *Why We Were in Vietnam* (1982). Thomas Powers, *Vietnam: The War at Home* (1973). Al Santoli, *Everything We Had* (1981). Herbert Schandler, *The Unmaking of a President: Lyndon Johnson and Vietnam* (1977). Neil Sheehan, *A Bright Shining Lie* (1988). R. B. Smith, *An International History of the Vietnam War: The Kennedy Strategy* (1985). Ronald Spector, *Advice and Support* (1983). Col. Harry Summers, *On Strategy* (1981). Wallace Terry, *Bloods* (1984). Thomas C. Thayer, *War Without Fronts* (1985). Wallace J. Thies, *When Governments Collide* (1980). James Thompson, *Rolling Thunder* (1980). Kathleen J. Turner, *Lyndon Johnson's Dual War: Vietnam and the Press* (1981). Irwin Unger, *The Movement* (1974). Marilyn Young, *The Vietnam Wars* (1991).

25: CULTURAL REVOLUTIONS

General Studies. John Morton Blum, *Years of Discord: American Politics and Society, 1961–1974* (1991). Peter N. Carroll, *It Seemed Like Nothing Happened* (1982). Allen J. Matusow, *The Unraveling of America* (1984). Kim McQuaid, *The Anxious Years* (1989). William O'Neill, *Coming Apart* (1971).

1968. Dan T. Carter, *The Politics of Rage: George Wallace, The Origins of the New Conservatism, and the Transformation of American Politics* (1995). David Caute, *The Year of the Barricades* (1988). Lewis Chester, Godfrey Hodgson, and Lewis Page, *American Melodrama* (1969). David Farber, *Chicago 68* (1988). Marshall Frady, *Wallace*, rev. ed. (1976). Godfrey Hodgson, *America in Our Time* (1976). Charles Kaiser, *1968 in America* (1988). Norman Mailer, *Miami and the Siege of Chicago* (1968). Arthur M. Schlesinger, Jr., *Robert Kennedy and His Times* (1978). Ben Stavis, *We Were the Campaign* (1969). Theodore White, *The Making of the President, 1968* (1969).

The New Left and the Counterculture. Edward Bacciocco, Jr., *The New Left in America* (1974). Ronald Berman, *America in the Sixties* (1968). Wini Breines, *Community and Organization in the New Left* (1983). Peter Clecak, *Radical Paradoxes* (1973). Peter Collier and David Horowitz, *Destructive Generation: Second Thoughts About the Sixties* (1989). Margaret Cruikshank, *The Gay and Lesbian Liberation Movement in America* (1992). Morris Dickstein, *Gates of Eden* (1977). Joan Didion, *Slouching Towards Bethlehem* (1967); *The White Album* (1979). John Diggins, *The American Left in the Twentieth Century* (1973). Sara Evans, *Personal Politics* (1979). Lewis Feuer, *The Conflict of Generations* (1969). Richard Flacks, *Youth and Social Change* (1971). Todd Gitlin, *The Whole World Is Watching* (1981); *The Sixties:*

Years of Hope, Days of Rage (1987). Paul Goodman, *Growing Up Absurd* (1960). David Harris, *Dreams Die Hard* (1983). Maurice Isserman, *"If I Had a Hammer . . .": The Death of the Old Left and the Birth of the New Left* (1987). Joseph Kelner and James Munves, *The Kent State Coverup* (1980). Kenneth Keniston, *Young Radicals* (1968); *Youth and Dissent* (1971). Richard King, *The Party of Eros* (1972). James Kunen, *The Strawberry Statement* (1968). Lawrence Lader, *Power on the Left* (1979). Klaus Mehnert, *Twilight of the Young* (1978). James Miller, *"Democracy in the Streets": From Port Huron to the Siege of Chicago* (1987). Charles Reich, *The Greening of America* (1970). W. J. Rorabaugh, *Berkeley at War* (1989). Theodore Roszak, *The Making of a Counter Culture* (1969). Kirkpatrick Sale, *SDS* (1973). Irwin Unger, *The Movement* (1974). Milton Viorst, *Fire in the Streets* (1979). Jon Wiener, *Come Together: John Lennon and His Time* (1984).

Indians, Hispanics, Asians. Rodolfo Acuña, *Occupied America*, 2nd ed. (1981). Larry W. Burt, *Tribalism in Crisis: Federal Indian Policy, 1953–1961* (1982). Vine Deloria, Jr., *Custer Died for Your Sins* (1969); *Behind the Trail of Broken Treaties* (1974). Ronald Dewing, *Wounded Knee: The Meaning and Significance of the Second Incident* (1985). Douglas E. Foley, *From Peones to Politicos: Class and Ethnicity in a South Texas Town, 1900–1987* (1988). Peter Iverson, *The Navajo Nation* (1981). Oscar Lewis, *La Vida* (1969). D'Arcy McNickle, *Native American Tribalism* (1973). Matt Meier and Feliciano Rivera, *The Chicanos* (1972). David M. Reimers, *Still the Golden Door: The Third World Comes to America* (1985). Julian Samora, *Los Mojados* (1971). Stan Steiner, *The New Indians* (1968). Ronald Takaki, *Strangers from a Distant Shore: A History of Asian Americans* (1989); *A Different Mirror: A History of Multicultural America* (1993). Ronald Taylor, *Chavez and the Farm Workers* (1975). Wilcomb Washburn, *Red Man's Land/White Man's Law* (1971). Charles F. Wilkinson, *American Indians, Time, and the Law* (1987).

Feminism. William Chafe, *The American Woman* (1972). Nancy Cott, *The Grounding of Modern Feminism* (1987). Marian Faux, *Roe v. Wade* (1988). Jo Freeman, *The Politics of Women's Liberation* (1975). Betty Friedan, *The Feminine Mystique* (1963). Carol Gilligan, *In A Different Voice* (1982). Cynthia Harrison, *On Account of Sex: The Politics of Women's Issues, 1945–1968* (1988). Susan M. Hartmann, *From Margin to Mainstream: Women and American Politics Since 1960* (1989). Alice Kessler-Harris, *Out to Work: A History of Wage-Earning Women in the United States* (1982). Ethel Klein, *Gender Politics* (1984). Kristin Luker, *Abortion and the Politics of Motherhood* (1984). Robin Morgan, ed., *Sisterhood Is Powerful* (1970). Rosalind Petchesky, *Abortion and Women's Choice* (1984). Sheila Rothman, *Woman's Proper Place* (1978). Winifred Wandersee, *On the Move: American Women in the 1970s* (1988). Gayle Yates, *What Women Want* (1975).

26: THE IMPERIAL PRESIDENCY

Nixon and the World. Seyom Brown, *The Crisis of Power* (1979). Lloyd Gardner, *The Great Nixon Turnaround* (1973); *A Covenant with Power* (1984). Seymour Hersh, *The Price of Power* (1983). Roger Hilsman, *The Crouching Future* (1975). Arnold Isaacs, *Without Honor: Defeat in Vietnam and Cambodia* (1983). Walter Isaacson, *Kissinger* (1992). Marvin Kalb and Bernard Kalb, *Kissinger* (1974). Henry A. Kissinger, *White House Years* (1979); *Years of Upheaval* (1982); *Diplomacy* (1994). David Landau, *Kissinger: The Uses of Power* (1972). Robert S. Litwak, *Detente and the Nixon Doctrine: American Foreign Policy and the Pursuit of Stability* (1984). Timothy Lomperis, *The War Nobody Lost—and Won* (1984). Roger Morris, *Uncertain Greatness* (1977). Harland Moulton, *From Superiority to Parity* (1973). John Newhouse, *Cold Dawn* (1973). Michael Oksenberg and Robert Oxnam, eds., *Dragon and Eagle* (1978). Gareth Porter, *A Peace Denied* (1975); *Vietnam* (1979). Thomas Powers, *The Man Who Kept* the Secrets (1979). William Quandt, Decade of Decision (1977). Franz Schurman, The Foreign Policies of Richard Nixon (1987). William Shawcross, Sideshow: Nixon, Kissinger, and the Destruction of Cambodia (1978). Richard Stevenson, The Rise and Fall of Detente (1985). John Stockwell, In Search of Enemies (1977). Robert Stookey, America and the Arab States (1975). Robert D. Schulzinger, Henry Kissinger: Doctor of Diplomacy (1989). Tad Szulc, The Illusion of Peace (1978).

Nixon and His Presidency. Stephen Ambrose, Nixon: The Triumph of a Politician, 1962–1972 (1989). Richard Barnet, The Lean Years (1980). Fawn Brodie, Richard Nixon: The Shaping of His Character (1981). Vincent Burke and Vee Burke, Nixon's Good Deed (1974). John Ehrlichman, Witness to Power (1982). John R. Greene, The Limits of Power: The Nixon and Ford Administrations (1992). H. R. Haldeman, The Haldeman Diaries: Inside the Nixon White House (1994). Joan Hoff, Nixon Reconsidered (1994). J. C. Hurewitz, ed., Oil, the Arab-Israeli Dispute, and the Industrial World (1976). R. L. Miller, The New Economics of Richard Nixon (1972). Daniel P. Moynihan, The Politics of a Guaranteed Income (1973). R. P. Nathan et al., Monitoring Revenue Sharing (1975). Richard Nixon, RN: The Memoirs of Richard Nixon (1978). Herbert Parmet, Richard Nixon and His America (1989). Raymond Price, With Nixon (1977). James Reichley, Conservatives in an Age of Change: The Nixon and Ford Administrations (1981). William Safire, Before the Fall (1975). Joan Edelman Spero, The Politics of International Economic Relations (1977). Michael Tanzer, The Energy Crisis (1974). Theodore H. White, The Making of the President, 1972 (1973). Bob Woodward and Scott Armstrong, The Brethren (1980).

Nixon and Watergate. Fawn Brodie, Richard Nixon: The Shaping of His Character (1981). Richard Cohen and Jules Witcover, A Heartbeat Away (1974). Len Colodny and Robert Gettlin, Silent Coup (1991). John Dean, Blind Ambition (1976). James Doyle, Not Above the Law (1977). Fred Emery, Wa-

tergate: The Corruption of American Politics (1994). Stanley J. Kutler, The Wars of Watergate (1990). J. Anthony Lukas, Nightmare: The Underside of the Nixon Years (1976). Bruce Mazlish, In Search of Nixon (1972). Richard M. Nixon, RN: The Memoirs of Richard Nixon (1978). Jonathan Schell, The Time of Illusion (1975). Arthur M. Schlesinger, Jr., The Imperial Presidency (1973). Michael Schudson, Watergate in American Memory: How We Remember, Forget, and Reconstruct the Past (1992). William Sirica, To Set the Record Straight (1979). Maurice Stans, The Terrors of Justice (1984). Theodore H. White, Breach of Faith (1975). Garry Wills, Nixon Agonistes (1970). Bob Woodward and Carl Bernstein, All the President's Men (1974); The Final Days (1976).

27: THE RISE OF AMERICAN CONSERVATISM

The Ford Presidency. James M. Cannon, Time and Chance: Gerald Ford's Appointment with History (1994). Gerald Ford, A Time to Heal (1979). John R. Greene, The Limits of Power: The Nixon and Ford Administrations (1992). Robert T. Hartmann, Palace Politics (1990). Gerald Ter Horst, Gerald Ford (1975). Richard Reeves, A Ford Not a Lincoln (1976). A. James Reichley, Conservatives in an Age of Change: The Nixon and Ford Administrations (1981). Edward and Frederick Schapsmeier, Gerald R. Ford's Date with Destiny: A Political Biography (1989). James L. Sundquist, The Decline and Resurgence of Congress (1981).

The Carter Presidency. Jack Bass and Walter Devries, The Transformation of Southern Politics (1976). James Bill, The Eagle and the Lion (1988). Zbigniew Brzezinski, Power and Principle (1983). Jimmy Carter, Why Not the Best? (1975); Keeping Faith (1982). Rosalynn Carter, First Lady from Plains (1984). Steven Gillon, The Democrats' Dilemma: Walter Mondale and the Liberal Legacy (1992). Betty Glad, Jimmy Carter (1980). Erwin Hargrove, Jimmy Carter as President (1989).

Steven B. Hunt, *The Energy Crisis* (1978). Haynes Johnson, *In the Absence of Power* (1980). Charles O. Jones, *The Trusteeship Presidency* (1988). Hamilton Jordon, *Crisis* (1982). Walter LaFeber, *Panama Canal* (1978). Clark Mollenhoff, *The President Who Failed* (1980). A. Glenn Mower, Jr., *Human Rights and American Foreign Policy* (1987). William B. Quandt, *Decade of Decisions* (1977); *Camp David* (1986). Barry Rubin, *Paved with Good Intentions* (1983). Lars Schoultz, *Human Rights and U.S. Policy Toward Latin America* (1981). Gaddis Smith, *Morality, Reason, and Power* (1986). Strobe Talbott, *Endgame* (1979). Jules Witcover, *Marathon* (1977). James Wooten, *Dasher* (1978). Cyrus Vance, *Hard Choices* (1983).

The New Right. Sidney Blumenthal, *The Rise of the Counter-Establishment* (1986). George Nash, *The Conservative Intellectual Movement in America Since 1945* (1979). Burton Yale Pines, *Back to Basics* (1982). David W. Reinhard, *The Republican Right Since 1945* (1983). Kirkpatrick Sale, *Power Shift: The Rise of the Southern Rim and Its Challenge to the Eastern Establishment* (1975). Peter Steinfels, *The Neo-Conservatives* (1979). John K. White, *The New Politics of Old Values* (1988). Clyde Wilcox, *God's Warriors: The Christian Right in Twentieth Century America* (1992). John Woodridge, *The Evangelicals* (1975).

The Reagan Presidency. Frank Ackerman, *Reaganomics* (1982). Laurence I. Barrett, *Gambling with History* (1984). Bill Boyarsky, *The Rise of Ronald Reagan* (1968). Paul Boyer, ed., *Reagan as President: Contemporary Views of the Man, His Politics, and His Policies* (1990). William J. Broad, *Teller's War: The Top-Secret Story Behind the Star Wars Deception* (1992). Lou Cannon, *Reagan* (1982); *President Reagan: The Role of a Lifetime* (1990). Joan Claybrook, *Retreat from Safety: Reagan's Attack on American Health* (1984). Robert Dallek, *Ronald Reagan: The Politics of Symbolism* (1984). Ronnie Dugger, *On Reagan* (1983). Thomas Byrne Edsall, *The New Politics of Inequality* (1984). Anne Edwards, *Early Reagan* (1987). Rowland Evans and Robert Novak, *The Reagan Revolution* (1981). Benjamin Friedman, *Day of Reckoning: The Consequences of American Economic Policy Under Reagan and After* (1988). Jack Germond and Jules Witcover, *Blue Smoke and Mirrors: How Reagan Won and Why Carter Lost the Election of 1980* (1981); *Wake Us When It's Over: Presidential Politics of 1984* (1985). George Gildner, *Wealth and Poverty* (1981). Fred I. Greenstein, ed., *The Reagan Presidency* (1983). William Greider, *The Education of David Stockman and Other Americans* (1982). Haynes Johnson, *Sleepwalking Through History: America in the Reagan Years* (1991). Jonathan Lash, *A Season of Spoils: The Story of the Reagan Administration's Attack on the Environment* (1984). Robert Lekachman, *Greed Is Not Enough: Reaganomics* (1982). Jane Mayer and Doyle McManus, *Landslide: The Unmaking of the President, 1984–1988* (1988). Charles Noble, *Liberalism at Work: The Rise and Fall of OSHA* (1986). Peggy Noonan, *What I Saw at the Revolution: A Political Life in the Reagan Era* (1990). John L. Palmer and Isabel V. Sawhill, eds., *The Reagan Experiment* (1982). Michael J. Piore and Charles F. Sabel, *The Second Industrial Divide* (1984). Frances Fox Piven and Richard A. Cloward, *The New Class War: Reagan's Attack on the Welfare State and Its Consequences* (1982). Nancy Reagan, *My Turn* (1989). Richard Reeves, *The Reagan Detour* (1985). Donald T. Regan, *For the Record* (1988). Michael Rogin, *Ronald Reagan: The Movie* (1987). Michael Schaller, *Reckoning with Reagan: America and Its President in the 1980s* (1992). C. Brant Short, *Ronald Reagan and the Public Lands: America's Conservation Debate, 1979–1984* (1989). Hedrick Smith, *The Power Game* (1988). Hedrick Smith et al. *Reagan: The Man, the President* (1980). David A. Stockman, *The Triumph of Politics* (1986). Sidney Weintraub and Marvin Goodstein, eds., *Reaganomics in the Stagflation Economy* (1983). F. Clifton White and William Gil, *Why Reagan Won* (1982). Theodore H. White, *America in Search of Itself* (1982). Garry Wills, *Reagan's America* (1987).

Reagan and the World. Seweryn Bialer and Michael Mandelbaum, eds., *Gorbachev's Russia and American Foreign Policy* (1988).

Raymond Bonner, *Weakness and Deceit: U.S. Policy and El Salvador* (1984). Tom Buckley, *Violent Neighbors* (1984). Steven Emerson, *Secret Warriors: Inside the Covert Military Operations of the Reagan Era* (1988). Thomas L. Friedman, *From Beirut to Jerusalem* (1989). Alexander Haig, *Caveat: Realism, Reagan and Foreign Policy* (1984). Jane Hunter et al., *The Iran-Contra Connection* (1987). David E. Kyvig, ed., *Reagan and the World* (1990). Walter LaFeber, *Inevitable Revolutions*, rev. ed. (1984). Richard A. Melanson, *Reconstructing Consensus: American Foreign Policy Since the Vietnam War* (1991). John Newhouse, *War and Peace in the Nuclear Age* (1989). Robert O. Pastor, *Condemned to Repetition: The United States and Nicaragua* (1987). Charles D. Smith, *Palestine and the Arab-Israeli Conflict*, 2nd ed. (1992). Strobe Talbott, *Deadly Gambits* (1984); *The Master of the Game: Paul Nitze and the Nuclear Peace* (1988). Daniel Wirls, *Buildup: The Politics of Defense in the Reagan Era* (1992). Bob Woodward, *Veil: The Secret Wars of the CIA* (1987).

28: MODERN TIMES

The Post Cold-War World. Bernard Gwertzman and Michael T. Kaufman, eds., *The Collapse of Communism* (1990). Paul Kennedy, *The Rise and Fall of the Great Powers* (1987). Robert Kuttner, *The End of Laissez Faire: National Purpose and the Global Economy After the Cold War* (1991). John Mueller, *Policy and Opinion in the Gulf War* (1994). Henry R. Nau, *The Myth of America's Decline: Leading the World Economy in the 1990s* (1990). Joseph Nye, *Bound to Lead: The Changing Nature of American Power* (1990) H. Norman Schwarzkopf, *It Doesn't Take a Hero* (1992).

Politics After Reagan. E. J. Dionne, *Why Americans Hate Politics* (1991). Thomas Ferguson and Joel Rogers, *Right Turn* (1986). William Greider, *Who Will Tell the People?* (1992). Robert S. McElvaine, *The End of the Conservative Era: Liberalism After Reagan* (1987). Kevin Phillips, *The Politics of Rich and Poor: Wealth and the American Electorate in the Reagan Aftermath* (1990). Adolph L. Reed, Jr., *The Jesse Jackson Phenomenon* (1986). Bob Woodward, *The Agenda* (1994).

Post-Liberal Culture. Peter N. Carroll, *It Seemed Like Nothing Happened* (1982). Pete Clecak, *America's Quest for the Ideal Self* (1983). Jim Hougan, *Decadence: Radical Nostalgia, Narcissism, and Decline in the Seventies* (1975). Christopher Lasch, *The Culture of Narcissism* (1978). Edwin Schur, *The Awareness Trap* (1976). Daniel Yankelovich, *New Rules: Search for Self-Fulfillment in a World Turned Upside Down* (1981).

Economy and Society. Carl Abbott, *The New Urban America: Growth and Politics in the Sunbelt Cities* (1981). Michael A. Bernstein and David E. Adler, *Understanding American Economic Decline* (1994). Barry Bluestone and Bennett Harrison, *The Deindustrializing of America* (1982). Connie Bruck, *The Predator's Ball: The Junk Bond Raiders and the Man Who Staked Them* (1988). Bryan Burroughs and John Helyar, *Barbarians at the Gate: The Fall of RJR Nabisco* (1990). Elizabeth Fee and Daniel M. Fox, eds., *AIDS: The Burdens of History* (1988); *AIDS: The Making of a Chronic Disease* (1992). Gerald N. Grob, *From Asylum to Community: Mental Health Policy in Modern America* (1991). Robert Heilbroner and Lester Thurow, *Five Economic Challenges* (1983). John Langone, *AIDS: The Facts* (1988). Frank Levy, *Dollars and Dreams: The Changing American Income Distribution* (1987). Michael Lewis, *Liar's Poker* (1989). Eric Marcus, *Making History: The Struggle for Gay and Lesbian Equal Rights, 1945–1990* (1992). Robert Reich, *The Work of Nations: Preparing Ourselves for Twenty-first-Century Capitalism* (1991). Kirkpatrick Sale, *Power Shift* (1975). Jonathan Schell, *The Fate of the Earth* (1982). Arthur Schlesinger, Jr., *The Disuniting of America* (1992). Bruce J. Schulman, *From Cotton Belt to Sunbelt: Federal Policy, Economic Development, and the Transformation of the South, 1938–1980* (1991). Randy Shilts, *And the Band Played On: Politics, People, and the AIDS Epidemic* (1987). James B. Stewart, *Den of Thieves* (1991).

Studs Terkel, *The Great Divide* (1988). John Woodridge, *The Evangelicals* (1975). Daniel Yergin, *The Prize* (1991).

Gender and Family. Mary Francis Berry, *Why ERA Failed* (1986). Susan M. Bianchi, *American Women in Transition* (1987). Nancy Caraway, *Segregated Sisterhood: Racism and the Politics of American Feminism* (1991). Andrea Dworkin, *Right-Wing Women* (1983). Barbara Ehrenreich, *The Hearts of Men: American Dreams and the Flight from Commitment* (1983). Jonathan Kozol, *Rachel and Her Children: Homeless Families in America* (1988). Kristin Luker, *Abortion and the Politics of Motherhood* (1984). Jane Mansbridge, *Why We Lost the ERA* (1986). Donald G. Mathews and Jane Sherron De Hart, *Sex, Gender, and the Politics of E.R.A.: A State and the Nation* (1990). Rosalind Pechesky, *Abortion and Woman's Choice* (1984). Harrell R. Rodgers, Jr., *Poor Women, Poor Families* (1986). Hilda Scott, *Working Your Way to the Bottom: The Feminization of Poverty* (1985). Ruth Sidel, *Women and Children Last* (1986). Suzanne Staggenborg, *The Pro-Choice Movement: Organization and Activism in the Abortion Conflict* (1991). Winifred D. Wandersee, *On the Move: American Women in the 1970s* (1988).

Nonwhites in the 1970s and 1980s. Ken Auletta, *The Underclass* (1981). Frank D. Bean and Marta Tienda, *The Hispanic Population of the United States* (1987). Derrick Bell, *And We Were Not Saved: The Elusive Quest for Racial Justice* (1987). James D. Cockcroft, *Outlaws in the Promised Land: Mexican Immigrant Workers and America's Future* (1986). John Crewden, *The Tarnished Door: The New Immigrants and the Transformation of America* (1983). Vine Deloria, Jr., *American Indian Policy in the Twentieth Century* (1985). Leslie W. Dunbar, ed., *Minority Report* (1984). Marian Wright Edelman, *Families in Peril* (1987). Douglas Glasgow, *The Black Underclass* (1980). Andrew Hacker, *Two Nations: Black and White, Separate, Hostile, Unequal* (1992). Michael Katz, *The Undeserving Poor: From the War on Poverty to the War on Welfare* (1989). Nicholas Lemann, *The Promised Land: The Great Black Migration and How It Changed America* (1989). Carl Nightingale, *On the Edge: A History of Poor Black Children and Their American Dreams* (1993). David M. Reimers, *Still the Golden Door* (1985). Carol B. Stack, *All Our Kin: Strategies for Survival in a Black Community* (1975). Stan Steiner, *The New Indians* (1968). William Julius Watson, *The Truly Disadvantaged* (1987); *When Work Disappears* (1996).

Picture Credits

Chapter 16: 324, UPI/Bettmann; 333, U.S. Coast Guard Photo; 337, UPI/Bettmann; 339, National Archives; 343, National Archives. **Chapter 17:** 349, The Bettmann Archive/Bettmann; 352, Corbis/Bettmann; 354, UPI/Bettmann; 361, Library of Congress; 364, Gordon Parks/Library of Congress. **Chapter 18:** 375, Franklin D. Roosevelt Library Collection; 381, UPI/Corbis/Bettmann; 384, Topham/The Image Works; 385, The Bettmann Archive/Bettmann. **Chapter 19:** 393, UPI/Bettmann; 398, UPI/Bettmann; 401, UPI/Corbis/Bettmann; 404, UPI/Bettmann. **Chapter 20:** 408, IBM; 415, Whirlpool Corporate Communications Department; 417, AP/Wide World Photos; 420, Culver Pictures; 422, AP/Wide World Photos; 423, NASA. **Chapter 21:** 431, AP/Wide World Photos; 433, Library of Congress; 435, UPI/Bettmann; 438, UPI/Bettmann; 442, G. Villet/Life Magazine (c) Time, Inc. **Chapter 22:** 449, U.S. Department of State; 450, UPI/Bettmann; 453, Washington D. C. Public Library; 456, AP/Wide World Photos; 459, AP/Wide World Photos; 460, UPI/Bettmann. **Chapter 23:** 464, UPI/Bettmann; 468, UPI/Bettmann; 471, Yoichi R. Okamoto/LBJ Library Collection; 476, UPI/Bettmann; 477, UPI/Bettmann; 480, Topham/The Image Works; 482, AP/Wide World Photos. **Chapter 24:** 486, Peace Corps; 488, UPI/Bettmann; 494, AP/Wide World Photos; 497, Yoichi R. Okamoto/LBJ Library Collection; 499, AP/Wide World Photos; 501, UPI/Bettmann. **Chapter 25:** 504, Topham/The Image Works; 507, AP/Wide World Photos; 518, UPI/Bettmann; 522, AP/Wide World Photos; 526, Jean-Claude LeJeune/Stock, Boston. **Chapter 26:** 533, John Filo/Valley News Dispatch, Tarentum, Pennsylvania; 536, UPI/Corbis/Bettmann; 538, UPI/Bettmann; 549, UPI/Bettmann; 551, Richard Nixon Library and Birthplace, Yorba Linda, California. **Chapter 27:** 554, AP/Wide World Photos; 557, Carter Presidential Library; 559, UPI/Bettmann; 567, UPI/Bettmann; 573, David Powers/Stock, Boston. **Chapter 28:** 577, Ronald Reagan Library, Simi Valley, California; 584, Official White House Photograph; 595, UPI/Bettmann; 599, AP/Wide World Photos; 603, Reuters/Bettmann.

Index

Page references followed by "f" indicate illustrations. Page references followed by "m" indicate maps.